Adobe® Captivate® 3

The Definitive Guide

Brenda Huettner

Wordware Publishing, Inc.

Library of Congress Cataloging-in-Publication Data

Huettner, Brenda.
Adobe Captivate 3 : the definitive guide / by Brenda Huettner.
p. cm.
Includes index.
ISBN-13: 978-1-59822-049-0
ISBN-10: 1-59822-049-7 (pbk.)
1. Captivate (Electronic resource). 2. Computer animation. I. Title.
TR897.7.H838 2008
006.6'96--dc22 2008016886
CIP

2320 Los Rios Boulevard
Plano, Texas 75074

Printed in the United States of America

ISBN-13: 978-1-59822-049-0
ISBN-10: 1-59822-049-7
10 9 8 7 6 5 4 3 2 1
0805

All inquiries for volume purchases of this book should be addressed to Wordware Publishing, Inc., at the above address. Telephone inquiries may be made by calling:

(972) 423-0090

Dedication

For my daughter, Heidi, because I am always inspired by her determination, insight, and sense of style in all things.

About the Author

Brenda Huettner is a writer, speaker, and consultant with over 20 years of experience in the technical publications field. She has written manuals, help systems, procedures, proposals, and training material for a variety of corporate clients, and has published several books on technical topics. She is a Fellow of the Society for Technical Communication, a senior member of the Administrative Council of the IEEE Professional Communication Society, and a member of the Usability Professionals Association. A regular presenter at conferences across the country, Brenda speaks on documentation, management, and career issues. Brenda lives in Arizona with her husband and two children, and is the publisher of Harry A. Franck's World War II narrative, *Winter Journey through the Ninth*.

Contents

Foreword

I have known Brenda for many years and we have met regularly at industry events all over the world, including my home country, Germany, so I was thrilled when she told me about this book. It will quickly guide you through all the powerful features of Captivate to develop engaging training products, without requiring any programming or Flash development skills.

My own background is in marketing. Before Captivate existed, I was tasked to develop online demonstrations of our software products. At the time, the available tools left me frustrated and annoyed with their limited functionality. If I moved my mouse to the wrong spot while recording, I wasted many hours recapturing the same tasks over and over until I finally got it right. For example, if I forgot to turn off my reminder window, it popped up while I was recording the screen. Since my reminders obviously had nothing to do with the demonstrated tasks, I had to painstakingly edit video segments to remove the little pop-up, which resulted in missing pieces of the mouse moving over the screen. In addition to the recording and editing problems, I had to face access issues. The file formats I used were video formats that required special codecs, which were not always installed on all customers' machines. (If you don't know what a codec is, don't worry. Captivate does not need codecs. If you *do* know about codecs, you may have experienced browser and loading issues of your content and, as a result, frustrated users.) Some files were so large that they never loaded on viewers' browsers. As an author of marketing and basic training content, I was not satisfied with the process and needed a simpler, faster, and more effective way of developing content, which I helped develop into what became Macromedia Captivate.

I have been the product manager and now marketing manager of Captivate from the first release, originally titled RoboDemo (2002), to the current version. Over those few years, we have collected and received a lot of customer feedback that the development team has turned into new feature sets. The product has quickly grown from a simple demonstration tool to a very powerful software simulation application that has reached the leadership position for simulations and rapid authoring in the e-learning industry. Ease of use, including the ability to change the captured mouse path and update screen shots, combined with interactivity, learning guidance, and an innovative approach, make Captivate a popular choice for rapid training development and the tool has won many industry awards.

Instructional designers can easily use Captivate to create Flash-based training content and thereby benefit from the ubiquity of the Flash Player. Since no programming skills are required, all training professionals can quickly develop and update online training themselves. Our customer Safety-Kleen Systems is a great example. Their technical training manager Frank Hanfland told us that Captivate helped increase course production, reduced development cost, and increased employee productivity. Instead of one course per month, the training team now develops five courses and costs were reduced more than $600,000. Nearly all instructional designers have to face the same challenges: no time and no budget. As seen in Frank's case, Captivate can make a significant difference addressing both these challenges.

Cost savings and rapid development are not the only benefits to Captivate. The key to providing effective training is the ability for the student to practice in a safe and simplified environment where corrective feedback is provided. My first recorded demonstrations for the web were more than 45 minutes long—and they were just that: demonstrations. Customers had to simply watch, which can quickly become very boring. There were far too many steps shown in one large non-reusable, non-interactive segment. Captivate provides so much more flexibility than these video recordings I developed back then. As an author, you can take advantage of the many benefits I and thousands of other e-learning content developers experience. You can create small, reusable learning objects, and then combine them in different ways using the viewer-controlled menu functions. Or you can deploy these objects through a learning management system, your existing online Help system, or through web-based support or help desk pages. You can add interactivity with branching to create realistic practice scenarios. Captivate supports many different interaction types and its simulation recording modes even add the interactions automatically for you. No coding or scripting skills are required—Captivate is designed to empower the everyday user (like myself; I am definitely not a programmer) to create engaging learning content.

You will be surprised at the many different types of content you can create. This book guides you from learning the basics about creating your first demonstration all the way to using interactive features and creating e-learning content. Try out the different features today and let your creative juices flow. Captivate has so much power that you can use it for more than just demos or simulations.

Please share your engaging and interesting training scenarios with us and other users—we are always looking for great examples to include in our customer showcase. Now, let Brenda skillfully guide you through Captivate's features and have fun!

Silke Fleischer
Product Manager, Captivate
San Diego, California

Acknowledgments

No man is an island, and no book can be brought to press without the effort and support of many people. I'd like to thank:

Silke Fleischer and Sandra Nakamura, who consistently came through with help, even at the last minute.

John Hedtke, who never wavered in his belief in my ability to write this book.

All the thoughtful, helpful people who devote their time and expertise to helping others in the online forums and the Captivate community.

Brenda Huettner
bphuettner@p-ndesigns.com

Introduction

Captivate software allows you to create interactive Flash movies quickly and easily with automatic recording functions, text captions, mouse tracking, and more. You can easily add e-learning capabilities with quizzing functions and branching, or create stand-alone movies that could run on a kiosk. Captivate 3.0 includes a variety of greatly enhanced functionality. Some of the features include:

- Automatic screen capture with smart full-motion recording
- Multi- or single-mode recording for screen capture
- Automatic recording of web applications
- AutoText captions
- Audio recording and editing
- Edit, Storyboard, and Branching views
- XML file export and import for easy localization
- Project templates
- Microsoft PowerPoint import
- Randomized quizzing and question pools
- Rollover and zoom functions
- Highlights and grayouts
- Text animations
- Animated slide transitions
- Rich media and image support
- SCORM/AICC compliance (LMS integration)
- Questionmark Perception support
- Multiple output formats
- Skins and menus
- Handouts
- Accessible content

How This Book Is Organized

This book covers Captivate 3.0 software functionality in 14 chapters.

Chapter 1: Installing and Configuring Captivate

Chapter 1 reviews the system requirements for Captivate and describes how to get the software set up. You can use this information for either a purchased copy of Captivate or for the trial version that is available for download at www.adobe.com. This chapter also describes how to activate your software license if you've purchased a copy of Captivate.

Chapter 2: Getting Ready to Make Movies

This chapter covers some of the basics of designing movies. These are things you should consider before you begin any project, like creating a project plan and identifying the resources you'll need.

Chapter 3: Creating Your First Movie (Just the Basics!)

This chapter steps you through an entire movie from recording to publishing. It will give you a good understanding of movie basics.

Chapter 4: Recording a Movie

This chapter describes the various recording options, defines "full-motion recording," and shows how to record a variety of movie types.

Chapter 5: Creating Movies without Recording

This chapter covers alternative ways of creating a movie. For example, you can start with a blank movie and add individual screen shots or images, create a movie of just questions, or import a PowerPoint file.

Chapter 6: Working with Slides

This chapter covers the basics of how slides work, and describes how to add, delete, or hide slides from view.

Chapter 7: Editing a Single Slide

This chapter describes the editing functions that apply to a single slide, such as how to work with the elements on a slide and how to change the timing of slide display. You'll also learn how to prevent changes to a slide and how to work with the slide background.

Chapter 8: Defining What the User Hears—Adding Audio

This chapter describes how to record audio within Captivate, either while recording or after. It also covers how to import and edit existing audio clips.

Chapter 9: Defining What the User Does—Adding Interactivity

This chapter describes how to add interactivity through elements such as click boxes, text entry boxes, and rollover images and captions. Use interactivity to create software simulations or simply to make your movies more engaging to viewers.

Chapter 10: Creating e-Learning Content

This chapter describes how to add quizzing functionality to your movies with a variety of question types. You can enter the correct answers and determine which slides display based on the viewer input. This chapter also discusses how to create question pools for random question display and how to store the answers that each viewer gives.

Chapter 11: Working with the Branching View

This chapter covers the functions available from the Branching view. This view lets you see the way the slides work together, and view the various possible paths through your movie.

Chapter 12: Using Captivate Tools

This chapter describes the additional tools that come with Captivate, such as a spell checker, bandwidth analyzer, and notes for each slide. You'll also learn about MenuBuilder, a tool that allows you to combine multiple movies in a single menu.

Chapter 13: Refining the Movie

This chapter shows you how to edit your movie as a whole by adding elements that cross all slides. For example, you can define the look and content of the playback controls, or control the way the movie starts and ends. This chapter also describes movie-level functions such as saving or hiding movies.

Chapter 14: Generating Captivate Output

This chapter describes how to generate a variety of output types. In addition to standard SWF movie files, you can integrate with other packages, zip files on the fly, or export just the text to Microsoft Word documents.

Conventions Used in This Book

Boldface text in a procedure indicates a button, link, or menu item that you should select. You can usually select these items with either the mouse or the keyboard.

Tip: A tip provides a helpful hint or useful technique.

Note: A note calls out specific information relevant to the current discussion.

Chapter 1

Installing and Configuring Captivate

This chapter describes how to get your copy of Captivate up and running. You'll also learn about the online and telephone options for activating your software, as well as deactivation options.

System Requirements

Before you begin installation, ensure that the system you'll be using has at least the following minimum configuration:

- Intel Pentium 4, Intel Centrino, Intel Xeon, or Intel Core Duo (or compatible) processor
- Microsoft Windows XP with Service Pack 2, Windows 2000 with Service Pack 2, or Windows Vista Home Premium, Business, Ultimate, or Enterprise (certified for 32-bit editions). Note: Trial version not supported on Windows 2000.
- 512 MB of RAM (1 GB recommended)
- 700 MB of available hard disk space (additional free space required during installation)
- DVD-ROM drive
- 800 x 600 screen resolution (1,024 x 768 recommended)
- Internet or phone connection required for product activation
- Software and accessories for publishing and recording

- Microsoft Internet Explorer 6 or later
- Adobe Flash Player 7 or later

Note: Flash Player must be installed before the Captivate software will start up. If you don't have Flash installed, the Captivate installation will attempt to download a copy of Flash from the Internet for you.

Note: If you're going to be recording sound for your demonstrations, you'll also want a microphone, speakers, and a sound card.

Installing the Software

The setup wizard for Captivate software makes most of the installation process automatic, so if you've used an installation wizard before, you can probably skip this section. The steps you'll follow are the same whether you're installing a trial version or a fully licensed version of Captivate. If you have a software license, you'll also need to activate your software.

If you're going to be installing a licensed version of the software at this time, you may want to make sure your Internet connection is up and running before you being installing. This will make it easier to activate and register your software during the installation process.

To download a trial version of the Captivate software, open your Internet browser and follow these steps:

1. Navigate to the Captivate web site (www.adobe.com/products/captivate).
2. Click **Download a free trial.**
3. In the window that appears, you'll need to sign in to the Adobe site. If you do not have an Adobe password account, click **Create an Adobe account** and enter the required information (your name, requested login ID, password, etc.) If you already have an Adobe account, enter your ID and password, then click **Sign in.**
4. Once you're signed in, confirm your address and indicate which (if any) of the Adobe communications you'd like to receive. There may also be a short survey that you can take. This screen also

includes links to the Adobe Terms of Service and Privacy policies. Click **Continue** to display the available trial downloads.

5. Select the appropriate Captivate version from the drop-down menu and click **Download**.
6. When the download is complete, open the executable file to begin the installation process. You will need to extract the zip file and save it to your system.

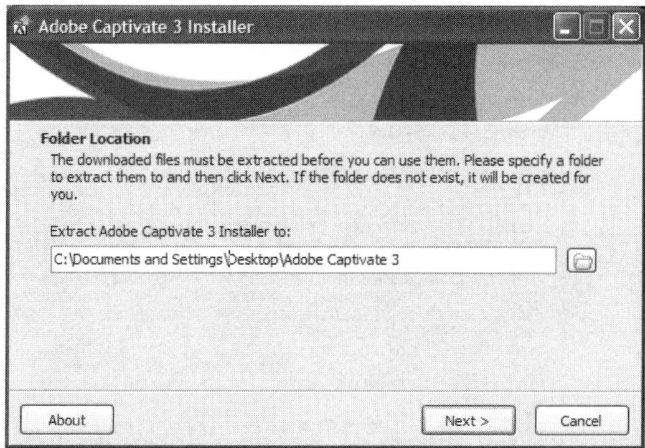

Figure 1-1. Extract the files.

7. Click **Next** to extract the files to the specified location. The welcome screen displays. Click **Next** to display the license agreement, and continue with step 3 below to complete the installation process.

To install the Captivate software using a purchased copy of the software, close all other programs, then follow these steps:

1. Insert the CD into your computer's CD-ROM drive. The installation wizard should start automatically and display a welcome message on your screen. Click **Next** to display the license agreement and skip to step 3.
2. If nothing displays on your screen, you'll have to run the setup program manually. You can do this in either of two ways:
   - Choose **Run** from your Start menu, click **Browse**, then type in your CD drive letter and a colon followed by the command **setup.exe**. For example, you might type D:setup.exe. Then click **OK**.

- Open your Windows Explorer by clicking on **My Computer**, then browse to your CD-ROM drive and double-click on the **setup.exe** icon.

The welcome screen displays. Click **Next** to display the license agreement.

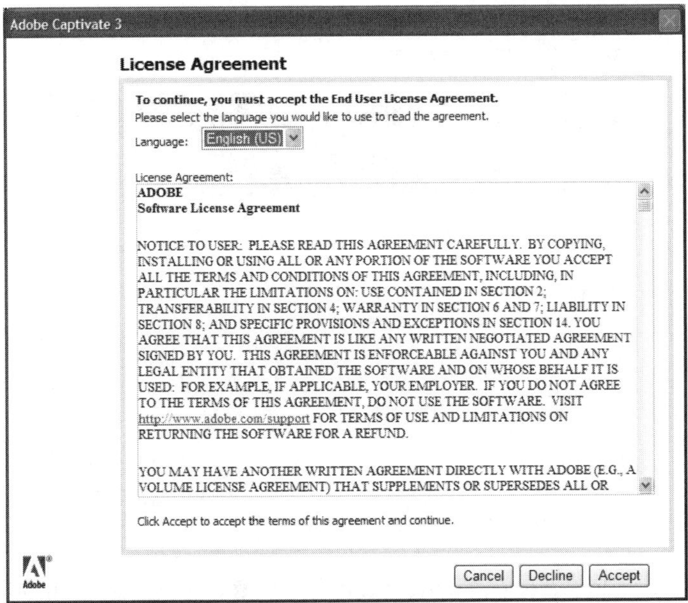

Figure 1-2. The license agreement screen.

3. You must agree to the terms of this agreement whether you are installing a licensed version or a trial version of Captivate software. Use the scroll bar to display the entire agreement.

4. After you've read the agreement, click **Accept** to display the software setup screen. At this point, you'll have a fully-functioning copy of Captivate whether you've purchased the software or are using the trial version. However, if you don't enter a serial number within 30 days, the software will stop working. You must *activate* the product (online or by telephone, as described in the next section) to enter and verify your serial number and license.

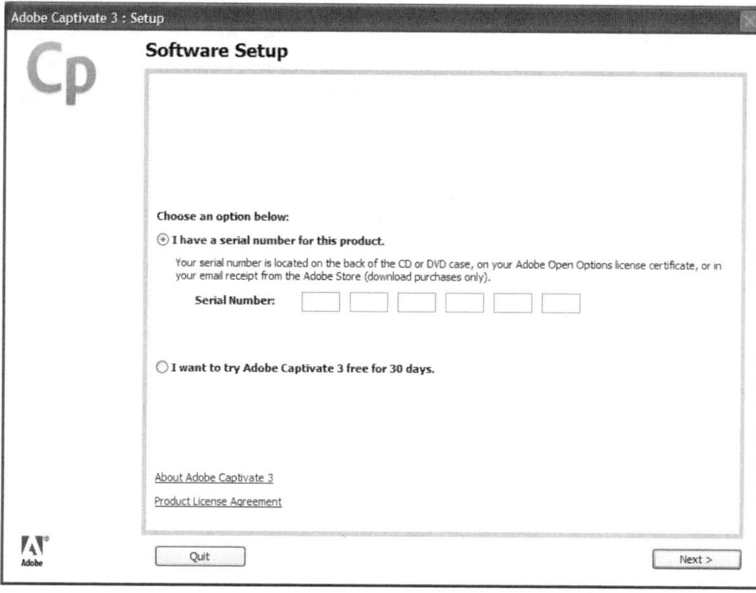

Figure 1-3. The software setup screen.

5. If you want to just try out the software, click the **I want to try Adobe Captivate 3 free for 30 days** button. This will allow you full access to the Captivate product, but it can only be used for 30 days from the day you install it. Otherwise, click the **I have a serial number for this product** button and type your serial number in the boxes provided. Enter four digits in each box.
6. Click **Next.** If this is your first version of Captivate, skip to step 8. If you have purchased an upgrade version of Captivate, and have removed the older version of Captivate from your system (or are installing on a new system), you'll see the upgrade screen.
7. For upgrade versions only, enter the version number and serial number of your OLD version of Captivate.
8. Click **Activate** to begin the activation process. The activation process identifies your system configuration with the specified serial number. This should only take a few seconds, depending on your connection speed. When the process is complete, a success window displays.
9. Click **Next** to display the Captivate main menu.

Note: Activation is required to use the Captivate software after the 30-day trial period. Registration is not required at all. However, you can always choose to register later by selecting the Register option from the Help menu within the Captivate software.

Telephone Activation

If the computer on which you'll be using Captivate does not have an Internet connection, or for any reason you choose not to activate your software online, you'll have to use the telephone method of activation. This takes a bit longer than the online version and requires a touch-tone phone. You'll need to be able to type confirmation numbers into your computer while on the telephone.

Tip: Make sure you have your Captivate serial number handy before beginning this process. You'll need to enter it on your touch-tone telephone.

1. Start up the software by double-clicking the **Captivate** icon. If you've already activated your software, the system will go directly to the main Captivate window, and you can skip this procedure. If you haven't yet activated this copy of the software, the Captivate activation screen displays.

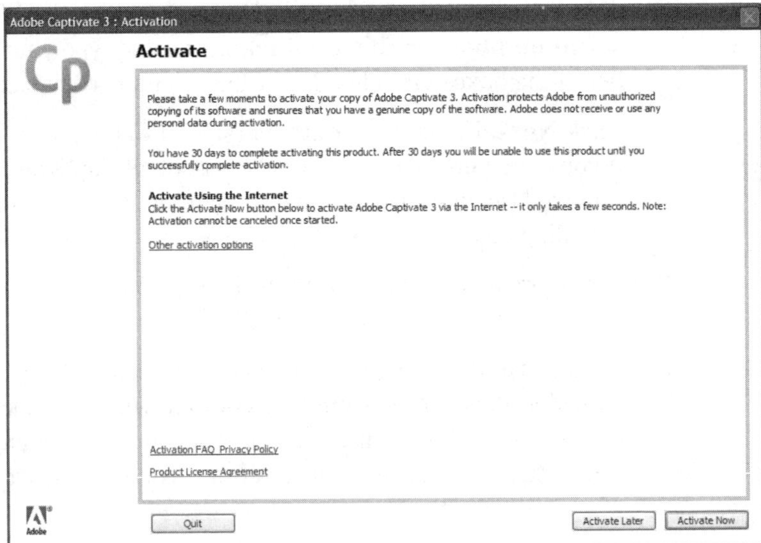

Figure 1-4. Choose an alternate activation method.

Note: If you've just installed the software, your Captivate activation screen may already be displayed.

2. Click the **Other activation options** link to begin the telephone activation process.

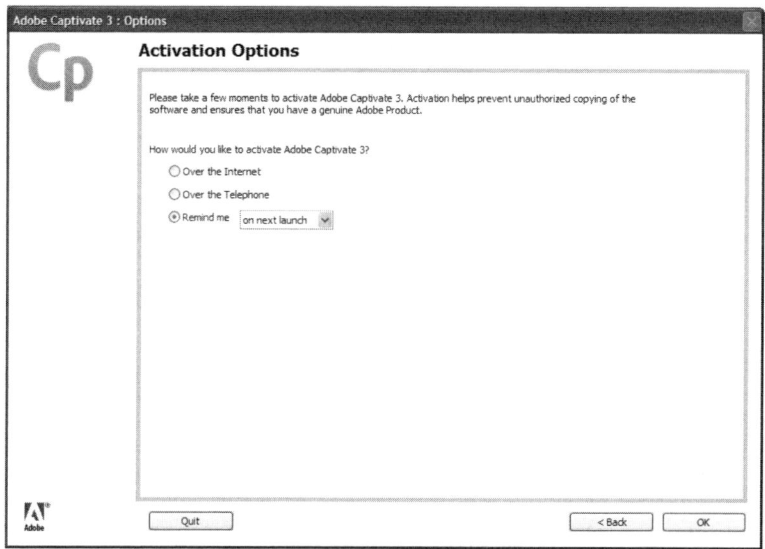

Figure 1-5. Choose telephone activation.

3. Choose **Over the Telephone** to display the phone activation entry screen.

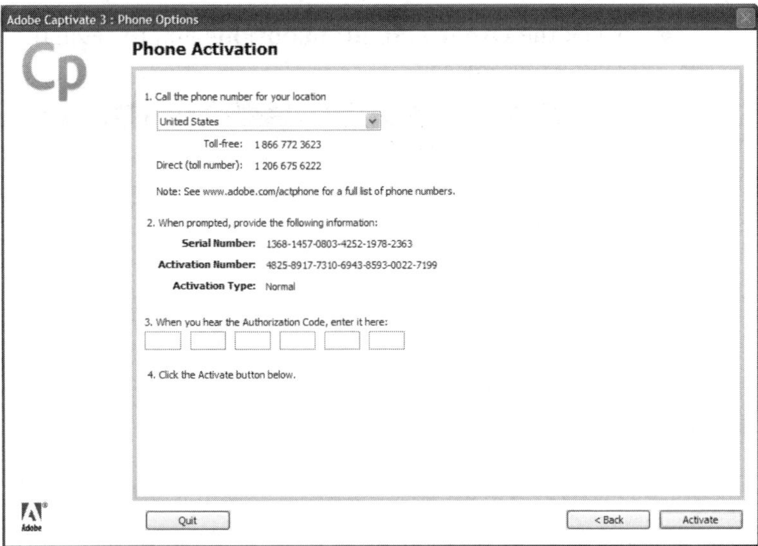

Figure 1-6. Enter your serial number and specify your country.

4. Choose your location from the drop-down list. This will allow the system to display the correct phone number for you to call.
5. Call the number on the activation worksheet to get to the automated activation system. Listen carefully to the prompts!
6. For each set of numbers, enter the digits on your telephone. You'll hear a confirmation of the numbers. Press the # key to continue entering numbers, or press the * key to re-enter each set of numbers.
7. When all of your groups of numbers have been entered correctly, the system will verify that the license number you've entered can be activated on this machine.
8. Once verified, you'll hear a series of confirmation numbers. Type the numbers into your activation worksheet as you hear them, then either press the * key to listen to the set of numbers again or press the # key to move on to the next set of numbers.

Note: This number is unique to your system configuration and cannot be used with other setups. You must get a unique confirmation number for each installation of Captivate software.

9. Click **Activate** to complete the activation process and display the registration screen.

10. Registration is an online process that requires an Internet connection. If your system does not have an Internet connection, simply click **Remind Me Later** to close the registration screen and display the Captivate main menu.

Deactivation

Each copy of Captivate software comes with an end-user license agreement that specifies the number of times you may install Captivate. For most people, the EULA specifies that you may have up to two installations, as long as you don't use them concurrently. For example, you may share one license between a home machine and a work machine, or between a desktop and a laptop PC. If for any reason you need to change computers or significantly change your hardware configuration, you'll need to deactivate one of your licenses so that you'll be able to activate Captivate on the new system.

Note: As soon as you deactivate your license, the software will stop working but will remain on your system. You may reactivate the software as long as you do not exceed the limit of active copies specified in your EULA.

The following steps require an active Internet connection.

To remove the license from your system, follow these steps:

1. From the Captivate main menu, click the **Help** menu, then choose **Deactivate** to display the deactivation screen.

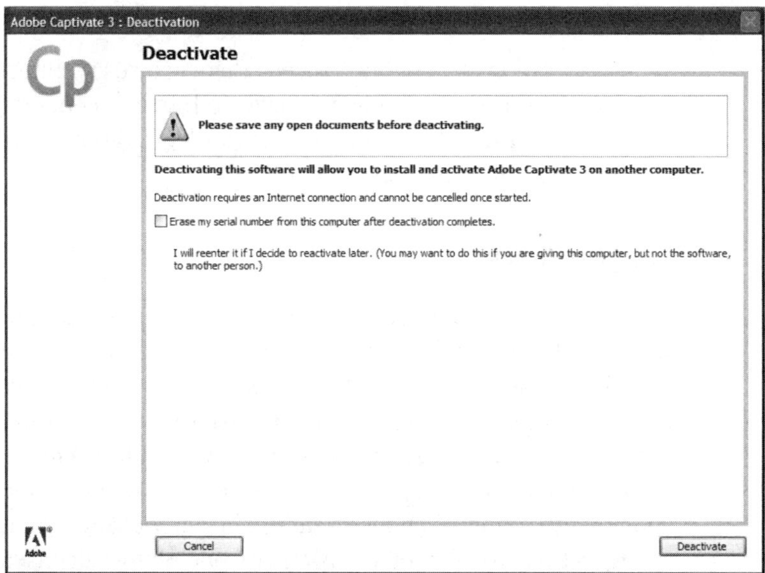

Figure 1-7. Deactivate your software license.

2. Click **Deactivate**. The Captivate license on your current system will be immediately disabled, and you'll be able to install and activate the software on another system.

Summary

This chapter described the steps you'll need to take to get your Captivate software up and running. We also covered how to activate your software license so you can use Captivate past the 30-day trial period and how to deactivate your license when you want to move Captivate to a new computer.

The next chapter describes the planning stages that go into making a movie with Captivate.

Chapter 2

Getting Ready to Make Movies

This chapter describes the steps you should take before beginning to use the Captivate software. Good planning and organization up front will help you to make better movies!

We'll assume that you already have good communication skills, including a good grasp of grammar and full understanding of the topic or software you're going to be teaching or demonstrating. This chapter will discuss the factors you'll need to consider in order to create a fast-paced, exciting movie. We'll also review some basics of project planning and general preproduction issues.

What Makes a Good Movie?

Captivate can be used for a myriad of purposes, such as product demonstrations, tutorials, quizzes, assessments, training, and even simple slide shows. But like any tool, it can create poor output just as easily as great output.

A good movie delivers the information that the viewer needs in a way that the viewer can understand. It is timely, accurate, and helpful. It ISN'T boring, overly repetitious, or excessively long or complicated.

What Is Your Goal?

The very first thing you'll need to think about is the goal of your movie. If, for example, you are creating a demo to sell a product, you'll want to take a very different approach than if you're creating an e-learning course that students use to get a certain type of certification. One is "flashier" with perhaps more animation; the other requires significant consideration of things like minimum passing scores and integration with other learning systems.

You can use Captivate to create a complex, interactive movie that plays only the sections that are appropriate to each user and tracks a variety of user input for grading and integration with a learning management system. You can also use Captivate to create a quick demonstration of a specific task that can be incorporated into standard online Help systems. Captivate has the flexibility to do these things and more, but this flexibility means that it's up to you to decide what you need and how to implement it. You'll also save time later if you make these decisions before you begin.

Note: Throughout this book, you'll see references to both movies and projects. Though similar, they aren't quite the same. Captivate stores the information you enter in project files (with the extension .cp) that can be used to create a variety of output movies (for example, a standard Flash file with the extension .swf or an executable program file with the extension .exe). When you create or edit a movie, you are actually creating or editing the project files. The movie itself (the output) isn't created until you "publish" it (see Chapter 14).

When you first create a movie with Captivate, you'll need to specify what type of movie you're making. Though there are other types, the two primary ones are software simulation and scenario simulation. A software simulation is primarily a demonstration-type movie that may be used for training purposes. A scenario simulation assumes that someone will be interacting with the movie, usually by clicking areas on the screen or answering questions in a training environment. This typically includes a grading or assessment component, and may integrate with an external learning management system (LMS).

There are four basic types of movies (and many variations):

Table 2-1. Movie types

This type of movie:	Does this:	Interactive	Graded	Branching
Demonstration	Shows the viewer how to do something.	No	No	No
Training simulation	Shows the viewer what to do and lets the viewer do it.	Yes	No	No
Assessment simulation	Teaches the viewer with a combination of demonstration and training simulations, and then stops periodically to evaluate how well the viewer learned the topic.	Yes	Yes	No
Scenario simulation	Incorporates branching to display specific slides based on the viewer's input.	Yes	Yes	Yes

Of course, once you get going you may find that you need to combine elements of different movie types into your current project. Captivate allows you full flexibility in adding any type of element to any type of movie. For example, though you're doing primarily a demonstration, you may want to insert a question that requests feedback from the viewers. Or you may create a series of demonstrations that lead up to an assessment. But for planning purposes, it is helpful to understand the types of movies you can create and the elements that go into each.

Elements of a Demonstration

Use a demonstration when you don't expect the viewer to interact with the movie. For example, this is very useful as a component of online Help or product demos or sales tools. A demonstration could be run from a web site, or even a stand-alone kiosk. Demonstration movies generally use captions and animations to show where the action is happening on the screen, but do not pause for the viewer's input at any point. A sample screen from a demonstration might look like this:

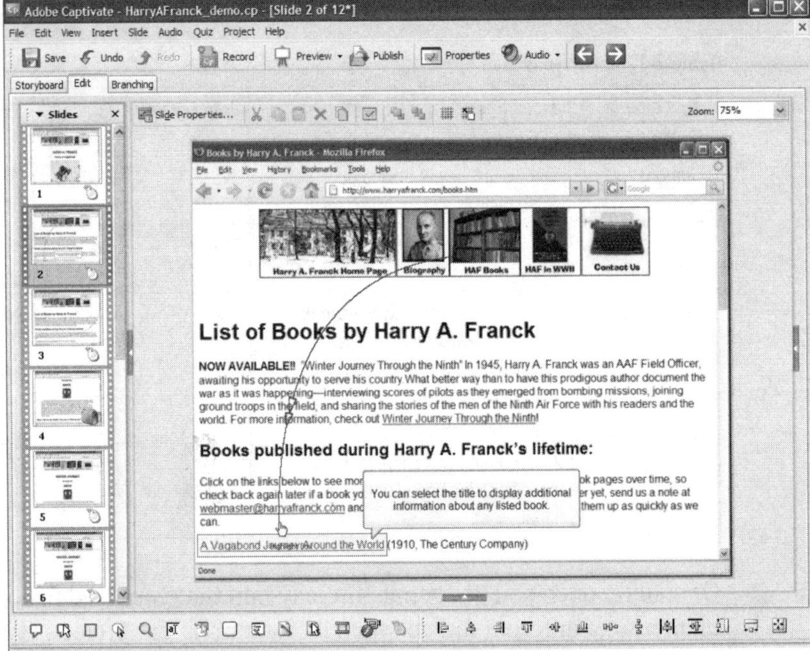

Figure 2-1. Demonstrations show how to do something.

The demonstration displays a text box that describes the action, and you can have an animation that shows a cursor moving to perform the action. You can even include audio that describes the action, or simply play a click noise to emphasize the action. The action (in this case, clicking on a text box) occurs within the movie without interaction from the viewer.

Elements of a Training Simulation

A training simulation builds on a demonstration movie by pausing at certain points to allow the viewer to interact with the movie. Like a demonstration, this type of movie can include text captions, highlight boxes, animations, and cursor movement. You can define a variety of parameters for each interaction, such as the number of attempts the viewer can make for each task, or different feedback messages that display depending on whether or not the viewer performs the correct task.

After the viewer performs a task, you can define which part of the movie to display next (the destination). For example, if the viewer

can't successfully click a certain box, you may want to replay the part of the movie that described that box. Or, if the viewer performs a series of tasks correctly, you may want to skip ahead to a more advanced part of the movie. This sort of interactivity, combined with the multiple destination options, ensures that the viewer is performing the correct actions at each step in the movie.

A sample training simulation movie screen might look like this:

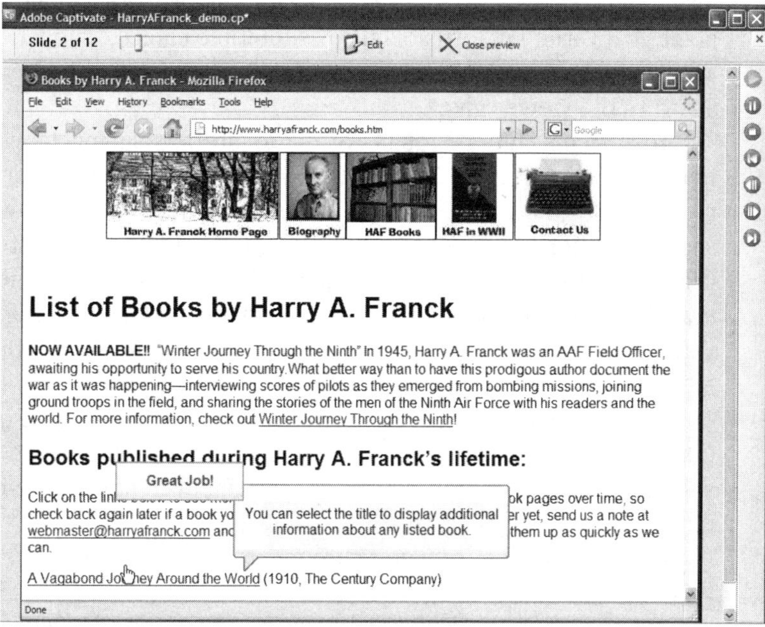

Figure 2-2. Training simulations wait for viewer interaction.

The simulation displays instructions in a text box and highlights the area the viewer is supposed to click. If the viewer actually clicks in the correct area, a "success caption" displays (in this case, the text "Great Job!") and the movie can then continue.

If, for example, the viewer clicked on a different area (such as the Winter Journey Through the Ninth link above), then you could have a "failure caption" display, or allow another try, or go back and restart the movie.

Elements of an Assessment Simulation

An assessment simulation incorporates the interactivity of a training simulation and adds true e-learning functionality. As the viewer works through the movie, interacting as you've defined, you can track and store the results of each interaction. Like a training simulation, you can specify different destinations depending on whether the user performs the correct action. In addition, you can insert questions at any point, in a variety of formats (such as multiple choice, true/false, short answer, and more), and specify destinations and feedback based on the answers the viewer gives.

You can manage the results of all the interactions for the whole movie and specify how the results will be delivered to you. For example, you may just want a text file e-mailed to you, or you may want all answers integrated into an existing learning management system (LMS). Captivate can produce output in formats compatible with several e-learning standards. If you're integrating with an existing system, you can specify whether you want to track results for each interaction or send just a summary of interactions throughout the movie.

You can also create questions that are not scored, such as questions that ask for comments or suggestions, or ask the viewer to enter subjective ratings for various things. You can even have those results e-mailed to you.

A sample screen from an assessment simulation might look like Figure 2-3.

For each question slide, the movie pauses while the viewer enters appropriate answers. In the example in Figure 2-3, you can see a matching question where the viewer is to match up the countries with the books that discuss them. This particular viewer got it right—you can see the "correct" caption on the slide. Depending on your goals, you may decide not to allow retries, or you may allow unlimited retries. Note also that this slide is the first of two question slides for this particular movie. The viewer can submit the answers, go back to check on the instructions in the previous parts of the movie, or skip this question altogether by clicking the Skip button. When you create an assessment simulation, you'll have full control over which buttons appear at which points in the movie.

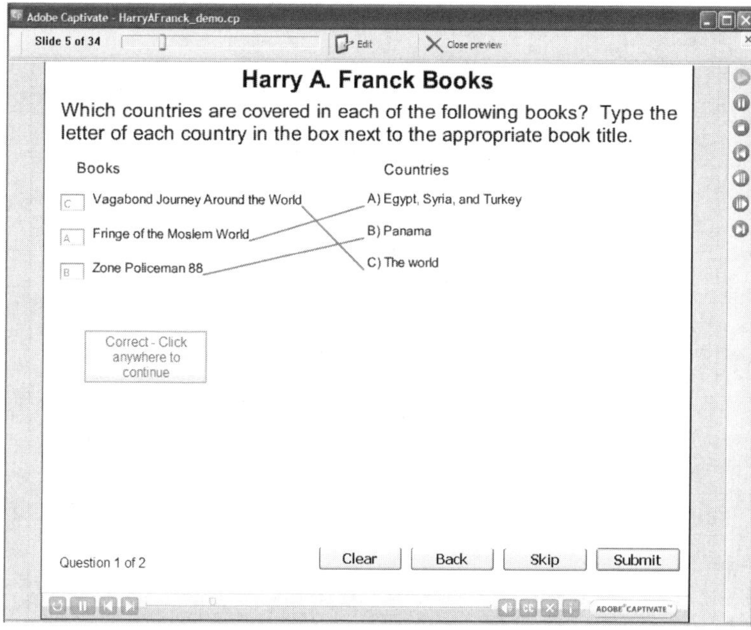

Figure 2-3. Assessment simulations add questions and tracking functionality.

Elements of a Scenario Simulation

Scenario-based learning presents a student (in our case, the viewer) with a situation or problem that must be solved, and a selection of options from which to choose at various points throughout the learning experience. In Captivate, you can create this type of learning using the branching functionality to display a list of options, and then display different slides based on which option the viewer chooses.

Unlike assessment simulations, scenario simulations typically have multiple options or branches for each question slide. Each branch may have many questions and branches of its own, creating a fairly complex "tree" of possible paths through your movie. Captivate has tools to help create and manage the display of these various paths.

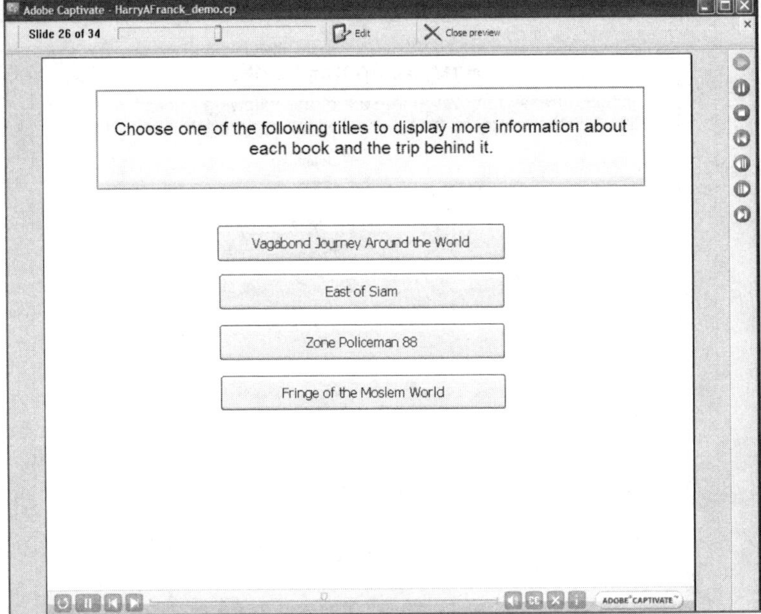

Figure 2-4. Scenario simulations make use of branching.

Elements of Slide Design

As you create your movie, much of your slide design will be determined by the screens that you capture as you move through the software you're demonstrating or simulating. However, you should also ensure that the elements you add are well-designed and consistent throughout your movie. For example, if you display a failure message in red on one slide, it should be in red on all slides. When you create questions, make sure they all use the same font and that the font you choose is easy to read.

A style guide for your movie can be a helpful tool to maintain consistency. There are lots of books on style guides and design, so we won't go into detail here. However, some elements you'll want to consider are:

- Backgrounds. Although Captivate allows you to use any image as a background, whether you've got a screen shot or another image or just text on a slide, use discretion when designing your slide backgrounds. A busy background distracts from the point you're trying to make.

- Text font, size, and color. This may vary by type of text but should remain consistent for all similar text types.
- Text phrasing and tense. Generally, use a command only when you are inserting an interactive element and want to tell the viewer to do something. If the caption is not for an interactive element, use a statement. For example, if the viewer sees "Click this button to advance to the next slide," he or she is likely to try to click the button. If it is simply a demonstration, consider using a phrase such as "This button advances to the next slide."
- Timing issues. You don't want to have one slide go by too fast and another too slow.
- Spelling and grammar. Make a list of words that are unique to your product or software or industry and use them consistently. And by all means, use the Captivate spell checker (see Chapter 12)!
- Animation. Though this can enliven a movie, too much animation becomes distracting. If your words are flying all over the place, the viewer will be watching the animation and not reading your important message.
- Color scheme. Make sure that the colors you pick for text boxes and highlight boxes show up well on your background or on your screen shots. For example, viewers may not be able to see a light blue highlight box if it is highlighting a blue button.

Planning Is Everything

Okay, this isn't a new concept. Before you even start up the Captivate software, you need to begin planning exactly what you want your viewers to take away from the experience. Some of the questions you'll need to answer include:

- Who will be watching this movie?
- What is the audience's current skill level?
- What hardware and software will they be using?
- What do they need to know *right now*?
- How much interactivity do they need?
- What determines success or failure?

- Will their progress or results be tracked, and if so, how?
- When does the finished product need to be delivered?

A comprehensive plan that answers all of these questions will serve as a guideline for the entire project and ensure that you end up with a movie that meets your audience's needs.

Elements of a Project Plan

There are lots of resources that talk about good project planning. Basically, a good plan will have the following minimum components:

- Executive summary
- Overview
- Audience
- Technical information
- Task list
- Schedule
- Script and/or storyboard

Executive Summary

The executive summary is a brief description of the scope and purpose of the project. Keep this short and sweet—it should never be more than one page long.

Overview

Here's where you can get into detail that you left out of the executive summary. Include the scope, purpose, and goals for the finished project, and summarize the rest of the sections in the plan.

Audience

The more information you have about the people who will be viewing this movie, the more accurately you can fulfill their needs. You're likely to have more than one audience category. For example, you may be creating a tutorial that shows novice users how to perform a task, but this same tutorial may also be used by instructors, expert users who perform the task only occasionally, or managers checking up on their employees. For each potential viewer type, you should look at:

- What they are doing (the specific task they're trying to accomplish)
- Their skill level (with the product, with movies, and with computer systems in general)
- The environment in which they're likely to be working

Technical Information

The technical information describes what the project will look like when it is completed and what hardware or software you expect the viewers to have. This includes any standards or style guides you may have and the graphic look and feel you want, as well as specific output type. Captivate software has a wide variety of output options, including:

- Flash files (.swf)
- Executable files (.exe)
- Stand-alone files for Windows, Linux, and Mac
- Handouts (Microsoft Word files)

You'll want to specify the level of interactivity. Will you include quizzes? Scoring? Interactive demos that require user input? You should also specify additional effects you'll use, such as audio, animations, or other customizations. Will you use a narrator? Will there be sound effects?

Task List

You know what you're doing and what it takes to make it happen, but there may be other people in your company who are not aware of the specific steps required to create this project. List all the tasks that need to be accomplished and who will accomplish each of them. Make sure you include all of the stakeholders in your project, including the writer, editor, reviewer, tester, approver, and any other personnel who may need to participate. This is particularly important if you're going to be asking for time from people in other departments—such as a QA department or usability group.

Note: Although you may include names at this point, be aware that things could change. This document is a tool that will need to be updated frequently throughout your project.

The tasks will vary for each project, but a good starting list of tasks is as follows:

- Create plan
- Review plan
- Revise plan
- Approve plan
- Learn product or topic
- Create script/storyboard
- Review script/storyboard
- Revise script/storyboard
- Approve script/storyboard
- Create movie files
- Create auxiliary files (animations, sound, etc.)
- Create sample output file
- Review sample output file
- Revise as needed
- Integrate with other software
- Final approval
- Project review and wrap-up

Be very specific with the tasks, particularly those that you expect to be accomplished by other groups. If you expect the usability department to run a test on your movie, say so here so that there are no surprises later. Similarly, list the people you'll need for technical reviews. Often you'll want to include informational review passes by various levels of management, even though you may not expect feedback from them.

Though the exact names may change as the project goes forward, you are more likely to get the support you need if you get buy-in from everyone up front.

Schedule

The schedule is simply your estimate of the amount of time you think needs to be allocated for each of the tasks in your list, along with an approximate completion date for each. Particularly for larger projects, make sure you take into account holidays, vacations, staff meetings, and other non-productive times. You'll also need to include a statement of assumptions that lists factors that could delay your project (such as slow reviewer turnaround, changes to code-freeze dates, or other issues you may hit).

Be aware that any schedule you set will change, and the larger the project, the more likely it is that something will go wrong. Some things are simply out of your control, such as when the software screens will be ready for you to capture or how fast the technical reviewers turn around and approve your output. The best you can do is to track the actual schedule against your estimates, and adjust the next project accordingly. As you go through subsequent projects, you'll be able to come up with increasingly accurate data, and this will help you make better estimates on future projects.

Scripts and Storyboards

If you're writing a manual, you start with an outline. If you're building a house, you need architectural drawings. When you create a Captivate movie, you can use either a script or storyboards to plan the content.

- Scripts, like in Hollywood, are printouts of the text that will be in the movie. In this case, you may also include directions such as "user clicks the Next button" or whatever is appropriate to your project. The more detail you include in your script, the smoother your project will go. Scripts can also be useful in the review process, if you need to get input or sign-off before actually creating a movie.
- Storyboards are graphic representations of your movie, usually consisting of a series of screen shots that represent the major components of the movie. The storyboards may be rough sketches on paper or more of a prototype done electronically, depending on your skills and available time.

Obviously, the script will have to describe some of the graphics, and storyboards will have some text. Both approaches are used to organize

your content and, most importantly, to get sign-off or approval before you invest a lot of effort into the final movie.

As you plan out the movie, you'll want to think about the components. In addition to screen shots, lessons, and questions (if you have any), make sure you plan for the extra elements that complete the movie. For example, you may want to include:

- Title page
- Credits page
- Copyright page
- Opening/closing graphic or splash screen
- Introductory material, such as prerequisites and/or assumptions you've made about the audience experience and skill level. This section often includes discussion of special navigation features you may have in the movie.
- The body of your movie (demonstration, simulation, or assessment slides)
- Feedback mechanism, which can be as simple as including an e-mail address or contact information at the end of the movie, or as complex as creating text boxes for viewer input and having the content e-mailed to you
- Ending, such as a final slide that lets the viewer know the movie is over

Planning Paths through Your Movie

As you build your movie with Captivate, there are numerous places where you can pause the movie to await viewer interaction. For each place you pause, you can specify where the movie will resume based on the viewer's input. For example, you may want to replay the introductory portions of the movie if the viewer didn't answer the first set of questions correctly. Or you may want to allow the viewer to skip some sections if they get a pre-test type of questioning correct. These paths through the movie are sometimes called branching or contingency branching.

As you think about your questions and interactive components, it's often helpful to create a diagram of potential paths through your movie. For example, a very basic flowchart showing three lessons might look like this:

Introduction
Yes
Lesson 1: Navigation
Menu Items
Text Links
Scroll Bars
Assessment/Quiz
Pass?
No
Yes
Lesson 2: Message Board
Reading Messages
Posting Messages
Assessment/Quiz
Pass?
No
Yes
Lesson 3: Books
Vagabond Journey
Zone Policeman 88
Fringe of the Moslem World
Winter Journey through the Ninth
Assessment/Quiz
Pass?
No
Yes
Final Assessment

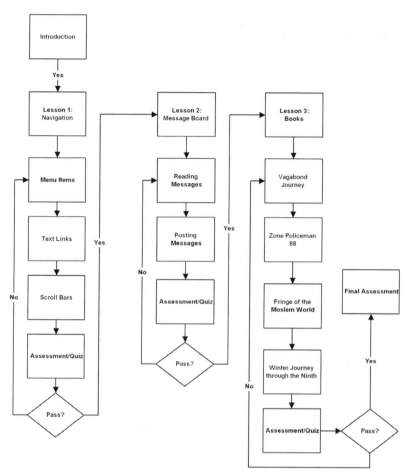

Figure 2-5. Plan out your paths.

The decisions—marked on Figure 2-5 with Pass? and Yes and No paths—can be easily entered in Captivate by specifying a different location depending on whether or not the viewer correctly answers the assessment or question. Note that you can also use this type of branching for any type of interactive element such as buttons (repeat the lesson if the Repeat button is clicked) or text entry boxes (where the viewer types Repeat to go back or Continue to go ahead).

Evaluating Your Movie

As a final step in your movie-making process, you should always check to see whether or not you met the goal or goals you set out in the first step. If you were simply including a demonstration in a Help system, you'll need to use methods outside of Captivate to track its success. For example, you may want to check with your call center to see if the movie helped reduce support calls for that particular function. For movies with more interactivity and assessment options, you can look at statistics like the percentage of viewers who answer each question, the percentage of correct answers, or the overall scores for the whole movie.

Obviously, you can go back and edit this movie to make it better. You should also document the lessons you learn from each movie so that when you plan the next project, you'll have a good base of experience from which to work.

Summary

This chapter reviewed a number of the things you'll need to think about to create a useful movie that meets your goals. The following chapter steps through the basics of making a simple movie in a very short time.

Chapter 3

Creating Your First Movie (Just the Basics!)

Captivate is powerful and flexible, and you can make your movies as intricate and interactive as you want. However, you will always start with a basic movie. This chapter describes how to make a basic movie with Captivate using the auto-record feature. Follow along and create a demonstration from start to finish!

Overview

Captivate allows you to capture the movement of your cursor and the resulting screen images with just a few keystrokes. To make the simplest form of movie—one that you can modify and enhance later—there are only a few basic steps:

1. Decide what you're going to record (discussed in more detail in Chapter 2).
2. Turn on the Captivate recording function, and then perform the tasks you want included in the movie.
3. Preview the project and make changes as necessary.
4. Publish the movie for others to use.

For the rest of this book, we'll be creating movies about the web site dedicated to Harry A. Franck, a well-known travel author from the early part of last century.

Recording with Captivate

To create your first movie, you'll need to decide what the movie will be about. For this example, we'll create a demonstration that shows how to navigate the various pages within a web site. Before you begin, ensure that the web site or whatever application you'll be recording is open and ready to go. If you want to follow along with our example, open up the website www.harryafranck.com in your preferred Internet browser.

1. Start the Captivate software by double-clicking the **Captivate** icon.

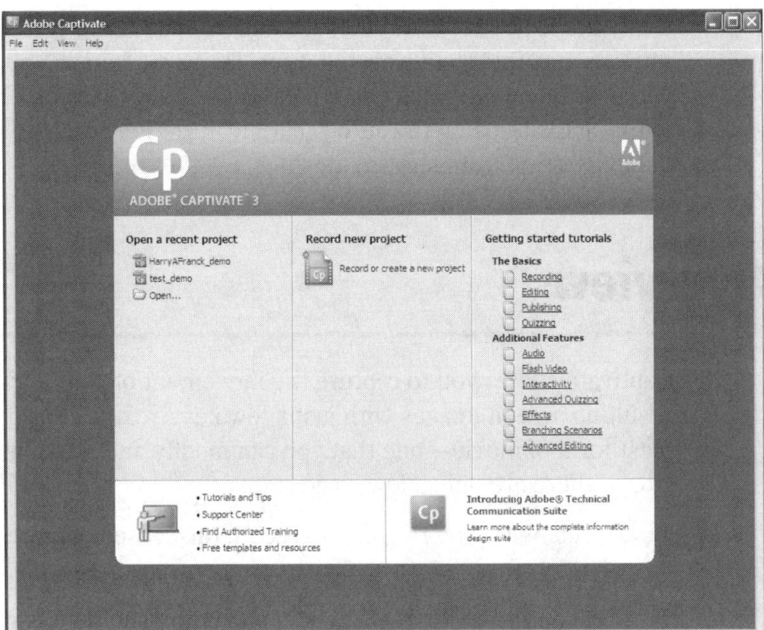

Figure 3-1. Start Captivate.

2. Click **Record or create a new project** to display the New project options window, as shown in Figure 3-2.

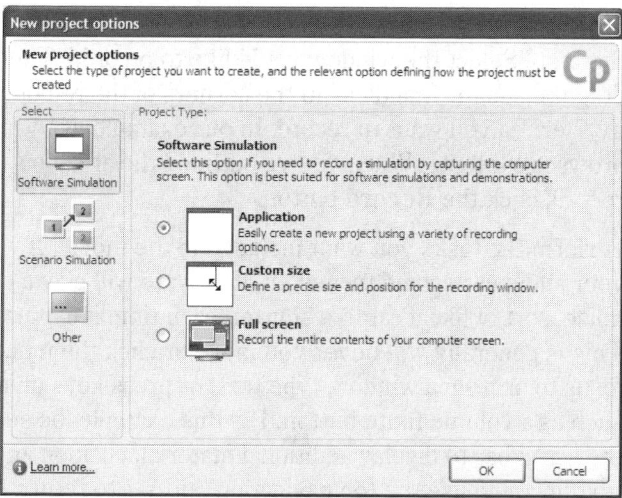

Figure 3-2. Choose the type of project.

3. We're going to be creating a demonstration for an application (the browser), so the default selections of **Software Simulation** and **Application** are fine. You'll still get a chance to set your window size in the next step. Click **OK** to display a red outline and the recording control box. Anything within this outline will be recorded to the movie file.

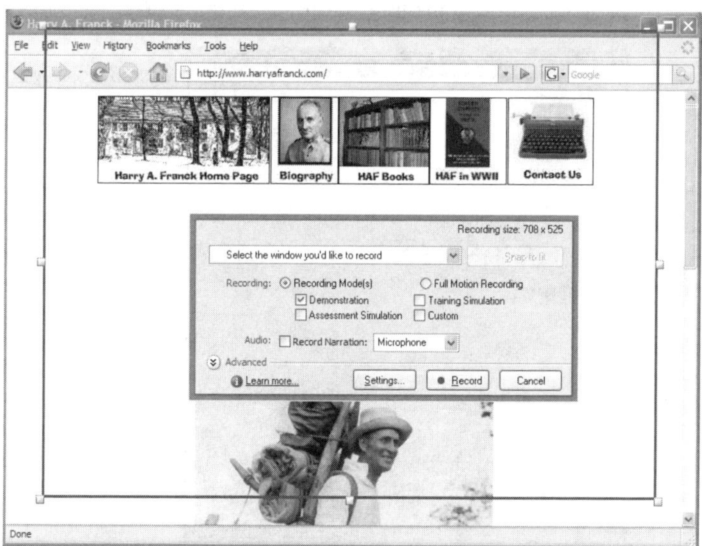

Figure 3-3. Specify the area to record.

4. First, choose the browser window from the drop-down containing the text "Select the window you'd like to record." Then click and drag the square "handles" in the corners of the red outline to specify the area you want to record. In our example, we want just the browser contents. When you've outlined the area you want to record, click the **Record** button.

5. Perform the tasks you want included in the movie. If you've got your audio set up and turned on, Captivate will play a clicking noise, sort of like a camera shutter, each time it captures a screen. This is generally whenever you move or click the mouse, change focus to or from a window, type text, or press keys on the keyboard such as a volume mute button. For this example, be sure to use the scroll bar to display additional material, click on an internal text link, and use the top navigation buttons to return to the main page.

Tip: Take your time when recording a movie, making sure that each screen is fully loaded and appears the way you want it to before you go on to the next task. You'll make a better movie if you proceed slowly while recording.

6. When you've finished all the tasks, press the **End** button on your keyboard to stop recording. Captivate will ask for a name for your project. Enter a project name, then click **OK**.

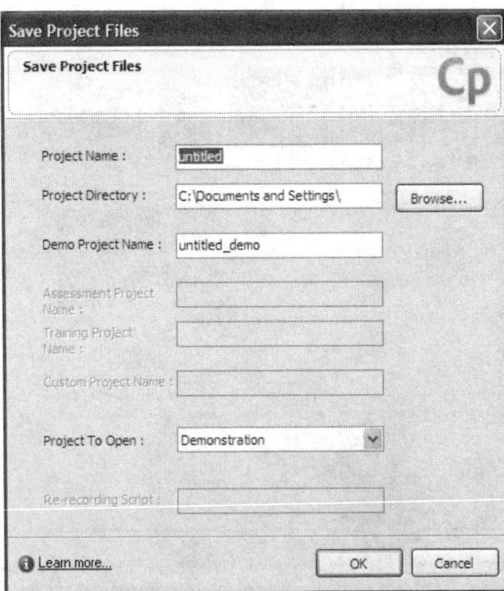

Figure 3-4. Specify a name for your movie project file.

Captivate displays a status message as it converts the stored images to SWF files, and then displays the movie on the Storyboard window.

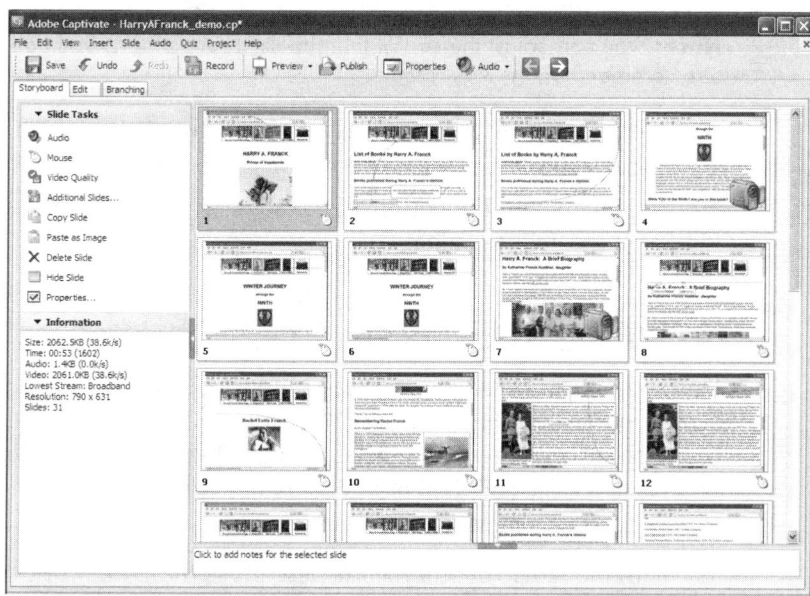

Figure 3-5. The captured screens display in the Storyboard window.

Previewing and Editing Movies

Once you've completed recording a movie, Captivate displays the movie in the Storyboard window. From here, you can preview the movie or make changes as necessary (including adding interactivity as described in Chapter 9).

There are five basic components of the Storyboard window:

- Menu bar—Located at the top of the screen, the menu bar allows you to access the various Captivate functions that apply to the entire movie (such as Save or Publish).
- Slide Tasks—On the left side of the screen, the Slide Tasks area lists the functions that you can perform on individual segments within your movie. Note that the Edit and Branching tabs (just above the Slide Tasks list) give you access to even more functions.
- Slideshow—The largest area of the screen, this area shows a "thumbnail" icon for each captured screen. You can select multiple

slides for easier, faster edits, or you can make changes to individual slides from here.

Note: You can adjust the size of thumbnails through the Thumbnail Size command on the View menu.

- Information—This area displays information about the movie, such as size and run-time length.
- Comments—At the bottom of the screen, this area displays notes about the selected slide.

Previewing Your Movie

Once you've recorded your actions, Captivate stores each captured screen and the actions associated with it as a slide. You can preview the movie at any time to see what it will look like. Captivate will generate an SWF file and then play it on your screen.

To preview a movie:

1. With the movie in Storyboard view, press the **F4** key or choose **Project** from the Preview menu.
2. The preview window includes some movie control buttons on the right side of the window. You can use these controls to play, pause, stop, or fast forward the movie preview, just as you would a VCR.

   As you watch, you'll notice a variety of elements that Captivate has automatically added to the movie for you:

   - Each slide is given a default display time.
   - A sound plays that represents each mouse click.
   - Some areas are surrounded by a highlight box.
   - Captions with default text are added in some places.

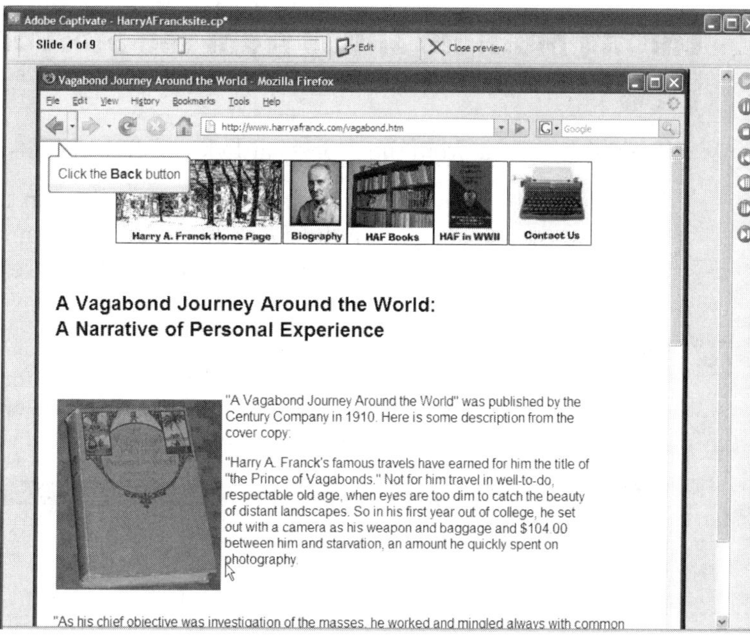

Figure 3-6. Some text has been added automatically, such as "Click the Back button" in the above example.

3. When the preview is complete, you can use the controls on the right of the screen to view it again or to step backward through the preview.
4. When you're finished watching the preview, click the **Close preview** button.

For this sample movie, Captivate added some text to the link we clicked. However, it isn't exactly the phrasing we want to use. We can easily edit this one slide later in Edit view. In addition, we notice that some of the slides do not display long enough for the viewer to be able to read all of the text. But this is easy to fix, and can be done right from the Storyboard view, so we'll do that first.

Editing Multiple Slides from the Storyboard View

To edit the movie from the Storyboard view, follow these steps:

1. Select the slides you want to edit by clicking once on the first slide, then holding down the **Shift** key and clicking on the last of the slides you want to change. The selected slides are highlighted.

Tip: If you double-click on a slide, you'll automatically open the slide in Edit view. While there are times you'll want to do this, for now you want to remain in Storyboard view. Simply click the Storyboard tab on the left side of the screen to return to Storyboard view.

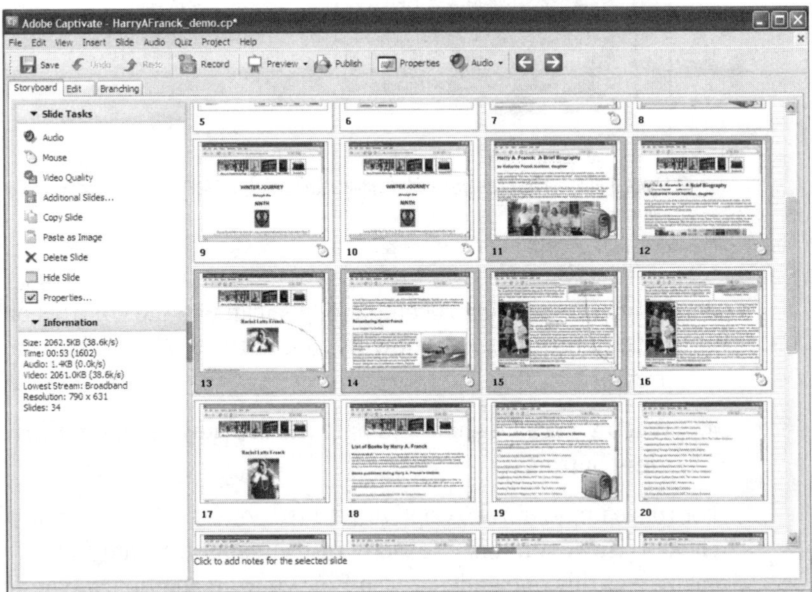

Figure 3-7. Select the slides you want to edit.

2. Choose one of the Slide Tasks functions on the left side of the screen by clicking on it. For our example, we'll click **Properties**.

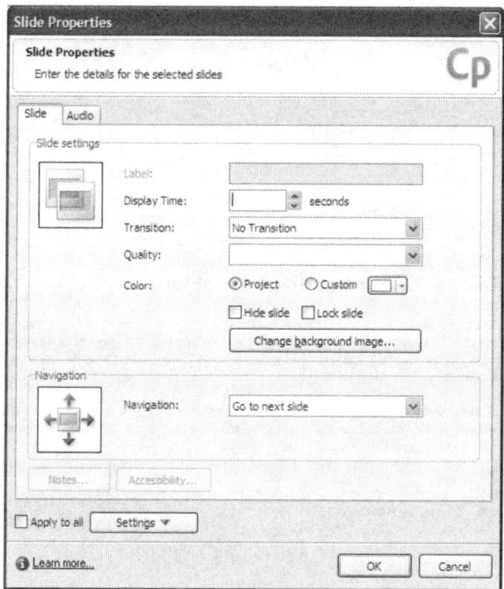

Figure 3-8. Enter the Display Time in the Slide Properties window.

3. In the Display Time box, type the time, in seconds, that you want each slide to remain on the screen.
4. Click **OK** to close the Slide Properties window.
5. Click **Save** at the top of the Captivate screen.

Tip: You could skip these last two steps, but it's better to save frequently. You never know when you might be interrupted!

6. Enter a name for the movie—in our case, we're calling it **HarryFranck_navigation**—and then click **Save.** Captivate automatically appends the suffix .cp (for Captivate project).

Editing a Single Slide from the Edit View

To make changes to a single slide, you'll want to go to the Edit view. This view has some of the same functionality as the Storyboard view, plus more. To make changes in the Edit view, follow these steps:

1. Open the slide you want to edit in Edit view in either of two ways:
   - Select the slide you want to change by clicking on it once, then click the **Edit** tab on the left side of the window.
   - Double-click the slide you want to edit.

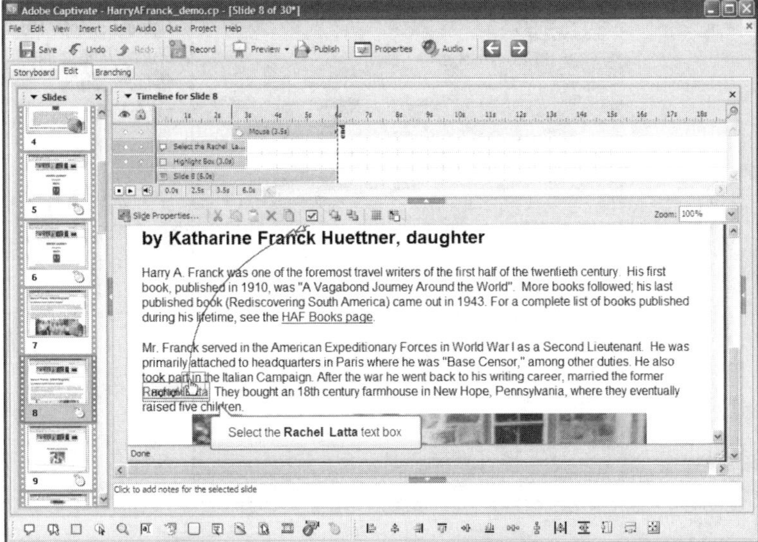

Figure 3-9. View a slide in Edit view.

2. Take a moment to locate the different elements of the Edit view and the slide we're viewing. The Edit view displays the selected slide in the main portion of the view. You'll also see the surrounding slides in a column on the left side of the screen and a "timeline" across the top of the slide. This shows you exactly how long each element on the slide appears on the screen. For this example, you can see there are three components:
   - Mouse track showing that the mouse movement comes up from the bottom of the screen to stop on a link.
   - Text box that says, "Select the **Rachel Latta** text box."
   - Highlight box that outlines the text of the link that was clicked.
3. Double-click on the element, either in the timeline or on the slide itself, to display the properties for that element. In our example, we want to change the text in the text box. Double-clicking on the text box itself displays the Text Caption window.

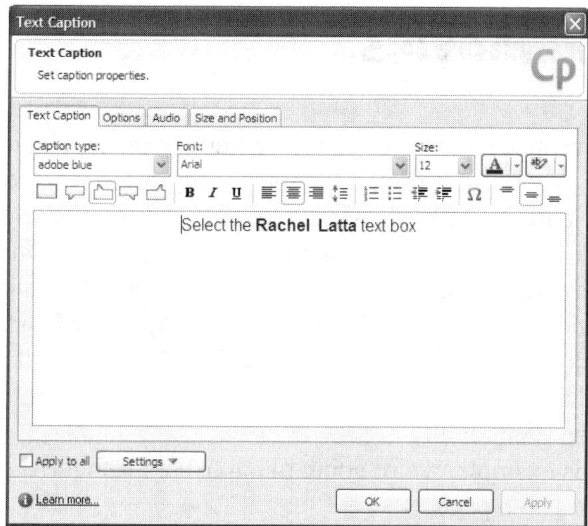

Figure 3-10. Change the text in the Text Caption window.

4. Make changes to the text as necessary. Note that you can change the font, size, color, and other attributes just as you would in standard word processing packages. Simply select the text you want to change, then select the new attributes for the selected text. For this example, we're changing the wording to "Click the **Rachel Latta** text box."
5. Click **OK** when you are done to close the Text Caption window and return to the Edit view display.
6. Click **Save** to save your changes.

Note: Sometimes you'll need to adjust the size of a text caption after editing text. To do this, drag the appropriate caption handle to resize the caption.

Publishing Movies

Once you've made whatever edits you need to make, you must publish the movie to convert it from a Captivate project file (CP) to an actual Flash movie file (SWF). The Captivate publishing function can also create additional files that can be used to view the Flash movie. For example, if you publish to a web page, you may set the publish feature to automatically create the HTML file that plays your Flash movie. If you publish to a stand-alone executable file, Captivate will create the EXE file that contains your movie. For more details on publishing options, see Chapter 14.

For this example, we're going to publish a Flash file designed for viewing on a web page.

1. From the open project, in either Storyboard or Edit view, click the **Publish** icon to display the publishing options.

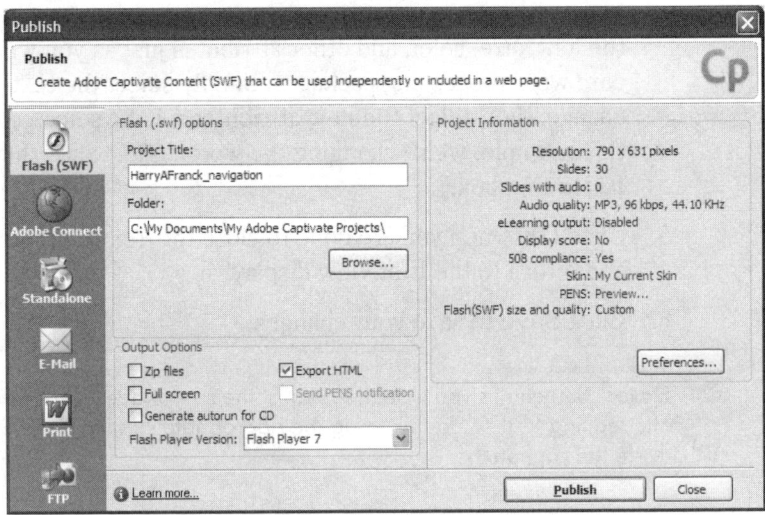

Figure 3-11. The Publish options window.

2. Click the **Flash (SWF)** icon to create a Flash movie.
3. Captivate enters a default name for the output movie that is the same as the name of the saved project. You can change this by typing a new name in the Project Title text box.
4. Captivate will store the output you publish in a new folder in the folder with your current Captivate project files. You can change this by typing a new location in the Folder text box.
5. Under Output Options, ensure that the **Export HTML** box is checked. Captivate will create an HTML file that automatically plays the published movie.
6. Click **Publish**. Captivate generates the movie, much as it did in the preview window. It also creates the HTML file necessary to publish your file on a web page and displays a message when complete. Captivate will prompt you if a new folder needs to be created.

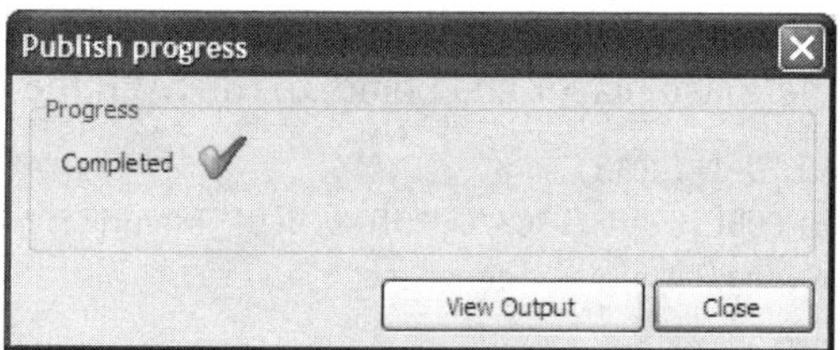

Figure 3-12. Publish the movie, then view the output.

7. Click **View Output** to see exactly what the movie will look like. For our HTML example, the movie will play in your default browser. Note that the movie playback controls appear at the bottom of your movie.

Figure 3-13. The playback controls display at the bottom of the movie.

8. The controls allow the viewer to play, back up, stop, or view the movie from any point, just as the preview controls worked, similar to a VCR. The playback controls also include an icon with the letter *i* (for information). This is where you can include information about the movie, your company, or yourself. Click the **i** icon to display the default information. To customize the information in this box or to change the look of all of the playback controls, see Chapter 13.

PROJECT CREATED BY
Brenda Huettner
bphuettner@harryafranck.com
www.harryafranck.com
2007
Adobe Captivate 3

Figure 3-14. Display the project information window.

9. When the movie is finished, you can use the playback controls to view the movie again or you can simply close the browser window.

Your movie is stored in the folder you specified as an SWF file. There's also another file in that folder with the same name as your movie but with the extension .htm. This is your HTML output. Although this isn't a book on writing HTML, you can see that the coding is fairly simple. It calls the Flash player and points to the SWF file you created.

```
<!-- saved from url=(0013) -->
<!DOCTYPE HTML PUBLIC "-//W3C//DTD HTML 4.01 Transitional//EN"
"http://www.w3.org/TR/html4/loose.dtd">
<html>
<head>
<meta http-equiv="Content-Type" content="text/html; charset=utf-8">
<title>HarryFranck_navigation</title>
</head>

<body>
<center>
<object classid="clsid:D27CDB6E-AE6D-11cf-96B8-444553540000"
codebase="http://download.adobe.com/pub/shockwave/cabs/flash/swflash
.cab#version=6,0,29,0" width="862" height="650" ID="Captivate1">
  <param name="movie" value="HarryFranck_navigation.swf">
  <param name="quality" value="high">
  <param name="menu" value="false">
  <param name="loop" value="0">
  <embed src="HarryFranck_navigation.swf" width="862" height="650"
     loop="0" quality="high" pluginspage="http:
     //www.adobe.com/go/getflashplayer"
     type="application/x-shockwave-flash" menu="false"></embed>
</object>
```

```
</center>
</body>
</html>
```

Summary

This chapter showed you how to create a simple demonstration, make a few minor edits, and publish the movie for viewing on the web. The rest of this book goes into more detail about the many additional features and functions in Captivate, starting with the next chapter about choosing recording options.

Chapter 4

Recording a Movie

When you begin a Captivate project, you'll generally record some actions on your computer, then go back and make changes or add interactivity. Although recording can be simple, you have a lot of options throughout the recording process. This chapter will cover these recording options and describe how to ensure that you capture the screens you'll need for your movie. To create a movie without recording screens, see Chapter 5.

Preparing to Record a New Movie

When you begin a Captivate project, you'll start by specifying the type of project you want to create using the Software Simulation options. A software simulation captures a series of screens as you perform tasks on your desktop, allowing you to set a variety of recording options as you go. Whichever options you choose, you'll still be able to edit the files to create the exact type of movie you want.

Before You Record

Be aware that Captivate will capture everything that is on your screen within the designated recording area. Before you begin recording, you may want to check for some elements that may distract from the point of your movie.

Open programs—If you're going to be recording the full screen or if your recording area includes the bottom taskbar, you may want to ensure that all extraneous software packages are closed. Also, be aware that if you have other programs running, such as an e-mail client or instant messaging software, any notifications or pop-up windows that happen to display while you're recording will be captured in the Captivate movie. Close programs to remove their icons from the taskbar.

Background—Don't use a multicolored, textured, or otherwise busy background. This can distract from your movie and make it hard to see mouse movement over the background.

Icons—If your recording area is full screen or allows for space between program application windows, your movie will include any icons that are on your desktop. Make sure that you are displaying only those icons that belong in your movie.

Copyrights—Ensure that you have permission to use whatever screen images or audio you plan to capture.

Tip: If you run through your movie a couple of times before you begin recording, you'll become more comfortable with the script or storyboards and can identify and hopefully resolve any problems that occur without storing error messages as part of your movie.

Specifying the Recording Area

When you begin recording a new movie, you'll need to specify which part of the screen you want to record (the recording area). Follow these steps:

1. Start the program you want to record, then start the Captivate software. The first screen you'll see is the Captivate main menu.

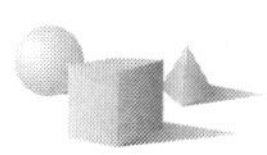

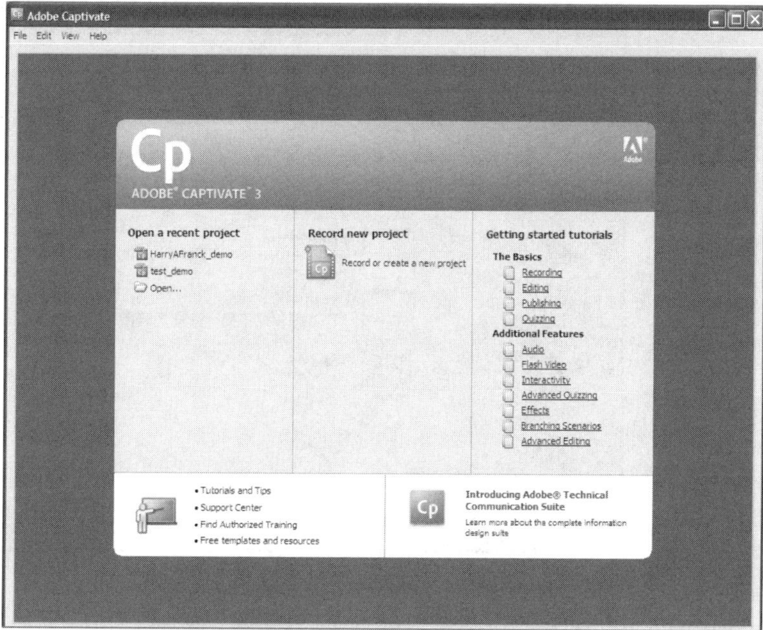

Figure 4-1. Start with the main menu.

2. Click **Record or create a new project** to open the New project options window.

   The first thing you'll need to decide is whether you're creating a software simulation or a scenario simulation. This chapter describes the Software Simulation process; the Scenario Simulation wizard is described in Chapter 5. If neither of these options covers the type of project you want, see the section "Creating Other Types of Projects" in Chapter 5.

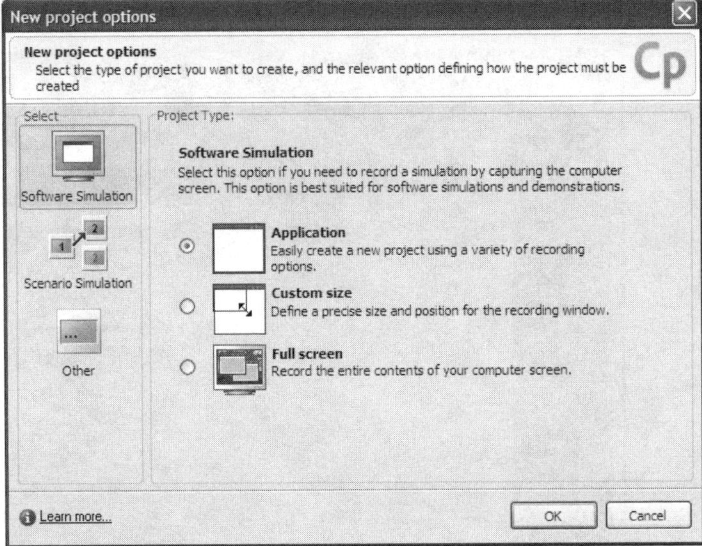

Figure 4-2. Choose the project type.

3. To begin a Software Simulation project, first click **Software Simulation**. You then need to specify the amount of area on your screen that you want to record. There are three options:
   - Application—This option identifies all of your open windows and automatically sets the recording area to fit the application window that you specify.
   - Custom size—This option allows you to choose from a list of preset window sizes (or specify a custom size of your own) regardless of the open windows. Anything that occurs within the specified area will be recorded.
   - Full screen—This option records your entire computer screen, even if you move from one application to another.

   Choose the appropriate option and then click **OK** to display your own computer screen with the recording area options. If you choose Full screen, the entire screen will be recorded. If you choose Application or Custom size, you'll see the default recording area outlined in red.

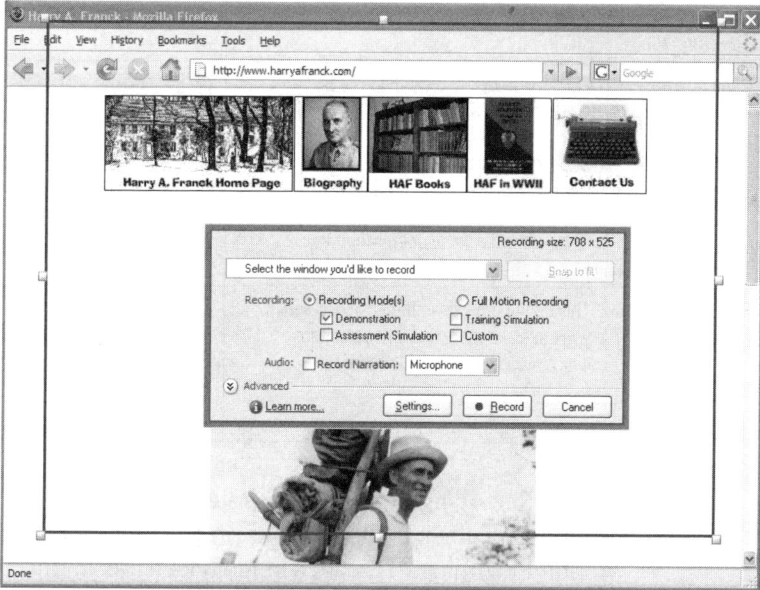

Figure 4-3. Define the recording area.

4. You can modify the recording area by clicking and dragging any of the square "handles" on the sides and corners of the red recording area box or by clicking anywhere within the red box and dragging it to a new location. The size of the movie area will be displayed in the control box in the center of your screen. Depending on the recording type, you'll also have the following additional options:

Table 4-1. Settings for the recording area

For this recording type:	Do this:	The control box looks like this:
Application	Click the down arrow at the top of the window to display a list of your open windows, then click the title of the window you want to record. By default, the red recording area encloses the exact window you specify.	

For this recording type:	Do this:	The control box looks like this:
Custom size	Enter the height and width in pixels. or Choose from the list of Preset window sizes. or Choose from a list of open windows.	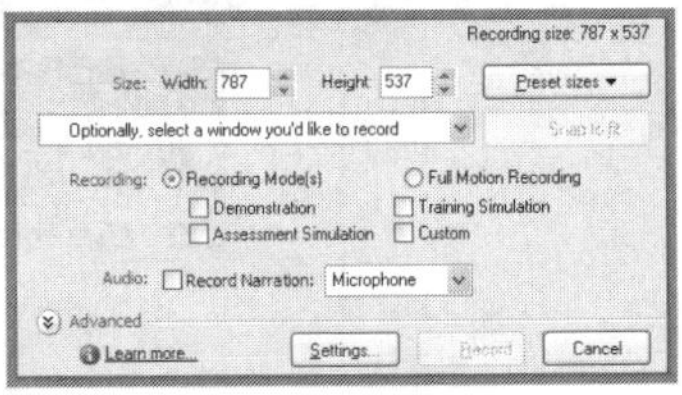
Full screen	This option defaults to the entire screen. If you have two monitors, you can choose which monitor you want to record.	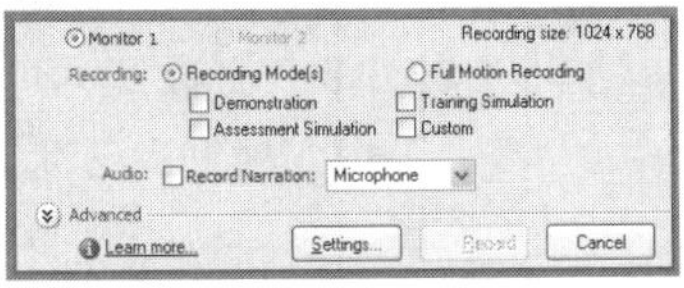

5. Set the Recording Mode options to determine which features will be automatically included in your project. You can choose Full Motion Recording to create a single video file, or choose any of the listed recording modes.

Table 4-2. Recording modes

Choose this mode:	To use these default settings:
Demonstration	Tracks mouse movement, automatically creates captions and highlight boxes.
Assessment Simulation	Automatically creates click boxes with a failure caption and text entry boxes for text fields with a failure caption. Captions and mouse movement are not included.
Training Simulation	Creates click boxes with hint and failure captions and text entry boxes for text fields with a failure caption. Captions and mouse movement are not included.
Custom	Allows you to choose which of the available elements (such as captions, mouse movement, highlight boxes, click boxes, and text entry boxes) will be included in the project file.

6. If you want to record audio while you're capturing your movie file, click the **Record Narration** option to select it; then choose the input method for your audio (microphone, line-in, or a pre-existing audio file on your system).

For any of the three recording types, you may modify additional settings, as described in the following section.

Modifying the Recording Settings

You can change the way that Captivate records your movies and the keys that activate the Captivate recording functions. You'll probably only need to set these options occasionally—subsequent movies will use the most recent settings you specified.

1. Set the recording area of the movie as described in the previous section.
2. In the control box for the recording, click the **Settings** button to view the categories of recording options.
3. Choose **Settings** from the Category list on the left side of the window to specify which components will be captured during automated recording.

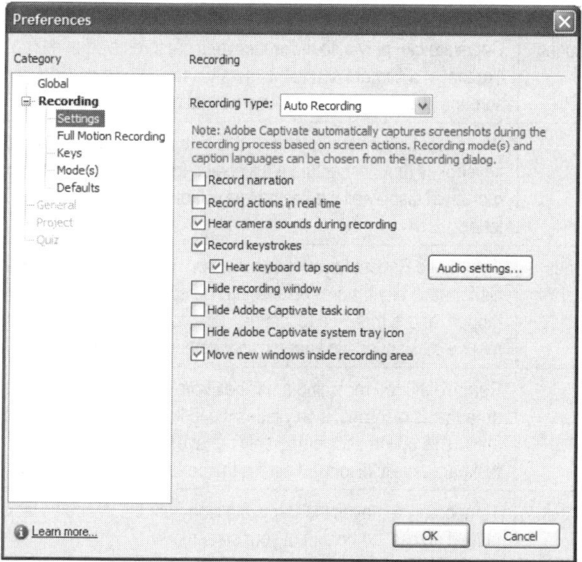

Figure 4-4. Set the options for recording in the Preferences window.

4. On the Recording Settings screen, set the Recording Type to **Auto Recording** or **Manual Recording.** If you choose Manual Recording, the selected elements will be captured when you click the PrntScrn button during recording. If you choose Auto Recording, the selected elements will be captured on each action you perform

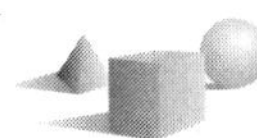

(click the mouse, open a window within the specified recording area, press a key on the keyboard, or drag and drop).

5. For each recording type, specify the following additional options by clicking the boxes to check or uncheck each option. Note that this sets the default options for the captured screens—they can all be changed at any time in the Edit view. Available options are:

Table 4-3. Recording settings

Check this option:	To do this:
Record narration	Record audio while you're recording the visual portion of the movie. You must have a microphone set up for this to work.
Record actions in real time	This feature causes Captivate to record at the same rate you perform actions. So, for example, if it takes you 10 seconds to move the mouse across the screen and click a button, the resulting slide will take 10 seconds to display that action. Without this option selected, Captivate adjusts the time for mouse movements and other actions based on default settings.
Hear camera sounds during recording	Captivate can play a sound whenever it captures a screen. The sound, sort of like that of a camera shutter, is merely a tool to help you identify when the screens are captured. The sound will not be part of the finished movie.
Record keystrokes	When you type on the keyboard, this setting will cause Captivate to store the keystrokes (but not capture a full screen for each character typed). The finished movie will display all the keystrokes without the overhead of a full screen per letter.
Hear keyboard tap sounds	If you have Record keystrokes turned on, you can have Captivate play a sound file for each key it stores. The sound file sounds like a keyboard key being tapped, and is merely a recording tool—you will have the option later of adding mouse click sounds to your movie whether or not this feature is turned on.
Hide recording window	Remove the red recording area lines from the screen. This does not change the area that is recorded; it only hides the indication of the outline of the recording area. This option also temporarily removes the Captivate icon from the Windows taskbar (usually displayed across the bottom of your screen).
Hide Adobe Captivate task icon	Temporarily removes the Captivate icon from the Windows taskbar (usually displayed across the bottom of your screen).
Hide Adobe Captivate system tray icon	Temporarily removes the Captivate icon from the Windows system tray (in the lower-right corner of your screen).
Move new windows inside recording area	When the application you are recording launches new windows or dialog boxes, they are placed inside the recording area to the extent possible. In cases where new windows are larger than the recording area, some of the area on the right and bottom of the new window or dialog box may be missed.

6. Click **OK** to save your changes, or **Cancel** to close the window without saving your changes.

7. Choose **Full Motion Recording** from the categories on the left side of the screen to define when you want to use the Full Motion recording options.

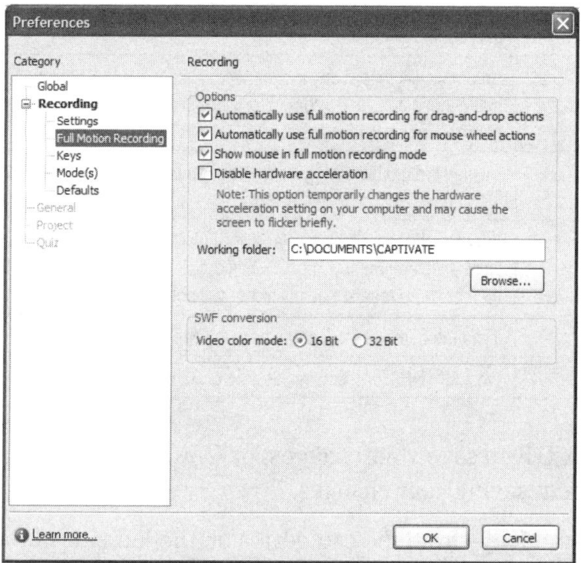

Figure 4-5. Set the Full Motion recording options.

8. From the Full Motion Recording screen, specify when you want to use the Full Motion feature. This feature automatically records more screens during drag-and-drop or mouse actions to give you a smoother movie. The extra screens are stored in one slide and indicated on the slide by a movie icon.

Tip: Full Motion recording delivers a very smooth movie, but also requires extra resources such as disk space and memory. Use this feature sparingly for the most efficient movies.

Table 4-4. Full Motion recording options

Check this option:	To do this:
Automatically use full motion recording for drag-and-drop actions	Automatically record any drag-and-drop actions in Full Motion mode. This will make these actions (such as dropping an image into a folder or using a scroll bar) appear smoother.
Automatically use full motion recording for mouse wheel actions	Automatically record any mouse wheel actions in Full Motion mode. This will make these actions (such as dropping an image into a folder or using a scroll bar) appear smoother.
Show mouse in full motion recording mode	Display the mouse during drag-and-drop Full Motion animations.
Disable hardware acceleration	Increase the resources available for Full Motion capture by turning off the hardware acceleration. If you check this option, you'll see a flicker on your monitor as the hardware resets, but this flicker will not appear in the finished movie.
Working folder	Type the name of the folder where the Full Motion recording will be saved.
SWF conversion	Choose 16 Bit for a smaller file size or 32 Bit for a greater range of color options.

9. Click **OK** to save your changes, or **Cancel** to close the window without saving your changes.
10. Choose **Keys** from the categories on the left side of the screen to define the keystrokes you'll use to control the recording process.

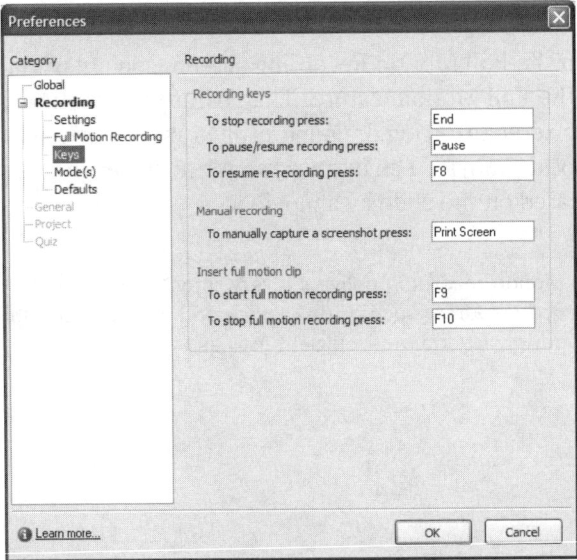

Figure 4-6. Set recording key options to control movie recording.

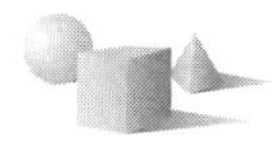

Note: Throughout this book, we'll use the default keystrokes to indicate recording stop and start instructions.

11. To change any of the recording keys, click in a text box and press the key combination you want to use (such as Alt+F2 or Ctrl+F4). You cannot use the Escape, Enter, Tab, Spacebar, F1, or Backspace keys, since these have other meanings within Captivate. You cannot use the Shift key unless it is in combination with either Alt or Ctrl (such as Shift+Ctrl+F3).

Tip: If you change the recording keys, make sure you write down the new keystrokes, particularly if you change the "end recording" keystroke.

12. Click **OK** to save your changes, or **Cancel** to close the window without saving your changes.
13. Choose **Mode(s)** from the Category list on the left side of the window to define the components that will be automatically added while recording. You can set different components for each of the available recording modes.

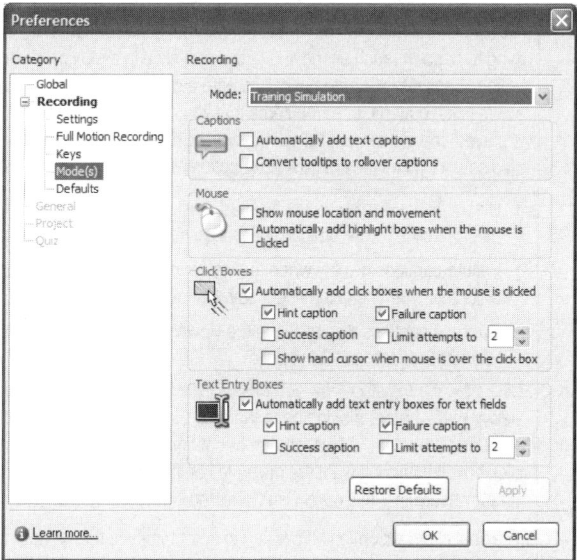

Figure 4-7. Set Mode(s) options to determine which elements will be captured.

14. Specify the recording mode for which you want to set options by choosing from the drop-down list. Depending on which mode you choose, some of the displayed options may be inactive.
15. Click to select each of the available options, or click a check mark to deselect an option. Remember that even if you don't choose them here, you can always add options later. If at any time you want to return to the default options, click the Restore Defaults button.

Table 4-5. Mode(s) options

For this type of element:	Specify these options:
Captions	Captions are the instructions that the system automatically adds when you perform an action, such as "Click the File menu." Select the Automatically add text captions box to specify that you want captions for the selected recording mode. If the application you're recording uses tooltips (small text boxes that display when you move the cursor over certain areas of the screen) you can have Captivate automatically convert these tooltips to rollover captions.
Mouse	If you select Show mouse location and movement, Captivate will be able to simulate the mouse movement on the final movie. If you select the Automatically add highlight boxes option, then Captivate will insert a partially transparent shaded box over each link or button that you click while recording.
Click Boxes	A *click box* defines an area on the screen that a viewer can click to cause something to happen (such as moving to the next slide in a movie). If you activate this option, Captivate will automatically create a click box the size and shape of the active links, buttons, or menu items that you click while recording. When the movie is played, the viewer must click in the click box to continue the movie. You may also select which types of click box captions will be automatically generated: • Hint captions display on the finished movie when the viewer moves the cursor over the click box. A typical hint caption might be "Try clicking on the File menu." • Failure captions display when the viewer clicks somewhere outside of the click box. This type of caption might say "Not quite, try again!" • Success captions display when the viewer clicks in the click box. This might say "Congratulations" or "Good Job!" Click box options also allow you to specify how many incorrect clicks you'll let the viewer make before moving on to the next slide. Select the Limit attempts to box and enter a number to limit the number of times the viewer can click outside the click box. If you don't want the movie to continue unless the viewer clicks correctly, simply ensure that this option isn't selected. The final click box option allows you to determine whether or not the cursor will change to a hand shape when the viewer moves it over the click box.

For this type of element:	Specify these options:
Text Entry Boxes	Text entry boxes allow the viewer to actually type into the box. Captivate will compare the typed text to your predefined answers to determine whether or not the typed text is "correct." Like click boxes, you have a variety of options based on whether or not the text is entered correctly. • Hint captions display on the finished movie when the viewer moves the cursor over the text entry box. A typical hint caption might be "Type the answer here." • Failure captions display when the viewer types incorrect text. This type of caption might say "Not quite, try again!" • Success captions display when the viewer types the correct text. This might say "Congratulations" or "Good Job!" Text entry box options also allow you to specify how many times you'll let the viewer type incorrectly before moving on to the next slide. Select the Limit attempts to box and enter a number to limit the number of times the viewer can type the text. If you don't want the movie to continue unless the viewer types correctly, simply ensure that this option isn't selected.

16. Click **OK** to save your changes, or **Cancel** to close the window without saving your changes.
17. Choose **Defaults** from the categories on the left side of the screen to define the appearance of the automatically generated captions and highlight boxes.

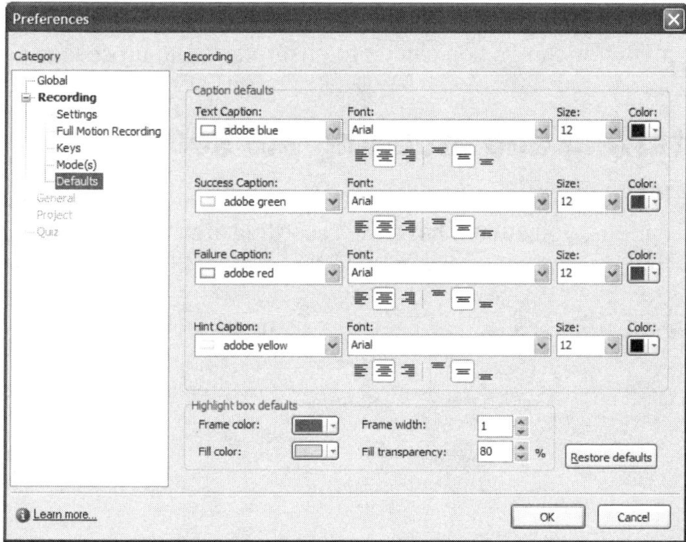

Figure 4-8. Set Defaults options to specify caption and highlight box appearance.

18. Choose from the drop-down lists for each type of caption to specify the appearance of the box that outlines the caption.
19. Specify the font face, size, color, and justification of the text within each caption type. Remember that this area is defining the default appearance of each caption type; you'll be able to customize them later if you want to.
20. Choose the color, width, and transparency for the highlight boxes. Like the captions, highlight boxes may be edited individually later.
21. Click **OK** to save your changes, or **Cancel** to close the window without saving your changes.
22. Once you've set all the recording options, click **OK** to return to the recording control box. From there, you can begin recording your movie as described in the following section.

Recording Actions on Your Screen

Once you've defined the area of the screen you want to record, turn on the Captivate recording function, then simply perform the tasks you want included in your movie. Although this is a simple process, there are a few things you can do to ensure that the process goes smoothly.

Starting and Stopping the Recording Process

When you've set the recording area and specified the recording options, you should have the recording area indicated by a red outline (unless you're recording the full screen) and the control box displayed.

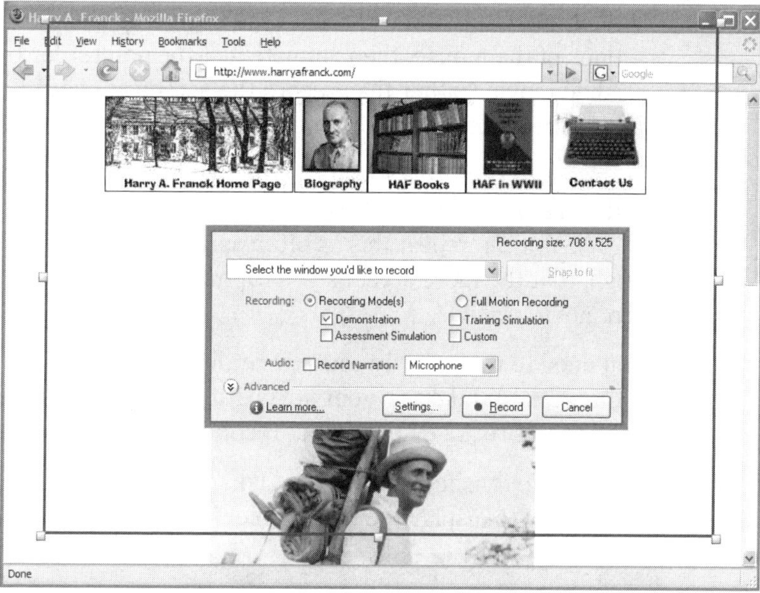

Figure 4-9. Start recording.

When you're ready to start recording, follow these steps:

1. In the control box, click **Record**.
2. Begin to perform the actions you want to record. If auto capture is on, Captivate will automatically capture the screen (and play a camera shutter sound) whenever you:
   - Click the mouse
   - Change focus from one window to another
   - Press any key on the keyboard
   - Click the mouse while it is in the recording area

   While you're recording, Captivate will also automatically insert the following components (based on your option settings):

   - Click boxes—These are areas that the viewer will click in during playback.
   - Highlight boxes—These are areas of particular interest that are highlighted.
   - Captions—Text instructions, such as "Click here."
   - Pointer movement—The mouse movement itself is not captured unless you are recording in Full Motion mode. Most of

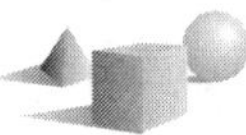

the time, Captivate will record the beginning and ending positions of the mouse, then animate just the pointer for the finished movie (rather than record the screen at every intermediate pointer location).

3. If you want to capture a specific screen while recording, press the **Print Screen** key (or whatever you've set as the manual recording key). You can repeat this as often as you like. Remember, though, that the more screens you capture, the larger your finished movie will be.
4. If you need to temporarily pause recording for any reason, press the **Pause/Break** key on your keyboard. You can then press the same Pause/Break key to resume recording when you are ready.
5. When you've finished with all the tasks you want to record, press the **End** key to display the Save Project Files window.

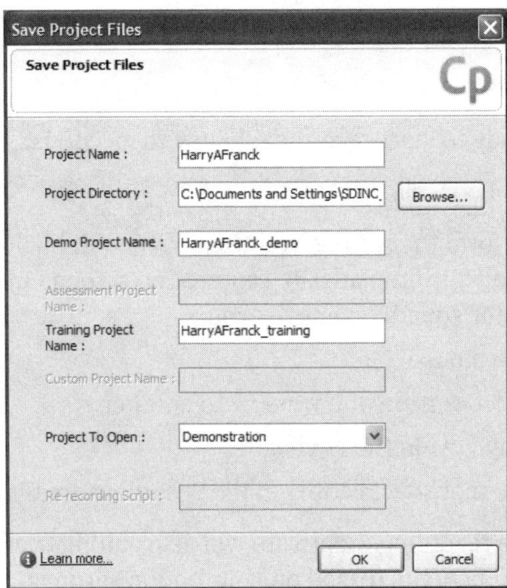

Figure 4-10. Specify the file names and location.

6. Enter a name for the project. Notice that if you've specified that you want to capture more than one type of project, Captivate allows you to enter a unique name for each type. The default project names use the project name as the base name, and add indicators for the project type (such as HarryAFranck_demo and

HarryAFranck_training). Click **OK** when you've specified all the names you want. The screens you've captured will appear as slides in the Captivate project.

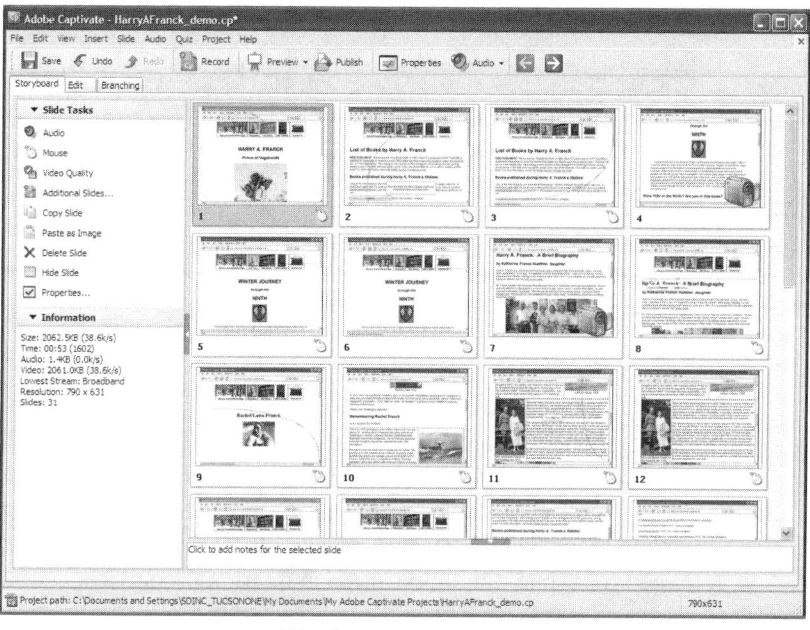

Figure 4-11. When complete, the project appears in the Storyboard view.

High-resolution Recording

Captivate allows you to create realistic movies and maintain relatively small file sizes because it does not use full animation for every action. Instead, Captivate captures a single screen, and then stores information to create the animated elements (such as typing or pointer movement) separately. Rather than store 30 copies of the same screen per second (or whatever your setting is), Captivate only captures a new frame when the screen changes. This keeps the disk space, file size, and memory resources fairly low.

However, there are several instances when you may want to capture a higher number of frames, such as when you're scrolling down a window. For these instances, Captivate will automatically switch to Full Motion recording mode and actually capture a higher number of frames per second than normal recording.

By default, Full Motion recording mode starts automatically whenever you drag and drop an icon or image, or draw within a graphics program. You can change the default at any time.

Table 4-6. Full Motion controls

To cause this:	Do this:
Manually start Full Motion recording while recording a movie.	Press F9.
Manually end Full Motion recording while recording a movie.	Press F10.
Stop the Full Motion recording from automatically starting on drag-and-drop or drawing actions.	In the Full Motion Recording screen of the Preferences window, deselect the Automatically use full motion recording for drag-and-drop actions option.

Once you've captured a Full Motion action, it will appear on your Storyboard view as a movie within a single slide, represented by a movie camera icon. You can edit this slide as you would any other, treating the Full Motion movie clip as you would any other element on the slide (see Chapter 7). You can also double-click on the movie camera icon to display the Full Motion animation properties.

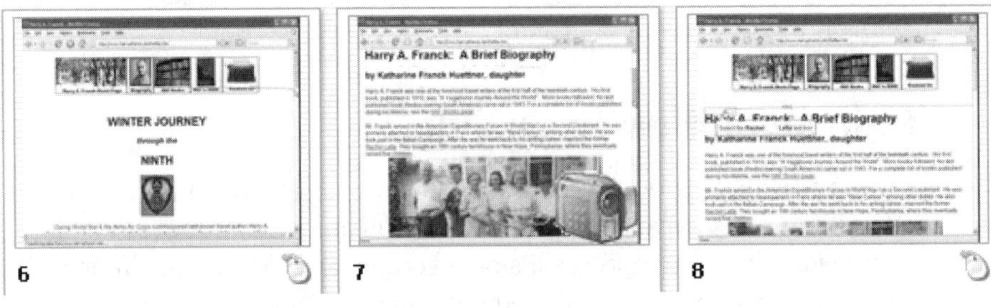

Figure 4-12. The movie camera icon indicates Full Motion recording within a slide.

Summary

This chapter described how to create new movies and some basic recording functions. The next chapter will describe how to create different types of movies without recording screen actions.

Chapter 5

Creating Movies without Recording

The previous chapter described how to create a movie by recording the keystrokes and screen images as you perform tasks on your computer system. Sometimes, however, it is more efficient to create movies in ways other than recording screen actions. This chapter describes how to use the Scenario Simulation wizard, as well as how to create blank movies, movies from image files, and movies from PowerPoint files.

Creating a Scenario Simulation

The Scenario Simulation wizard helps you create scenario or interaction-based training content that isn't necessarily tied to software simulations, such as training for soft skills or sales presentations. The Scenario Simulation wizard automatically creates the appropriate slides which you can then edit as needed.

To use the Scenario Simulation wizard, follow these steps:

1. Start the Captivate software. The first screen you'll see will be the Captivate main menu.
2. Click **Record or create a new project** to open the New project options window.
3. Click **Scenario Simulation**.

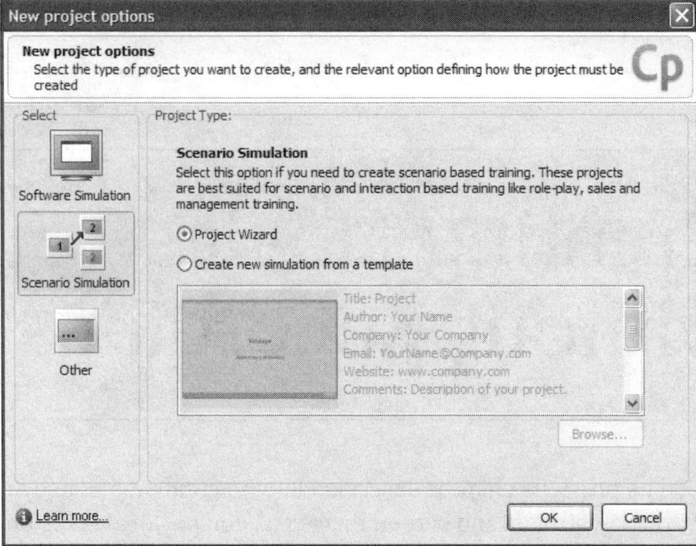

Figure 5-1. Begin the Scenario Simulation wizard.

4. Choose **Project Wizard**, and then click **OK** to display the Scenario Simulation project options.

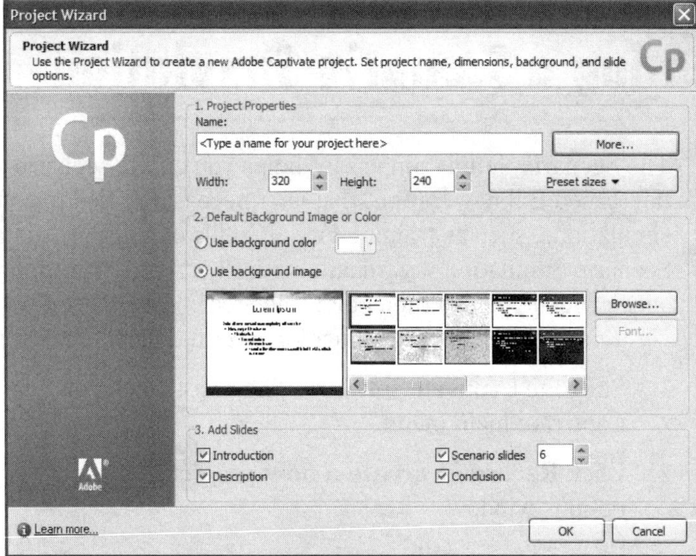

Figure 5-2. Specify the Scenario Simulation options.

5. Enter a name for the project, and specify the size (in pixels) for the resulting movie.

Tip: Remember that the larger the movie dimensions, the larger your movie file will be. Also, keep your audience in mind. If they do not have high-resolution monitors, they may not be able to view the larger movies.

6. Click the **More** button to enter information about the movie and your company. This information will appear when the viewer of the movie clicks the Information button.

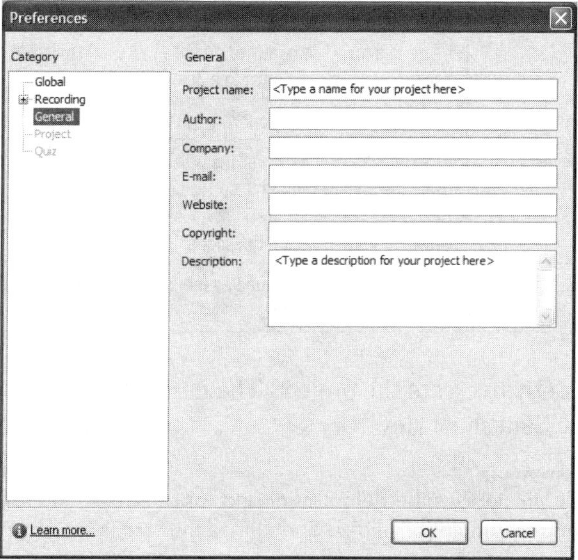

Figure 5-3. Specify the information that will appear in the Information window.

7. Enter as much or as little information as you want in the Preferences window. When finished, click **OK** to save your changes and return to the Scenario Simulation options.

8. Specify either a default background color for your slides or a default background image from the displayed images. If you have a specific image or template you want to use, click the **Browse** button to point to the file.

Tip: The displayed backgrounds are actually taken from the Captivate/Templates directory that is installed with the Captivate software. You can copy any existing PowerPoint template to this directory to display your corporate look and feel for use with Captivate movies.

9. Define the number and type of slides you want in the base project. Remember, of course, that you can add or change slides as much as you need to—this just gives you a starting place. The available slide types in the wizard are shown in Table 5-1.

Table 5-1. Scenario Simulation slide types

This type of slide:	Looks like this:
Introduction	Large text for a title centered on the slide, with a full-slide graphic in the background. This is similar to a Title slide in PowerPoint.
Description	Large text, like the Introduction, but the graphics are more minimal.
Scenario slides	This defaults to question slides with Clear, Skip, and Submit buttons, using the specified graphic background. Note that if you included Scenario slides, you'll also get a Results slide that summarizes the viewer's answers to the questions.
Conclusion	Uses the same background as the Introduction slide, but is placed at the end of the movie.

10. Click **OK** to create the project. The designated slide types appear in the Slideshow view.

Note: Captivate uses the default font and font size to create the text in scenario simulation slides. Sometimes the font is too large (see slide 9 in Figure 5-4) or too small. You can change the font size or any other property as needed (see Chapter 7, "Editing a Single Slide").

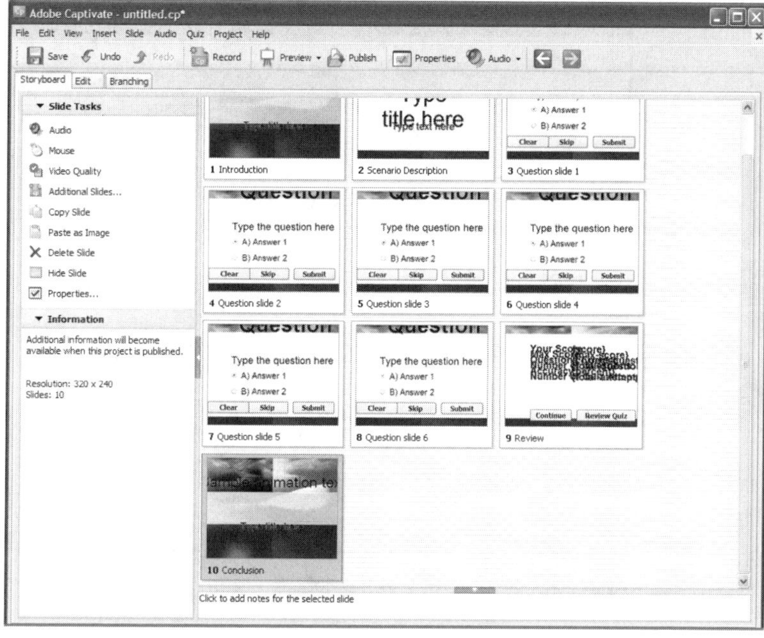

Figure 5-4. Introduction, question, and conclusion slides in a scenario simulation.

Creating Other Types of Projects

Creating a Blank Project

A blank project consists of one blank slide and all of the movie settings. This can then be used as a template to ensure that all movies use the same settings. Or you might create a blank project with the intention of recording slides later. To create a blank project, follow these steps:

1. Start the Captivate software. The first screen you'll see will be the Captivate main menu.
2. Click **Record or create a new project** to open the New project options window.
3. Click **Other** to display the project types that do not involve recording.

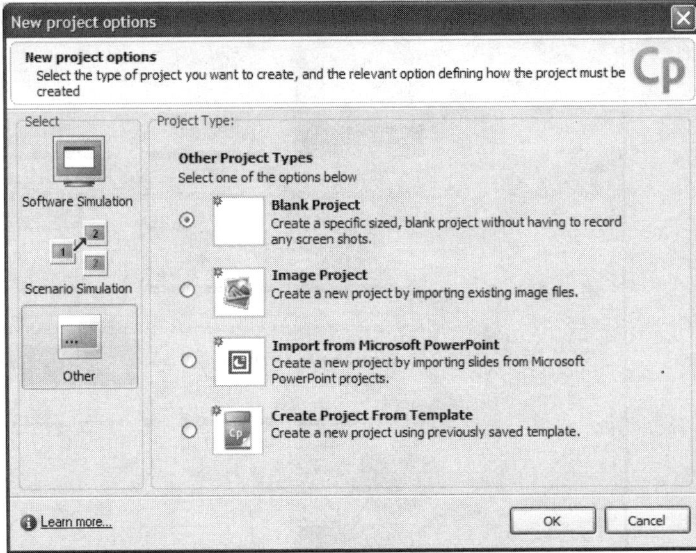

Figure 5-5. Choose to create a blank project.

4. Choose **Blank Project**, and then click **OK** to display the Blank project window.
5. Choose from the list of predefined window sizes, or enter a custom size.

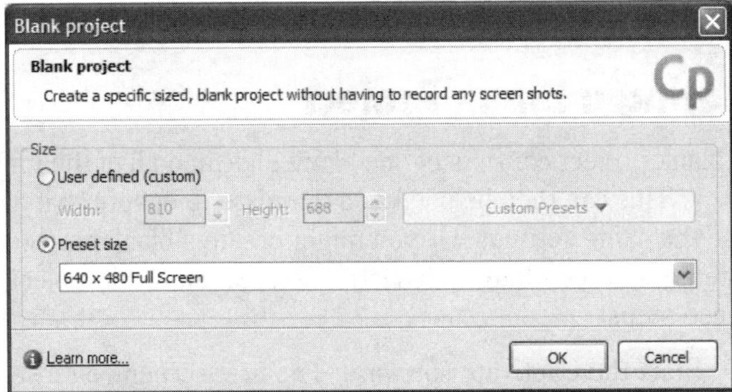

Figure 5-6. Specify a size for the blank project.

Note: Remember that the larger the window size, the larger your movie file will be. Also, keep your audience in mind. If they do not have high-resolution monitors, they may not be able to view the larger movies.

6. Click **OK** to see your single blank slide in Storyboard view.

Creating an Image Project

If you have a series of images, you can create a slideshow type of movie by simply importing the images into the project. Valid image formats include JPEG, GIF, PNG, BMP, ICO, EMF, POT, and WMF.

Tip: Although you can add images to this project later, it's easiest if all of your images are in the same folder. That way, you can import them all at once when you create the project.

To create an image project, follow these steps:

1. Start the Captivate software. The first screen you'll see is the Captivate main menu.
2. Click **Record or create a new project** to open the New project options window.
3. Click **Other** to display the project types that do not involve recording.

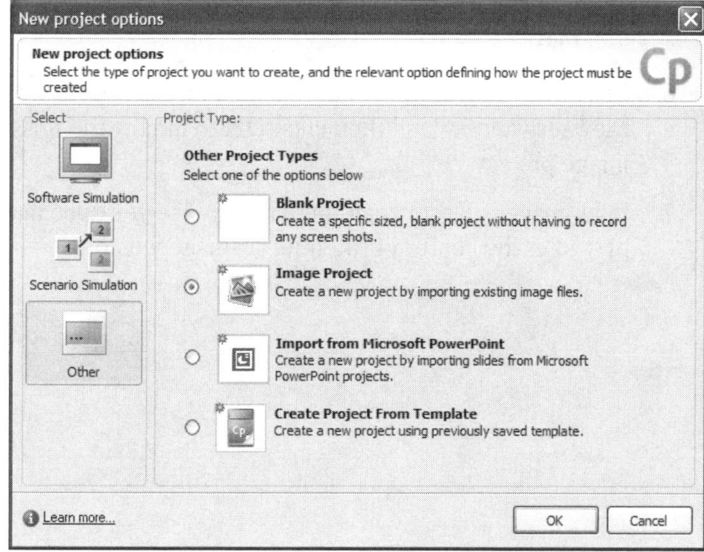

Figure 5-7. Choose to create an image project.

4. Choose **Image Project**, and then click **OK** to display the Image project window.

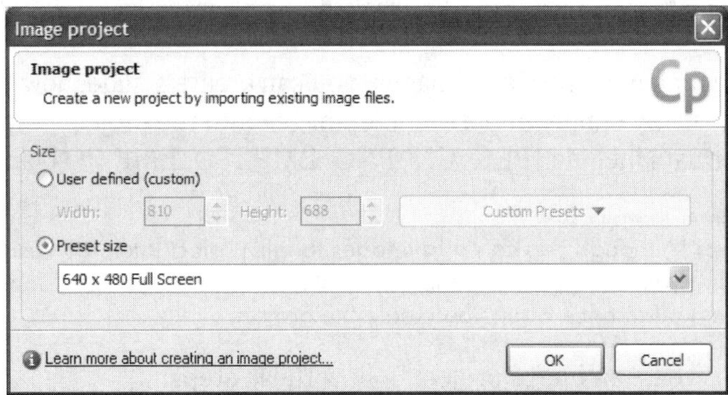

Figure 5-8. Select the image window size.

5. Choose from the list of predefined window sizes or enter a custom size, and then click **OK** to display a browser window.

Tip: Remember that the larger the window dimensions, the larger your movie file will be. Also, keep your audience in mind. If they do not have high-resolution monitors, they may not be able to view the larger movies.

6. Select the images you want included in this project from the browser window, and then click **OK** to import the images into your image project.
7. If an image is larger than the window size you specified, it is displayed in the center of the Import Image window.

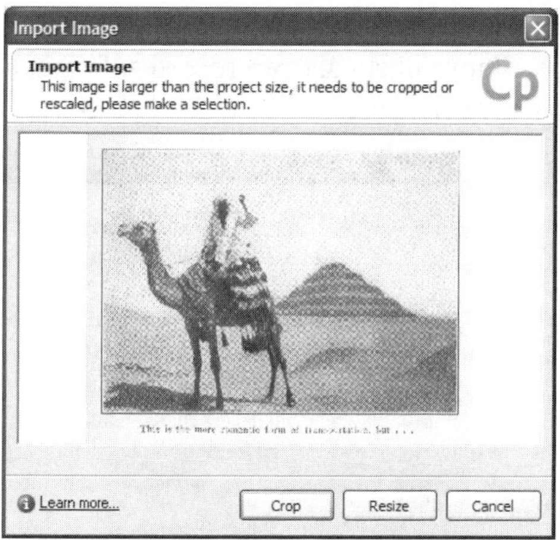

Figure 5-9. Crop or resize images to fit the window.

8. Choose whether you want to crop the image or resize it to make it fit.
   - Crop—Cuts the image to fit, removing equal amounts of the image from all sides. You'll end up with whatever is in the center of the image. In this example, the Crop command would take away some of the sky and the desert on the right side of the picture, and it would also cut off the camel's head and feet.
   - Resize—Resizes the image until the height fits within the designated space. This may mean that you'll end up with white areas on either side of the image. You'll lose some resolution, as tiny elements get more difficult to see.

9. Images appear as individual slides in the project file. You can add elements, import more images, even record additional actions, just as you would in any other project.

Figure 5-10. An image project in Edit mode.

Tip: If your pictures are much larger than the slides, or if you want to crop them off-center (for example, to get just the camel's head instead of just the saddle area), you may want to edit them in an external graphics editing package.

Creating a Project from PowerPoint Slides

As you've seen by now, movies created with Captivate are based on slide images that the software automates in a variety of ways. If you have a set of PowerPoint slides, you can use them as the basis of a movie by importing the slides into Captivate.

1. Start the Captivate software. The first screen you'll see will be the Captivate main menu.
2. Click **Record or create a new project** to open the New project options window.
3. Click **Other** to display the project types that do not involve recording.

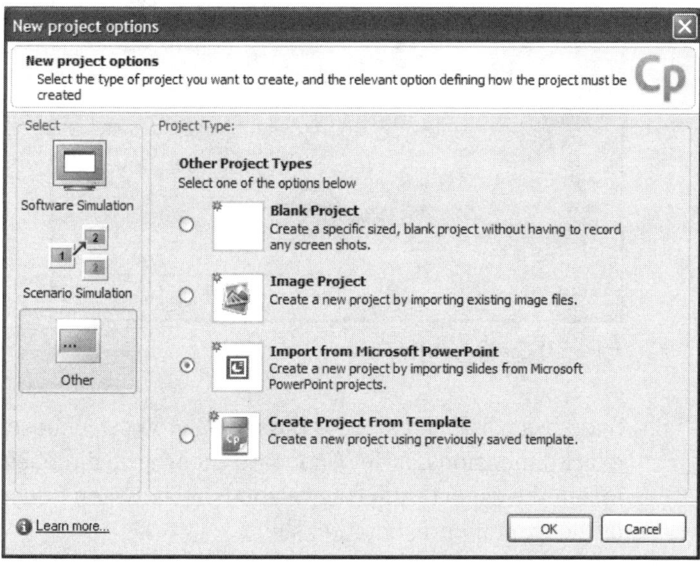

Figure 5-11. Choose to import PowerPoint slides.

4. Choose **Import from Microsoft PowerPoint**, and then click **OK** to display a slide browser window.

Chapter 5

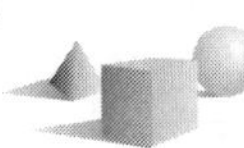

5. Choose the PowerPoint file you want to import, and then click **Open** to display the Convert PowerPoint presentations window.

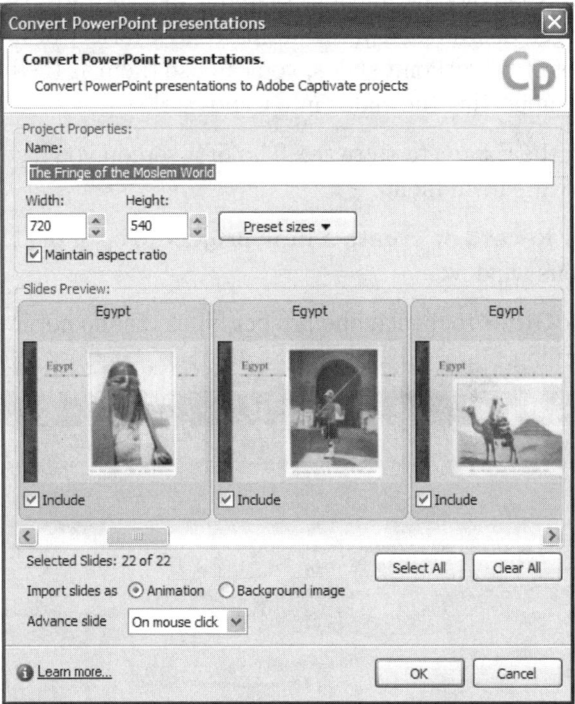

Figure 5-12. Specify PowerPoint import options.

6. Specify a name and size for the movie. You can choose to specify exact dimensions, or let Captivate choose the dimensions that best match the aspect ratio (the relationship between height and width) of the existing presentation slides.
7. The Slides Preview area of this window displays all the slides from the specified presentation. By default, all slides have the Include check box selected. If there are slides that you don't want to import into the project, simply click the **Include** check box to deselect it. You can also use the **Select All** or **Clear All** buttons to specify which slides you want to include.
8. Indicate whether you want the PowerPoint slides to be the background image of the project slides or imported as animations. This

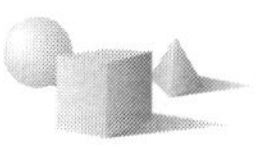

choice will be based on the amount of animation you have on each slide within the original presentation. If you choose Background image, each slide is imported as an image. If you choose Animation, each slide is imported as a single Flash (SWF) animation.

Note that custom graphic animations built in PowerPoint are only imported if you choose to import slides as animations.

9. Specify whether you want the slides to advance on a mouse click or automatically by choosing an option from the Advance slide drop-down. If you choose to advance slides by mouse click, Captivate will automatically insert a click box over each of the slides. If you choose to advance slides automatically, Captivate will use the PowerPoint timings to determine how long each slide is displayed.

10. When you've finished entering the options, click **OK** to convert the PowerPoint presentation to a Captivate project and display the project in Slideshow view.

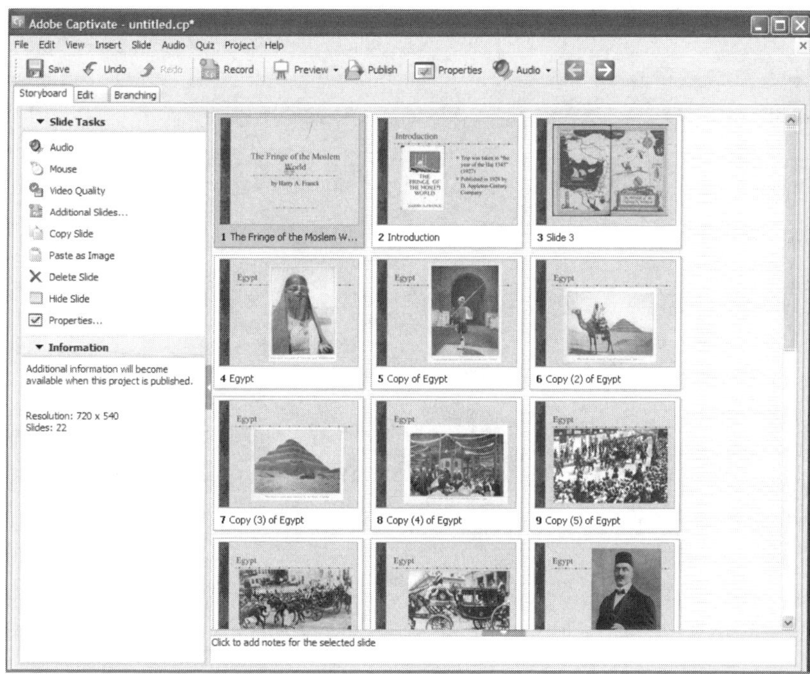

Figure 5-13. Each PowerPoint slide becomes a Captivate slide.

Summary

This chapter described the various ways you create movies that don't necessarily start with capturing screen actions. The following chapter describes how to modify your slides for further customization.

Chapter 6

Working with Slides

Captivate allows you to customize exactly how the finished movie looks. You can rearrange or delete slides, edit the way the elements on the slide look, or change the way the mouse moves. You can adjust the speed the movie plays and how the viewer navigates through your movie. This chapter discusses how to add different types of slides and how to delete slides from your project.

Slide Basics

Each time you capture a screen, Captivate stores it as a slide. Each slide has its own properties, such as transitions and timing, and may also have additional components, such as captions or highlight boxes. When you publish and then play the movie, the timing of the slide components and the transitions from slide to slide work together to create a seamless series of actions.

When you view your movie in Storyboard view, each slide is shown in miniature, with small icons representing the different components of the slide. If you've used the automatic features of Captivate, you'll see a variety of elements associated with each slide (such as captions or highlight boxes). Each slide also has associated properties, such as the length of time it will be displayed or the way you want to transition to the next slide.

Tip: Do not confuse slides with "frames." A regular movie such as you see in theaters is composed of a series of frames. Each frame displays for a fraction of a second, with tiny changes between frames that look like movement when the movie is played. In Captivate movies, a slide is more like the background on which other things happen. Slides typically remain on the screen for many seconds, and the elements on them that move (such as a mouse cursor) are stored as separate animation instructions.

In Edit view, the full slide is shown with the actual components. For example, the mouse cursor path will display, not just the icon representing mouse movement. The Edit view also includes some icons for slides surrounding the current slide.

We've already seen that some slides can also contain high-resolution mini-movies (such as when you record click-and-drag actions). You can also add other types of multimedia elements, as described later in this book:

- Adding sound to your project is described in Chapter 8.
- Working with animations is described in Chapter 7.
- Adding interactivity is described in Chapter 9.

Viewing Slides

There are two primary modes for viewing your slides:

- Storyboard view—Shows all of your slides, with associated icons that indicate the elements associated with each slide.
- Edit view—Shows a single slide and all the elements on it. Edit view can also display a "filmstrip" view of the other slides in the project. The filmstrip displays icons representing the slides in the movie, but in a single line on the edge of the currently selected slide.

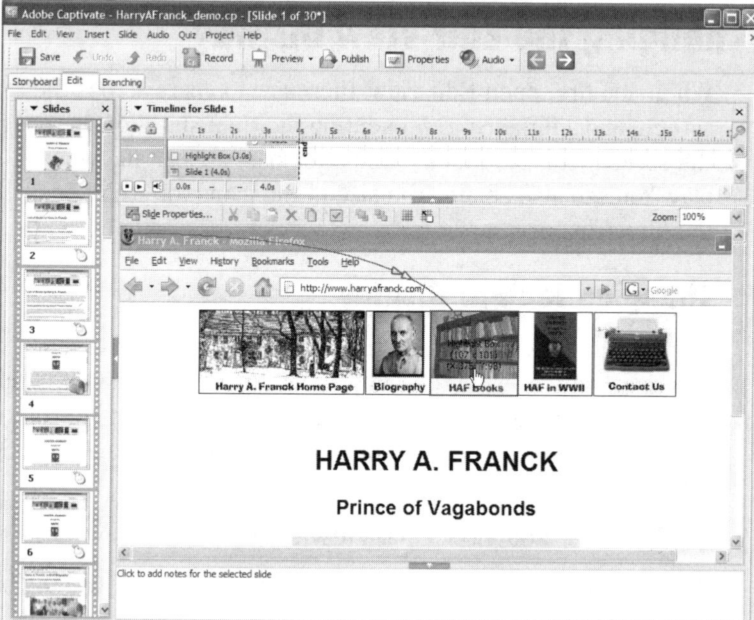

Figure 6-1. Viewing a movie in Edit view.

To display a slide in Edit view, do one of the following:

- From Storyboard view, click on a slide to select it, then click the **Edit** tab.
- From Storyboard view, double-click on a slide.
- From Branching view, click on a slide to select it, then click the **Edit** tab.
- From Branching view, double-click on a slide.
- From Branching view, right-click on a slide, then select **Edit Slide** from the context menu.
- From Edit view, use the filmstrip scroll bar to display the slide you want to edit, then click on that slide.
- From the Edit view menu bar, click the right-facing arrow to display the next slide in sequence, or click the left-facing arrow to display the previous slide.

Changing the Edit View Display

When you first open Edit view, there are toolbars across the top of the screen, and a filmstrip representing multiple slides down one side of the screen. You can modify which toolbars appear and where they display. You can also change the size of the icons (or "thumbnails") within the filmstrip.

Changing Toolbar Display

You can turn the toolbars on and off as often as you like. For example, you may want to leave the toolbars you use most frequently open all of the time, even though that leaves less room for the slide you're editing. You can also move the toolbars around as you like. To do this, follow these steps:

1. From the Edit view, click **View** to display the View menu.
2. Choose **Toolbars** from the View menu to display the toolbar options.

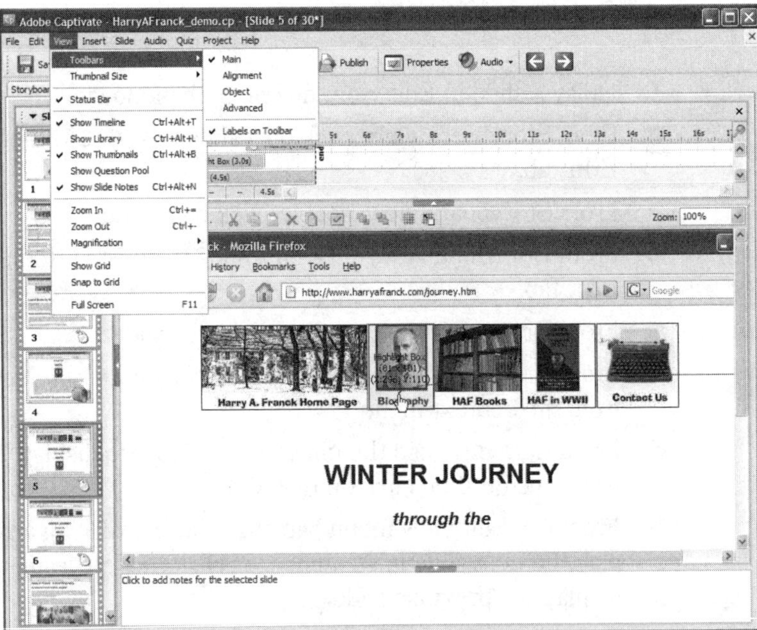

Figure 6-2. Use the View menu to change the Edit view toolbar display.

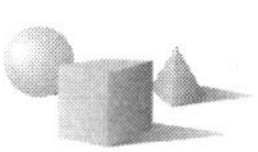

3. Display any of the listed toolbars by clicking on the toolbar name to check it, or hide a toolbar by clicking on the name to remove the check mark. In the example in Figure 6-2, the Alignment, Object, and Advanced toolbars have been turned off; only the Main toolbar is displayed.

Note: When you click a toolbar name, the View menu changes to reflect the choice you made, then closes immediately. You'll know if the display changed by looking for the toolbar. Simply open the View menu again to continue modifying your display.

4. To change the location for each toolbar, first display the toolbar as described in step 3. Move your cursor to the vertical dotted line on the toolbar until the cursor changes to an icon with four arrows. Hold down the mouse button and drag the toolbar to a new location. You can place the toolbars on any side of the Captivate window, or move them to the center of the Captivate window where they'll be opened in their own separate "floating" windows. You can move these windows around as needed, and even move them off the Captivate window altogether (such as to a second monitor).

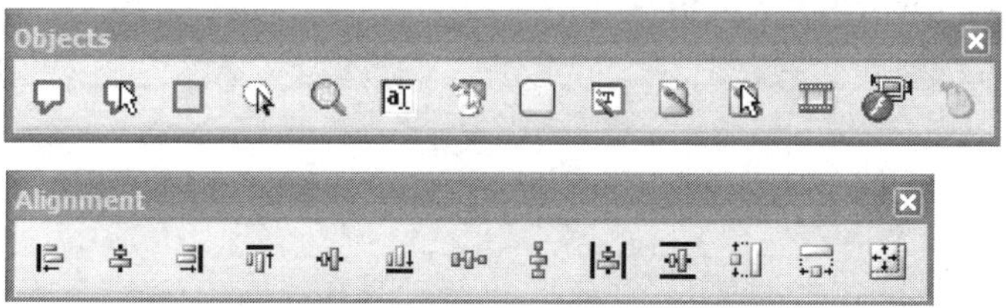

Figure 6-3. The Object and Alignment toolbars can display in separate windows.

Modifying the Filmstrip Display

Like the toolbars, the filmstrip can be on or off, and you can change the position of the filmstrip on the screen. You can also change the size of the slide icons (called thumbnails). For example, you may want to make the icons smaller (so you can see more slides at once) and display the filmstrip across the bottom of the screen.

There are two ways to turn the filmstrip display on:

- From the Edit view, click **View** to display the viewing options, then click **Show Thumbnails**.
- Hold down the **Control** and **Alt** keys on your keyboard, and then press the letter **B**.

There are three ways to turn the filmstrip display off:

- From the Edit view, click **View** to display the viewing options, then click **Show Thumbnails** to deselect it.
- Hold down the **Control** and **Alt** keys on your keyboard, and then press the letter **B**.
- Click the **X** icon in the upper-left corner of the displayed filmstrip.

To change the location of the filmstrip, move your cursor to the vertical dotted line on the side of the title bar until the cursor changes to an icon with four arrows. Hold down the mouse button and drag the filmstrip to a new location. You can place the filmstrip on any side of the Captivate window, or move it to the center of the Captivate window where it will be opened in its own "floating" window. You can move floating windows around as needed, and even move them off the Captivate window altogether (such as to a second monitor).

To change the size of the slide icons, click the **View** menu, choose **Thumbnail Size** to display the size options, then click the size option you want (Small, Medium, or Large). Alternatively, right-click on any thumbnail, then select the desired size from the Thumbnail Size option on the context menu.

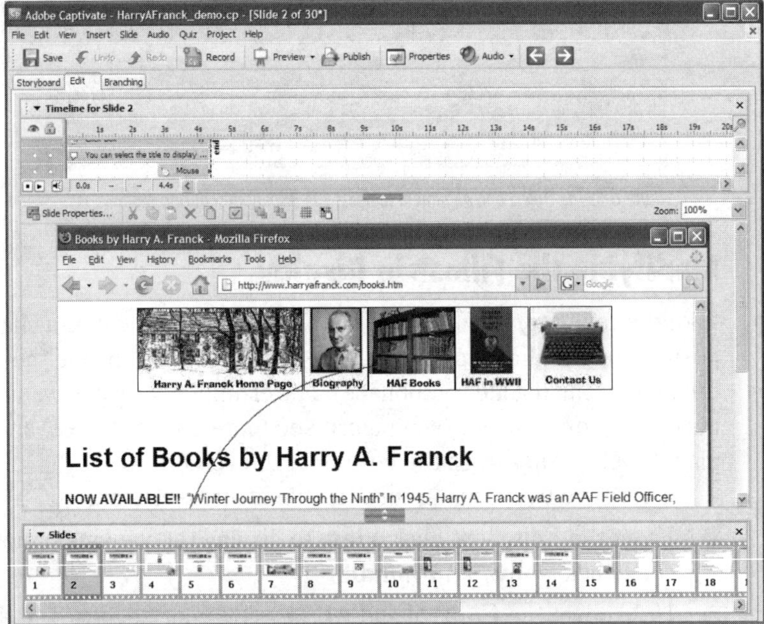

Figure 6-4. Display the filmstrip with small thumbnails at the bottom of the screen.

Naming a Slide

You can assign a name to each slide by entering a slide label. The label will appear underneath the slide in Storyboard view and in the film-strip portion of the Edit view. This can be useful if you have a lot of similar slides or if you're viewing the slides as small thumbnail icons. It can also be very helpful if you plan to construct a lot of branching for your movie (especially if you do not have a detailed storyboard or script).

Tip: You don't have to name all the slides, but it is useful to label at least the first slide for each task in your movie.

To name a slide:

1. Open the slide that you want to name in Edit view.
2. Double-click the slide, click the **Slide Properties** button, or choose **Properties** from the Slide menu to open the Slide Properties window.
3. In the Slide Properties window, click the **Slide** tab.

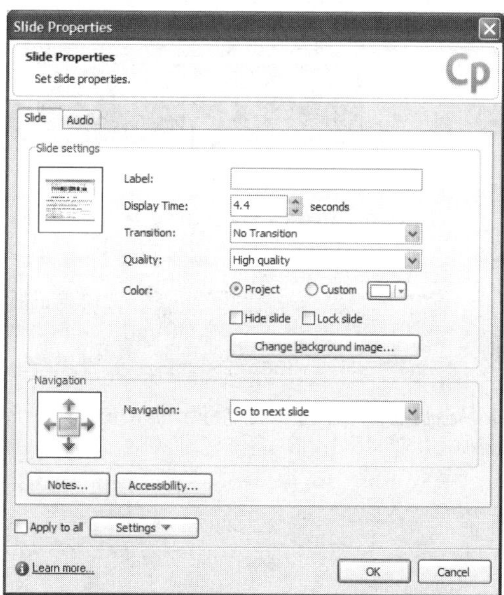

Figure 6-5. Add a slide label in the Slide Properties window.

4. In the Label box, type a short description of the slide. You can use spaces or punctuation as needed. For example, you might enter "List of Books" on the slide that begins that portion of the movie. Keep the labels short, since they may be truncated in your display, depending on your monitor settings and thumbnail size. For example, a large thumbnail may show the first 20 characters, while a medium thumbnail may only show the first six characters.

Tip: Even if the label under the slide is truncated, you can still view the full label by moving the cursor over the slide thumbnail.

5. Click **OK** to close the Slide Properties window and display the new label.

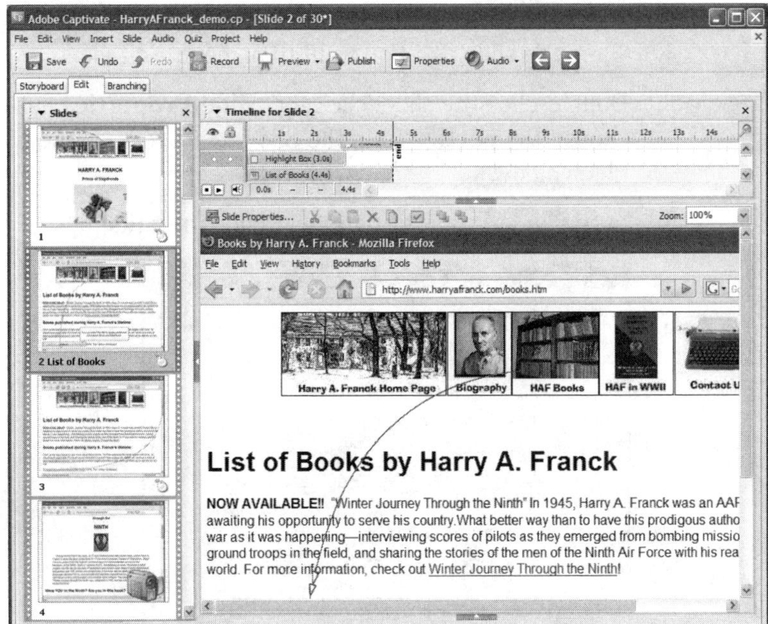

Figure 6-6. View the slide label in the filmstrip. Here, the filmstrip is shown on the left side of the screen as large thumbnails.

Adding a Slide

You can add or delete slides from either the Edit view or the Storyboard view. The steps for adding a slide vary depending on the type of slide. There are six main slide types.

Table 6-1. Types of slides

Slide Type	Description
Blank	This is a slide with absolutely nothing on it. You can import elements later or use it as a spacer.
Question	A question slide includes questions that the viewer is to answer. This type of slide turns your movie into an e-learning lesson. (See Chapter 10 for more details about e-learning.)
Random Question	Captivate allows you to create a set of questions in a "question pool." This type of slide will randomly display one of the questions from the specified pool.
Image	This type of slide contains an image. Image slides are useful for the first slide in a movie or to separate sections of your movie. You can use a logo, photo, or any other graphic you want. When you add this type of slide, you'll point to the image file you want to use. Make sure the image exists before you begin adding it. Images can be in JPG, JPEG, GIF, PNG, BMP, ICO, EMF, or WMF format.
PowerPoint	This lets you import Microsoft PowerPoint slides directly into your Captivate project.
Animation	This type of slide contains an animation, like a movie within your movie. As you add this type of slide, you'll point to the file you want to use. Make sure the animation file exists before you add this type of slide. Animations can be in SWF, animated GIF, or AVI format, among others. Your animation slide can even be another movie created with Captivate that you want to embed into the current project.

Once you've added the new slides to your project, you can add more elements to them as described in later sections of this chapter. For example, you can add animations to an image slide or put questions into a slide that started as part of a PowerPoint presentation.

The rest of the sections in this chapter describe the blank, image, PowerPoint, and animation slides. For question and random question slides, see Chapter 10.

Adding a Blank Slide

You can insert blank slides anywhere in your project. You can use them as placeholders for information you want to add later, or you can create the slide and add elements to it right away. Once you've created the slide, you can add elements such as images, text, and animation. You can even turn it into a question slide or add interactivity as described in later chapters.

To add a blank slide, follow these steps:

1. Open the project to which you want to add a blank slide.
2. Choose the location for the new slide within your project by selecting the slide immediately before the one you want to add. For example, if you have the first slide open, the new slide will be inserted as slide number 2. You can move slides around later if you need to.
3. From the Insert menu, choose **Blank Slide**. The new blank slide appears in your project.

Adding an Image Slide

An image slide is simply a slide with an image on it. When you're recording new actions, you're actually creating image slides where the image is a screen capture (the movements and other elements are added separately). You can add an image slide anywhere in your project. The image can be any stored file, such as a corporate logo or product photo. This is particularly useful as an opening, or when you're introducing a new section of the movie, or for ending the movie.

Before you begin, check the image file you're going to use. It should meet these conditions:

- The image must be in one of the valid Captivate image formats (JPG, JPEG, GIF, PNG, BMP, ICO, EMF, or WMF).
- The image should be approximately the same size as your movie. If the image is too big, Captivate can either resize or crop the image, but you may not get the exact results you expect.
- The image should be oriented the same way as the movie. For example, if you insert a vertical picture into a horizontally oriented movie, the slide will have white stripes on either side.

For example, to introduce a section of the movie about Harry Franck's family, we may want to start with an image slide containing a photo from his wedding in 1919. Figure 6-7 shows the original photo, then the resulting slide using the Captivate crop function, the resulting slide using the rescale function, and finally the slide as edited in the graphics package to match the movie size.

Tip: An image slide stores the image as the background of the slide. You may want to consider creating a blank slide and importing a graphic onto it. You'll get more image options that way.

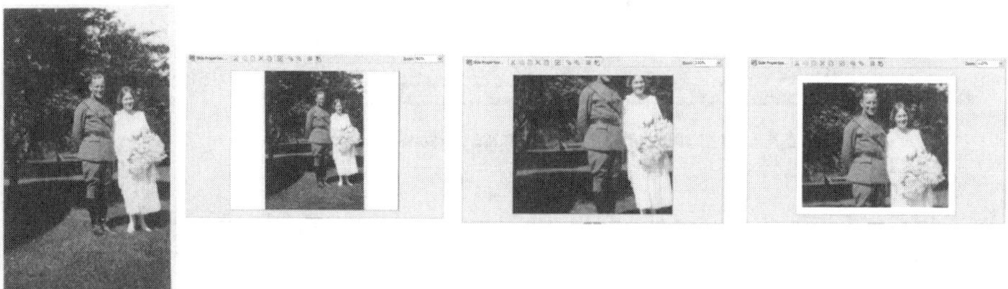

Figure 6-7. Original photo and three image slides (cropped, resized, and edited in a graphics package).

To create an image slide, follow these steps:

1. Open the project to which you want to add an image slide.
2. Choose the location for the new slide within your project by selecting the slide immediately before the one you want to add. For example, if you've got the first slide open, the new image will be inserted as slide number 2. You can move slides around later if you need to.
3. From the Insert menu, choose **Slide** and then **Image Slide** to open a browser window that defaults to the last picture folder you used.
4. Browse to the correct folder, then select the image you want to insert. If the image is the same size as the movie (or smaller), you'll see the image as a slide (and you're done!). If the image is larger than the movie size, the Import Image window displays.

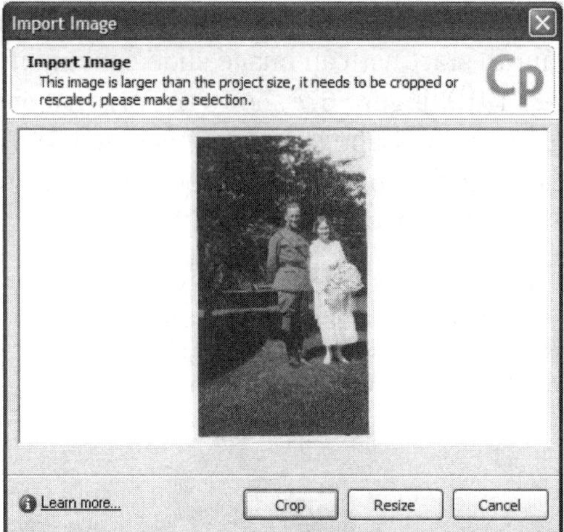

Figure 6-8. Crop or resize in the Import Image window.

5. Choose one of the following options to make the image fit the movie and display the image slide:
   - Crop—The edges of the image that exceed the movie size will be cut off, leaving the center of the image.
   - Resize—The entire image will be made smaller to fit in the movie.

Adding a PowerPoint Slide

Captivate can use existing PowerPoint slides as the basis for a project. When you add PowerPoint slides, some elements will be automatically converted to the Captivate format:

- Each PowerPoint slide will become one slide in the Captivate project.
- Any content on the PowerPoint Notes page will be copied to the Captivate Notes function.
- The PowerPoint slide title will be stored as the Captivate slide label.

However, any transitions or audio or other unique PowerPoint elements will not be carried over to the Captivate movie. Each slide will be assigned a default time by the Captivate software—you can go back and edit the timing and other properties as needed.

To add one or more PowerPoint slides to your Captivate project, follow these steps:

1. Open the project to which you want to add a PowerPoint slide.
2. Choose the location for the new slide within your project by selecting the slide immediately before the one you want to add. For example, if you've got the first slide open, the new slides will be inserted starting with slide number 2. You can move slides around later if you need to.
3. From the Insert menu, choose **Slide** and then **PowerPoint Slide** to open a browser window that defaults to the last folder you used.
4. Browse to the correct folder, and then select the presentation that contains the slide or slides you want to insert. The PowerPoint slide options window displays the slides in the current project.

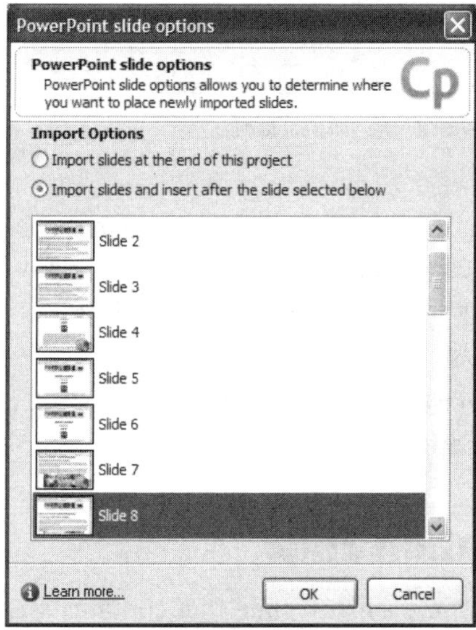

Figure 6-9. Select the PowerPoint slide options.

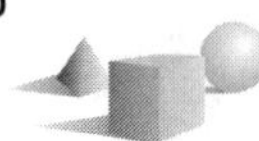

5. Specify whether you want to insert the new slide or slides after the currently selected slide or at the end of the slides, then click **OK** to display the Convert PowerPoint presentations window.

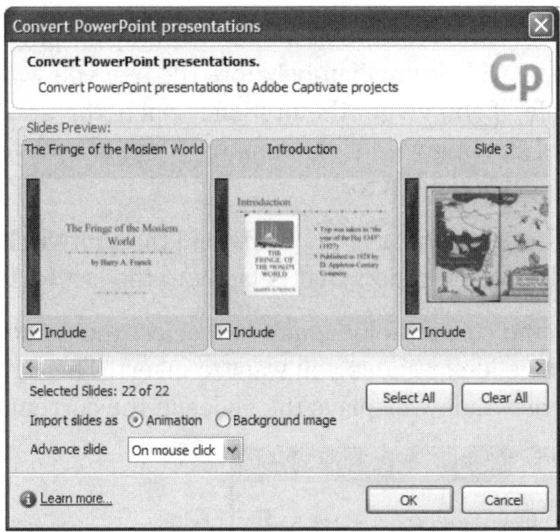

Figure 6-10. Choose the PowerPoint slides you want to add.

6. Click the slides you want to add until the screen displays a green check mark below each slide. Note that you can easily select all slides or clear all the check marks using the buttons at the bottom of the selection window.

7. Click **OK** when you're done to add the selected PowerPoint slides to your project as Captivate slides.

Adding an Animation Slide

An animation slide is simply a blank slide that contains an animation file. Captivate can import files in valid animation formats (including SWF, AVI, and animated GIF) into any project. When you add an animation slide, Captivate will create a blank slide and then place the animation file that you specify on that slide. Just like when you add an animation file to an existing slide, you can change the properties of the animation.

Tip: This process is useful when adding larger animations. To add smaller animated elements (such as an animated GIF or flashing arrow) to an existing slide, see the section in Chapter 7 titled "Importing Animations."

Before you begin, check the animation file you're going to use. It should meet these conditions:

- The animation must be in one of the valid Captivate animation formats (including SWF, AVI, or animated GIF).
- If the animation is going to fill your whole slide, it should be approximately the same size as your movie. You will be able to resize your animation if necessary as described in Chapter 7.
- The animation frame rate should be appropriate for the movie you're creating. Captivate will play all imported animations at the setting specified in the Captivate movie preference settings (usually 30 Flash frames per second).

1. Open the project to which you want to add an animation slide.
2. Choose the location for the new slide within your project by selecting the slide immediately before the one you want to add. For example, if you've got the first slide open, the new animation slide will be inserted as slide number 2. You can move slides around later if you need to.
3. From the Insert menu, choose **Slide** and then **Animation Slide** to open a browser window that defaults to the last folder you used.
4. Browse to the correct folder, then select the animation you want to insert. The icon for the animation appears on a new slide in your project.

Duplicating an Existing Slide

If you've got a slide just the way you want it, with borders or timing or transitions or whatever other elements you've added, you can use that slide as a starting point for other slides. The only difference between the slides will be in the label on the new slide—it will be prefaced with "Copy of" and then the original slide title. There are two ways to duplicate slides. The duplicate function copies the selected slide and inserts the copy into the movie immediately after the original slide.

The copy and paste function allows you to specify where you want the copy inserted.

To duplicate a slide, follow these steps:

1. Display the slide you want to duplicate, either by clicking on the slide in the filmstrip in Edit view or highlighting the slide in Storyboard view.

Tip: You can select more than one slide by clicking the first slide, then holding down the Control key before clicking each of the other slides you want to select. You can also select a series of sequential slides by clicking the first slide, holding down the Shift key, and then clicking the last slide in the series you want to select.

2. From the Edit menu, choose **Duplicate Slide** (or right-click on a slide and select **Duplicate Slide**) to insert a copy of the selected slide or slides into your movie immediately following the original slides.

To copy a slide and paste it somewhere else in the movie, follow these steps:

1. Display the slide you want to copy, either by clicking on the slide in the filmstrip in Edit view or highlighting the slide in Storyboard view.
2. From the Edit menu, choose **Copy Slide** to copy the selected slide or slides.
3. Specify the location for the new slide by selecting the slide immediately before the location of the new slides.
4. From the Edit menu, choose **Paste Slide**. The slides will be inserted into your movie immediately following the slide you selected in step 3.

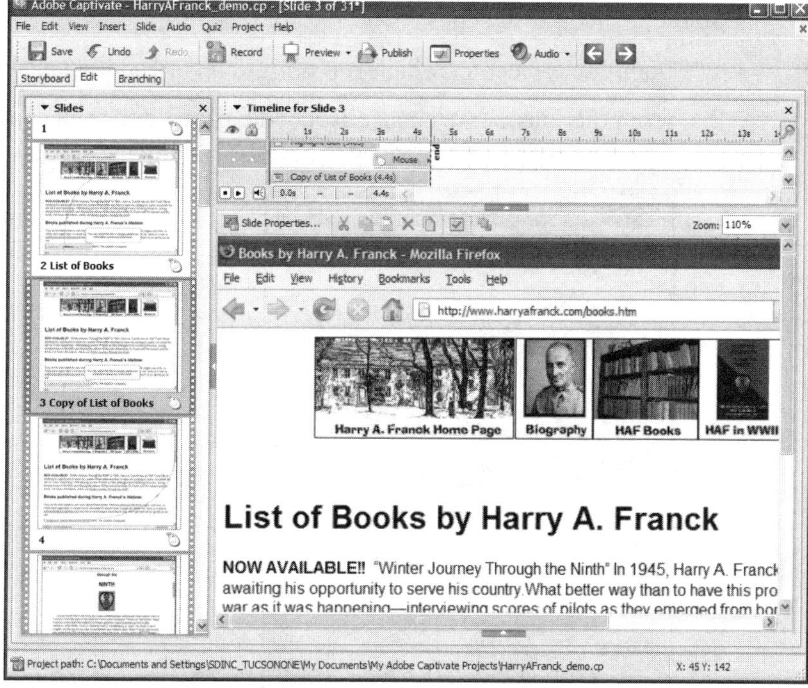

Figure 6-11. The new slide is an exact copy of the old slide (except for the slide label).

Recording Additional Slides

You can add new slides to an existing project by recording your screen actions. This works just like the recording function you used to create a new project (see Chapter 4). There are two main differences between recording a new project and recording new slides for an existing project:

- When recording new slides for an existing project, you need to specify where you want the newly recorded slides to be inserted.
- When recording new slides for an existing project, you cannot change the size of the recording window. It will default to the same size as the rest of the project.

To record additional slides:

1. Open the project for which you want to record additional slides.
2. From the File menu, choose **Record/Create**, and then choose **Additional Slides** to display the Record additional slides window.

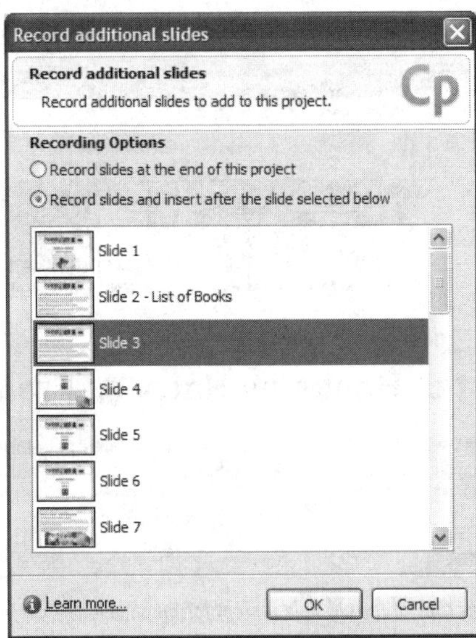

Figure 6-12. Specify a location for the newly recorded slides.

3. Specify the location for the new slides by clicking either the **Record slides at the end of this project** option or the **Record slides and insert after the slide selected below** option, then click a slide icon.

Tip: You can always move slides around later if you need to.

4. When you've specified the new location, click **OK** to display the recording window.

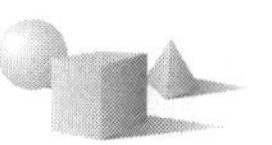

Figure 6-13. Set the recording area.

5. Because you're adding slides to a pre-existing project, you can't change the size or shape of the recording area—it is defined by the current project. However, you can move the red outline to a different area of the screen or move the underlying windows to the red outline. Once you have a window selected, the Snap to fit button changes that window to match the size of the recording area. You can also select any of the options or other settings as needed (see Chapter 4).

Tip: If you absolutely must add slides of a different size or shape than the original project, you can always record as a separate project and publish the movie and then embed the SWF.

6. Click **Record** to begin recording your new slides.
7. Perform the tasks you want to record, then press the **End** key to stop recording and import the new slides into your project.

Deleting a Slide

As you work on a Captivate project, there may be times when you want to remove a slide or series of slides. For example, if you made a mistake while recording a task, it is sometimes simpler to remove the incorrect slides and record a few new ones rather than start recording all over again. When you delete a slide, it is permanently removed from the project and from your computer.

To delete a slide, follow these steps:

1. There are a variety of ways to begin the deletion process. Do any one of the following:
   - From Storyboard view, click the slide to select it, then click **Delete Slide** in the Slide Tasks pane.
   - From Storyboard or Edit view, right-click on the slide to display the pop-up menu, then choose **Delete Slide**.
   - From Storyboard or Edit view, select the slide, then press the **Delete** key on your keyboard.
   - From Storyboard or Edit view (with the slide for deletion selected or displayed), choose **Delete Slide** from the Edit menu.

   Whichever method you use, a confirmation dialog appears:

   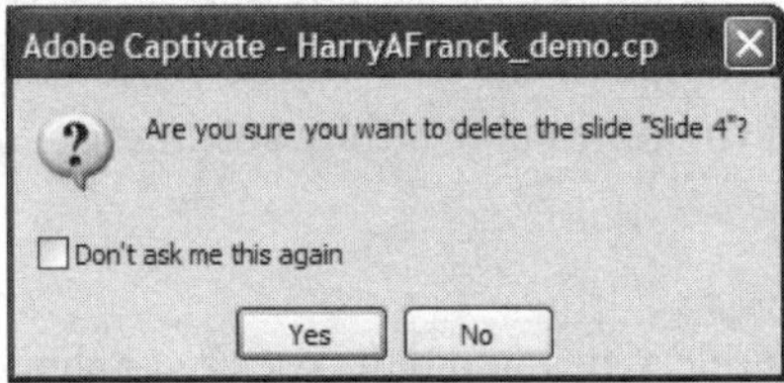

   Figure 6-14. Confirm that you want to delete a slide.

2. Confirm that you want to delete the slide by clicking **Yes**, or cancel by clicking **No**.

Hiding a Slide

There may be times when you don't want the viewers to see a slide, but you don't want to delete the slide either. Captivate has a hide function that allows you to leave the slide in your project but prevent the slide from appearing in the finished movie. For example, you may want to hide slides if they aren't yet finished, if you are using them as placeholders for some future component, or if you are creating one movie that will be delivered to multiple audiences and you want to keep some slides hidden from some of the audiences.

Hidden slides will remain in the project, and you'll be able to see them in both Storyboard and Edit mode. Hidden slides are indicated by a diagonal line through the slide number and will not be exported when you publish the Flash movie.

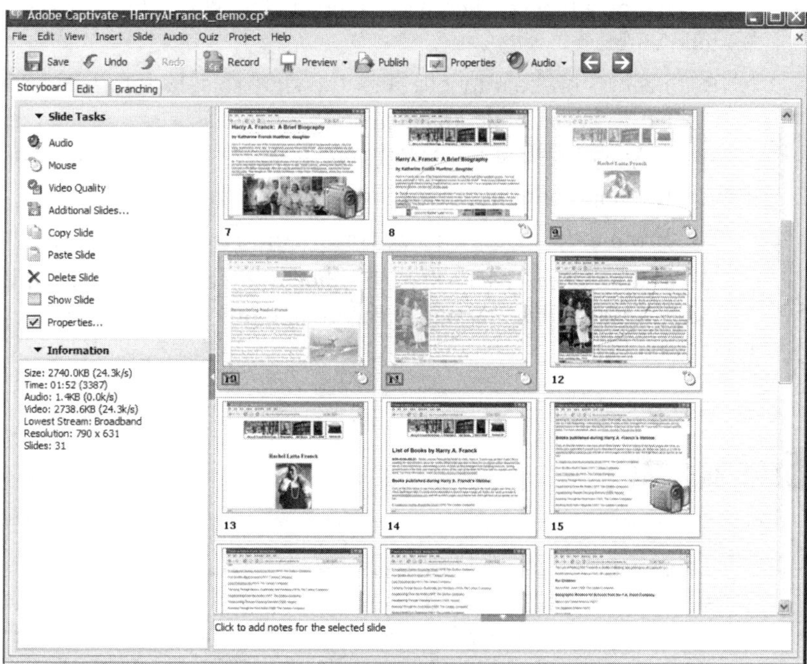

Figure 6-15. Slides 9, 10, and 11 are hidden and won't be in the published movie.

To hide a slide, do any one of the following:

- From Storyboard view, click the slide to select it, then click **Hide Slide** in the Slide Tasks pane.
- From Storyboard or Edit view, right-click on the slide to display the pop-up menu, then choose **Hide Slide**.
- From either view, choose **Hide Slide** from the Slide menu.
- From either view, select the slide, then hold down the **Shift** and **Control** keys on your keyboard and press the letter **H** on your keyboard.

Tip: Before distributing a movie with hidden slides, be sure to preview it carefully. It is very easy to hide one slide too many, and it can be very disconcerting for the viewers if you've hidden a slide that contains information they need.

To change a hidden slide back to normal viewing, do one of the following:

- From Storyboard view, click the slide to select it, then click **Show Slide** in the Slide Tasks pane.
- From Storyboard or Edit view, right-click on the slide to display the pop-up menu, then choose **Show Slide**.
- From either view, choose **Show Slide** from the Slide menu.
- From either view, select the slide, then hold down the **Shift** and **Control** keys on your keyboard and press the letter **H** on your keyboard.

Summary

This chapter described the various ways you can add, hide, and delete slides from your movie. It also explained the various views and the different types of slides. The following chapter describes how to add elements to and delete elements from a slide.

Chapter 7

Editing a Single Slide

After you've created a project full of slides, you'll usually need to go in and do a little bit of editing to get exactly the look or effect you want in your finished movie. No matter what type of slide you're working with, they all have the same basic components:

- Background, usually a screen capture or other image
- Visual elements such as text, captions, check boxes, mouse movement, etc.
- Transition information
- Audio (described in Chapter 8)

Most of the time, you'll be working in Edit view when you're editing a single slide.

Working with the Slide Background

When you look at a movie created with Captivate, most of what you see is the background of the slide. It is the surface on which the actions (such as mouse movement or the appearance of text captions) take place. The background of a slide will vary depending on the type of slide (and how you created it).

Table 7-1. Different types of slide backgrounds

This type of slide:	Uses this for a background:
Recorded slide	The image of the screen when you captured it.
Image slide	The image you specified when you created the slide.

This type of slide:	Uses this for a background:
Blank slide	The background of the slide is a solid color as specified in the background preferences for the movie.
PowerPoint slide	The original PowerPoint slide becomes the background. Note that once you've imported a PowerPoint slide into Captivate, you can no longer edit the text on the slides. However, you can add new text boxes to a slide with a PowerPoint background.
Question slide	The background of the slide is a solid color as specified in the background preferences for the movie.
Animation slide	The background of the slide is a solid color as specified in the background preferences for the movie.

You can't edit the contents of the background image within the Captivate software, but you can change the background of a slide to a new image. It's fairly simple to reimport the background into any slide, so if you need to make edits and have an external graphics program, you can make background changes. For example, if you've got a logo for a background, and your company logo changes, you can simply replace the old background logo with the new one. Any transitions or other elements on that slide remain in place.

In another example, sometimes when you're documenting a software product, a menu item might change. You could rerecord the slides that show that menu item, then edit the elements such as text captions or timings as necessary. Or you could copy the background image to your graphics package, change the one menu item, then replace the background of the slides with the new edited image. All of the other elements (captions, questions, click boxes, rollovers, buttons, etc.) will be retained.

Setting the Background Color

If you're working with slides that allow the background color of the project to show through (such as question slides, blank slides, or animation slides with an animation smaller than the movie size), you can specify the default background color for the entire project. By default, the background starts out as white.

To set a new background color, follow these steps:

1. Open the Captivate project.
2. From the Edit menu, choose **Preferences** to display the Preferences window.

3. From the list on the left of the window, choose Settings from the Project category to display the project settings.

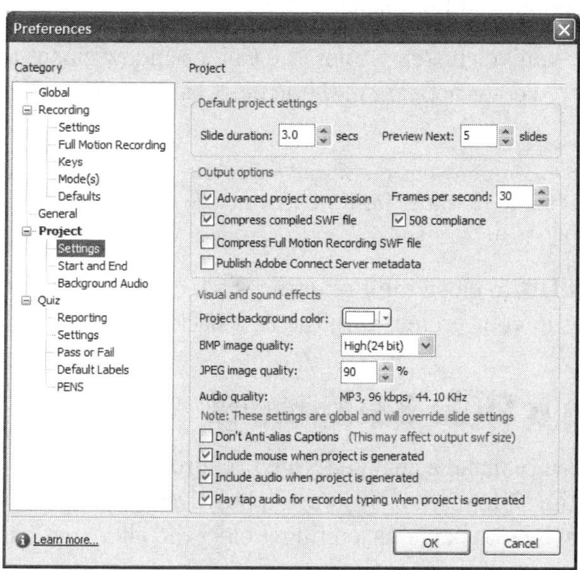

Figure 7-1. Set the background color in the Preferences window.

4. Note that the current background color is displayed in a small rectangular box under Visual and sound effects. To change the color, click on the down arrow in the color box to open the Color window.

Figure 7-2. Select a color for the background.

5. From this window, you can enter a color in any of the following ways:
   - Click one of the displayed colors.
   - Enter the hexadecimal value for the color (such as #000000 for black and #FFFFFF for white).
   - Click the **eyedropper** icon, then click any area on the screen to copy the color of that area.

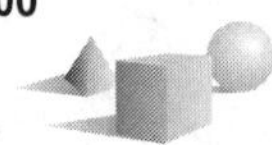

- Click **More Colors** to display the standard color selection tool. Use this option if you need to enter RGB values or Hue, Saturation, and Luminance values.

Once you've chosen a color, the Color window closes and the selected color appears in the Project background color box.

Tip: If your company has an official corporate color, you should be able to get the RGB values from your corporate art, marketing, or public relations department.

6. Click **OK** to close the Preferences window and update all the slides in your project with the new background color.

Copying a Slide Background

If you need to make a change to the background of a slide, you can easily copy the slide to your system clipboard, and then paste the slide into a graphics package for editing. Select the slide that has the background you want to copy, then use any of the following methods:

- Click the right mouse button to display the pop-up menu and choose **Copy Background.**
- From the Edit menu, choose **Copy Background.**
- Hold down the Shift and Control keys on your keyboard, then press the Y key (**Shift+Ctrl+Y**).

The background of the slide is stored as an image onto the clipboard. You can then paste it into any graphics package for editing as necessary or paste from the clipboard to the background of any other slide.

Inserting a New Background Image

You can insert any image file as a new background into any slide. This can be the image that you copied from the slide (and edited), or it can be an entirely new image. You also have a choice of choosing an image from the Captivate library or from any other location.

Using a Background Image from the Library

You can import any image from the Captivate library to use as a slide background. The image will be referenced from the slide rather than copied into it. This allows you to make changes, if necessary, to the image file in the library, and have those changes automatically display in all the slides that use that image.

1. Select the slide by clicking on it. You can be in Storyboard, Edit, or Branching view.
2. From the Slide menu, choose **Properties** (or double-click anywhere on the slide background) to display the Slide Properties window.
3. From the Slide Properties window, click the **Change background image** button. A list of the current backgrounds and images in the project displays.

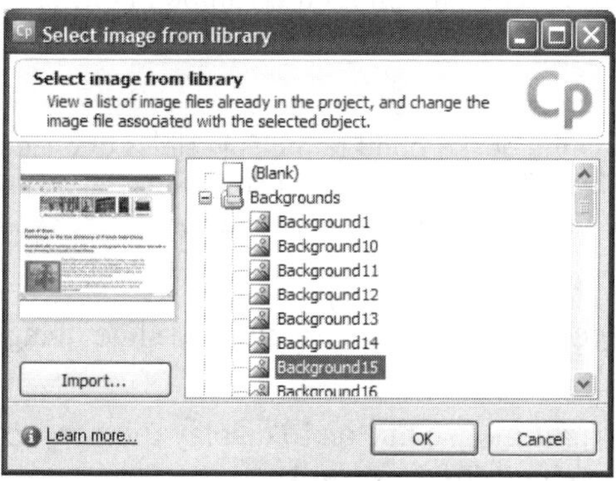

Figure 7-3. Change the background image by selecting a file from the library.

4. Use either of the following methods to select an image for the background of the slide:
   - Choose the background or image you want to use by clicking once on the file name to display a preview of the image in the left side of the window, then click **OK** to select that image and close the Select image from library window.

- If the image you want to use is not yet in the Captivate library, click the **Import** button to browse to the image location, then click **OK** to select the file, copy it to the slide background and into the Captivate library, and also close the Select image from library window.

Using a Background Image that Isn't in the Library

You don't have to use the Captivate library to insert a new background; you can cut and paste images from any other application.

1. From a graphics or image editing application, copy the image to your clipboard. This is usually done by pressing the Control and C keys (**Ctrl+C**) or using the software's Copy function.
2. Open the Captivate project that contains the slide or slides where you want to place the new background.
3. Select the slide by clicking on it. You can be in either Storyboard or Edit view.

Tip: You can update the background of multiple slides at once by selecting multiple slides. To select multiple slides, select the first slide, then hold down the Control key as you click additional slides you want to select.

4. Paste the image from the clipboard into the slide using one of the following methods:
   - Click the right mouse button to display the pop-up menu and choose **Paste as Background.**
   - From the Edit menu, choose **Paste as Background.**
   - Hold down the Shift and Control keys on your keyboard, then press the V key (**Shift+Ctrl+V**).
5. Click **Yes** to confirm that you want to replace the background of the selected slide. The new image will be placed on the slide, and all the original objects such as mouse movements, captions, or highlight boxes will remain where they were.

Adding and Editing Visual Elements

The real power of Captivate is not in the slide backgrounds or the screen capture images, but rather in the variety of elements that you can place on top of the background of the slides. Each element has a variety of options that you can set to fully customize the look and feel of your movie. The major elements are:

Text captions—Text captions contain words that describe the actions going on in each slide. These can be automatically generated by Captivate, or you can manually add them.

Highlight boxes—Highlight boxes surround specific portions of the screen that you want the viewer to notice. These can be automatically generated by Captivate, or you can manually add them.

Image boxes—In addition to using images as the backgrounds of your slides, you can add images to any slide in image boxes. This gives you more control over the display of your image than just using the image as a background.

Animations—You can import an existing animation file into a Captivate slide. Valid formats include SWF, AVI, and animated GIF files. Captivate comes with a variety of predefined animations, such as arrows and spinning boxes, as well as a collection of animation schemes you can add to your text.

Click boxes—A click box is an area that the viewer must click before the next slide will be shown. See Chapter 9 for more detail on this type of element.

Text entry boxes—Text entry boxes allow the viewer to enter information, as in quizzing or other interactive applications. See Chapter 9 for more detail on this type of element.

Rollover elements—This category includes rollover captions, slidelets, rollover images, and zoom boxes. These elements display in the finished movie when the viewer rolls the cursor over specified areas of the slide. See Chapter 9 for more detail on this type of element.

Buttons—Buttons can be used to give the viewer a choice of what to do next while viewing your movie. See Chapter 9 for more detail on this type of element.

Questions and Quizzes—Use to create e-learning applications, as described in Chapter 10.

Specifying Default Elements for Recording

When you record tasks for a movie, Captivate can automatically add various visual elements for certain actions. For example, text captions will be added whenever you:

- Select a menu
- Select an item from a menu
- Click on a button
- Click on a link
- Change a value in a list
- Select or deselect a check box
- Open a new window or dialog box

Captivate can also be set to automatically include highlight boxes or click boxes whenever you click the mouse or to record the mouse movements (or not). To specify whether or not Captivate should add elements automatically for you, you have to edit the recording options. To do this, follow these steps:

Note: You do not have to have an open project to change the recording options.

1. From the Edit menu, choose **Preferences** to display the Preferences window, then click on **Recording** from the categories on the left side of the window.

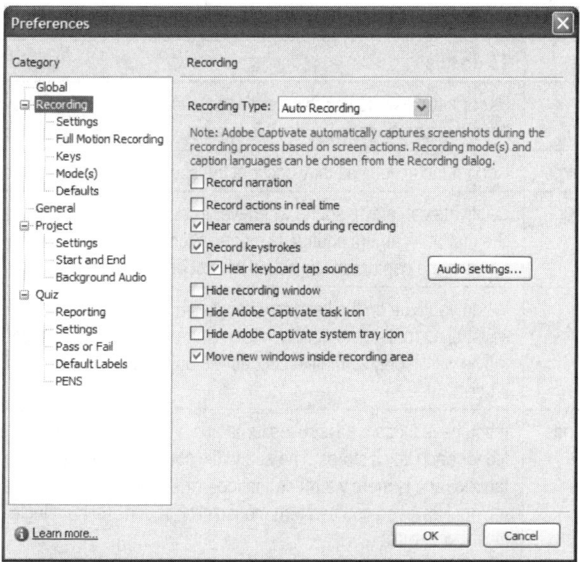

Figure 7-4. Specify recording settings in the Preferences window.

2. Set the Recording Type to **Auto Recording** or **Manual Recording**. If you choose Manual Recording, the selected elements will be captured when you press the PrntScrn key during recording. If you choose Auto Recording, the selected elements will be captured on each action you perform (such as click the mouse, open a window within the specified recording area, press a key on the keyboard, or drag and drop).

3. For each recording type, specify the following additional options by clicking the boxes to check or uncheck each option. Note that this sets the default options for the captured screens—they can all be changed at any time in the Edit view. Available options are:

Table 7-2. Recording options

Check this option:	To do this:
Record narration	Record audio while you're recording the visual portion of the movie. You must have a microphone set up for this to work.
Record actions in real time	Record the actions as they occur at the speed at which you perform them.
Hear camera sounds during recording	Captivate can play a sound whenever it captures a screen. The sound, sort of like that of a camera shutter, is merely a tool to help you identify when the screens are captured. The sound will not be part of the finished movie.
Record keystrokes	When you type on the keyboard, this setting will cause Captivate to store the keystrokes (but not capture a full screen for each character typed). The finished movie will display all the keystrokes without the overhead of a full screen per letter.
Hear keyboard tap sounds	If you have Record keystrokes turned on, you can have Captivate play a sound file for each key it stores. The sound file sounds like a keyboard key being tapped, and is merely a recording tool—the sounds will not be part of the finished movie. However, you can turn mouse click sounds (either single-click or double-click) on or off later.
Hide recording window	Remove the red recording area lines from the screen. This does not change the area that is recorded; it only hides the indication of the outline of the recording area. This option also temporarily removes the Captivate icon from the Windows taskbar (usually displayed across the bottom of your screen).
Hide Adobe Captivate task icon	Temporarily removes the Captivate icon from the Windows taskbar (usually displayed across the bottom of your screen).
Hide Adobe Captivate system tray icon	Temporarily removes the Captivate icon from the Windows system tray (in the lower-right corner of your screen).
Move new windows inside recording area	Ensure that all windows and pop-ups are fully captured when you record. If this is not selected, the recording process may inadvertently crop some of your windows.

4. Click **OK** to save your changes, or **Cancel** to close the window without saving your changes.
5. Choose **Full Motion Recording** from the categories on the left side of the window to define when you want to use the Full Motion recording options.

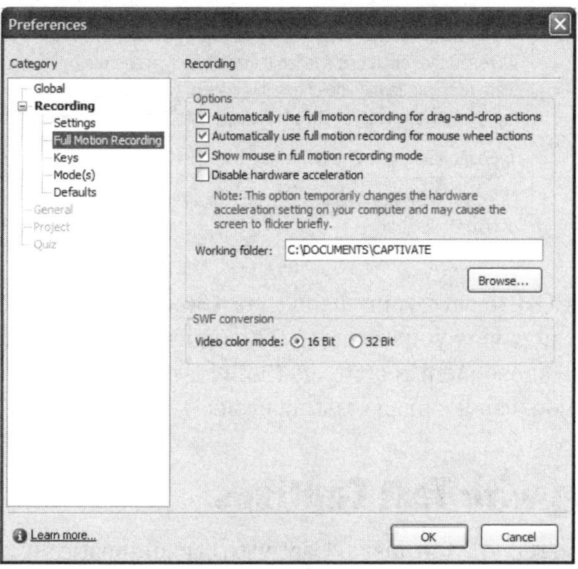

Figure 7-5. Set the Full Motion recording options.

6. From the Full Motion options, specify when you want to use the Full Motion feature. This feature automatically records more screens during drag-and-drop or mouse actions to give you a smoother movie. The extra screens are stored in one slide and indicated on the slide by a movie icon.

Tip: Full Motion recording delivers a very smooth movie, but also requires extra resources such as disk space and memory. Use this feature sparingly for the most efficient movies.

Table 7-3. Full Motion options

Check this option:	To do this:
Automatically use full motion recording for drag-and-drop actions	Automatically record any drag-and-drop actions in Full Motion mode. This will make these actions (such as dropping an image into a folder or using a scroll bar) appear smoother.
Automatically use full motion recording for mouse wheel actions	Automatically record any mouse wheel actions in Full Motion mode. This will make these actions (such as dropping an image into a folder or using a scroll bar) appear smoother.
Show mouse in full motion recording mode	Display the mouse cursor during drag-and-drop Full Motion animations.

Check this option:	To do this:
Disable hardware acceleration	Increase the resources available for Full Motion capture by turning off the hardware acceleration. If you check this option, you'll see a flicker on your monitor as the hardware resets, but this flicker will not appear in the finished movie.
Working folder	Type the name of the folder where the Full Motion video will be saved.
SWF conversion	Choose 16 Bit video color mode for a smaller file size or 32 Bit for a greater range of color options.

7. Click **OK** to save your changes, or **Cancel** to close the window without saving your changes. The options you've set will be used for all subsequent recordings (both for new projects and recording additional slides in an existing project).

Working with Text Captions

When you record your tasks, Captivate can automatically add some text captions to point out the specific tasks. For example, if you click on a link called "home page," Captivate will add a text caption that says "Click Here!" You can edit these captions, delete them, or create your own custom captions. For example, you may prefer to have the caption read "Click here to return to the home page."

You can also define the exact look of a caption, including the font, color, and size.

Adding Text Captions

Even if you use the automatic text captions, you may want to add a few captions of your own. For example, you could add a caption to point to a specific area of the screen or to insert a comment or special instruction. To add a text caption, follow these steps:

1. In Edit view, select the slide you want to edit.
2. From the Insert menu, select **Text Caption**, or click the Text Caption icon ( ) to display the New Text Caption window.

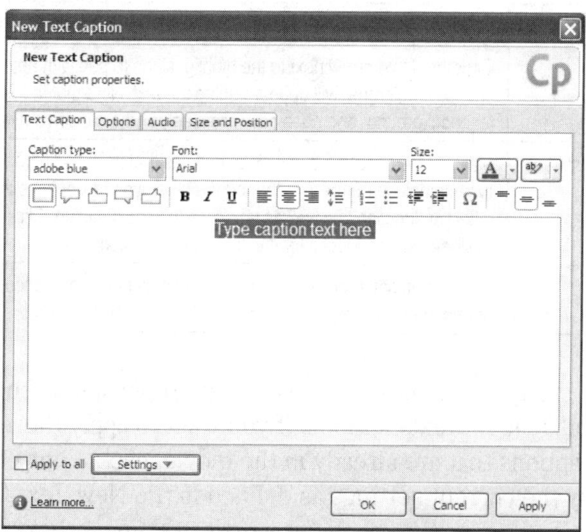

Figure 7-6. Add a caption with the New Text Caption window.

3. Type the text you want to display in the text caption.

Tip: Although the amount of caption text is unlimited, remember that it will be sitting on top of your slide background (which is often already very busy) and the more text you include, the smaller it will have to be to fit on the screen. The best captions are succinct and to the point. Use short, declarative phrases ("This is the main menu") or brief commands ("Click here to go to the next page").

4. If necessary, change the look of the caption by editing the following properties:

Table 7-4. Text caption properties

To change this:	Do this:
Caption type	Choose a caption type from the list. The caption type defines the shape and color of the outline that will be placed around the text, as well as the default text color (although you can change this).
Font	Choose a font for the text from the list. The list of fonts will be determined by the fonts available on your system.
Size	Choose a size for the text from the list.
Color	Click the down arrow next to the letter A to choose a color for the text.

To change this:	Do this:
Highlight	Click the down arrow next to the highlight icon (a pen with ab next to it) to choose a color that will appear behind the text. Note that this is a color for the text background, and does not necessarily fill the caption outline.
Caption outline style	Many of the caption types include outlines that point in different directions. In the example in Figure 7-6, the "adobe blue" type has options that point in four different directions as well as an option with no direction. Click any one of the outline icons to select it for the current text caption.
Text style	If you want, set standard text options such as font appearance, bullets, numbering, and alignment.

5. The changes you make to the caption properties will be applied to all subsequent text captions. If you want to apply these changes to all captions that are already in the movie, click **Apply to all** to apply the current settings as defined in the New Text Caption window. To view or change the properties settings, click the **Settings** button.

Tip: Note that if you change only part of a caption (such as making a single word bold or italicizing a phrase), these changes will not be applied to other captions.

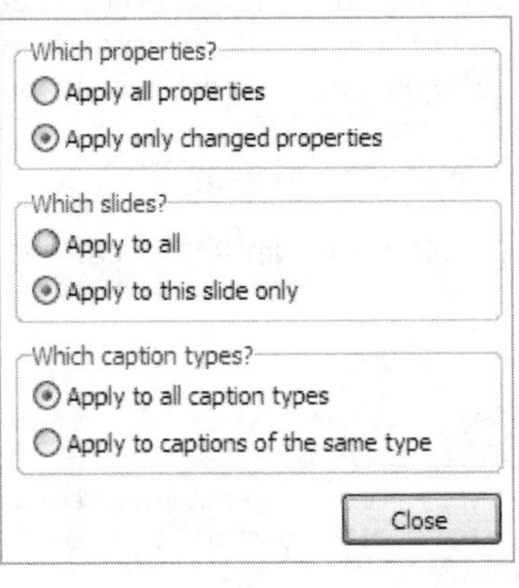

Figure 7-7. Apply settings to previously created captions.

6. You can click the Options tab to set timing and transitions as described later in this chapter, click the Size and Position tab to set the default size and position, or click the Audio tab to set audio properties, as described in Chapter 8.

7. Click **OK** to display the new caption in the center of the slide, as shown in Figure 7-8.

8. Using your mouse, click and drag the text caption to the desired location on the slide. You can also resize the caption box if necessary by clicking and dragging the corners of the outline.

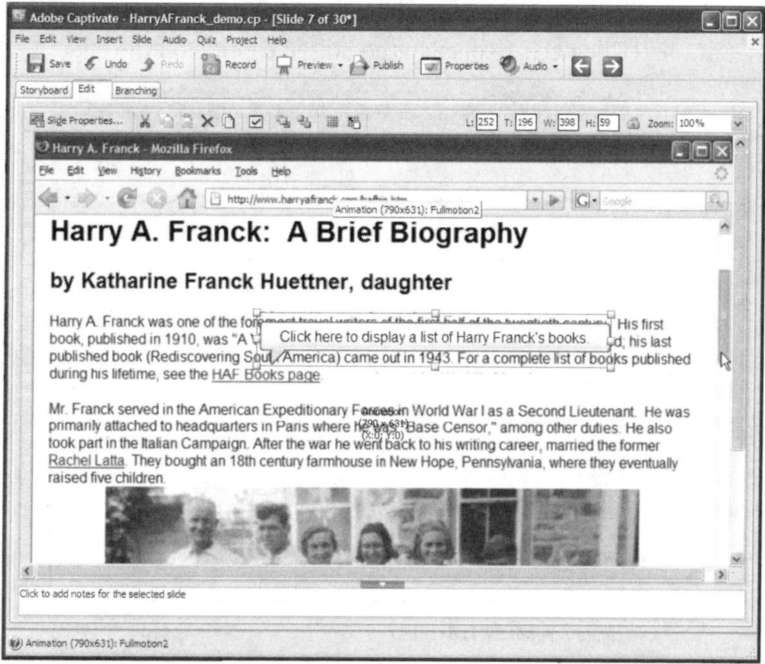

Figure 7-8. The new caption appears on the slide.

Editing Text Captions

Once you've created a text caption, you can move it around or resize it just like any other element on the slide. You can go back and edit the text as needed or change the look of the caption. You can also set the length of time the caption displays, as well as define the way the caption enters and leaves the screen during the movie (the transition).

1. In Edit view, select the slide you want to edit.
2. Double-click on the caption to open the Text Caption window (see Figure 7-9).
3. Make changes as necessary to the text caption properties. These are described in more detail in Table 7-4.

4. You can click the Options tab to set timing and transitions as described later in this chapter, click the Size and Position tab to set the default size and position, or click the Audio tab to set audio properties, as described in Chapter 8.
5. Click **OK** to display the edited caption on the slide.

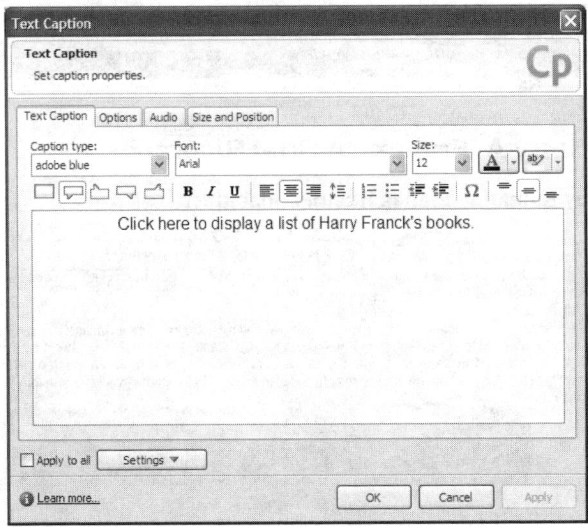

Figure 7-9. Edit the text caption.

Specifying Caption Language

Captivate automatically inserts captions as you record a software simulation. You can set the default language for these captions in the recording window that displays when you begin the recording process.

To change the caption language, follow these steps:

1. Click **Record or create a new project** to display the New project options window.
2. Select **Software Simulation**, then choose the type of project (Application, Full screen, or Custom size) to display the recording window. This window will display the mode and audio settings that you specified the last time you created a movie.

3. Click the double arrows next to the word Advanced to display additional options.

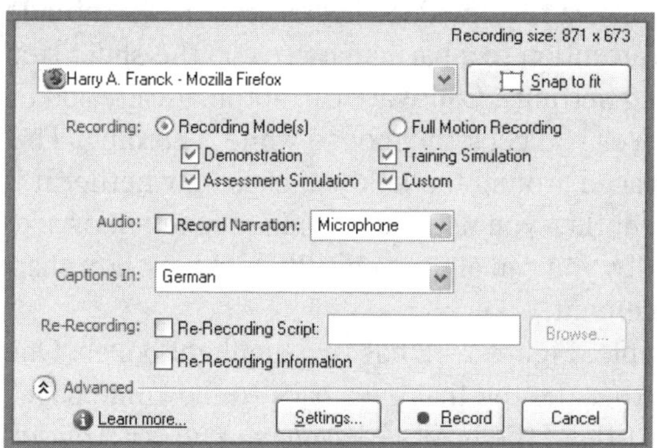

Figure 7-10. Specify caption language.

4. Choose a language for the captions from the Captions In drop-down list. Available options as of this printing are Chinese-simplified, Chinese-traditional, English, French, German, Italian, Japanese, Korean, Norwegian, Portuguese-Brazilian, Portuguese, Spanish, and Swedish. Note that only the captions will be translated into the selected language. The screen elements, such as buttons or menu items, remain in the original source language.

5. Click **Record** and continue to create the movie as normal. The finished movie will use the specified language for captions.

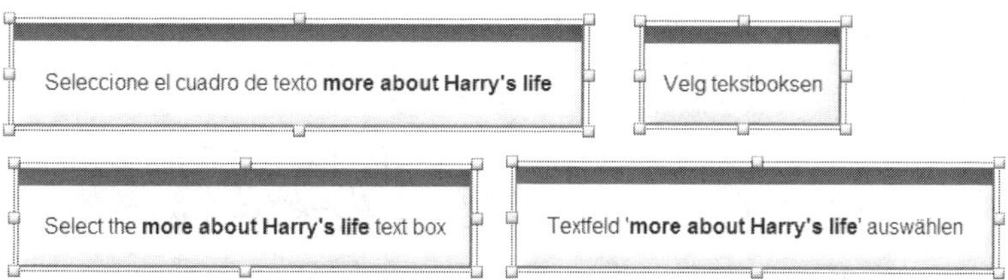

Figure 7-11. A caption in four languages.

Working with Highlight Boxes

A highlight box is a rectangular, shaded area that is intended to draw the viewer's attention to a particular area on the slide. Depending on your recording settings, Captivate can automatically add highlight boxes whenever you click the mouse while recording. The highlight box will be placed around the link you clicked, whether it is a button or a text link. Whether you use the automatic function or add highlight boxes manually, you can always edit the highlight box shape, color, size, and placement.

For example, Figure 7-12 has two highlight boxes. One is around the button across the top that goes back to the home page. The other is around the title of the book, *A Vagabond Journey Around the World*. Both highlight boxes are set to 50% transparency so that they show up clearly in this book; however, you may want to use a higher transparency so that viewers can see the button or text behind them. The words "highlight box" that appear in the center of the box will not appear in the finished movie. The currently selected highlight box, in this case the one around the text link, will display with small square handles in each corner and on the sides.

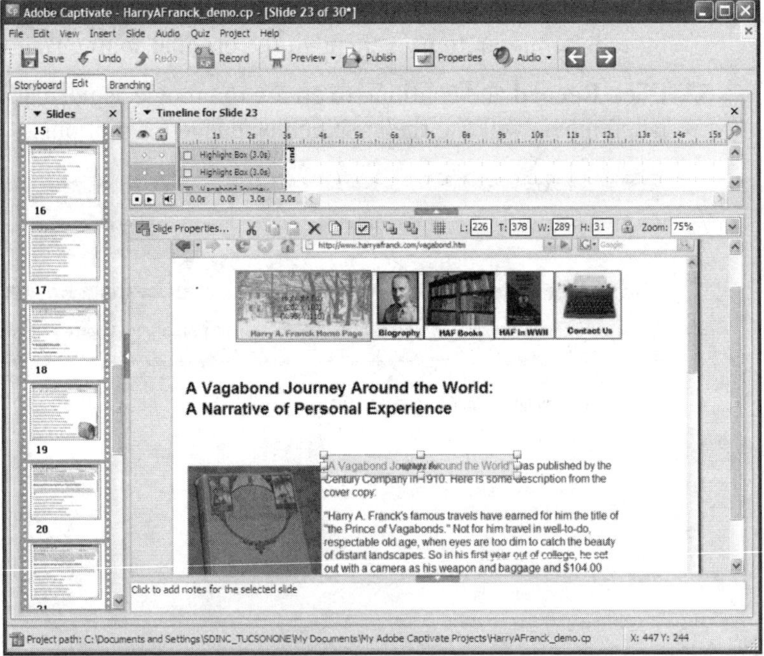

Figure 7-12. A slide with two highlight boxes.

Adding or Editing a Highlight Box

To add or edit a highlight box, follow these steps:

1. In Edit view, select the slide you want to edit.
2. To add a highlight box, from the Insert menu, select **Highlight Box**, or click the Highlight Box icon ( ) to display the New Highlight Box window. To edit an existing highlight box, double-click on the highlight box to display the New Highlight Box window.
3. If necessary, change the look of the caption by editing the following properties. As you make changes, the preview in the center of the window changes to reflect each new selection.

Table 7-5. Highlight box properties

To change this:	Do this:
Frame color	Click on the down arrow in the color box next to Frame color to display the Color window, and then choose a color for the border around the outside edge of the highlight box. This is usually a darker shade than the inside of the box.
Frame width	Specify the width, in pixels, for the border or frame of the highlight box. Set the width to 0 to remove the frame.
Fill color	Click on the down arrow in the color box next to Fill color to display the Color window, and then choose a color for the highlighting. This is usually a lighter shade than the frame of the box.
Fill transparency	Enter the percentage of transparency for the inside of the box. 0% would be completely solid; 100% would be completely transparent. Most of the time, you want something between these two values so that the highlight box is noticeable and yet the text behind the box still shows through.

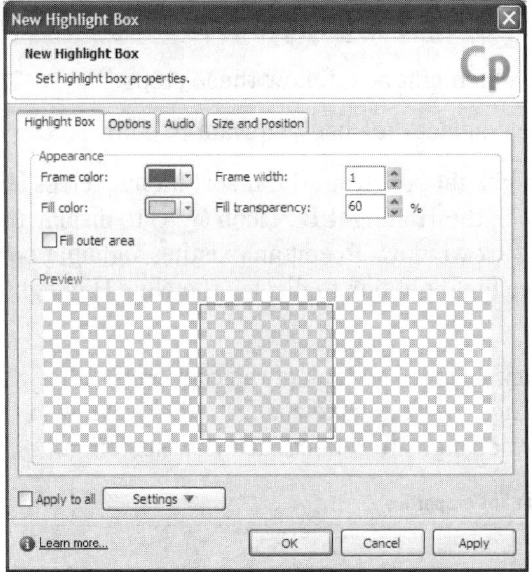

Figure 7-13. Set the new highlight box properties.

4. The changes you make to the highlight box properties will be applied to all subsequent highlight boxes. If you want to apply these changes to all highlight boxes that are already in the movie, click **Apply to all** to apply the current settings as defined in the New Highlight Box window. To view or change the properties settings, click the **Settings** button.

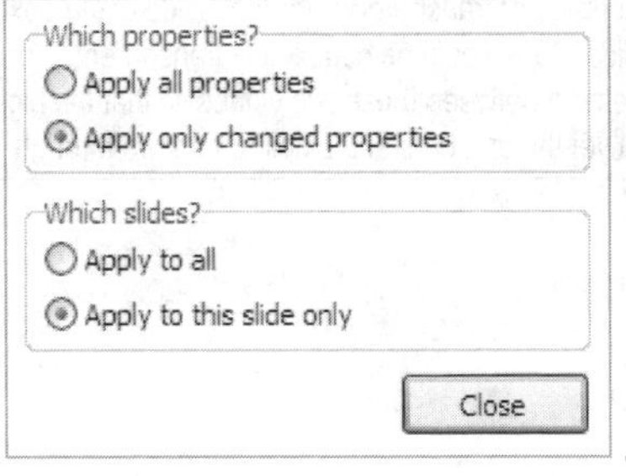

Figure 7-14. Apply settings to previously created highlight boxes.

5. You can click the Options tab to set timing and transitions as described later in this chapter, click the Size and Position tab to set the default size and position, or click the Audio tab to set audio properties, as described in Chapter 8.
6. Click **OK** to display the new highlight box in the center of the slide with the default size of 100 x 100 pixels.

7. Using your mouse, click and drag the highlight box to the desired location on the slide. You can also resize the highlight box if necessary by clicking and dragging the corners of the outline.

Working with Images

For most projects, you'll use an image or series of images as the background of each slide. In many cases, this will be a screen capture, logo, or photograph (see the section called "Working with the Slide Background" at the beginning of this chapter). When you create an image slide, you're importing an image as the background. Background images cannot be edited or changed within Captivate.

You can also import an image as an element on top of a slide background. Like other visual elements, the image can have unique timing and transition settings. You can resize the image or move it around on the slide. You can also specify a transparency setting for the image.

Valid image formats include JPEG, GIF, PNG, BMP, ICO, EMF, POT, and WMF.

Tip: Although you can add images of any size, this process works best with smaller images, such as an arrow or small icon or button that you will make interactive. If you need to import an image that will take up the entire slide area, see the section titled "Adding an Image Slide" in Chapter 6.

Adding or Editing an Image

Once you've imported an image, you can move it around or resize it just like any other element on the slide. You can also set the length of time it displays, as well as define the way the image enters and leaves the screen during the movie (the transition). You cannot, however, actually edit the image (such as change colors or erase parts of the image). For that type of task, you'll need to use an external graphics application.

To add or edit an image, follow these steps:

1. In Edit view, select the slide you want to edit.

2. To add a new image, from the Insert menu, select **Image**, or click the Image icon ( ) to display the images available in the last folder you used. Browse to the location of the image you want to

import, highlight the image name, and click **Open**. To edit an existing image, double-click on the image in the slide.

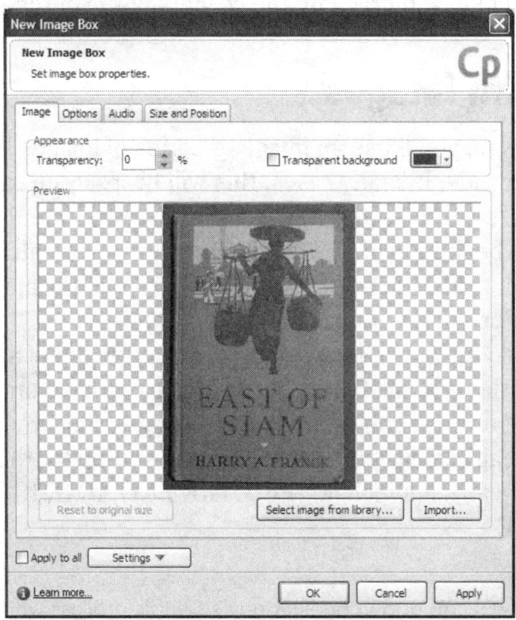

Figure 7-15. Import an image as an element on the slide.

3. The image you selected appears in the center of the New Image Box window. Enter the percentage of transparency for the image. 0% would be completely solid; 100% would be completely transparent.
4. You can specify that Captivate import the image but make the background color of the image transparent. For example, if you are adding a logo that is a custom shape, such as a shield, you might not want the rectangular outline of the image file to show.

Tip: Be careful to check your images after you import them, particularly if you use a transparent background. Captivate will make all areas that are the color of the background transparent. For example, if you have an image of a black circle with white lettering and a white background, and you make the white background transparent, then Captivate will make all white portions of the image transparent (including the letters). If this isn't the look you wanted, use a graphics program to make the background or the letters slightly different shades of white.

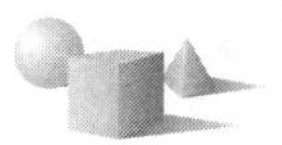

5. The changes you make to the image properties will be applied to all subsequent images. If you want to apply these changes to all images that are already in the movie, click **Apply to all** to apply the current settings as defined in the properties settings window. To view or change the properties settings, click the **Settings** button.

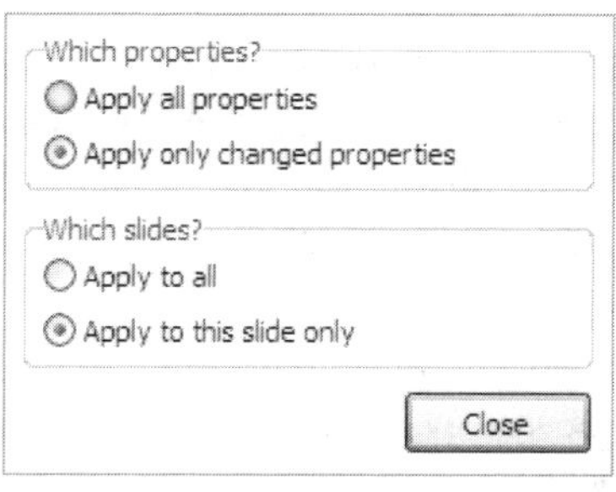

Figure 7-16. Apply settings to previously created images.

6. You can click the Options tab to set timing and transitions as described later in this chapter, click the Size and Position tab to set the default size and position, or click the Audio tab to set audio properties, as described in Chapter 8.
7. Click **OK** to display the new image in the center of the slide.
8. Using your mouse, click and drag the image to the desired location on the slide. You can also resize the image if necessary by clicking and dragging the corners of the outline.

Working with Animations

There are three types of animations within Captivate. The primary difference between the animation types is the way the files are created.

- Full-motion recordings are actually AVI animations that are created by Captivate and stored as Flash files that are displayed on a single slide. These full-motion recordings take up the full area of the slide and thus cannot be moved. The icon for the animation appears in the center of the slide. Full-motion recording is described in Chapter 4.
- Imported animations are files that were created outside of Captivate. Valid animation types for importing are AVI, SWF, FLA, FLV, and animated GIF files.

- Text animations are predefined animations that come with Captivate. Use these to make any text you enter move in various ways.

For all three animation types you can modify parameters such as transparency, timing, and transitions.

Importing Animations

You can import files in valid animation formats into your Captivate project. Like the full-motion recording, these mini-movies will be stored on a single slide. You'll be able to modify the placement of the animation, as well as the other standard element properties.

Tip: Captivate comes with a gallery of animated arrows and boxes that you can import into your movies. By default, they're stored in the Captivate\Gallery\SWF Animation folder.

To import an animation, follow these steps:

1. In Edit view, open the slide on which you want the animation.
2. From the Insert menu, select **Animation** or click the Animation icon ( ) to open the last-viewed folder.
3. Browse to the appropriate folder and choose the animation you want to import. For this example, we'll import an animation from the Captivate Gallery that shows a blue arrow moving diagonally downward (Captivate\Gallery\SWF Animation\Arrows\Blue Fade\downleft.swf).
4. Click **OK** to open the selected animation in the New Animation window. A preview of the animation displays on the left side of the window; statistics for the animation display on the right side of the window.

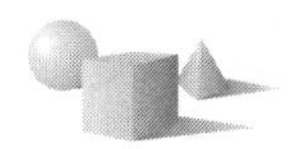

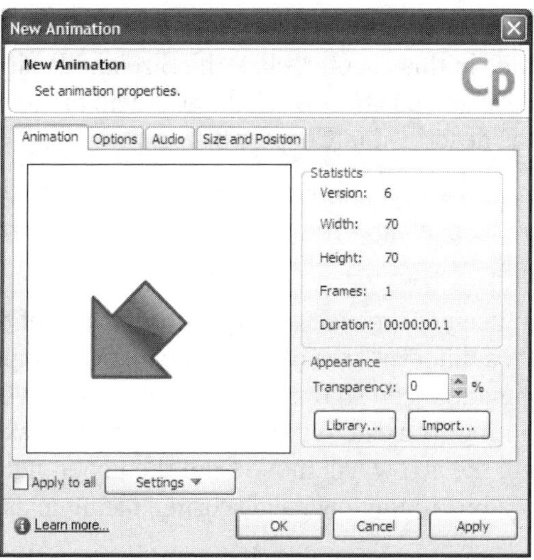

Figure 7-17. Insert an animation and set transparency.

5. If after viewing the preview you decide that it isn't the right animation, click the **Import** button to choose a new file.
6. Make changes as necessary to the Transparency setting. Remember, the lower the transparency setting, the less transparent (or more solid) the animation will appear.
7. The changes you make to the transparency will be applied to all subsequent animations. If you want to apply these changes to all animations that are already in the movie, click **Apply to all** to apply the current settings as defined in the New Animation window. To view or change the properties settings, click the **Settings** button.

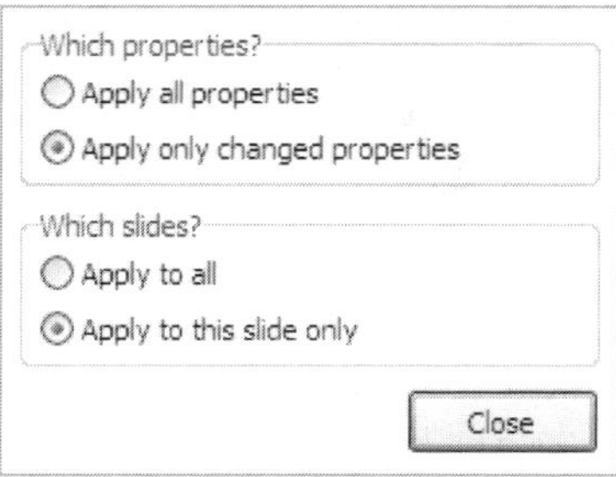

Figure 7-18. Apply settings to previously created images.

8. You can click the Options tab to set timing and transitions as described later in this chapter, click the Size and Position tab to set the default size and position, or click the Audio tab to set audio properties, as described in Chapter 8.
9. Click **OK** to display the animation on the slide. Note that the animation won't be playing—you'll just see an icon that represents the animation.
10. If necessary, use your mouse to click in the center of the image and drag it to a different area of the screen. For example, we might drag this animation icon so that the bottom corner (where the arrow is pointing) is close to the link for Harry Franck's books. When played, the arrow will move from the upper-right corner of the animation box to the lower-left corner, fading in as it moves.
11. If necessary, use your mouse to click on the square handles on the sides or corners of the animation, and then drag them outward or inward to create the size and shape you need.

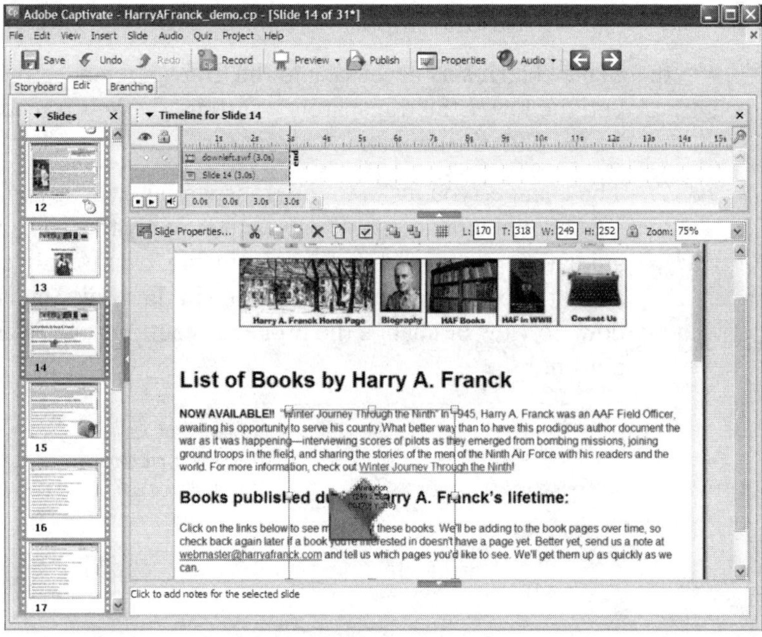

Figure 7-19. Move or resize the animation as needed.

Tip: Use the handles on the corners of the animation rather than the sides to maintain the aspect ratio (the relative height and width). This will prevent distorting the shapes.

Adding Text Animations

Captivate comes with a selection of animations specifically designed to add motion to the text that you enter. Some of the animations cause the text to enter or exit the slide in colorful or spectacular ways, while others make the letters in your text move about for the duration of the animation.

For example, you could have text shuffle in (like cards), spin like a top, pop in when bulbs break, or scroll onto the screen with a filmstrip effect. There are many others, but you'll have to view the list that comes with Captivate to see them all.

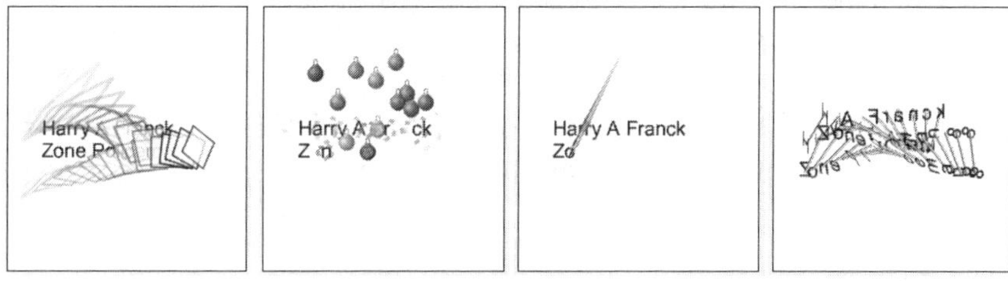

Figure 7-20. A few of the Captivate text effects.

To add text animation to a slide, follow these steps:

1. In Edit view, open the slide to which you want to add the text animation.
2. From the Insert menu, select **Text Animation** or click the Text Animation icon ( ) to display the New Text Animation window. The window displays the words "Sample Text" with the first animation from the list. In the following example, the "Aquarium" effect has blue-striped fish nibbling at the letters in the text. During the animation, more fish come in and continue nibbling until the letters are all gone.

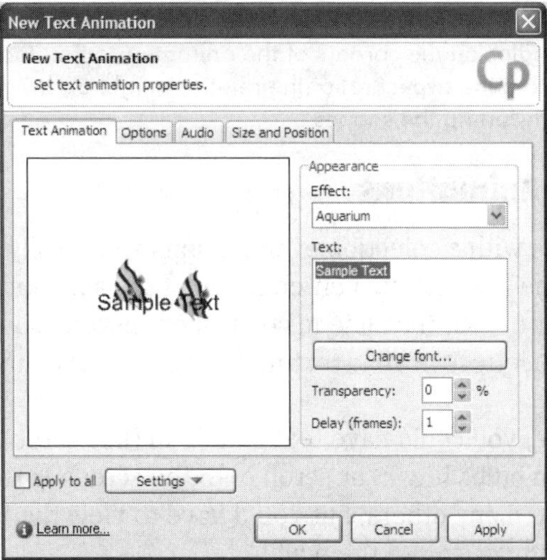

Figure 7-21. Type your text and choose a text animation effect from the list.

3. Type the text you want to animate in the Text box. Note that you can enter multiple lines of text and use any punctuation or special symbols.

Tip: There is no limit to the amount of text you can animate, but it works best if you animate smaller phrases rather than long strings of text. You can press the Enter key to create multiple lines of text in one animation, or you can create several one-line animations for the same slide.

4. Choose the animation effect you want from the Effect list. As you select from the list of animations, a preview of the selected animation will display on the left side of the window, using the words you've entered in the text box. For example, for a slide introducing Harry A. Franck books, we may want to create a title slide that makes it appear that a pen is writing out the letters on the slide. This is the animation called "Feather."

5. If you want to change the font, size, or color of your text, click the **Change font** button to display the Font window, and then choose the font, style, size, and color you want. For example, we may want to use a font that looks more like handwriting.

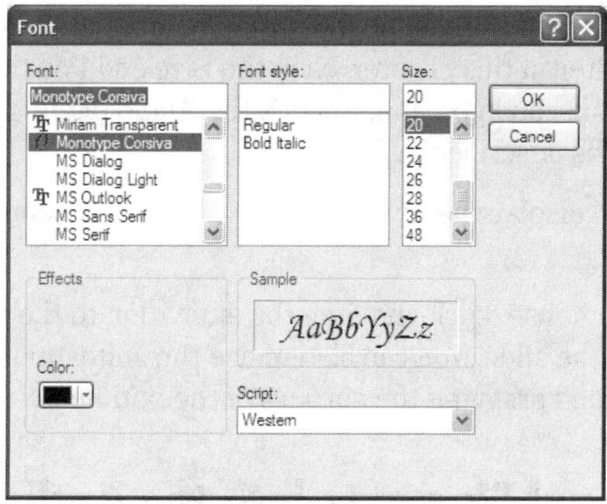

Figure 7-22. Specify font, size, and color for your text.

6. Click **OK** to close the Font window and display the changes in the New Text Animation window.
7. Make changes as necessary to the Transparency setting. Remember, the lower the transparency setting, the less transparent (or more solid) the animation will appear.
8. Specify the time delay between frames of the animation.

Note: This is in frames, not in seconds. A frame delay of 1 makes for a very fast, smooth movie. A higher delay between frames will cause the letters to come in (or fly out, or whatever the animation does) very slowly. Regardless of the frame delay, the animation will not run longer than the timing setting on the Options tab.

9. The changes you make to the animation properties will be applied to all subsequent animations. If you want to apply these changes to all animations that are already in the movie, click **Apply to all** to apply the current settings as defined in the New Text Animation window. To view or change the properties settings, click the **Settings** button.

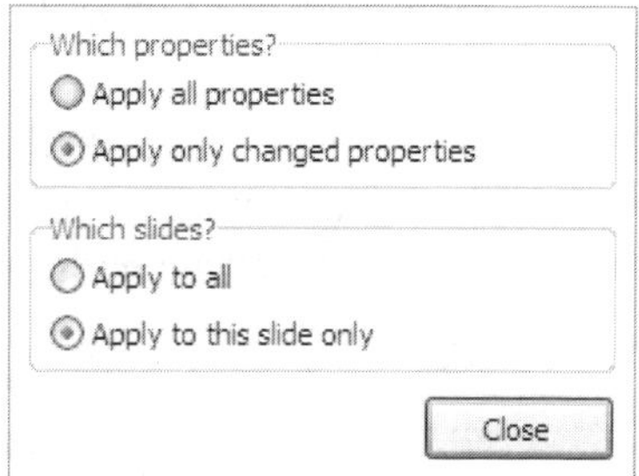

Figure 7-23. Apply settings to previously created text animations.

10. You can click the Options tab to set timing and transitions as described later in this chapter, click the Size and Position tab to set the default size and position, or click the Audio tab to set audio properties, as described in Chapter 8.

11. Click **OK** to display the new text animation in the center of the slide.

12. Using your mouse, click and drag the animation to the desired location on the slide. You can also resize the animation if necessary by clicking and dragging the corners of the outline.

Merging Visual Elements into the Background

As we've seen throughout this chapter, you can add elements on top of the background of any slide. These elements usually remain separate from the background so that you can modify them, move them around, and control their individual timing. However, there may be some instances where you want to merge an element into the background. For example, to make a type of watermark background, you could import an image of your logo as an object. This would allow you to edit the size, placement, and transparency of the logo to make it almost transparent. Then, merge the image into the background and use that background for other slides.

Note: Once you merge an object into the slide background, you can no longer edit that object.

To merge any object into the background of the slide, follow these steps:

1. In Edit view, add the object to a slide and make whatever changes you want. Remember, you won't be able to change the object after it is merged with the background.

2. Click once on the object to select it.

3. From the Edit menu, select **Merge into Background** (or right-click on the object and select Merge into Background) to display the confirmation dialog.

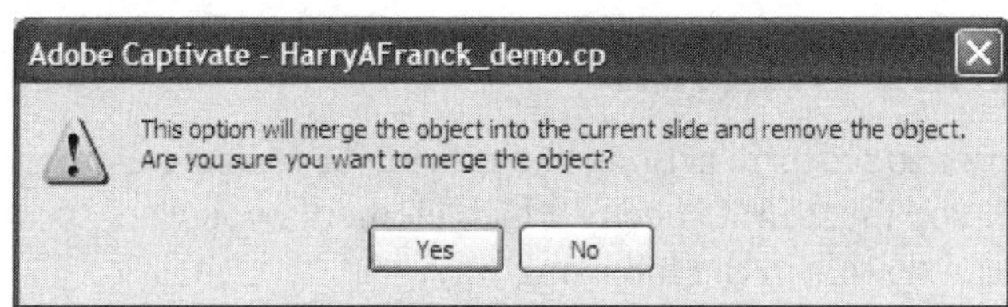

Figure 7-24. Merging an object and background cannot be undone.

4. Click **Yes** to complete the merge. Any objects you had selected are now part of the background of the slide.

Tip: If you merge animations into the background, the animations are converted to a single image. The result will display only the last frame of the animation.

Rearranging Elements on a Slide

Once you've inserted the various elements (such as images, animations, or captions) onto a slide, you can move them, resize them, align them with each other, or even delete them. The functions described in this section apply to all of the elements that you add on top of slides, but not to the background of the slides. If, for example, you've created an animation slide or an image slide, that animation or image is part of the slide background and not a separate object.

Tip: You can tell the difference between background and editable elements because the background elements do not have "handles" for resizing. Also, double-clicking a background will only display the slide's properties window (not the window for the element type).

Selecting Elements

In order to perform actions like moving or resizing elements on a slide, you must first specify which elements you want to work with. You can do this in the following way:

- Click once on an element to select it, either in the Edit view or from the timeline. The outline of a selected element displays small square boxes (called "handles") in each corner and on each side of the outline.

Tip: If you accidentally double-click on an element, the properties window for that element appears. Simply click Cancel to close the window. The element will remain selected.

To select multiple elements at once, do any one of the following:

- Click on one element to select it, then hold down the **Shift** key while you click on one or more subsequent elements.
- Click on one element to select it, and then from the Edit menu, choose **Select All**. Note that this option only becomes available after you've selected one object.
- Using the mouse, click anywhere on the slide, then hold down the left mouse button while you drag the mouse across the screen. This will draw a dotted line box, and any object within the box will be selected when you release the mouse button.

There are two elements in Figure 7-25: one text caption and one highlight box. The text caption has been selected and displays handles. The highlight box has not been selected.

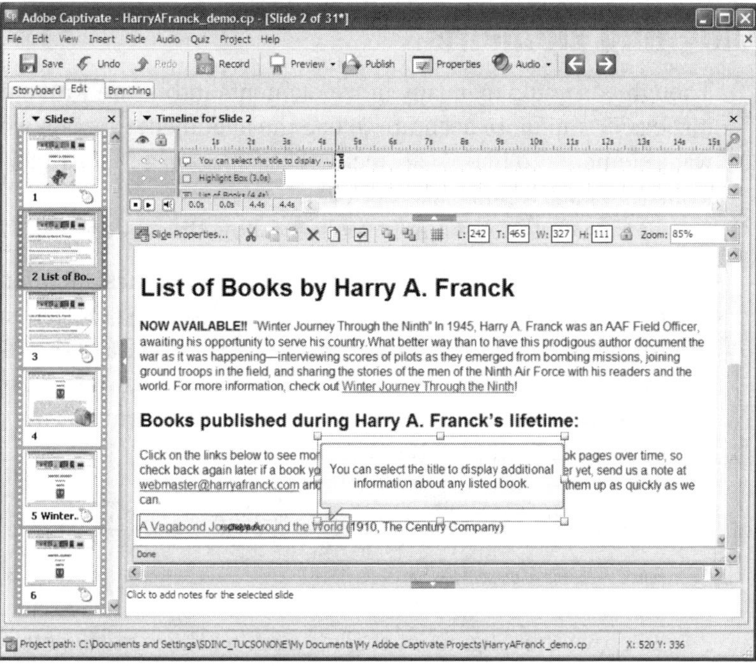

Figure 7-25. Selected elements, like this text caption, have "handles."

To remove the elements from selection, simply click once anywhere on the slide background.

Moving Elements

Once an element or set of elements has been selected, simply click anywhere within the selected element outline, hold down the mouse button, and drag the element to a new location.

For more exact placement of the element, use the up, down, left, or right arrow keys to move the element one pixel at a time in the direction of the arrow. This is sometimes referred to as "nudging."

If you're moving several elements at once, they will move as a group, retaining their positions relative to each other.

Aligning Elements

Though you could manually move elements into a line with each other, it is easier and more accurate to use the alignment function when you want elements to line up perfectly. There's even a toolbar of alignment icons that makes this task very easy.

To turn on the Alignment toolbar, follow these steps:

1. In Edit view, from the View menu, click **Toolbars** and then **Alignment** to select it, or right-click on any displayed toolbar and select Alignment. A check mark appears on the menu, and the Alignment toolbar displays in the location you last placed it. If you haven't displayed the Alignment toolbar before, the default location is across the bottom of the screen.

Figure 7-26. The Alignment toolbar.

2. To move the Alignment toolbar, click on the vertical dotted line on the far left (or top) of the toolbar, then drag the toolbar to a new location on any side of the Captivate screen. You can also drag the toolbar to the center of the screen to display it in a "floating" window.

When you align objects, Captivate will move all the elements you select in a line with the first one selected (the "anchor" element). You can easily see which is the anchor element because it will have white handles; subsequently selected objects will have black handles.

To align objects, follow these steps:

1. Select two or more objects.
2. Click the icon representing the type of alignment you want.

Table 7-6. Alignment options

Click this icon:	To align the elements like this:
	Align the left side of each element along the left side of the anchor.
	Align the horizontal center of each element along the horizontal center of the anchor.
	Align the right side of each element along the right side of the anchor.

Click this icon:	To align the elements like this:
	Align the top of each element along the top of the anchor.
	Align the vertical center of each element along the vertical center of the anchor.
	Align the bottom of each element along the bottom of the anchor.
	Space the elements so that there is an equal distance between the horizontal centers of each one.
	Space the elements so that there is an equal distance between the vertical centers of each one.
	Align the horizontal center of all elements, then center them horizontally on the slide.
	Align the vertical center of all elements, then center them vertically on the slide.
	Resize all elements so that they are the same height as the anchor.
	Resize all elements so that they are the same width as the anchor.
	Resize all elements so that they are the same height and width as the anchor.

Tip: If you change your mind about anything you do within Captivate, you can use the Undo function to step back through actions you've performed since you opened the project. Choose Undo from the Edit menu or press Ctrl+Z to undo the previous action.

Placing Elements with the Grid

For more precise placement of elements on a slide, you can display a grid in Edit view and specify the distance between both horizontal and vertical grid points. You can then either manually place elements on the grid, or you can have Captivate automatically place the elements along the lines formed by the grid points.

Note: The grid is a tool for placement of elements like captions, animations, and images. It will not display in the finished movie.

To use the grid for placing elements, follow these steps:

1. In Edit view, from the View menu, choose **Show Grid**. A grid composed of dots displays on the slide.

2. For finer control over placement, you can set the dots to be closer together. From the Edit menu, choose **Preferences** to display the Preferences window.
3. Click the word **Global** in the Category panel to display the global options.

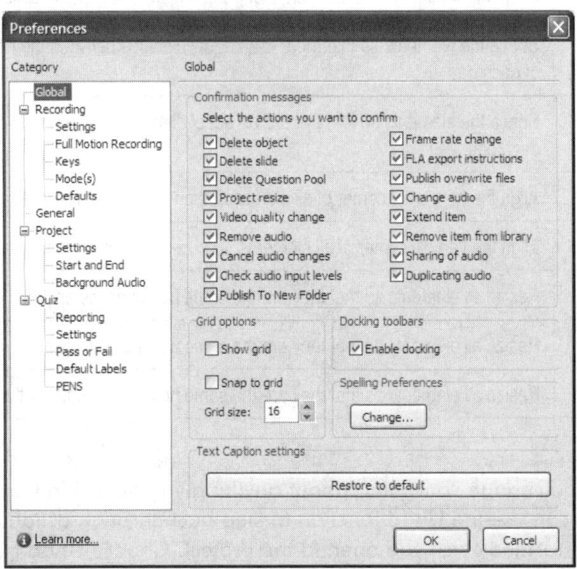

Figure 7-27. Set the grid size in the Global area of the Preferences window.

4. Click **Snap to grid** if you want Captivate to automatically place elements so that they are touching the nearest grid lines or click the checked box to turn off Snap to grid.

Tip: You can also turn Snap to grid on and off from the View menu. You don't have to open the Preferences window each time.

5. The default grid size is 16 pixels between each dot, both horizontally and vertically. Set this to the number that works for your project. Larger numbers allow more space between the grid dots; smaller numbers allow for more precise placement.
6. Click **OK** to close the Captivate Preferences window and return to the gridded slide.

If you selected Snap to grid, any element you move will automatically be placed along the grid. If you don't have Snap to grid turned on, you can still use the grid as a guideline for alignment.

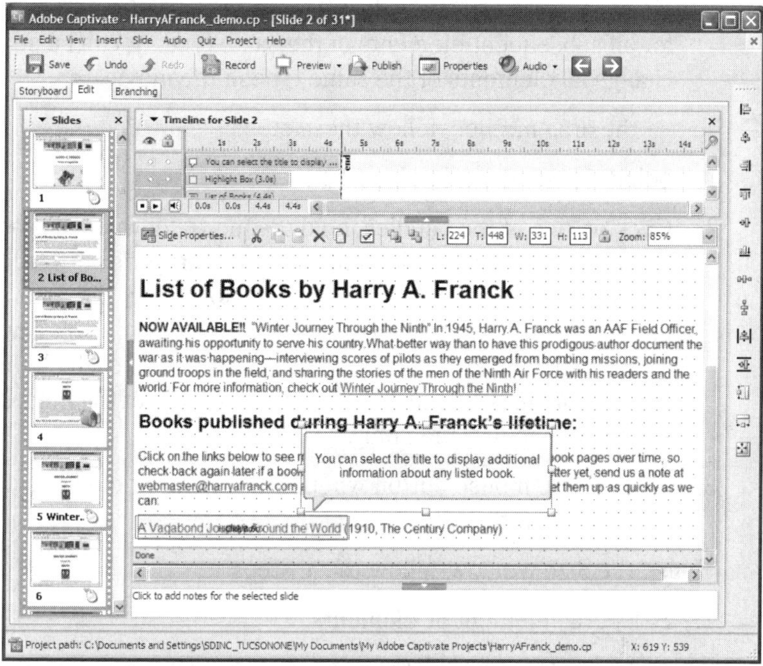

Figure 7-28. Text captions and other elements snap into alignment on the grid.

7. When you're finished moving things around, from the View menu, choose **Show grid** again to remove the check mark and turn off the grid.

Resizing Elements

Each element you add to a slide starts out with a default size. Captivate creates text captions so that they're just big enough to fit the text you enter. It imports animations and images at their original size, and bases the size of text animations on the font size and type of animation. You can change the size of any element using the handles on the corners and sides of the selected objects.

There are three ways to change the size of Captivate elements:

- Dragging the handles works just like it does in other applications. This is the quickest way to change a single element.

- Use the Size window. The Size window gives you more control, and is particularly useful when resizing several elements at once.
- Specify the size and placement on the Size and Position tab in the element's properties window. This option can store your changes for all subsequent elements of the same type, or can be set to change all elements of the same type in the movie.

To use the drag method, follow these steps:

1. Select the element or elements.
2. Click on one of the handles, hold the mouse down, and drag the handle away from the element to make it bigger or toward the center of the element to make it smaller. Hold down the Shift key and drag the handles in the corners of the element to maintain the aspect ratio and keep the same general shape of each element. Use the handles on the sides or top or bottom of the element to stretch in one direction only.
3. Release the mouse button when the element or elements are the size you want them to be.

To use the Size window, follow these steps:

1. Select the element or elements.
2. From the Edit menu, choose **Size** to display the Size window.

Note: If you've only selected one element, the shrink and grow options will not be available.

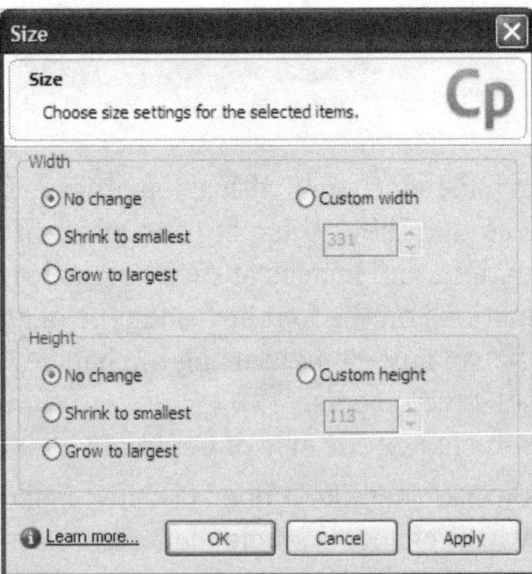

Figure 7-29. Set the exact size of an element.

3. Specify the width for the object or objects by selecting one of the following options:
   - No change—Leave this selected under Width if you only want to change height as in step 4.
   - Shrink to smallest—Select this to resize all of the objects to match the width of the smallest selected element.
   - Grow to largest—Select this to resize all of the objects to match the width of the largest selected element.
   - Custom width—Select this to specify an exact width, then enter a number in pixels for the width of each selected object.
4. Specify the height for the object or objects by selecting one of the following options:
   - No change—Leave this selected under Height if you only want to change width as in step 3.
   - Shrink to smallest—Select this to resize all of the objects to match the height of the smallest selected element.
   - Grow to largest—Select this to resize all of the objects to match the height of the largest selected element.
   - Custom height—Select this to specify an exact height, then enter a number in pixels for the height of each selected object.
5. Click **OK** when you're done to close the Size window and view the resized elements.

To use the Size and Position tab in the element's properties window, follow these steps:

1. Double-click the element to display the properties window.
2. Click the **Size and Position** tab.

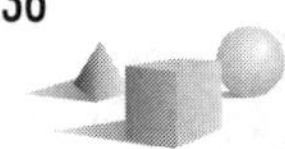

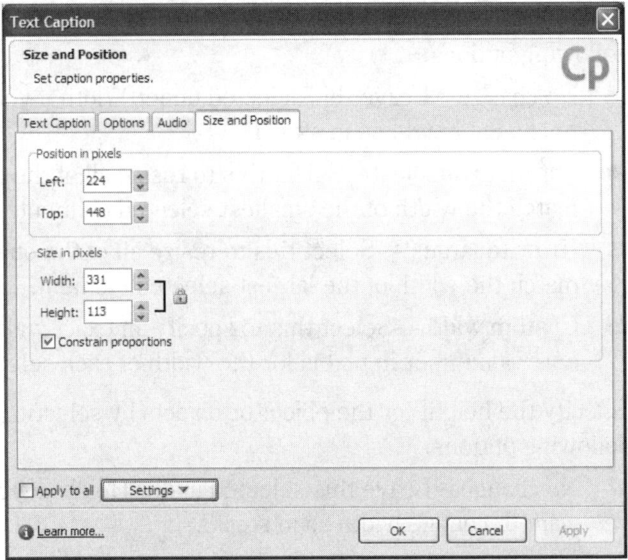

Figure 7-30. The Size and Position tab in the properties window adjusts an element's location (in this case, a text caption).

3. Specify the position of the element by entering the number of pixels the left edge of the element should be from the left of the slide, and the number of pixels the element should be from the top of the slide. For example, the very top leftmost position would show 0 in both the Left and Top boxes.
4. Specify the size of the element by entering the width and height in pixels. If you want to ensure that the proportion of width to height remains the same as you change the numbers, click either the Constrain proportions check box or click the lock icon to display a closed lock. This is similar to "Maintain aspect ratio" in other programs.
5. The changes you make to the element's properties will be applied to all subsequent elements of that type. If you want to apply these changes to all similar elements that are already in the project, click **Apply to all** to apply the current settings as defined in the properties window. To view or change the properties settings, click the **Settings** button.
6. Click **OK** to save your changes and close the window.

Deleting Elements

When you delete an element from a slide, you're deleting it permanently. Make sure this is what you want to do before you start to delete!

Tip: If you change your mind about anything you do within Captivate, you can use the Undo function to step back through actions you've performed since you opened the project. Choose Undo from the Edit menu or press Ctrl+Z to undo the previous action.

To delete an element, follow these steps:

1. Select the slide that contains the element you want to delete and open it in Edit view.
2. Select the element you want to delete.
3. Do any one of the following:
   - From the Edit menu, choose **Delete**.
   - Right-click on the element to display the pop-up menu, then choose **Delete**.
   - Press the **Delete** key on your keyboard.

   Whichever method you use, a confirmation dialog appears.

   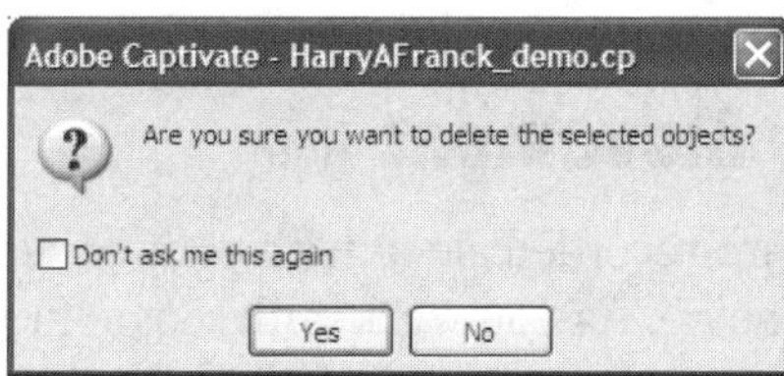

   Figure 7-31. Confirm that you want to delete the element.

4. Confirm that you want to delete the element by clicking **Yes**, or cancel by clicking **No**.

Tip: Although you can click the Don't ask me this again check box in the delete confirmation dialog to save a mouse click whenever you're deleting, it is a good idea to leave this unchecked. Once deleted, you cannot retrieve elements, and an extra confirmation step may one day save your project from accidental disaster.

Changing Cursor Movement

When you record actions on the screen, Captivate automatically stores the movements of your cursor as you move it around on the screen using the mouse or another pointing device. Rather than store the exact path, Captivate stores only the beginning and ending locations of the cursor on each slide. When the movie is played, Captivate fills in the cursor movement using the mouse settings you've entered for properties such as cursor icon, speed, path, and mouse click. One exception to this is if you record your movie in Full Motion recording mode. Full Motion recording captures the exact motions of your cursor.

Within Captivate, the cursor movement is also called the mouse movement, since it is typically created by recording your use of the mouse, although you can use other pointing devices such as a pen on a tablet. Sometimes the cursor is also called the pointer, even when it is a non-pointing icon such as a timer or cross-hatch.

Unlike other elements on a slide, you cannot delete cursor movement. You can, however, set the mouse movement so that it doesn't show. The beginning and end points are still stored, and you can show them again later if you need to, but the mouse cursor will not display on the slide in the finished movie.

Displaying Cursor Movement

The cursor movements are recorded along with your screen shots whenever you record a movie. As you work with movie files, you can turn the display of these movements on or off. There are three ways to do this:

- Set the default recording options for cursor movement display (on or off) before you record the movie. You can always override the cursor display for each slide later.
- Turn the cursor display on or off for a single slide through the Mouse menus.
- Set the cursor defaults with the Mouse Properties window. This window allows you to specify whether you want the new settings to apply to a single slide or become the new default for all slides.

To change the default cursor display, follow these steps:

1. From the Edit menu, choose **Preferences.**
2. From the displayed Preferences window, click the **Mode(s)** option under Recording in the Category panel on the left side of the window.

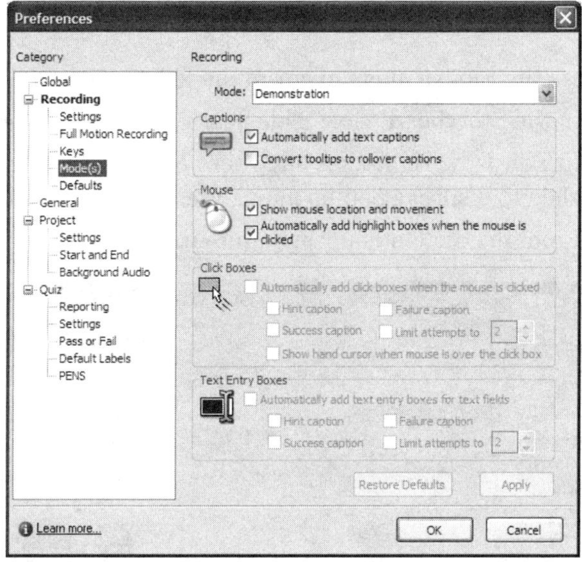

Figure 7-32. Set the recording options.

3. Specify the recording mode for which you want to change the default cursor display (Demonstration, Assessment Simulation, Training Simulation, or Custom). Remember that these are the options that display when you begin the recording process.
4. Click **Show mouse location and movement** to select it and display the cursor on your slides. Deselect this option to hide the cursor movement.
5. Click **OK** to close the Preferences window. All subsequent recordings, whether new movies or new slides in an existing movie, will use the new settings. The next time you record a movie, the cursor movement will display by default.

   You can turn the cursor movement on or off for specific slides using the Mouse menu options.

Note: Turning the display off does not remove the cursor movement from the file. It is just hidden until you turn it on again. Hiding the cursor movement on one slide does not change the cursor start positioning for the next slide, so you may appear to have a cursor pop out of nowhere if you hide cursor movement on a slide that actually had some movement. When you hide a slide, Captivate adjusts the start position of the cursor on the subsequent slide to match the previous slide.

Access the Mouse menu in any of the following ways:

- In the Storyboard view Slide Tasks pane, click **Mouse**.
- In Edit view, right-click anywhere on the background of the slide to display a pop-up menu, then choose **Mouse**.
- From the Slide menu, click **Mouse**.

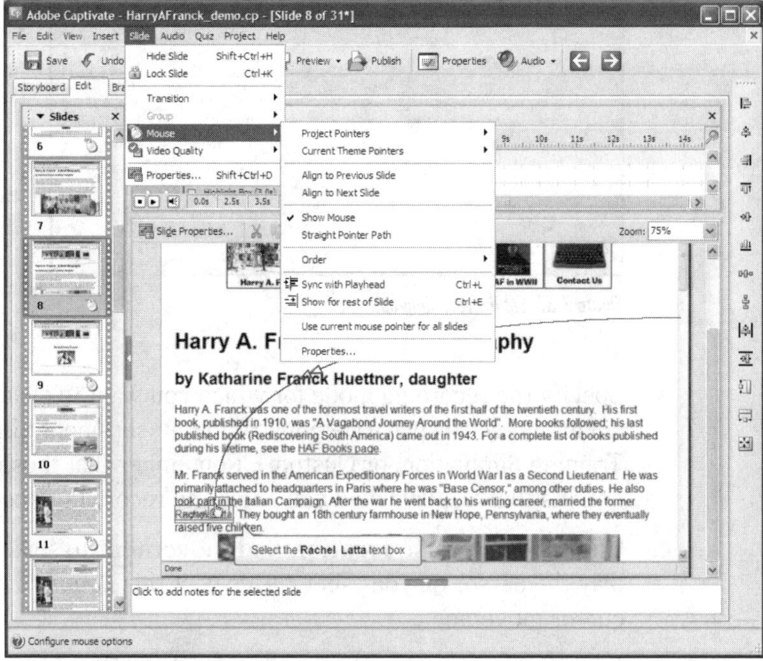

Figure 7-33. Display the Mouse menu options.

From the Mouse menu, select (or deselect) the **Show Mouse** option to turn the cursor movement display on or off.

Changing the Cursor Icon

For each slide, you can designate a different icon to be used as the cursor. You can choose from the variety of cursor icons that come with your Windows system, or you can use your own icon (as long as it is in valid Windows cursor format). For example, on some slides you may want to leave the standard image of a hand pointing to various objects; on other slides you may want to use a timer or cross-hatch.

To change the cursor icon, follow these steps:

1. Display the slide that contains the icon you want to change.
2. Display the Mouse menu by doing any one of the following:
   - In the Storyboard view Slide Tasks pane, click **Mouse.**
   - In Edit view, right-click anywhere on the background of the slide to display a pop-up menu, then choose **Mouse.**
   - Double-click on the cursor on the slide.
   - Double-click on the Mouse element in the timeline.
   - From the Slide menu, click **Mouse.**
3. Choose either **Project Pointers** (for a display of all icons in the cursor folder on your system) or **Current Theme Pointers** (for a display of the icons that match your current Windows theme).
4. Click the cursor icon you want to use for the current slide or select **Browse** to navigate to the file containing the icon you want to use.

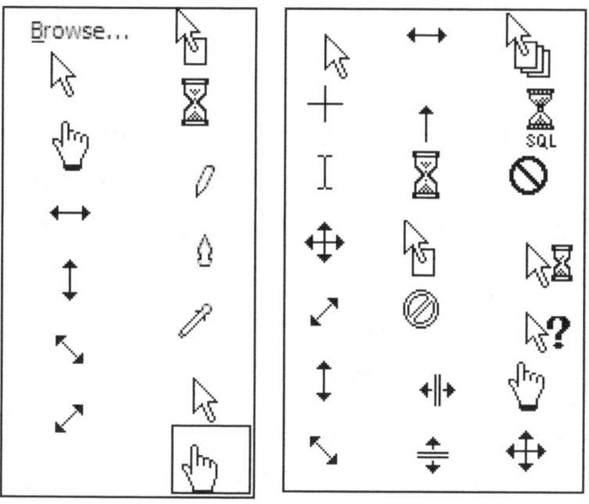

Figure 7-34. Choose a new icon for the cursor from either the project pointers or current theme pointers.

5. If you want to use the currently selected cursor for all the slides in the current movie, display the Mouse menu again (as in step 2) and choose **Use current mouse pointer for all slides**.

Changing the Cursor Path

Captivate stores the beginning and ending points of your cursor movements, then displays the path as a line between those two points. When you play the movie, the selected cursor icon moves along a path that represents the movement you made when recording the slides. Note that this isn't necessarily the same path you actually took—if you moved the mouse in a squiggly pattern or in circles, Captivate will still represent this as a direct line between the beginning and end points. In general, beginning and end points are set for each slide when you click the mouse button.

You can display the line either straight or curved, and you can move the end point of the movement to a new location. When you move the end point of a cursor path, Captivate automatically adjusts the start point of the path on the next slide to match, giving you a smooth transition when the movie is played. You can also move the starting point by selecting the cursor and dragging the red anchor to a new location.

To change the way the cursor moves across the screen, follow these steps:

1. In Edit view, select the slide with the cursor movement you want to change. Note that the path displays an arrow indicating the direction of movement. The arrow points toward the end point of the path, which displays the selected icon.
2. To change the path from curved to straight (or from straight to curved), open the Mouse menu in any of the following ways:
   - In the Storyboard view Slide Tasks pane, click **Mouse**.
   - In Edit view, right-click anywhere on the background of the slide to display a pop-up menu, then choose **Mouse**.
   - From the Slide menu, click **Mouse**.

   Then click **Straight Pointer Path** to select it (for a straight path) or click again to deselect it (for a curved path).

3. Change the end point of the path in any one of the following ways:
   - Click the icon at the end of the path, and drag it to a new location.
   - From the Mouse menu, choose **Align to Previous Slide** to move the end point of the current slide to match the end point of the previous slide. This will place the two points exactly on top of each other, making the cursor remain still for the duration of the current slide.
   - From the Mouse menu, choose **Align to Next Slide** to move the end point of the current slide to match the end point of the next slide. Because the end of the current slide is always the same as the beginning point of the next slide, this places the two points (beginning and ending) on the next slide on top of each other, making the cursor remain still for the duration of THAT slide.

As you move the end point on the current slide, the beginning point of the path on the next slide will also be changed.

Tip: If you change your mind about anything you do within Captivate, you can use the Undo function to step back through actions you've performed since you opened the project. Choose Undo from the Edit menu or press Ctrl+Z to undo the previous action.

Changing the Cursor Speed

Captivate automatically moves the cursor icon along the specified path. You can define how long this takes using the mouse properties. The faster the cursor moves, the less time the slide will take to play, but the more difficult it may be for the viewer to follow the cursor.

To set the cursor speed, follow these steps:

1. In Edit view, open the slide that contains the movement you want to edit.
2. Open the Mouse menu in any of the following ways:
   - In the Storyboard view Slide Tasks pane, click **Mouse**.
   - In Edit view, right-click anywhere on the background of the slide to display a pop-up menu, then choose **Mouse**.
   - From the Slide menu, click **Mouse**.

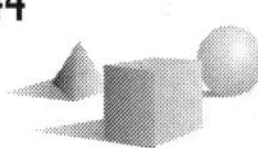

3. Choose **Properties** from the Mouse menu to display the Mouse Properties window.

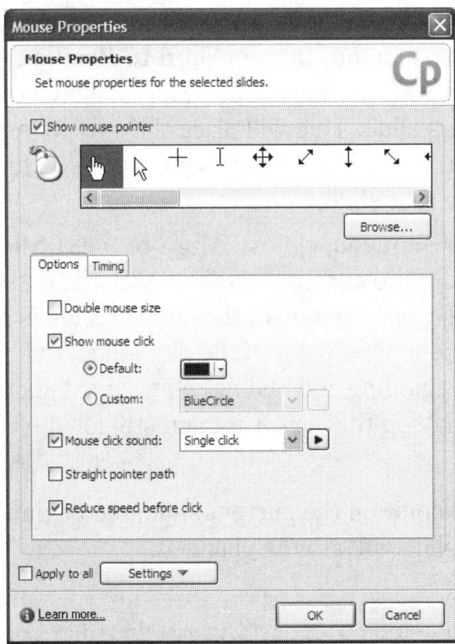

Figure 7-35. Set the cursor speed in the Mouse Properties window.

4. Click **Reduce speed before click** to slow the cursor down just before the end of the path. This allows relatively high-speed movement, but lets the viewer see where the clicks occur.
5. Click the **Timing** tab to display the timing options for the cursor movement.

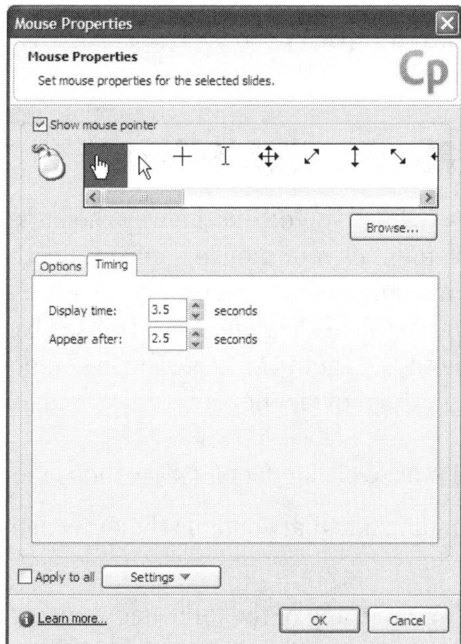

Figure 7-36. Set the length of time for the cursor movement.

6. Set the total length of time, in seconds, that you want the cursor to take to move between the beginning and end points by entering a number in the Display time box. You can enter time in one-tenth of a second increments.
7. Set the total length of time, in seconds, that you want the slide to appear BEFORE the cursor movement starts by entering a number in the Appear after box. You can enter time in one-tenth of a second increments.
8. The changes you make to the mouse properties will be applied to all subsequently created slides. If you want to apply these changes to all slides that are already in the movie, click **Apply to all** to apply the current settings as defined in the Mouse Properties window. To view or change the properties settings, click the **Settings** button.
9. Click **OK** to close the Mouse Properties window and display the slide.

Note: You can also set cursor speed using the timeline as described later in this chapter.

Adding Special Mouse Click Effects

There are two options that let you define the way the cursor movement mimics the movement of your mouse. Unlike the other elements, the cursor movement does not have a separate audio component, and although the mouse click effects are noises based on audio files, Captivate does not treat them like other audio components. They are linked to and part of the movement element and cannot be treated separately.

To set the special mouse click effects, follow these steps:

1. In Edit view, open the slide that contains the movement you want to edit.
2. Open the Mouse menu in any of the following ways:
   - In the Storyboard view Slide Tasks pane, click **Mouse**.
   - In Edit view, right-click anywhere on the background of the slide to display a pop-up menu, then choose **Mouse**.
   - From the Slide menu, click **Mouse**.
3. Choose **Properties** from the Mouse menu to display the Mouse Properties window, as shown in Figure 7-35.
4. Select **Show mouse click** to cause a small animation to display when the cursor reaches its end position on the path. This graphic represents the clicking of a mouse. By default, a small blue dot appears when the cursor reaches the end of the movement path.
5. If you've chosen to show the default mouse click graphic, select **Default**. You can change the color of the graphic by clicking in the color box (shown in Figure 7-35 as a dark box next to the word Default).
6. If you've chosen to show a graphic to represent the mouse click but don't want to use the default graphic, select **Custom** and then choose a graphic from the drop-down list. The box next to the list displays a preview of what each graphic looks like.

7. To play a sound when the cursor reaches the end of its movement path, select the **Mouse click sound** check box, then choose one of the available sounds (single click, double-click, or browse to choose a sound file of your own). Sound files must be in either WAV or MP3 format.
8. The changes you make to the mouse properties will be applied to all subsequently created slides. If you want to apply these changes to all slides that are already in the movie, click **Apply to all** to apply the current settings as defined in the Mouse Properties window. To view or change the settings, click the **Settings** button.
9. Click **OK** to close the Mouse Properties window and display the slide.

Changing the Timing of Elements on a Slide

When Captivate creates the Flash movie from your slides, each slide is displayed for a set length of time. The elements on each slide display in turn, also for a set length of time. You can create a wide variety of effects for your movie by modifying the length of time that each element displays and specifying when the element should appear on the slide.

There are two main functions that determine the length of time that a slide and the elements on it are displayed.

- Transitions set the way that an element appears on the slide and how the element is removed from the slide when the set element timing expires.
- Timing determines the length of time that each element is displayed and the delay, if any, between the display of the slide and the start of the element display. Timing can be set either through the element properties or with a unique Captivate tool called the timeline. This is a visual representation of the elements on a slide, placed along a graph that represents the total length of time the slide is displayed. It is very similar to the Flash Timeline, with most (though not all) of the same features.

Changing Element Transitions

The transitions for each element define the way the element enters and leaves the screen during the movie. You can set transitions for any elements except mouse movement, zoom areas, click boxes, and buttons. To set transitions for any element that allows transitions, follow these steps:

1. In Edit view, select the slide that contains the element you want to edit.
2. Double-click on the element to open the properties window for that type of element.
3. Click the **Options** tab to display transition parameters. For this example, we're looking at the New Highlight Box properties window, but the other elements use similar windows.

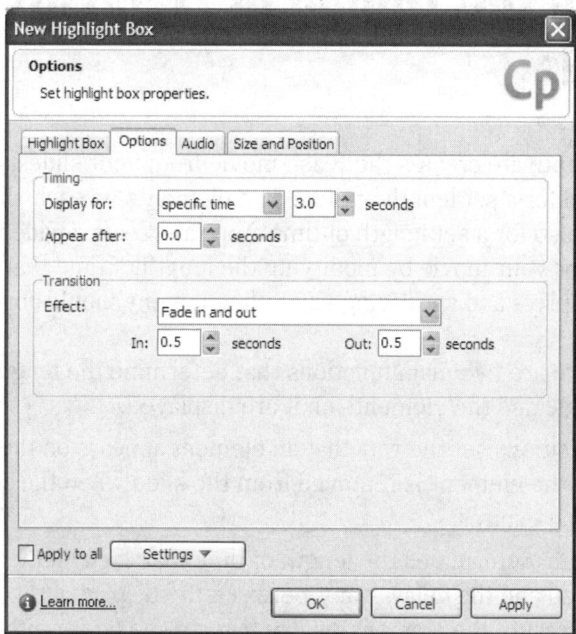

Figure 7-37. Set transitions in the element's properties window.

4. Choose a transition effect for the object.

- Fade in—The element will appear very dim at first and will gradually become more solid until it reaches the defined transparency setting.
- Fade out—The element will gradually become more transparent until it is gone from the slide display completely.
- Fade in and out—The element will appear dim, then gradually get more solid. Then it will gradually become more transparent until it is gone from the display completely.
- No transition—The element simply displays and then is removed after the specified timing.

5. For fading effects, you'll also need to specify how long or how gradual the effect should be. The default is 0.5 seconds.

Tip: It is usually best to show some restraint in adding effects to your movie. If you already have a lot going on, multiple animations and transition effects can be more distracting than entertaining.

6. The changes you make to the transition properties will be applied to all subsequently created elements of this type. If you want to apply these changes to all similar elements that are already in the movie, click **Apply to all** to apply the current settings as defined in the properties window. To view or change the properties settings, click the **Settings** button.
7. Click **OK** to close the window.

Changing Element Timing Properties

1. In Edit view, select the slide that contains the element you want to edit.
2. Double-click on the element to open the properties window for that type of element.
3. Click the **Options** tab to display timing properties. For this example, we're looking at the New Animation properties window, but the other elements use similar windows.

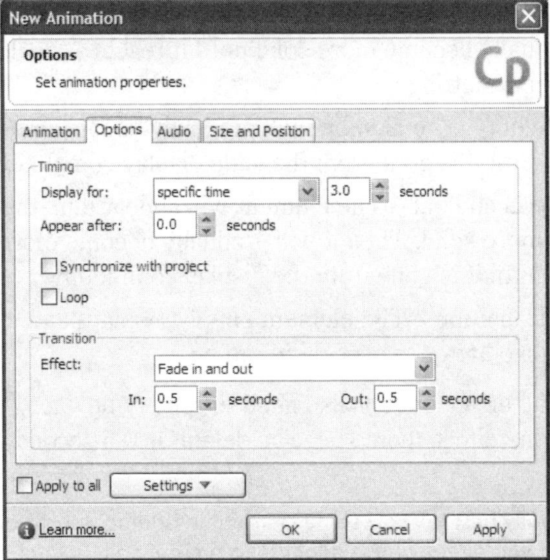

Figure 7-38. Set the timing parameters.

4. Set the length of time the element will display by choosing one of the following from the list of Display for options:
   - Specific time—Enter the number of seconds you want the element to display. If you enter a time longer than the current length the slide is displayed, the slide timing will be adjusted to the new length of time. For example, if your slide is currently set to display for 3 seconds, and you enter 5 seconds in the animation timing area, the slide timing will be extended to display for 5 seconds. You can enter times in increments of one-tenth of a second.
   - Rest of slide—Displays the element for as long as the slide is displayed.
   - Rest of project—Displays the element for the rest of the entire movie.
   - Duration of Animation (Animation and Text Animation elements only)—Displays the element for the length of time needed to display the entire animation.

Tip: If you use the rest of project setting, make sure you test the whole project. This setting makes it easy to accidentally cover up important information on a later slide without realizing it.

5. You can specify that the element displays a certain length of time after the slide first appears by typing a number of seconds in the box labeled **Appear after**. Leave this number set to 0.0 if you want the element to display as soon as the slide displays. You can enter times in increments of one-tenth of a second.

Note: If you've specified a duration for an element, the slide will display for at least as long as the total of the Appear after and the Display for times. For example, a Display for setting of 5 seconds and an Appear after setting of 3 seconds would display the slide a total of 8 seconds.

6. The New Animation properties window has two unique check boxes that the other option windows don't have:
   - Synchronize with project—This option lets you control the length of time that the animation plays using the timeline (see the next section).
   - Loop—This option plays the animation continuously for as long as the animation is displayed.
7. The changes you make to the timing properties will be applied to all subsequently created elements of this type. If you want to apply these changes to all similar elements that are already in the movie, click **Apply to all** to apply the current settings as defined in the properties window. To view or change the properties settings, click the **Settings** button.
8. Click **OK** to close the window.

Using the Captivate Timeline

While working in Edit mode, you can display the Captivate timeline for a quick view of the elements on the slide and when each will display. Instead of opening the properties of each element, then adjusting the timing, you can simply drag the elements on the timeline to specify when each will display and for how long.

Understanding the Timeline Basics

The timeline itself is a horizontal representation of the duration of a slide, with a ruler across the top that marks out the slide display in seconds. Each element is represented by a rectangular box in the

timeline. By default, most elements are displayed as soon as the slide is displayed. Many will remain on display for the full time that the slide is displayed.

To display the timeline, you must be in Edit view. Then go to the View menu and select Show Timeline.

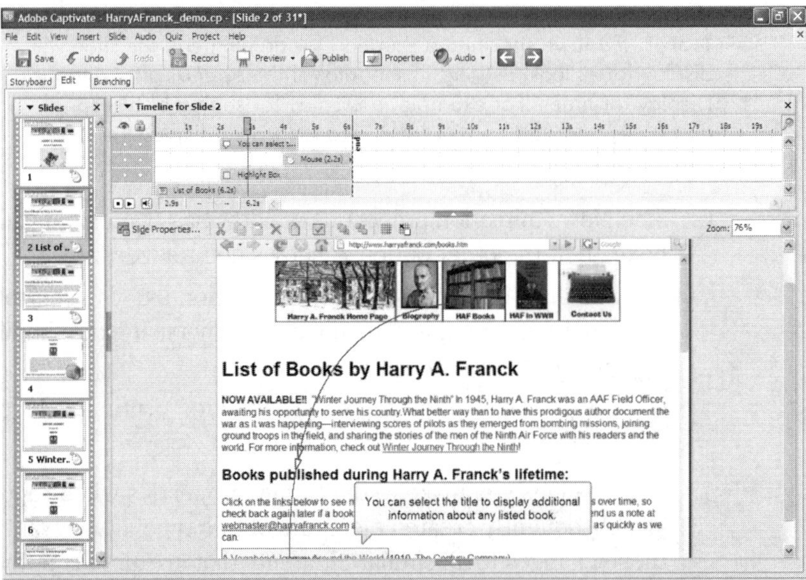

Figure 7-39. View the slide elements on the timeline.

In Figure 7-39, the timeline displays a "stack" of three elements plus the slide itself (on the bottom of the stack). This particular slide will be displayed for 6.2 seconds. The slide displays the background for 2 seconds, then the highlight box and text caption display. After the slide has been displayed for 4 seconds, the mouse element (representing the cursor movement) displays and begins to move along the designated cursor path. This will take 2.2 seconds to go from beginning to end. Though the highlight box remains visible for the rest of the slide, the text box disappears shortly after the mouse element begins.

The timeline controls are displayed at the bottom of the timeline. The first two allow you to preview elements on the slide, just as they will appear within the movie. The first, a square icon, stops the preview, and the second, a triangular icon, starts the preview. As you preview the slide, a red line moves across the timeline, indicating the time on the slide. This red line is the playhead, and you can use it to

view exactly what the slide looks like at any given point; you also can drag the playhead to see how objects (including audio) will play back.

Tip: This feature can delay a little when you have more complex animations and audio. Proper levels of available system memory help tremendously in using this handy feature.

There is also a scroll bar that is part of the timeline in case the slide lasts longer than the displayed amount of time (in this case, 19 seconds or so).

To use the timeline, click on an element in the timeline and drag it to the desired position on the timeline. You can change either the length of time the element displays (the duration) or the amount of time before or after the element displays.

- Click in the center of the element on the timeline, then drag the entire element. The duration of the element remains the same, but the amount of time before and/or after the element will change.
- Move the cursor to the right side of the element in the timeline until the cursor becomes a set of vertical lines. This indicates that you're on the edge of the element. Click and drag the edge outward or inward to change the duration of the element.
- Drag the right side of a timeline object to a different position to lengthen or shorten the time the element is displayed.
- Drag the center line in a timeline object to change the pause location.

For example, if you want the slide to display for two seconds before the cursor begins to move, you would click in the center of the mouse movement element on the timeline and drag it until the left edge of the element is at the 2-second line on the timeline. Similarly, you might move the highlight box so that it only displays after the 3 seconds that the text caption displays.

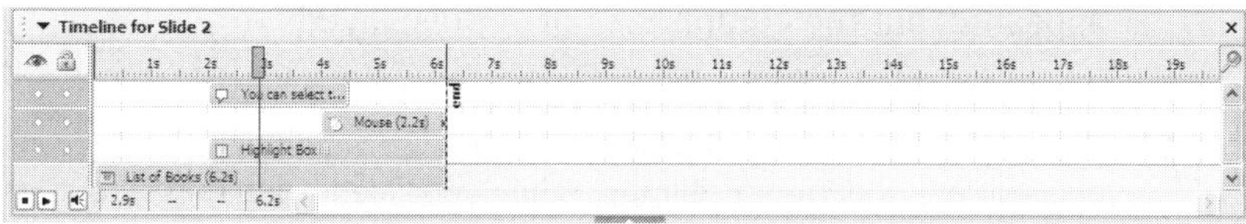

Figure 7-40. Make changes to element timing on the timeline.

Note: If you stretch or drag an element on the timeline past the duration for the whole slide, the slide duration (as represented by the bottom of the stack) will automatically be extended.

Previewing a Slide

There are several ways to preview the way a slide will look when it is played.

- Click the **Preview** icon (Preview), then choose **Play this slide**.
- Press **F3** to display from the playhead to the end of the slide.
- Press the **Spacebar** to display from the playhead to the end of the slide.
- On the lower portion of the timeline, click the **Play** icon (▶).
- Drag the playhead ( ) across the timeline.

Note that previewing a single slide does not let you preview interactive elements. You must preview multiple slides to access interactive features.

In any preview, the playhead, represented by a vertical red line, moves across the timeline as the slide plays. If you use the playhead method to preview your slide, you can stop and examine the way the slide will look at any given point in the display.

To manually move the playhead, click on the rectangle at the top of the red playhead line and drag the playhead across the timeline. This is called "scrubbing" the playhead. It's a common tool in movie editing software and it can be done in reverse as well as forward to check animation, movement, etc., and is powerful for quickly checking and adjusting timing.

In Figure 7-40, the playhead is at 2.9 seconds into the slide display. At this point in the preview, the text caption and highlight box have appeared, but the cursor has not yet displayed.

Tip: As you move the playhead, the slide elements will display according to the timing settings. When you release the mouse button and the playhead stops moving, all elements will display, regardless of the location of the playhead. To see just the elements at that particular moment, click the top of the playhead and hold the mouse button down as if you were dragging the playhead.

Setting Element Timing Using the Timeline

In addition to the ability to move elements individually, the timeline includes some functions that let you set the timing for elements by moving the elements on the timeline using shortcuts. You can use any of these shortcuts for a single element, or you can select several elements in the timeline and move them all at once.

To select multiple elements, click on any element to select it, then hold down the Control key and click on additional elements.

Once you've selected the element or elements for which you want to set a timing option, do any of the following:

Table 7-7. Using the timeline to set timing options

To set this timing:	Do this:	Or use these keys:
Start the element as soon as the slide displays.	Click and drag the element or elements to the left side of the timeline.	
Start the element at the time indicated by the current position of the playhead.	Right-click to display a pop-up menu, then select Sync with Playhead.	Ctrl+L
Extend the timing of the element so that it remains visible for the whole time the slide is displayed.	Right-click to display a pop-up menu, then select Show for rest of slide.	Ctrl+E
Shorten the whole slide duration.	Click the end of the slide element and drag it toward the beginning of the slide. Each element will move as needed to fit in the allotted time. Note that you can't make the slide duration shorter than the timing for the longest element.	

Changing the Timeline Display

Like the other Captivate toolbars, you can turn the timeline display on and off as needed. In addition, you can change the size of the displayed timeline and the amount of time that it is displayed.

To change the way the timeline displays, follow these steps:

1. If it isn't already displayed, display the timeline. In Edit view, from the View menu, choose **Show Timeline**.
2. To change the position of the timeline, click on the vertical dotted line in the top-left corner of the timeline ( ) to display a four-headed arrow, then hold down the left mouse button and drag the timeline to a new location. Note that the timeline will display in a new window but remain horizontally oriented.

Note: If you move the timeline to the top or the bottom of the slide display, it will "dock" or become part of the slide window.

3. You can change the size of the increments in the ruler that represents seconds in the timeline. For example, if you currently are showing 19 or 20 seconds on the timeline, but only need 5 or 6, you could make the increments larger. Valid ruler display options are tiny, small, normal, medium, and large. The actual number of seconds that will display for each option varies by the type of monitor you have and your system display settings. To change the seconds on the timeline ruler, do one of the following:
   - Click the **magnifying glass** icon in the upper-right corner of the timeline to display a list of size options, and then click the one you want.
   - Click anywhere on the **timeline ruler**, then use your mouse wheel to scroll through the available ruler sizes.

Preventing Changes to a Slide

After you've made all these edits to a slide to make it exactly what you want, you can lock the slide so that the objects on it cannot be moved, deleted, or changed. Locking a slide prevents changes to the elements on the slide, but it does not prevent changes to the slide as a whole. In other words, although no one but you will be able to delete the captions from a locked slide, anyone would be able to move the whole slide to another part of the movie or change the slide transitions.

Tip: Anyone with access to these Captivate project source files can lock (or unlock) any slide or element on a slide. Though this feature is very useful to prevent accidental or unintended changes, it does not prevent others from unlocking and making changes.

Another method of preventing accidental changes is to temporarily hide elements on a slide. Like the lock elements feature, the hide feature can easily be undone by anyone.

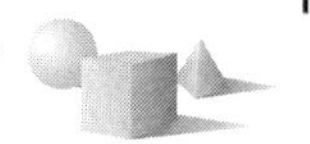

Locking a Slide

To lock a slide, do any of the following:

- From the Slide menu, choose **Lock Slide**.
- Right-click on the slide to display the pop-up menu, then choose **Lock Slide**.
- Click the **Properties** icon or double-click the slide to display the properties window, then click the **Lock Slide** check box.
- Press **Ctrl+K** on your keyboard.

Locking or Hiding Individual Elements on a Slide

You can also prevent changes to individual elements on a slide by locking just those elements. Or you can hide individual elements from the slide (though they'll still appear on the timeline). On the far left side of the timeline is a matrix of radio buttons with an eye icon and a lock icon in the top row.

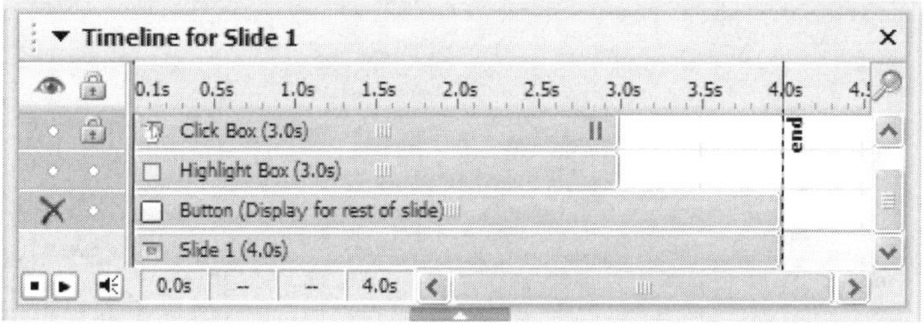

Figure 7-41. Locking individual elements on a slide prevents changes.

To lock an object on the slide, click in the column under the lock icon and in the row for the selected element. To unlock the element, click that same radio button to deselect it. To lock all elements in the slide, click the lock icon itself.

To hide an element on the slide, click in the column under the eye icon and in the row for the selected element. To view the element, click that same radio button to deselect it. To hide all elements on the slide, click the eye icon itself.

In Figure 7-41, the click box is locked and the button is hidden.

Summary

This chapter described how to work within a single slide. It covered the slide background, adding and editing various types of elements, and adjusting the timing and transitions for a slide. The next chapter will discuss how to record and add audio to your movie.

Chapter 8

Defining What the User Hears—Adding Audio

Captivate allows you to add sound to your movies, either by recording sounds as you record the visual elements or by adding separate audio files later. You can add sounds to a single element on a slide, for the duration of a slide, or even for the whole movie. For example, you may want to include special sounds for certain actions (like getting a question right—or wrong) or narrate your actions on the screen. You can also include sound files as needed for accessibility purposes or simply add some background music that plays throughout the movie.

Like other elements (see Chapter 7), you can move audio files around on the timeline, or copy, paste, and delete them as needed. You can also adjust the sound level so that your audio volume is consistent from slide to slide.

Recording New Audio Files

There are several ways to record audio in Captivate. You can record a voice narration while you're recording a project, you can record audio for an existing project, you can record individual audio files for each slide, or you can record audio for each individual element (such as a click box or caption). Before recording any audio, you must first set up the appropriate audio equipment and calibrate it for use with Captivate.

Setting Up Audio Equipment

In order to record audio files for use with Captivate, you must have the following minimum configuration:

- Computer with sound card to record the audio.
- Microphone with stand. The better your microphone, the more professional your audio will sound. You'll need the stand to avoid unnecessary noises from microphone movement.
- Speakers so that you can hear the recorded audio.

In addition, you may want to consider some of the following equipment to ensure a clean audio file:

- Microphone preamplifier to boost the signal of the microphone.
- Headphones to use while recording to avoid distracting feedback.
- Recording software that lets you edit audio files or create sound effects. Choose whichever software works for you, but it must be able to create MP3 or WAV formatted files.

Once you've got everything set up, you'll need to calibrate the audio input to make sure that Captivate can recognize your microphone and your voice. Each time you begin to record an audio session, Captivate displays a message asking you if you want to check your recording levels. You can calibrate each time you record, or you can do it whenever you begin a session or change hardware, even if you aren't recording anything at the time.

To have Captivate calibrate your recording levels without recording anything, follow these steps:

1. Make sure your microphone is plugged in and turned on.
2. Open an existing Captivate project.
3. From the Audio menu, choose **Settings**.

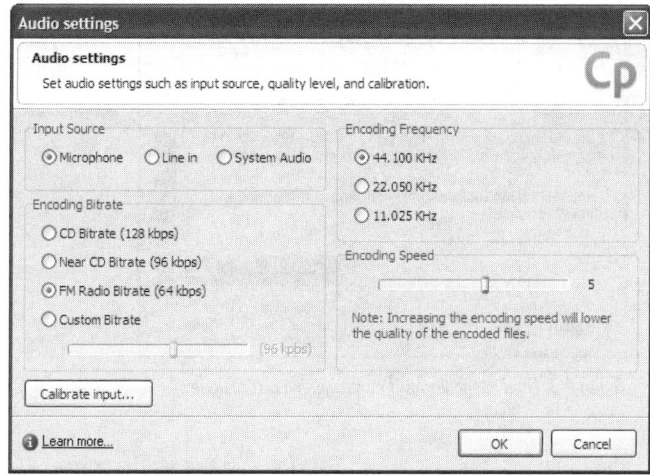

Figure 8-1. Display the Audio settings window.

4. Click the **Calibrate input** button to display the Calibrate audio input window.

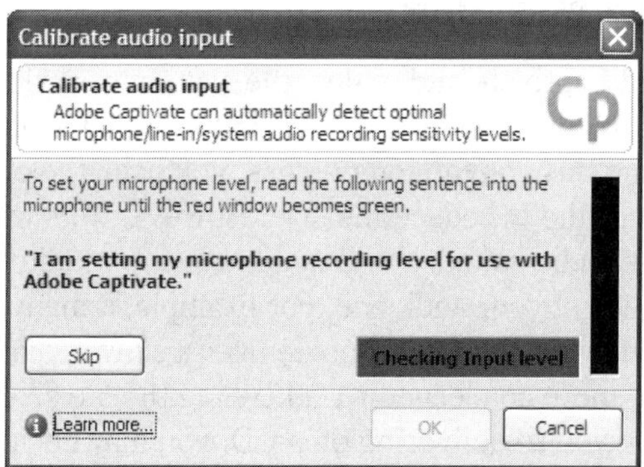

Figure 8-2. Speak into the microphone to set the audio levels.

5. As soon as the Calibrate audio input window displays, start speaking into the microphone with a normal voice. Read the sentence on the window, or say anything else you like. As you speak, the meter level indicator will move, and as soon as the system has a good audio level setting, the text message will turn green and switch from "Checking Input Level" to "Input level OK."

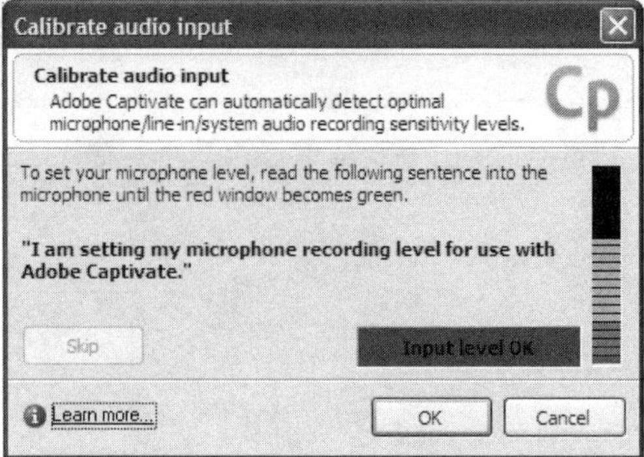

Figure 8-3. Captivate indicates if an acceptable recording level exists.

6. Once the level is set, click **OK** to close the Calibrate audio input window.
7. Click **OK** to close the Audio settings window.

Setting Audio File Size

When you record Captivate audio files, the system records your voice in WAV format and then converts it to MP3 format for storage with each slide. During this conversion process, you have the option of also compressing the audio to reduce file size. However, this will also lower the quality of the audio sound. You'll need to set the audio options based on the needs of your audience. For example, if many of your viewers will be downloading your movie over a slower, dial-up connection, you may be more concerned with keeping the file size small. On the other hand, if you're delivering on a CD, you may decide to set the audio to a higher quality even though it increases the file size.

To set the audio recording quality, follow these steps:

1. Make sure your microphone is plugged in and turned on.
2. Open an existing Captivate project.
3. From the Audio menu, choose **Settings**.

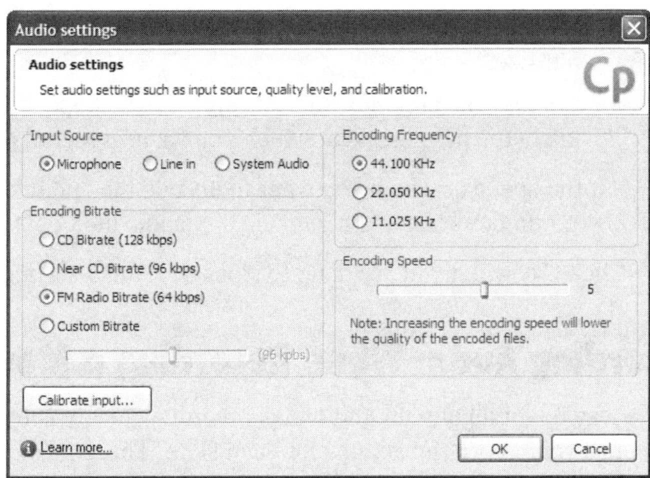

Figure 8-4. Set audio quality.

4. Choose one of the available sources for audio input:
   - Microphone
   - Line in
   - System Audio
5. Choose one of the encoding frequencies. This is the number of times per second the original sound wave is translated into digital form. A higher frequency results in a more accurate digital representation of the sound.
   - 44.100 KHz—The most frequent sampling; gives the highest quality (near CD quality)
   - 22.050 KHz—Comparable to FM radio
   - 11.025 KHz—Fewer samples per second, resulting in lower quality sound; generally considered equivalent to telephone quality, but actually a little higher
6. Choose one of the encoding bitrates. This specifies the amount of audio information (in kbps) that will be stored per second of a recording:
   - CD Bitrate (128 kbps)—This setting gives you the highest quality, and largest file size.
   - Near CD Bitrate (96 kbps)—This setting is close to CD quality, but creates a smaller file size.

- FM Radio Bitrate (64 kbps)—This setting creates the smallest file size.
- Custom Bitrate—For this setting you must specify the rate in kilobytes per second at which you want to record the audio.

7. Set the speed at which you want to encode the audio for output. A lower number creates a higher-quality audio file.
8. Click **OK** when you are done to close the Audio settings window.

Recording Audio While Recording a Movie

One way to get all of your audio files recorded quickly is to record them as you record the actions for each slide. This sort of narration is easy to do—you just talk aloud as you move the mouse or click through your application. Captivate will record your voice and store it as a series of audio clips, one for each slide that you create.

Note: For more details on the non-audio options available while recording, see Chapter 4.

To record audio while you're creating a new movie with Captivate, follow these steps:

1. Start the program you want to record, and then start the Captivate software. The first screen you'll see is the Captivate main menu.
2. Click **Record or create a new project** to open the New project options window.
3. Choose the type of project you want to create to display the recording options window.

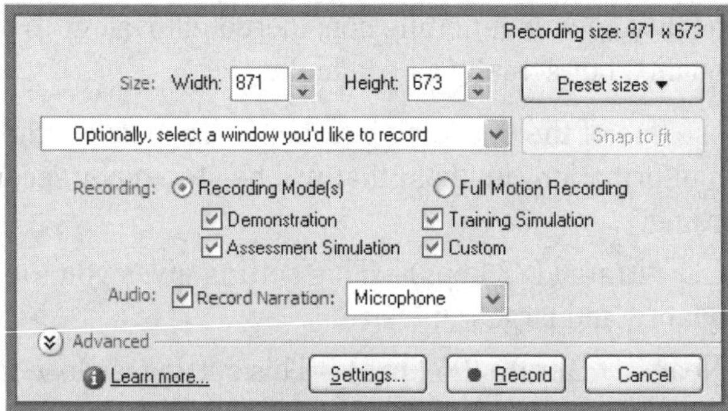

Figure 8-5. Set narration in the recording options window.

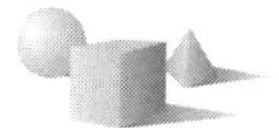

4. Select the **Record Narration** check box to turn on the audio recording when you begin the movie.
5. Choose the audio input method from the drop-down box (Microphone, Line In, or System Audio).

Note: If you have Record Narration selected, you won't have the option to turn on camera sounds. The camera sounds are tools that help you record; even when turned on, they don't play in the finished movie.

6. Click **Record.** If this is the first time you're recording audio this session, a message displays. If you've recorded audio already, skip to step 10.

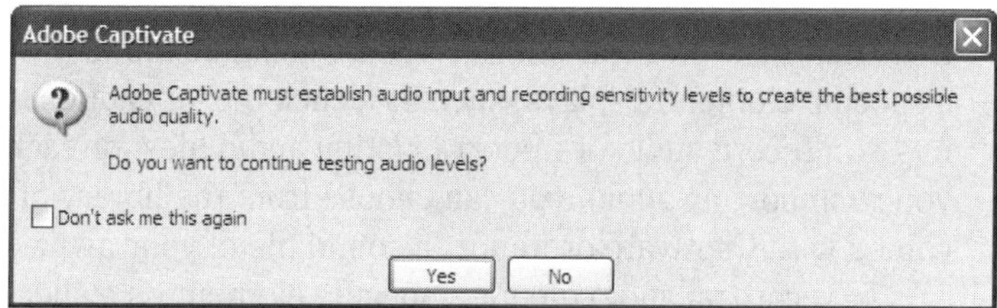

Figure 8-6. Determine whether or not you want to calibrate your microphone.

7. Click **Yes** to begin calibration.

Tip: Even though you don't have to calibrate for each recording session (you can click No or even turn off the message by selecting Don't ask me this again), it is a good idea to test the audio levels each time you record. This will help identify the myriad little things that can go wrong between recording sessions, such as a shift of cables that loosens a connection or something being placed on a table that blocks the microphone enough to impact audio levels.

8. When the calibration is complete, click **OK** to close the Calibrate microphone window.
9. Click **Record** to begin recording screens and audio.
10. After clicking Record, a series of three countdown windows displays to let you know exactly when to begin speaking. Perform the actions you want to record, and speak into the microphone to create the audio.

Tip: For easier editing later, do not speak while you are doing actions, but instead speak and then click the mouse or choose a menu item. Remember, each slide gets a separate audio file, and each time you click usually creates a new slide. You don't want to end up with half a word on one audio file and half on the next. Although they should play seamlessly when you publish the movie, splits like this could make adding or deleting slides more difficult.

11. When you finish, press the **End** key to stop recording, generate the slides and audio files, and display the new project in Storyboard view.

Recording Audio for Individual Elements

In some cases, you may want to record an audio file that will play when a specific element displays, such as a click box or caption. Captivate lets you record audio or import existing audio files for each element. If you're importing audio, you can choose from the library of sounds that comes with Captivate or import a sound file of your own.

To record an audio file for a specific element on a slide, follow these steps:

1. Open the slide that contains the element to which you want to add audio.
2. Double-click the element to display the properties for that element.
3. Click the **Audio** tab to display the audio properties. Figure 8-7 shows the audio settings for a text caption, but all elements have similar audio properties.

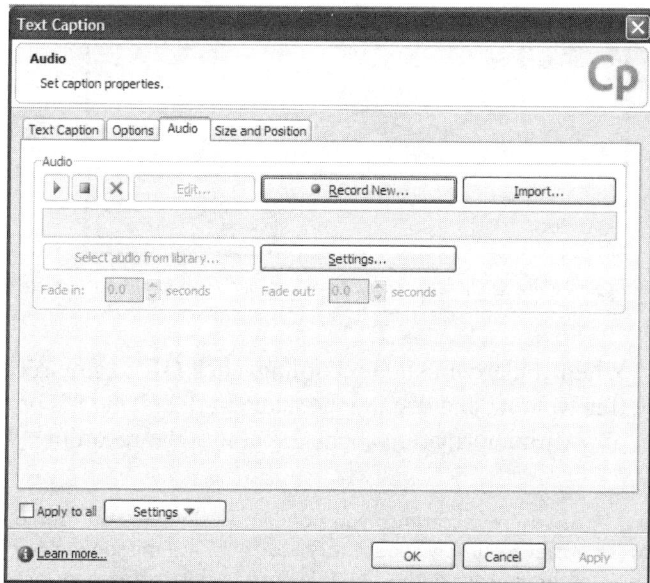

Figure 8-7. View, record, or edit audio files.

4. Click **Record New** to display the Record Audio window. If this is the first time you're recording audio this session, a message displays. If you've recorded audio already, skip to step 7.
5. Click **Yes** to begin calibration.

Tip: Even though you don't have to calibrate for each recording session (you can click No or even turn off the message by selecting Don't ask me this again), it is a good idea to test the audio levels each time you record. This will help identify the myriad little things that can go wrong between recording sessions, such as a shift of cables that loosens a connection or something being placed on a table that blocks the microphone enough to impact audio levels.

6. When the calibration is complete, click **OK** to close the Calibrate microphone window and display the Record Audio window.
7. Click **Record** to begin recording audio for this element.
8. Begin speaking into the microphone. The Record Audio window displays a status bar that shows the audio level and a timer. The following example shows a recording of about seven seconds.

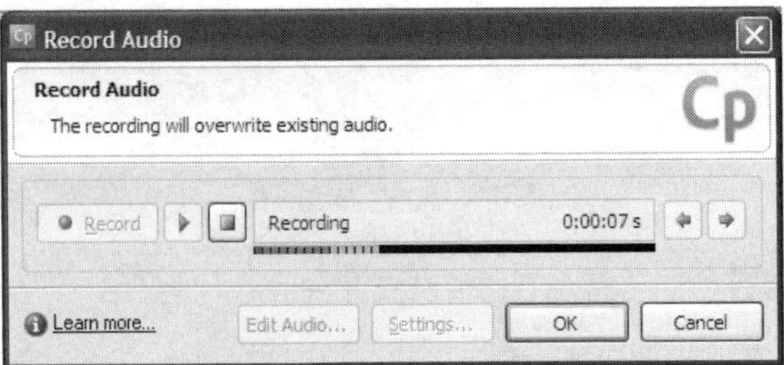

Figure 8-8. The Record Audio window displays the audio level and time as you record.

9. When you are finished recording, click **OK** to stop recording, close this window, and display the audio in the element's properties window with information about the new audio recording.

Tip: If, as you're recording, you notice a mistake in your audio, it may be easier to simply repeat (and correct!) the misspoken portion as part of the current audio file. It is easy to delete the incorrect audio later.

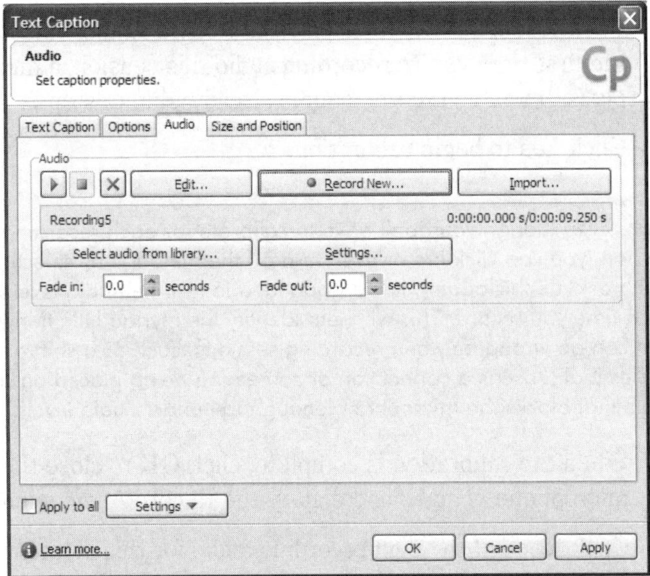

Figure 8-9. The properties window displays information about the recorded audio.

10. Click **OK** to close the properties window.

Recording Audio for an Existing Slide

You can record new audio files for each individual slide, rather than for a single element or for the entire movie. When you record slide narration, you have the option to preview the action on the slide as you record, as well as to see the captions and any notes you may have stored with the slide. You can then read this text while recording, much as an actor would read a script. The resulting audio file is associated with the slide; by default, it begins when the slide is first displayed. You can change the timing of the audio for each slide or do other audio editing as necessary. This is particularly useful if you've already recorded audio for an entire movie and just need to change one or two slides.

To record new audio for an existing slide, follow these steps:

1. Open the slide to which you want to add audio.
2. There are two ways to begin recording for a slide:
   - Double-click the background of the slide (not on any elements) or click the **Properties** icon to display the properties for that slide. Click the **Audio** tab to display the audio properties, then click **Record New** and choose **Record this Slide** from the drop-down menu.
   - Click the **Audio** icon at the top of the Captivate screen (in any view) and choose **Record this Slide** from the drop-down menu.

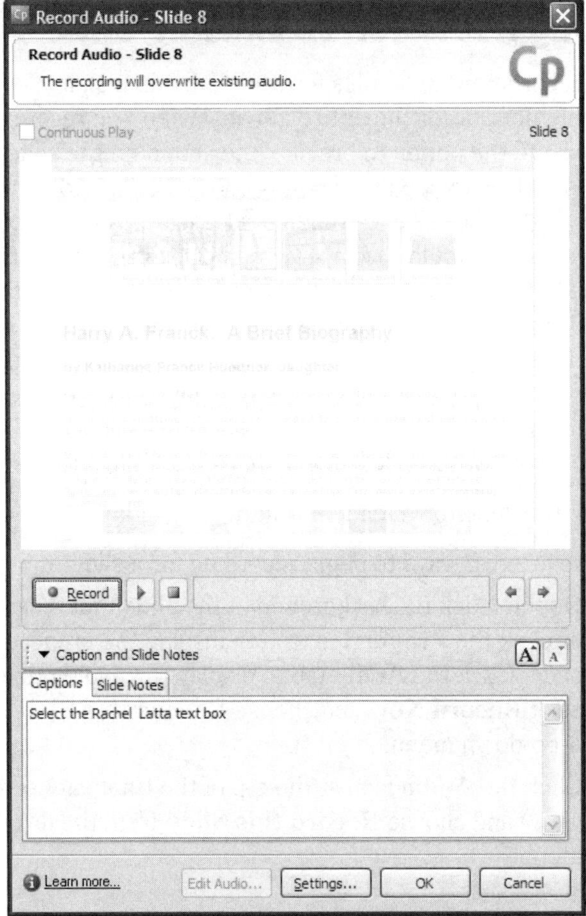

Figure 8-10. The Record Audio window displays captions and slide notes.

3. If this is the first time you're recording audio this session, a message displays. If you've recorded audio already, skip to step 6.
4. Click **Yes** to begin calibration.

Tip: Even though you don't have to calibrate for each recording session (you can click No or even turn off the message by selecting Don't ask me this again), it is a good idea to test the audio levels each time you record. This will help identify the myriad little things that can go wrong between recording sessions, such as a shift of cables that loosens a connection or something being placed on a table that blocks the microphone enough to impact audio levels.

5. When the calibration is complete, click **OK** to close the Calibrate microphone window and display the Record Audio window.

6. Click **Record** to begin recording audio for this slide. You'll see a preview of the slide and a timer that shows how much time is left for the slide as the various elements display. For example, animations will run, captions will display or dissolve, and the cursor will move across the screen (if you've defined them to do so).

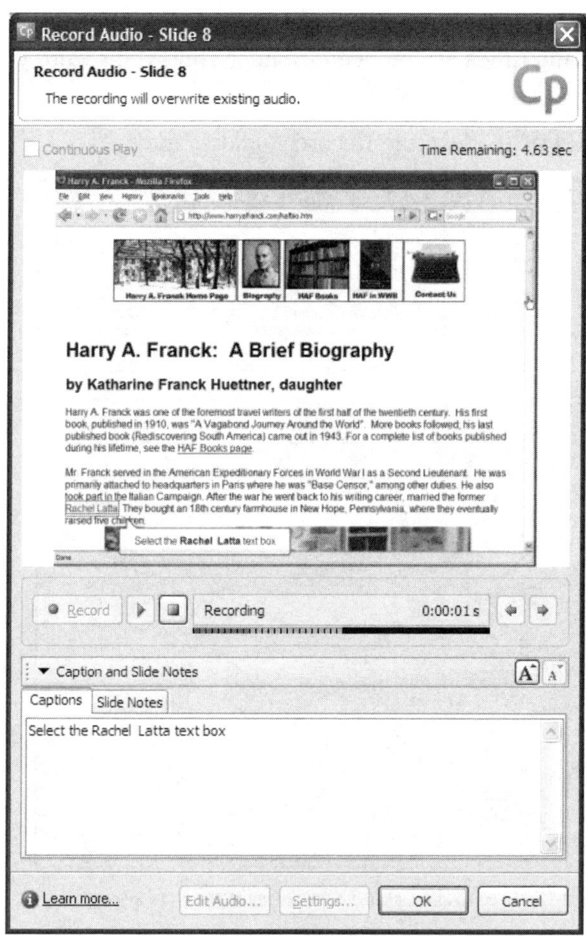

Figure 8-11. The elements move on the slide preview as you record.

7. Begin speaking into the microphone. You won't get the countdown display as when recording audio with screens, but you will see a progress bar with a timer that lets you know that the voice is being captured.

8. When you are finished recording, click the square blue **Stop audio** button (■) to stop recording and save your audio.

   You can then play the audio you just recorded by clicking the triangular **Play audio** button (▶). You can rerecord audio for the slide as many times as you need to. Each time you record you'll overwrite the previous audio file.

9. Click **OK** to close the Record Audio window.

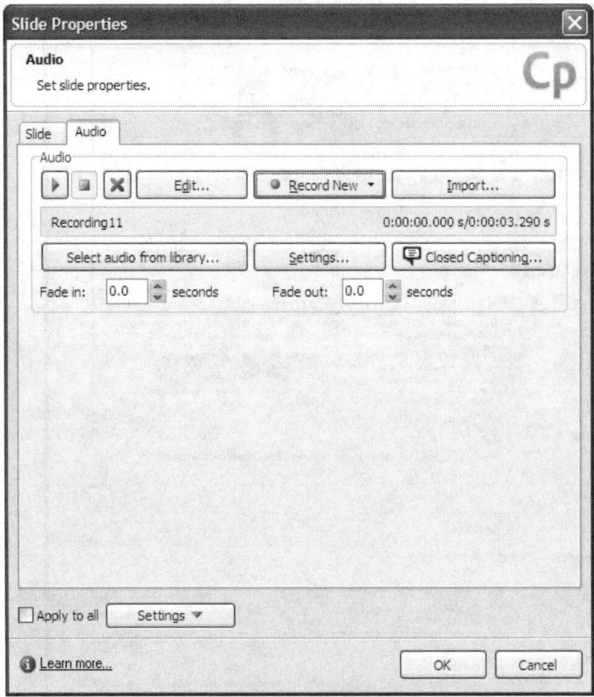

Figure 8-12. The audio information is displayed in the properties window.

10. If you began recording from the properties window, click **OK** to close the window.

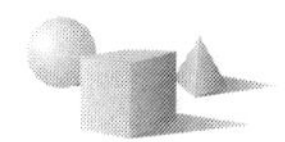

Chapter 8

Recording Background Audio for a Movie

You can record new audio files that will run in the background throughout the entire movie. When other audio elements play (such as for a caption or for a slide), Captivate can automatically lower the volume of the background audio. If the background audio file is shorter than the movie length, Captivate can repeat the background audio in a loop until the end of the movie.

To record background audio, follow these steps:

1. From the Edit menu, choose **Preferences** (or from the Audio menu, choose **Background Audio**).
2. In the Preferences window, click **Background Audio** under the Project heading in the Category list if it isn't already selected.

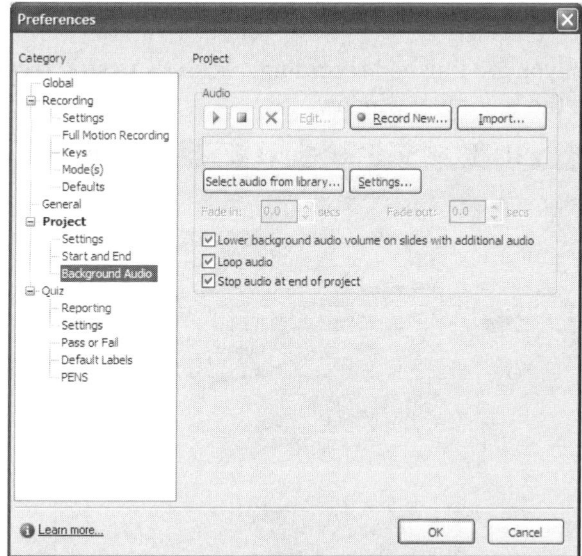

Figure 8-13. Record background audio.

3. Click **Record New** to display the Record Audio window. If this is the first time you're recording audio this session, a message displays. If you've recorded audio already, skip to step 6.
4. Click **Yes** to begin calibration.

Tip: Even though you don't have to calibrate for each recording session (you can click No or even turn off the message by selecting Don't ask me this again), it is a good idea to test the audio levels each time you record. This will help identify the myriad little things that can go wrong between recording sessions, such as a shift of cables that loosens a connection or something being placed on a table that blocks the microphone enough to impact audio levels.

5. When the calibration is complete, click **OK** to close the Calibrate microphone window and display the Record Audio window.
6. Click **Record** to begin recording background audio for this movie.
7. Begin recording your background audio. You won't get the count-down display as when recording audio with screens, but you will see a progress bar with a timer that lets you know that the voice is being captured.
8. When you are finished recording, click **OK** to stop recording and close the recording window.

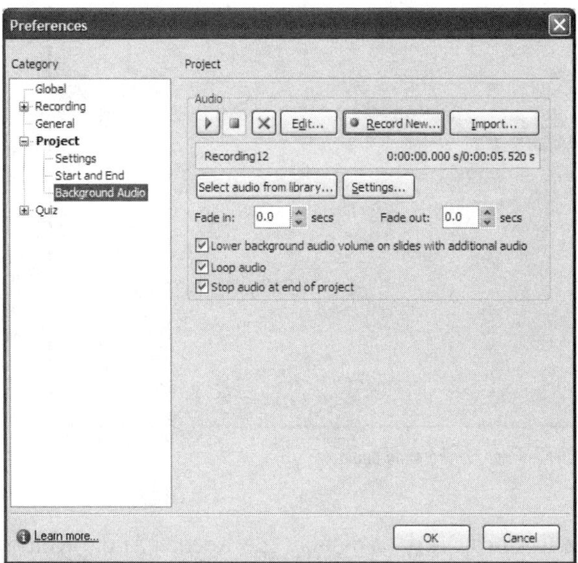

Figure 8-14. The audio information displays in the Preferences window.

9. Click the check box to lower the volume of the background audio on slides that have other audio elements on them. If the check box

is not selected, the background audio will play at the same volume even when other audio is playing.

10. Click the **Loop audio** check box to repeat the background audio so that it will last as long as the movie lasts. If the check box is not selected, the audio file will play through just once.
11. Click the **Stop audio at end of project** check box if you want the audio to end when the project ends. If this check box is not selected, the audio will play until the end of the audio file, even if the project is finished.
12. Click **OK** to close the Preferences window.

Chapter 8

Importing Existing Audio Files

If you already have audio files that you want to add to your Captivate movie, you can do so in any of the following ways:

- Add existing audio to an element on a slide.
- Add existing audio to an entire slide or series of slides.
- Add existing audio to the background of a movie.

The existing audio must be in either WAV or MP3 format. If you use WAV format, Captivate will automatically convert the files to MP3 format for inclusion in your movie.

Tip: Captivate comes with a gallery of existing audio elements. By default, these are stored in Captivate\Gallery\Sound. The import audio function defaults to this location.

Adding Audio to Individual Elements

You can add audio to any of the elements on a slide, such as buttons, click boxes, and success/failure captions. You can add voice files if you have them or sound effects such as a ringing bell or buzzer. When you associate audio with an element, the audio will not begin to play until the element appears on the slide. To add existing audio to an element, you can either choose from an audio file that exists within your project already or you can browse to import a file elsewhere on your system.

To add an audio file to a specific element on a slide, follow these steps:

1. Open the slide that contains the element to which you want to add audio.
2. Double-click the element to display the properties for that element.
3. Click the **Audio** tab to display the audio properties.

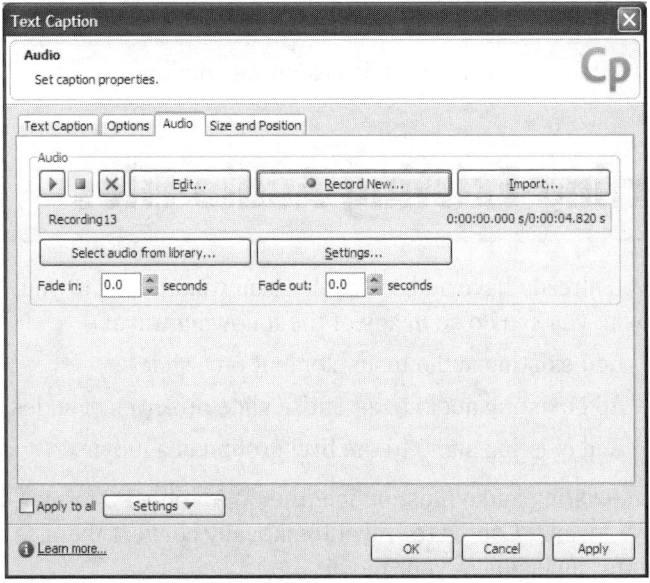

Figure 8-15. View, record, or edit audio files.

4. Click **Import** to display the most recently used folder of sound files, or click **Select audio from library** to display the list of sound files in the current movie.

Note: Unless you've imported an external library, the audio library will display only those individual audio files you've already imported or recorded in the current movie. If you don't have any audio in the current movie yet, the Select audio from library button will not be available.

5. Click the name of the audio file you want to play when the element appears, then click either **OK** (for Select audio from library) or **Open** (for Import).

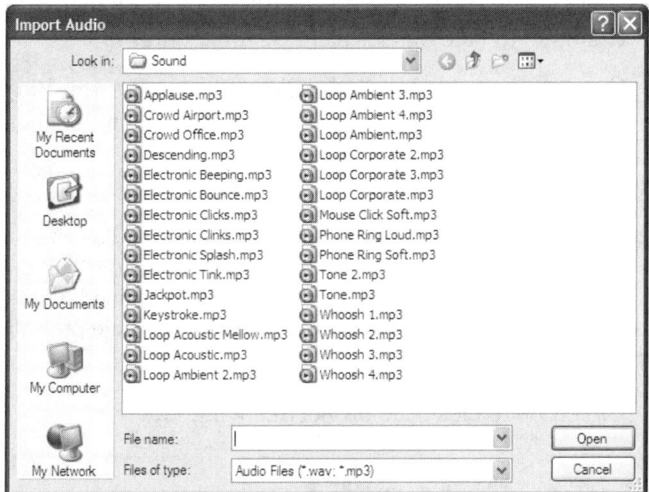

Figure 8-16. You can choose sounds from any location.

Figure 8-17. You can choose from sounds in the library.

Tip: If you're choosing audio from the library, you can click the Play icon (a dark triangle above the sound wave image) to hear what each audio file sounds like before you select it.

6. You can specify a fade-in time to start the sound file gradually or a fade-out time to make the sound file gradually get softer as it ends. Enter a time in seconds in the Fade in or Fade out boxes. You can specify fade times with an accuracy of a tenth of a second. For example, to fade out for half a second, enter 0.5.
7. Once you've added an audio file, you can click the **Play** icon to hear how it will sound or preview the audio in the slide timeline (see Chapter 7).

Tip: Though the Play icon lets you know how the audio will sound, this audio preview may not incorporate all of the options that are part of the overall slide. For example, if you have defined a fade-in time delay, you'll need to preview the slide (or the whole project) in order to see this delay.

8. Click **OK** to close the properties window.

Adding Audio to a Slide

You can add audio to an entire slide. This type of audio begins playing as soon as the slide displays. Unlike audio attached to elements, you can modify the audio to begin or end whenever you like within the slide timeline. To add existing audio to a slide, you can choose from an audio file that exists within your project already, or you can browse to import a file from elsewhere on your system.

To add an audio file to a slide, follow these steps:

1. Open the slide to which you want to add audio.
2. Double-click anywhere on the background of the slide (not on an element) to display the properties for that slide.
3. Click the **Audio** tab to display the slide audio properties.

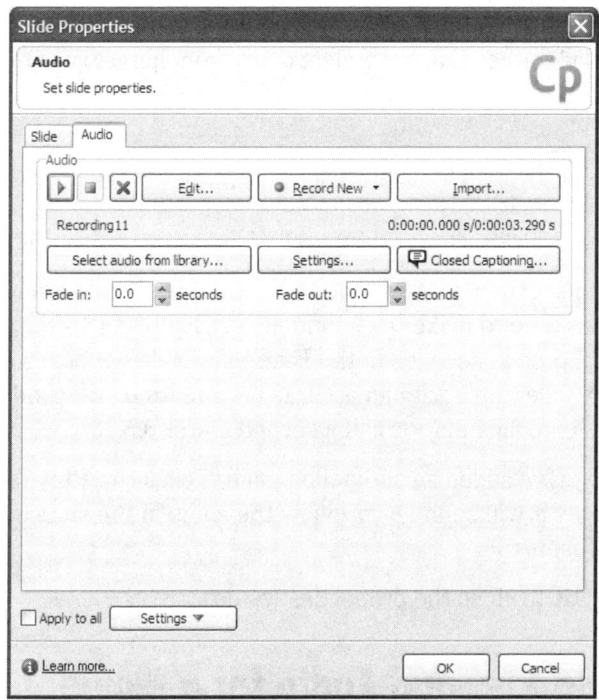

Figure 8-18. The Slide Properties window.

4. Click **Import** to display the most recently used folder of sound files, or click **Select audio from library** to display the list of sound files in the current movie.

Tip: You can also import audio from the Captivate sound library by selecting the slide, then choosing Import from the Audio menu. This option does not let you choose from files already in the movie.

Note: Unless you've imported an external library, the audio library will display only those individual audio files you've already imported or recorded in the current movie. If you don't have any audio in the current movie yet, the Select audio from library button will not be available.

5. Click the name of the audio file you want to play for this slide, and then click either **OK** (for Select audio from library) or **Open** (for Import).

Tip: If you're choosing from the audio library, you can click the Play icon (a dark triangle above the sound wave image) to hear what each audio file sounds like before you select it.

6. You can specify a fade-in time to start the sound file gradually or a fade-out time to make the sound file gradually get softer as it ends. Enter a time in seconds in the Fade in or Fade out boxes. You can specify fade times with an accuracy of a tenth of a second. For example, to fade out for half a second, enter 0.5.
7. Once you've added an audio file, you can click the **Play** icon to hear how it will sound or preview the audio in the slide timeline (see Chapter 7).
8. Click **OK** to close the properties window.

Adding Background Audio for a Movie

Background audio plays for the entire movie, regardless of which slide is displayed or how long the slide is on the screen. When other audio elements play, you can lower the volume of the background audio. If the background audio file is shorter than the movie length, you can repeat the background audio in a loop until the end of the movie.

To add background audio to a movie, follow these steps:

1. From the Edit menu, choose **Preferences** (or from the Audio menu, choose **Background Audio**).
2. In the Preferences window, click **Background Audio** under the Project heading in the Category list if it isn't already selected.

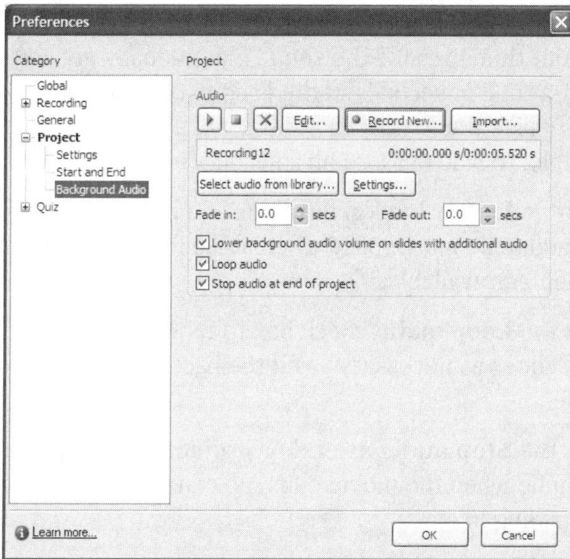

Figure 8-19. Import background audio.

3. Click **Import** to display the most recently used folder of sound files, or click **Select audio from library** to display the list of sound files in the current movie.

Note: Unless you've imported an external library, the audio library will display only those individual audio files you've already imported or recorded in the current movie. If you don't have any audio in the current movie yet, the Select audio from library button will not be available.

4. Click the name of the audio file you want to play for this slide, then click either **OK** (for Select audio from library) or **Open** (for Import).

Tip: If you're choosing from the audio library, you can click the Play icon (a dark triangle above the sound wave image) to hear what each audio file sounds like before you select it.

5. You can specify a fade-in time to start the sound file gradually or a fade-out time to make the sound file gradually get softer as it ends. Enter a time in seconds in the Fade in or Fade out boxes. You can specify fade times with an accuracy of a tenth of a second. For example, to fade out for half a second, enter 0.5.
6. Click the **Lower background audio** check box to play the current audio file more softly when audio for specific slides or elements is available.
7. Click the **Loop audio** check box to repeat the current audio file as many times as necessary to fill the background of the entire movie.
8. Click the **Stop audio at end of project** check box to stop playing the audio when the movie ends, no matter where in the audio file that ending hits.
9. Click **OK** to close the Preferences window.

Viewing and Removing Audio Files

Once you've got audio in your movie, you can easily check to see the status of all the audio files in a single place. You don't have to open each individual element's audio properties window. You can play the files, or you can remove them from your movie. You can also export the MP3 audio files you've created in Captivate for use with other programs.

Note: You cannot change the audio properties from this view. To make changes to the audio, such as replacing a file or adjusting timing, go to the audio file properties as described in the section called "Editing Audio Files."

To view the audio for your whole movie, follow these steps:

1. From the Audio menu, select **Advanced audio** to display the Advanced Audio Management window.

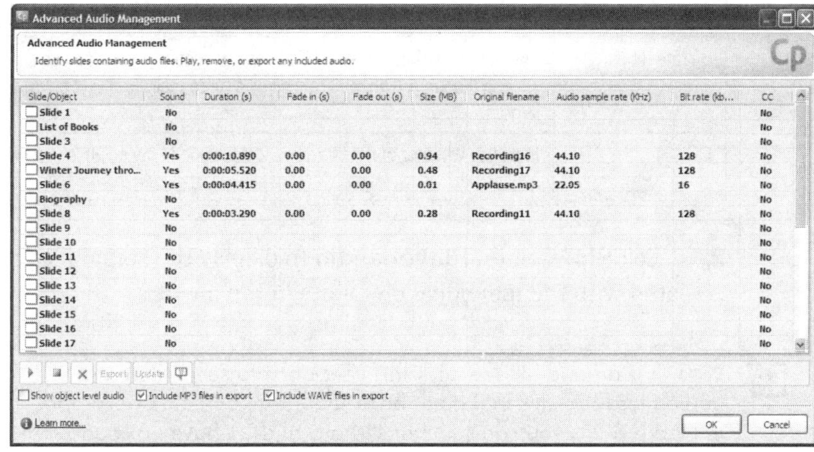

Figure 8-20. Display the sound files for the whole movie.

The Advanced Audio Management window displays a row of information for each slide in the movie, and also includes a row for the background audio, if any.

Tip: You may need to resize the window to display all of the information, or use the scroll bars across the bottom and on the side of the window.

Table 8-1. Audio file properties

This column:	Displays this information:
Slide object	The slide number or slide label if there is one or name of object.
Sound	Yes indicates that there is an audio file associated with the slide; No indicates there isn't. Note that this does not include audio for individual elements unless you check the Show object level audio option. Therefore, a slide may contain objects with audio but still show up on this window with a No.
Duration (s)	The length of the sound file in seconds.
Fade in (s)	Specify the length of time in seconds for the fade in.
Fade out (s)	Specify the length of time in seconds for the fade out.
Size (MB)	The size of the sound file in megabytes.
Original filename	The name of the sound file. Note that Captivate automatically names the files as you record them.
Audio sample rate (Hz)	An indicator of the sound quality set during recording. A higher sample rate gives a more realistic sound but requires a larger file size. The sample rate for CD-quality audio is 44,100 samples per second, expressed in kilohertz.

This column:	Displays this information:
Bit rate (kbps)	The number of bits the audio file uses per second, expressed as kilobits per second (kbps). A higher bit rate gives a more realistic sound but requires a larger file size.
CC	Indicates whether or not there is a text version of the audio for use with closed captioning.

2. Click **Show object level audio** to display the sound files associated with the individual elements in the movie.

Tip: It is a good idea to click this check box to see if there are audio files for slides that don't have slide-level audio. For example, in Figure 8-21, you can see that slides 8 and 11 have no sound, but the text captions on those slides have associated audio files.

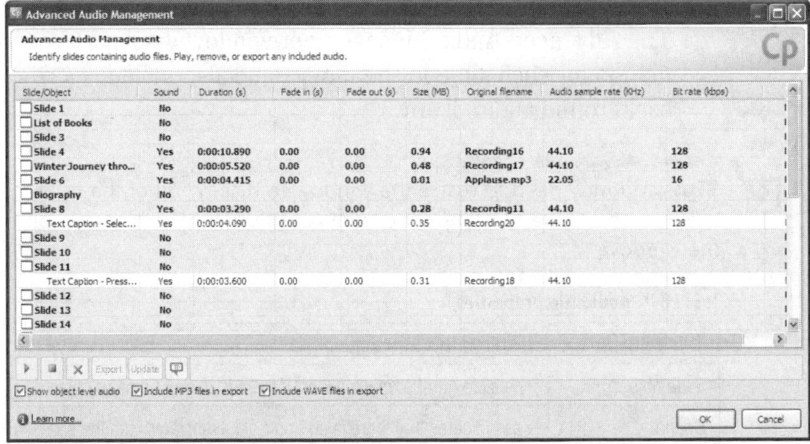

Figure 8-21. Display the sound files for each element.

3. To play a file, click anywhere on the row for that file to select it, and then click the **Play** icon (▶). You can click the **Stop** icon (■) to stop the file, or simply let it play until it is done.

4. To copy an audio file from within your Captivate movie to a different location on your system, select the file and then click **Export** to display a window that lets you browse to an appropriate folder. Click **OK** in the folder window to export both the MP3 and WAV versions of the audio file to the selected destination folder.

Tip: Once you remove a file that was created within Captivate, it will be removed entirely from your movie and from your system. If you think you might want to use the audio file again, in this or other movies, export the file as described in step 4.

5. To remove a file from the movie, click anywhere on the row for that file to select it, and then do either of the following:
   - Right-click to display a pop-up menu, and then choose **Remove**.
   - Press the **Delete** key.

   Click **OK** in the confirmation dialog that displays to complete the file removal.
6. When you finish, click **OK**.

Editing Audio Files

Captivate includes a basic audio editing tool that lets you adjust the audio files to fit your needs. You can add silence (described in Table 8-3), delete parts of the audio, or adjust volume for an audio file. For example, you may want to remove a single word rather than rerecord the whole audio clip. Or you may want to remove some of the extra silence that is often recorded at the beginning and ending of an audio file.

Tip: Don't remove all of the silence—you need a little bit of space at the beginning and end of each file so that if the audio plays near another piece of audio it will sound more natural. You may also want to use a small sample of silence in other places within your movie to maintain ambient room noise and create a seamless effect.

To edit an audio file, follow these steps:

1. Open the audio file properties window for the specific type of element.

Table 8-2. Audio properties windows

For this type of element:	Do this:
Element (such as click box or caption)	In Edit view, double-click the element on the slide, and then click the Audio tab.
Slide	Double-click the background of the slide to display the properties, and then click the Audio tab.
Background Audio	Choose Background Audio from the Audio menu.

2. From the audio properties window, click the **Edit** button to open the Edit Audio window.

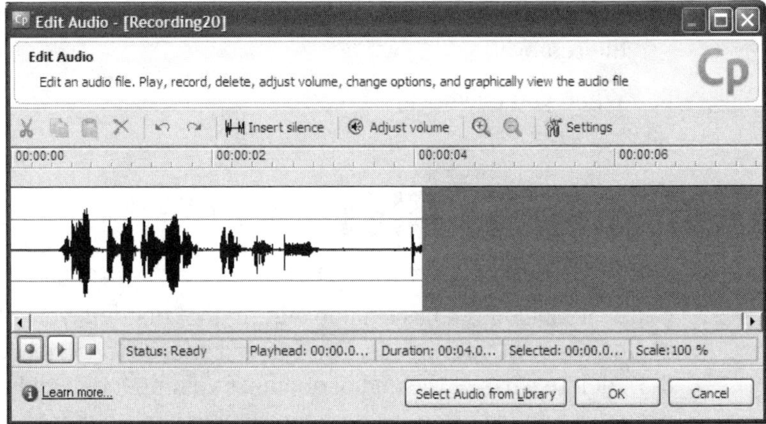

Figure 8-22. Open the audio file to edit it.

3. Set the display of the audio file to one that is appropriate for your needs by clicking the magnifying glass icons with the plus or minus signs. For example, Figure 8-22 shows an audio file that lasts 4.1 seconds. Click the "plus" magnifying glass icon to zoom in on the file so that you can see the audio components more clearly or the "minus" to zoom out and see more of the audio file.

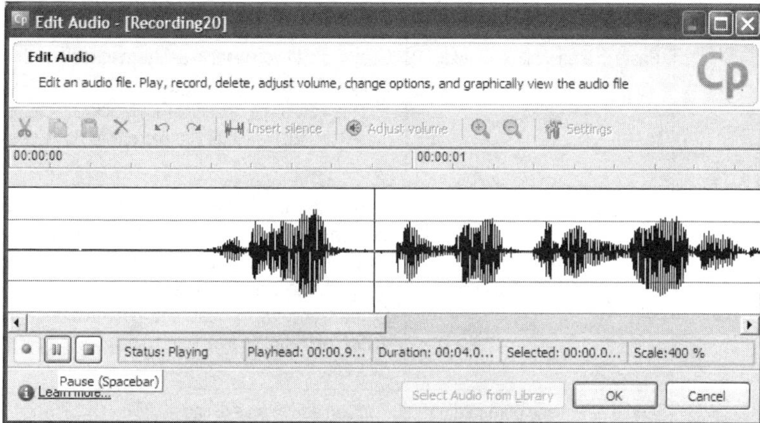

Figure 8-23. Zoom to display the audio file in an appropriate size.

4. Click the **Play** icon to play the audio file. As the file plays, a vertical line called the playhead moves across the window to indicate exactly which part of the displayed file is playing at any moment. In Figure 8-23, for example, the playhead indicates that 0.9 of a second of the audio has played. In this example, that's just about between the first two words. Notice that as the audio is playing, the Play icon changes to two vertical lines to become a Pause icon. You can hit the Pause icon or the Stop icon at any time. You can also select a portion of the audio and press the Spacebar key to preview the selected portion only.
5. Make any of the following edits to your audio file:

Table 8-3. Edit options for audio files

To make this change:	Do this:
Select a specific piece of audio	Click on the audio graphic and drag the cursor to highlight a specific area.
Delete a part of the audio	Select the part you want to delete, then right-click and choose Delete (or press the Delete key) to remove the audio from the file.
Copy a part of the audio	Select the part you want to copy, then right-click and choose Copy (or press Ctrl+C) to copy the audio to the clipboard.
Cut a part of the audio	Select the part you want to cut, then right-click and choose Cut (or press Ctrl+X) to cut the audio from the audio file.

To make this change:	Do this:
Paste in a new piece of audio	Copy the part you want to paste, then click on the audio graphic so that the playhead displays in the location where you want to add the new piece of audio. Right-click and choose Paste (or press Ctrl+V). Note that you can only cut and paste audio within a single file.
Add silence	Click on the audio graphic so that the playhead displays in the location where you want to begin a period of silence, and then click the Insert silence button. A window displays that allows you to specify the length of the silence and lets you choose a location for the silence (at the playhead location or the beginning or the ending of the audio file). Enter a number in seconds, and then click OK.
Add a new piece of recording	You can add to an existing audio file by clicking the Record button. The new audio will be inserted starting at the point where the playhead is displayed. Tip: This can be tricky. It works best if your audio setup is exactly as it was when the original audio was recorded.
Undo a change	Click the Undo icon in the menu across the top of the window.

Tip: Use discretion when editing audio files. It is all too easy to make audio edits that cause your file to sound stilted or awkward or to create something that doesn't make sense. Often, it is easier and quicker to rerecord the entire audio file.

6. If necessary, you can adjust the volume of the entire audio file or simply a portion of it. For example, if the person speaking turned slightly while recording, a word or two may be quieter than you like. You can select these words in the audio graphic and make them a little bit louder. To display the Adjust Volume window, click the **Adjust volume** button.

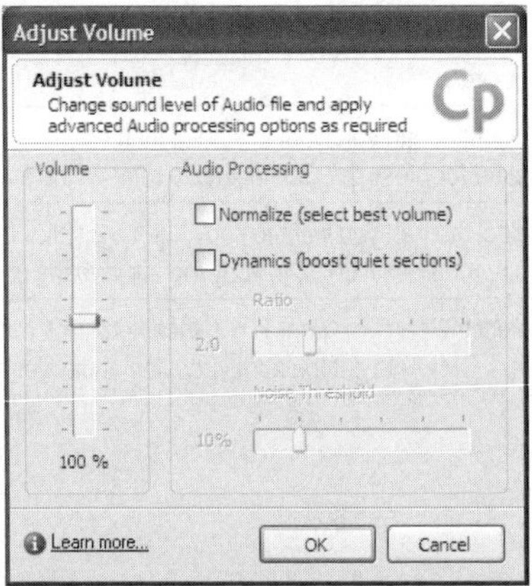

Figure 8-24. Adjust volume as needed.

7. Move the Volume slider up (to make the audio louder) or down (to make the audio quieter) to change the volume of the selected portion of the audio file.
8. You can also adjust the audio by selecting either (or both) of the following audio processing options:
   - Normalize—Adjusts the sound volume automatically. This will keep the sound level consistent across the selection or entire audio clip.
   - Dynamics—Automatically increases the volume for the quietest portions of the audio file. You can set a maximum ratio to specify the factor by which the quietest audio should be increased. You can also set a noise threshold, which specifies the relative volume of the quietest audio that you want to amplify. For example, you may have an audio file where most of the sound is at an acceptable level, but some portions are too quiet. A ratio of 2 would double the volume of the quietest portions of the audio. A Noise Threshold setting of 10% would specify that portions of the audio that are 10% or less of the audio level of the rest of the file should NOT be amplified by that ratio (they are likely to be background noise).
9. Click **OK** to close the Adjust Volume window.
10. When you finish editing the audio file, click **OK** to close the Edit Audio window.

Changing Audio Timing

If you have audio files associated with individual elements, such as text captions or click boxes, the audio timing is controlled within the properties for that element. By default, the audio begins when the element displays. You can move the element on the timeline as described in Chapter 7 to prevent the various audio files from playing at the same time. For audio files that are associated with the slide background, you can use the Audio Timing control. For example, you can move the display of slides to let audio continue playing when the slide changes, or you can move the slide so that more than one audio file plays while the slide is displayed. You can also perform many of the editing functions that were available while editing each audio file (such as adding silence or copying and pasting bits of audio).

To change audio timing, follow these steps:

1. From the Audio menu, select **Edit timing**, then choose **Project**. You can also choose **Slide** from this menu to display the Edit Audio window for the selected slide (see the previous section, "Editing Audio Files"). The Edit Audio Timing window displays.

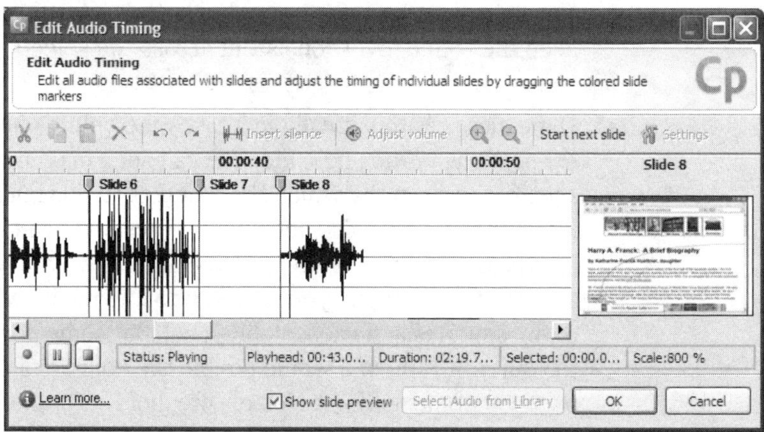

Figure 8-25. Display audio across all slides.

There is a timeline across the top of the window that indicates how far into the movie each portion of the video is. Like other timelines, there is also a playhead (shown in Figure 8-25 at about 42 seconds). This window also shows the slides across the top of the window, just beneath the timeline, and can show a preview of the current slide (where the playhead is) on the right side of the window. The audio for each slide, if any, displays as a graphic across the middle of the window. For example, in Figure 8-25, you can see that there are audio files associated with slides 5, 6, and 8, and that the audio for slide number 8 ends well before the slide ends.

2. Set the display of the audio file to one that is appropriate for your movie by clicking the magnifying glass icons with the plus or minus signs ( ).

3. Click the **Play** icon to play the audio file. Notice that as the audio is playing, the Play icon changes into two vertical lines to become a Pause icon. You can hit the Pause icon or the Stop icon at any time.

4. You can move the slide dividers ( ) at the top of the graphic to change the way the audio file is distributed across the slides. As you move each divider, you're changing the length of time each slide is displayed. The length of time the audio plays does not change.
5. If necessary, you can cut or paste the audio, insert silence, or use any of the other editing functions listed in Table 8-3.
6. You can add a sound file to the movie by clicking the **Import** button, then browsing to the file you want to add.
7. When you're finished editing the audio timing, click **OK** to close the window.

Summary

This chapter described the audio functions available with Captivate. You saw how to record new audio; how to add existing audio to elements, slides, and the entire movie; and how to use the audio editing functions. The following chapter describes how to add interactivity to your movie by inserting interactive elements and a variety of captions.

Chapter 9

Defining What the User Does—Adding Interactivity

When you recorded your actions on the screen, the recording options determined if the resulting movie would be a demonstration that the viewers would simply watch (and learn from) or a more interactive project where the movie pauses while the viewer clicks or types to move from one slide to another. Another type of interactivity allows the viewers to get more information using a rollover function. When the viewer moves the cursor over a certain spot, you can have either a text caption or an image display on the screen. This is particularly useful for functions similar to tooltips in other packages.

A very powerful feature of Captivate allows you to add multiple interactive elements to a single slide and specify different actions based on which element the viewer clicks. For example, you could replicate your main menu within the movie by putting a click box over each icon and then displaying different slides based on which box the viewer clicks. Or you could add buttons that skip over certain parts of the movie or allow the viewer to repeat various sections. Giving the viewer this type of flexibility and control over the way the movie plays is often called "branching" or "contingency branching" in e-learning applications. Captivate lets you display these options for presentation of slides in a Branching view (see Chapter 11 for more information on branching).

You can manually add these interactivity features to any slide in any movie, or you can have Captivate automatically add some

interactive elements, such as click boxes, while you're recording the movie. See Chapter 4 for more information on recording movies.

Adding Interactivity with Boxes and Buttons

There are three main types of interactive elements:

- Click boxes specify an area where the viewer should click.
- Text entry boxes specify an area where the viewer will type and the text will display on the slide.
- Buttons specify an area where the viewer will click, usually to go to another slide.

These interactive elements can be added automatically when you're recording a movie, or you can enter them manually for more exact control over how the viewer will interact with your movie.

Adding and Editing Interactive Elements

For each type of element, you'll need to specify a variety of properties:

- Instructions on what happens in the movie when the viewer successfully clicks in the specified area (such as go to the next slide or display a URL).
- Instructions on what happens in the movie when the viewer clicks outside of the designated area (or types an invalid text string).
- Optional captions that display on success or failure, or when the viewer moves the mouse over the specified interactive area.
- Timing, such as whether or not the movie should pause while awaiting viewer input.
- Audio, if necessary, as described in Chapter 8.
- Instructions on how you want Captivate to store information about the viewer's success or failure actions. This reporting information can then be imported into other e-learning applications.

When you add the basic interactive elements, you'll do so in the following major steps:

Step 1: Specify the type of interactive element and indicate how to proceed when the viewer interacts with the movie.

Step 2: For buttons only, define how you want the button to look.

Step 3: Set interactive element options, such as captions, timing, or audio.

Step 4: Adjust the interactive elements and associated components to place them exactly where you want on the slide and to display the text you want.

Step 1: Specify an Interactive Element

When you're adding interactivity, you'll need to decide which type of element you want to use.

Click boxes—Click boxes allow you to specify an area where the viewer should click. For example, you might use this if you want the movie to pause until the viewer clicks a specific link or clicks on a menu option.

Text entry boxes—Text entry boxes are rectangular areas where you want the viewer to type specific text. The text will display on the slide as it is typed; it must match any one of the correct answers that you provide before the movie will continue. You can display the outline of the box or not. Each text entry box defaults to having a submission button, but you can turn this off if you want to.

Note: The text entry box button is not the same as the regular interactive buttons and has only a subset of the interactive button functionality.

Buttons—Buttons are visual elements that you want the viewer to click. You can control the appearance of the button using either a text label or an image. To the end viewer, a button will appear to be very similar to a click box.

Tip: The main difference between a click box and a button is that the click box defines an area but doesn't have a visual component—the viewer can't see where a click box is without an additional element such as a highlight box.

To add an interactive element, follow these steps:

1. In Edit view, open the slide to which you want to add interactivity.
2. From the Insert menu, select the type of element you want to add (**Click box**, **Text entry box**, or **Button**) to display the properties window. The properties in the window will vary slightly depending on the element you choose, but most property options are the same for all interactive elements. Figure 9-1 shows the properties window for a text entry box.

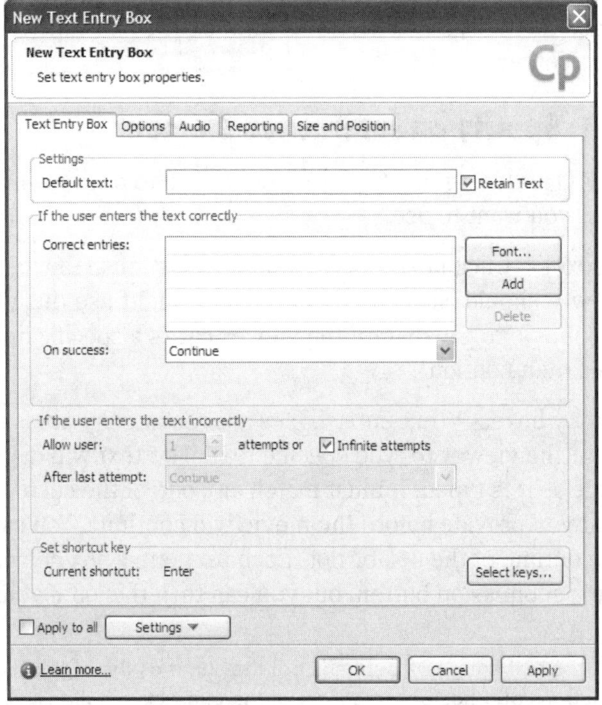

Figure 9-1. Set the interactive element properties.

3. *For text entry box elements only*, enter the text that you want to display when the viewer first sees the text box. This might be something like "type your name here". You can select the Retain Text check box if you want the text that the viewer enters to display on subsequent viewings of the text box (for the current instance of the movie only).

4. *For text entry box elements only,* enter the text that you want the viewer to type in the Correct entries box. Click on a row in the box, then type an answer exactly as you want the viewer to type it. You can enter as many correct answers as you like. Click the **Delete** button to the right of the Correct entries box to remove an entry, or click the **Font** button to set the way you want the text to look as the viewer types it.

5. For all interactive elements, choose from the **On success** drop-down list to specify what you want the movie to display when the viewer clicks within the click box. Valid options are listed in Table 9-1.

Table 9-1. Destination options based on viewer success (or failure) to perform certain actions

Choose this option:	For this effect:	Also enter this information:
Continue	Continue playing the rest of the current slide and the rest of the movie.	None necessary
Go to previous slide	Display the previous slide, and then continue the movie from that point, even if all the actions for the current slide have not yet been performed.	None necessary
Go to next slide	Continue on to the next slide in the movie, even if all the actions for the current slide have not yet been performed.	None necessary
Jump to slide	Display the specified slide and continue the movie from there.	Choose from the drop-down list of slides. Note that slide labels, if any, appear in the list instead of slide numbers. This makes it easy to find the slide you're looking for!
Open URL or file Open other project	Display the specified URL or file in the viewer's default browser, or play another Flash movie. The viewer must have an active Internet connection to view URLs, and the specified file or movie must exist on the viewer's system. Note that the URL will not be visible on the finished movie.	Enter the URL or file name, or browse to the location of the file by clicking the button with three dots (...). For movies, you can also choose from a drop-down list. Click the black triangle button to choose the type of window in which the URL or file will display. Valid options are Current, New, Top, or Parent.
Send e-mail to	Create an e-mail message to send to a specified address in the viewer's default e-mail program. The viewer will still have to fill in the message and subject and hit Send.	Enter the e-mail address to which you want the e-mail sent. Click the check box to indicate whether or not the current movie should continue playing.

Choose this option:	For this effect:	Also enter this information:
Execute JavaScript	Run JavaScript commands.	Enter the JavaScript code you want to run.
No Action	Take no action, not even continue the movie.	None necessary

6. By default, Captivate allows the viewer an unlimited (infinite) number of tries to get the correct action (click in the click box or on the button, or type the correct text in the text entry box). If you want to limit the number of attempts, click the **Infinite attempts** check box to deselect it, then specify the number of attempts you want to give the viewer. If you leave Infinite attempts selected, the movie will pause until the viewer gets it right. If you specified a number of attempts, choose an option from the **After last attempt** drop-down list to specify what you want the movie to display after the last unsuccessful attempt. Valid options are the same as for successful actions and are listed in Table 9-1.
7. *For button elements only,* choose the way you want the button to look by choosing from the Type drop-down menu (see "Step 2: Set Button Properties").
8. *For text entry box elements only,* click the **Options** tab and choose the way you want the entry box to display on the screen by selecting one of the following transition parameters:
   - Fade in—The box will appear very dim at first and will gradually become more solid until it reaches the defined transparency setting.
   - Fade out—The box will gradually become more transparent until it is eliminated from the slide display completely.
   - Fade in and out—The box will appear dim, then gradually get more solid. Then it will gradually become more transparent until it is eliminated from the display completely.
   - No transition—The box simply displays and then is removed after the specified timing.

   For fading effects, you'll also need to specify how long or how gradual the effect should be. The default is 0.5 seconds.

Tip: It is usually best to show some restraint in adding effects to your movie. If you already have a lot going on, multiple animations and transition effects can be more distracting than entertaining.

9. If you want to automatically apply the current settings to all elements of this type in the movie, click the **Apply to all** check box. Depending on the type of element, this check box may be on the main tab, on the Options tab, or unavailable at all.
10. Each interactive element has a default shortcut key that sends the action to the controls of the Flash movie. For example, the action for a click box defaults to a mouse click. The action for a text entry box defaults to the Enter key. You can change the shortcut key for each element by clicking the **Select keys** button to display the Shortcut key window.

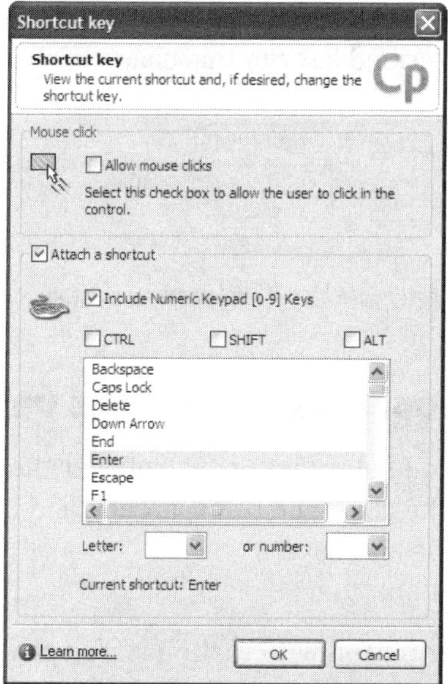

Figure 9-2. Set a shortcut key combination.

Select **Allow mouse clicks** to let the viewer use the mouse to click in the element. Select **Attach a shortcut** to activate the shortcut options, then choose a new key combination. You can choose any combination of keys, but don't choose so many that it is difficult for the viewer to enter them.

Tip: Try to avoid key combinations that are likely to conflict with other software. For example, F1 is often designated as a Help button, and Ctrl+C is often used for copy functions.

11. Click **OK** when you are done to close the Shortcut key window and return to the display of the properties window.
12. You may choose to enter the options as described in the following sections of this chapter or set audio properties (see Chapter 8). You can also set properties that relate to e-learning and quizzes, which are described in Chapter 10.
13. Click **OK** when you are done to close the properties window and view the new interactive element on your slide. The element will appear in the center of your slide, along with associated components, if any. For example, a text entry box will display with a button, and success or failure captions will display if you have them turned on (as described later in this chapter).

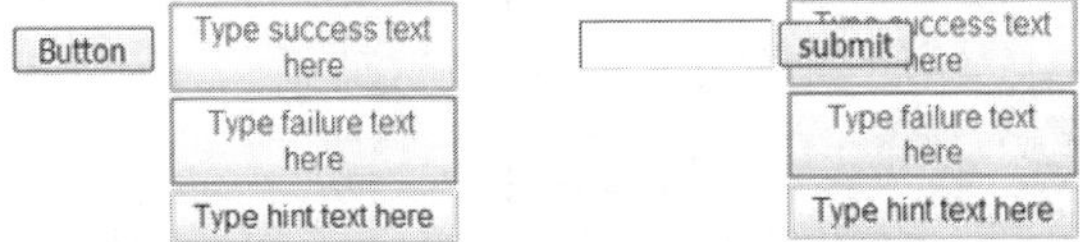

Figure 9-3. Buttons and text entry boxes often have several associated elements.

Step 2: Set Button Properties (for Buttons Only)

If you're adding a button, you have a lot of control over the appearance of the button. You can set the color and transparency, and either enter text for the button or choose an image.

There are three types of buttons:

Text button—A rectangular button with text on it. You can have the button itself be transparent, making it look like a text link. Or you can define the color, size, and style of the text. This button type is quick and easy to add but does not let you modify the color or shape of the button.

Transparent button—This type of button functions like a combination click box and highlight box, allowing the viewer to see the borders of the button and making full use of the interactive properties. By placing a transparent button on top of other elements on the

background of a slide, such as a menu item, icon, or background button, you can make it look like the menu item, icon, or background button is actually working.

Image button—A set of images that displays one at a time, depending on the state of the button:

- Up state is before the button is clicked.
- Down state is after the button has been clicked.
- Over state is when the mouse is over the button but hasn't been clicked yet.

To define the unique button properties, follow these steps:

1. From the Edit view, either create a new element as described in Step 1 (above) or double-click on an existing element to open the element's properties window.
2. Set the success and failure options just as you would for any other element, as described above.
3. Choose the button type from the drop-down list. Depending on the option you choose, the bottom portion of the properties window will change to reflect the different options available.
4. If you chose Text button, type the button text in the Button text box. You can click the **Font** button to change or hide the background and borders of the button (only the text displays in the movie).

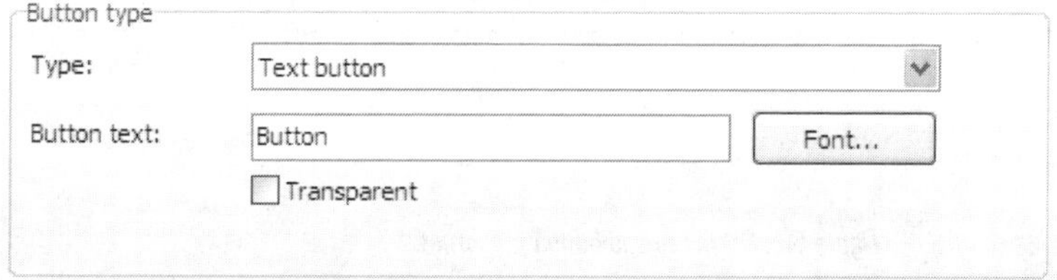

Figure 9-4. Set the text button properties.

5. If you chose Transparent button, choose the colors for the button by clicking on the Frame and/or Fill color box and then choosing a color from the palette. You can also set the width of the frame around the button, along with the transparency percentage. The default, 0%, is a solid button (not transparent at all). Set this to a

higher number (50% or 60%) to let the viewer see through the button to the background of the slide.

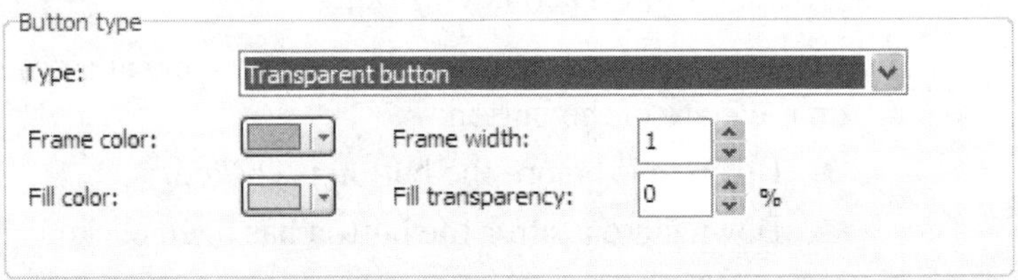

Figure 9-5. Set the Transparent button properties.

6. If you chose Image button, you'll be presented with three options. Captivate will display a different image for each of the three possible states of the button:
   - Up image (the first in the row of buttons) is displayed before the button is clicked.
   - Down image (the middle image) is displayed after the button has been clicked.
   - Over image (the third image in the row of buttons) is displayed when the mouse is over the button but hasn't been clicked yet.

   The default is to use three rectangles with varying interior colors to indicate the three possible image states.

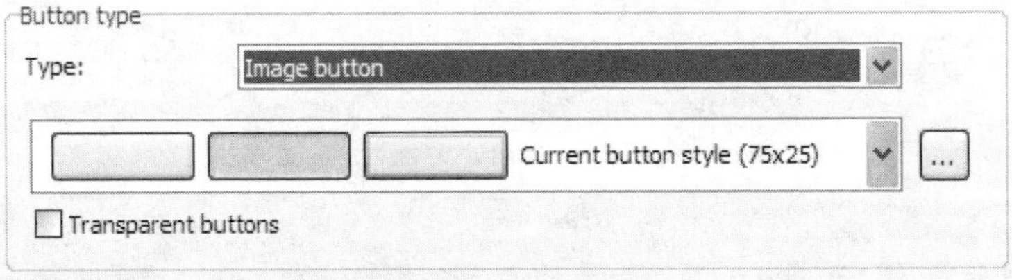

Figure 9-6. Set the Image button properties.

Click the **Browse** button (with three dots) to browse the folders on your system and choose an image for each of the three button states. You can also set the buttons to have a transparent color by selecting the **Transparent buttons** check box. When this is selected, Captivate will make whatever color is in the upper-left corner of the button image be transparent throughout the button

image. For most buttons, this allows the slide to show through the body of the button.

Tip: Captivate comes with a variety of buttons that you can use anywhere within your movie. They're usually stored in the default folder at Captivate\Gallery\Buttons. You can create your own buttons by following the naming conventions for the three button states and placing the corresponding graphics in this folder.

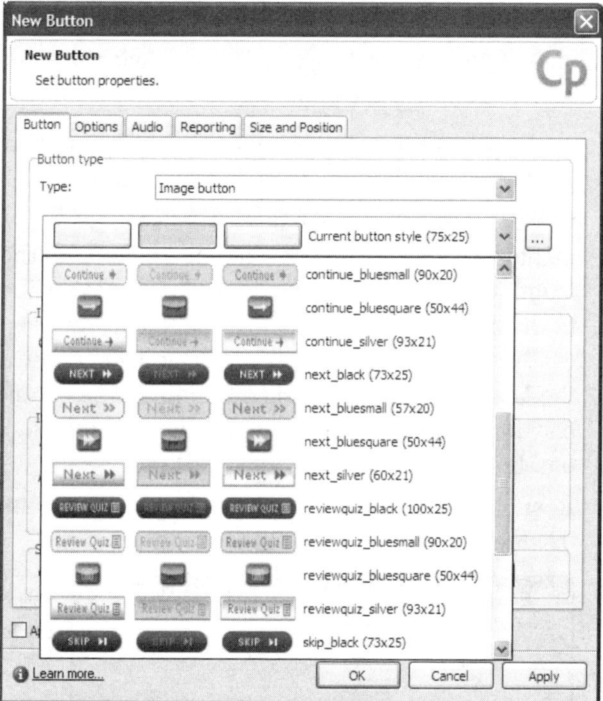

Figure 9-7. Samples of the gallery buttons in the Image button properties window.

7. You may choose to enter options for the button as described in the following sections of this chapter or set audio properties (see Chapter 8). You can also set properties that relate to e-learning and quizzes, which are described in Chapter 10.

8. Click **OK** when you are done to close the element's properties window and view the new button on your slide, along with the success or failure captions if you have them turned on (as described in the following section).

Step 3: Set Interactive Element Options

Each interactive element has a variety of additional options that you can set to control exactly how the element will behave when the movie is playing. To set the interactive properties, follow these steps:

1. From the Edit view, either create a new element as described in Step 1 (above) or double-click on an existing element to open the element's properties window.
2. Click the **Options** tab to view the options for the element. For example, if you are creating or editing a click box element, the available options are shown in Figure 9-8.
3. Set the length of time the element will display by choosing one of the following from the list of Display for options:
   - Specific time—Enter the number of seconds you want the element to display. If you enter a time longer than the current length the slide is displayed, the slide timing will be adjusted to the new length of time. For example, if your slide is currently set to display for 3 seconds, and you enter 5 seconds in the Display for area, the slide timing will be extended to display for 5 seconds. You can enter times in increments of one-tenth of a second.
   - Rest of slide—Displays the element for as long as the slide is displayed.

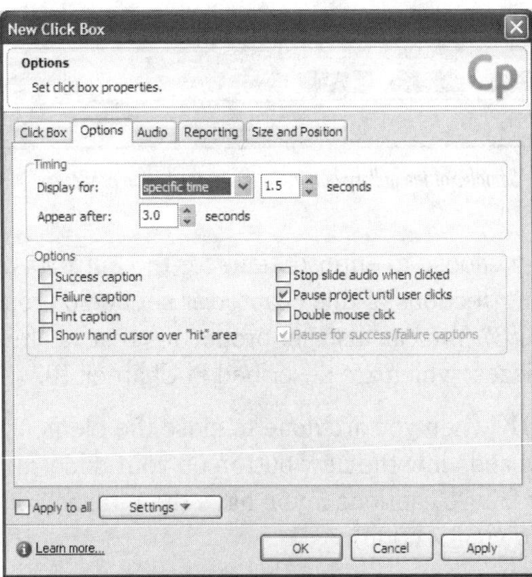

Figure 9-8. Set properties for a click box.

4. You can specify that the element displays a certain length of time after the slide first appears by typing a number of seconds in the box labeled "Appear after." Leave this number set to 0.0 if you want the element to display as soon as the slide displays. You can enter times in increments of one-tenth of a second.

Note: If you've specified a duration for the element, the slide will display for at least as long as the total of the Appear after and the Display for times. For example, a Display for setting of 5 seconds and Appear after setting of 3 seconds would display the slide a total of 8 seconds.

5. *For text entry boxes and buttons only,* specify the length of time after the element displays that you want to pause the movie and wait for the viewer input. For example, you may have other animation or mouse movement going on for 2 or 3 seconds after a text entry box first displays. Set the Pause project after setting to **3** seconds so that the action on the slide can complete before you pause the movie.

6. Click any of the following options to select it, or click on a selected item to deselect it.

Table 9-2. Options for interactive elements

Select this:	To cause this:
Success caption	Include a special text caption that displays when the viewer clicks in the box, presses the button, or types correct text.
Failure caption	Include a special text caption that displays when the viewer does not successfully click in the box, press the button, or type correct text.
Hint caption	Include a special text caption that displays when the viewer moves the mouse over the click box.
Show hand cursor over "hit" area	*For click boxes and buttons only,* change the cursor to a pointing hand icon when the viewer moves the mouse over the click box or button.
Stop audio when clicked	*For click boxes and buttons only,* stop playing slide audio file, if any, when the viewer clicks the click box or button. This option does not stop the background audio, which plays for the whole movie.
Pause project until user clicks	*For click boxes only,* stops the movie until the viewer clicks in the box.
Double mouse click	*For click boxes only,* allows viewers to double-click the click box.
Pause for success/ failure captions	Stops the movie until all success and failure captions have displayed.

Select this:	To cause this:
Show button	*For text entry boxes only*, displays a button that the viewer clicks to indicate the text entry is complete (like a Submit or Enter button). Note that this button is not the same as a fully interactive button; it is a component of the text entry box element.
Show text box frame	*For text entry boxes only*, displays a border around the text box.
Password	*For text entry boxes only*, causes the text that the viewer enters to be displayed on the screen as asterisks, just as many passwords display.
Case-sensitive	*For text entry boxes only*, requires that the viewer enter the text exactly as it is entered in the properties box, with all upper- and lowercase letters typed correctly.

7. You may choose to enter audio properties (see Chapter 8). You can also set properties that relate to e-learning and quizzes, which are described in Chapter 10.
8. To view the changes you've made and continue working in the properties window, click **Apply**. When you are done, click **OK** to close the element's properties window and view the new element on your slide, along with the success or failure captions and any other components you have turned on.

Step 4: Adjust Interactive Elements and Components

If you used the automatic functions to create interactive elements while recording, the elements are likely to be placed at the appropriate points in the slide (such as click boxes over links that you click and success or failure captions right next to the elements the viewer is supposed to click, such as menu icons). When you create new interactive elements on your slide, Captivate defaults to placing them in the center of the slide at a default size. You'll need to move and resize these elements as appropriate, exactly as you would move or resize or align any other element, by clicking and dragging the whole element to a new location or dragging the handles of the element to resize it (see Chapter 7). You can also move the associated components, such as success captions or hints.

In addition, you'll probably want to change the text that appears on the additional components of interactive elements. If you're adding new elements, the default text just says something like "Enter success text here." Even if you're using the automatically generated text, you may want to change the wording. You can also change the color schemes and other properties of the success, failure, and hint captions.

To change the appearance of interactive captions, follow these steps:

1. From Edit view, double-click on a success caption, failure caption, or hint caption to display the properties window, as shown in Figure 9-9.
2. Type the text you want to display in the caption.

Tip: While there is no limit to the amount of text you can include in a caption, remember that this caption will be sitting on top of your slide background (which is often already very busy) and the more text you include, the smaller it will have to be to fit on the screen. The best captions are succinct and to the point.

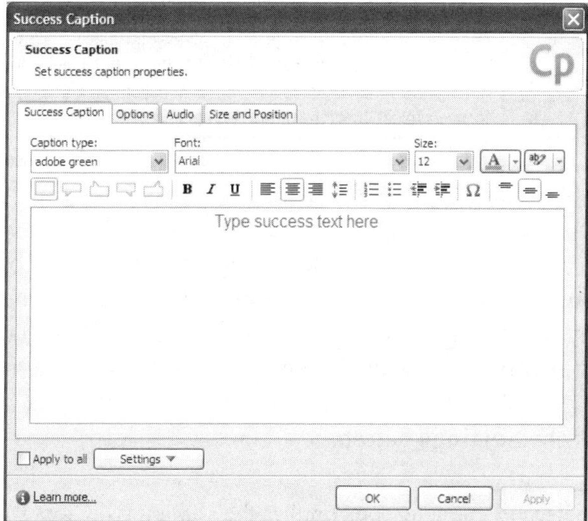

Figure 9-9. Enter new text in the Success Caption properties window.

3. If necessary, change the look of the caption by editing the following properties:

Chapter 9

Table 9-3. Interactive element caption properties

To change this:	Do this:
Caption type	Choose a caption type from the drop-down list. The caption type defines the shape and color of the outline that will be placed around the text, as well as the default text color (though you can change this). The icons below this field display the look of each caption type.
Font	Choose a font for the text from the list. The list of fonts will be determined by the fonts available on your system.
Size	Choose a size for the text from the list.
Color	Click the down arrow next to the letter A to choose a new color for the text. The text color does not change the color of the caption type outline.
Highlight	Click the down arrow next to the highlight icon (a pen with ab next to it) to choose a color that will appear behind the text. Note that this is a color for the text background, and does not necessarily fill the caption outline.
Caption outline style	Many of the caption types include outlines that point in different directions. In Figure 9-9, the "adobe green" type has options that point in four different directions as well as an option with no direction. Click any one of the style icons to select it for the current text caption.
Text style	If you want, set standard text options such as font appearance, bullets, numbering, and alignment.

4. The changes you make to the caption properties will be applied to all subsequent interactive element text captions. If you want to apply these changes to all captions that are already in the movie, click **Apply to all** to apply the current settings as defined in the properties window. To view or change the properties settings, click the **Settings** button.

Note: Selecting this check box applies the caption style, font type, font size, font color, and transition properties to all success or failure or hint captions in the movie. It does not change the wording of the text, nor does it change the text style (such as bold, italic, or justification).

5. You can click the Options tab to set timing and transitions as described in Chapter 7, or click the Audio tab to set audio properties as described in Chapter 8.

6. Click **OK** to close the properties window and display the new text.

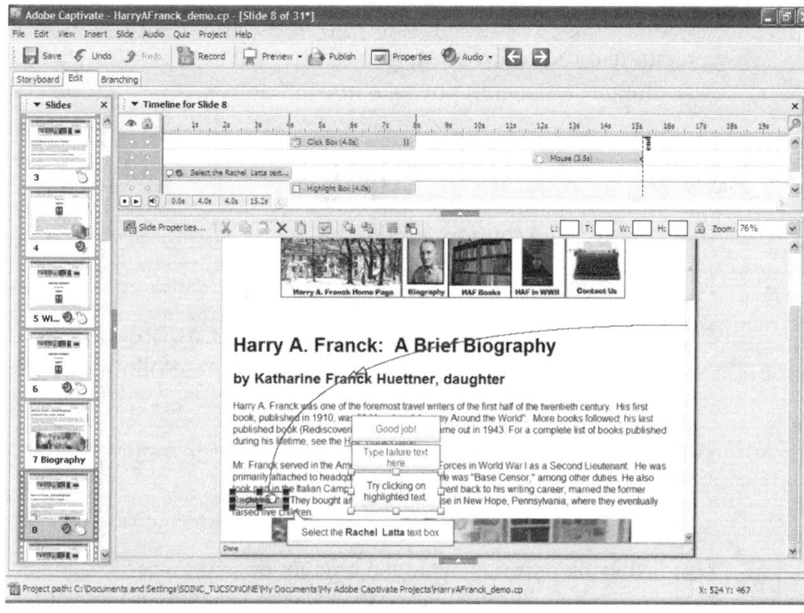

Figure 9-10. Modified version of interactive elements.

Figure 9-10 shows a click box with success, failure, and hint captions. Though you may not see it on the printed page, the three caption types display in the project using different colors as an added indicator of type. Also notice that the click box has been moved to the same place on the screen as the previously placed highlight box. This will ensure that the viewers see exactly where they're supposed to click.

Adding Interactivity with Rollovers

Rollover captions, rollover images, and rollover slidelets are a cross between the static elements (text captions and images) and their more interactive equivalents. The rollover elements are interactive in that they only appear if the viewer takes an action (like moving the cursor over the designated area). But they do not require this action. The movie will continue whether the rollover caption displays or not.

A rollover element consists of two components: the area that the viewer must "roll over" and the caption, image, or secondary slide that appears. Rollover captions are particularly useful when you're

documenting complex screens with many options. In such situations, you can use the rollover caption to create a sort of interactive job aid describing the use and purpose of each option.

Adding a Rollover Caption

To add a rollover caption, follow these steps:

1. In Edit view, select the slide you want to edit.
2. From the Insert menu, select **Rollover Caption** or click the Rollover Caption icon ( ) to display the New Rollover Caption window, as shown in Figure 9-11.
3. Type the text you want to display when the viewer rolls the mouse over the designated area.

Tip: While there is no limit to the amount of text you can include in a caption, remember that this caption will be sitting on top of your slide background (which is often already very busy) and the more text you include, the smaller it will have to be to fit on the screen. The best captions are succinct and to the point. Use short declarative phrases ("This is the main menu") or brief commands ("Click here to go to the next page").

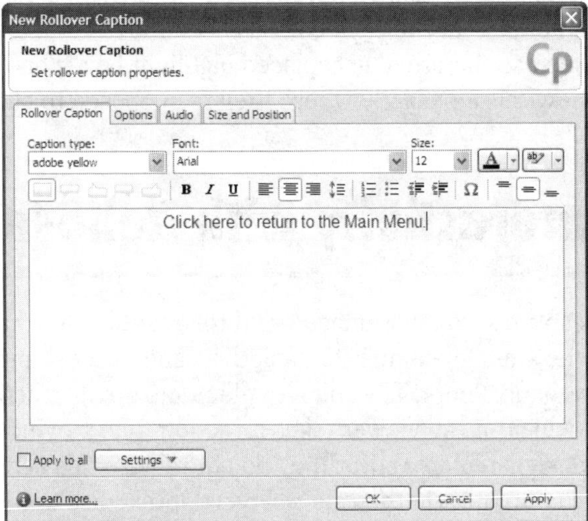

Figure 9-11. Set the rollover caption properties.

4. If necessary, change the look of the caption by editing the following properties:

Table 9-4. Rollover caption properties

To change this:	Do this:
Caption type	Choose a caption type from the list. The caption type defines the shape and color of the outline that will be placed around the text, as well as the default text color (though you can change this). The icons below this field display the look of each caption type.
Font	Choose a font for the text from the list. The list of fonts will be determined by the fonts available on your system.
Size	Choose a size for the text from the list.
Color	Click the down arrow next to the letter A to choose a new color for the text. The text color does not change the color of the caption type outline.
Highlight	Click the down arrow next to the highlight icon (a pen with ab next to it) to choose a color that will appear behind the text. Note that this is a color for the text background, and does not necessarily fill the caption outline.
Caption outline style	Many of the caption types include outlines that point in different directions. In the example above, the "adobe yellow" type has options that point in four different directions as well as an option with no direction. Click any one of the style icons to select it for the current text caption.
Text style	If you want, set standard text options such as font appearance, bullets, numbering, and alignment.

5. The changes you make to the caption properties will be applied to all subsequent rollover text captions. If you want to apply these changes to all captions that are already in the movie, click **Apply to all** to apply the current settings as defined in the properties window. To view or change the properties settings, click the **Settings** button.

Note: Selecting this check box applies the caption style, font type, font size, font color, and transition properties to all rollover captions in the movie. It does not change the wording of the text, nor does it change the text style (such as bold, italic, or justification).

6. You can click the Options tab to set timing and transitions as described in Chapter 7, or click the Audio tab to set audio properties, which are described in Chapter 8.

7. Click **OK** to display the new rollover caption and the text that you entered in the center of the slide.

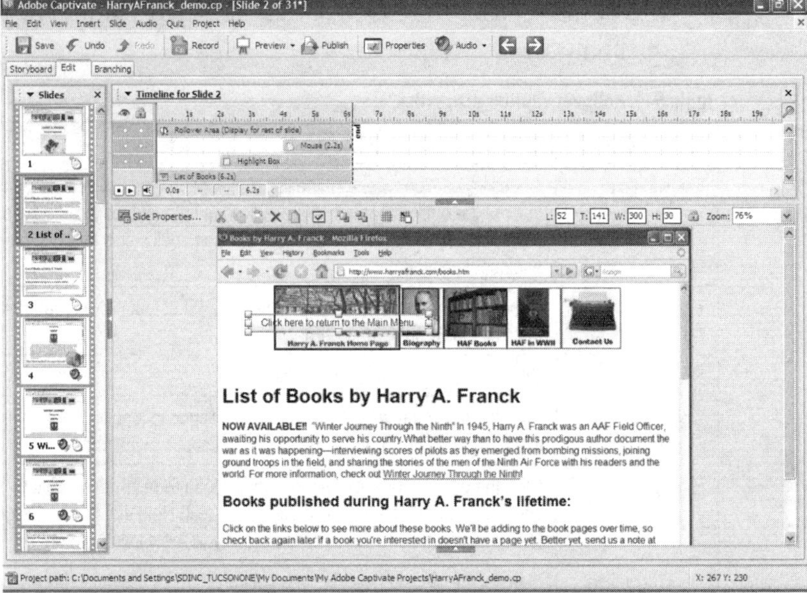

Figure 9-12. The new rollover caption appears on the slide.

8. Click and drag the text box to the location you want it to appear when the viewer rolls the mouse over the designated area.
9. Click and drag the rollover caption box—it's difficult to see, particularly if the slide is very busy—from the center of the slide to the area where you want the viewer to click. In this example, we'll drag the outline that surrounds the words "Click here to return to the Main Menu" to the top of the slide and resize it until it matches the width of the first icon in the menu.

Note that once the movie is running, the rollover captions will only display when the mouse is in the designated rollover area. If you have several rollover captions, don't worry if the text boxes pile up on each other. It may be difficult to see while you're editing, but they'll only appear one at a time during the movie. For example, if we continue adding rollover captions to the icons in the menu above, the result in Edit view looks like Figure 9-13. It will get even more crowded when we add click boxes and/or success and failure captions.

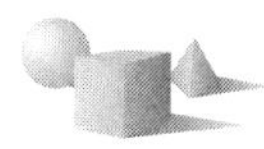

Tip: You can't see the rollover captions when you use the Play this slide function (by pressing F3). To see what the captions will look like when the movie is played, use either Preview from this slide (F8) or Preview Next 5 slides (F10) from the Preview menu.

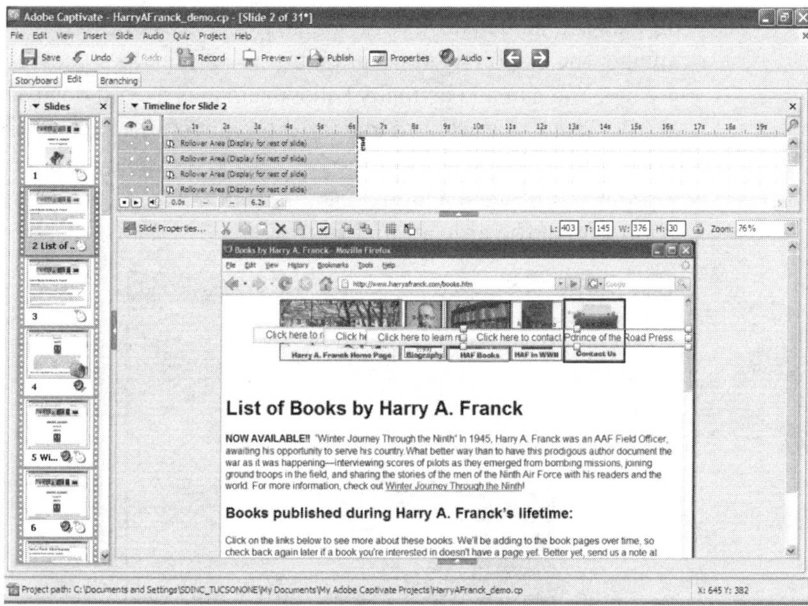

Figure 9-13. Many rollover captions pile up in the Edit view but display one at a time when the movie is played.

Adding a Rollover Image

To add a rollover image, follow these steps:

1. In Edit view, select the slide you want to edit.
2. From the Insert menu, select **Rollover image** or click the Rollover Image icon ( ) to display the images available in the last folder you used.

Tip: Captivate comes with a gallery of buttons that you can import as images. By default, they're stored in the Captivate\Gallery\Buttons folder.

3. You can use rollover images for many things, such as close-ups of the background or showing categorization icons. Remember, though, that a rollover image does not require a click; the viewer only has to roll the mouse over the designated area. For this example, we'll add a close-up of the background image. As the viewer moves the mouse around on a map to the area of the rollover image, the region displays in higher resolution as a separate image. You can add as many rollover images as you desire. Browse to the image you want to use for the rollover, then click **OK** to select the image and open the New Rollover Image properties window with the selected image in it. In this case, we've selected a closeup of the area around Jerusalem.

Figure 9-14. Import an image as an element on the slide.

4. The image you selected appears in the center of the window. Enter the percentage of transparency for the image. 0% would be completely solid; 100% would be completely transparent.

5. You can specify that Captivate import the image but make the background color of the image transparent. For example, if you are adding a logo that is a custom shape, such as a shield, you might not want the rectangular outline of the image file to show.

Tip: Be careful to check your images after you import them, particularly if you use a transparent background. Captivate will make all areas that are the color of the background transparent. For example, if you have an image of a black circle with white lettering and a white background, and you make the white background transparent, then Captivate will make all white portions of the image transparent (including the letters). If this isn't the look you wanted, use a graphics program to make the background or the letters slightly different shades of white.

6. The changes you make to the properties will be applied to all subsequent rollover images. If you want to apply these changes to all rollover images that are already in the movie, click **Apply to all** to apply the current settings as defined in the properties window. To view or change the properties settings, click the **Settings** button.

Tip: If you want the rollover area to be invisible, set the frame width to zero and the frame fill to 100% transparency.

7. You can click the Options tab to set transitions, as described in Chapter 7, or click the Audio tab to set audio properties, which are described in Chapter 8.
8. Click **OK** to display the new rollover image in your slide. By default, the rollover area and image are in the center of the slide.
9. Click and drag the image to the location where you want it to appear when the viewer rolls the mouse over the designated area.
10. Click and drag the rollover image box—it's difficult to see, particularly if the slide is very busy—from the center of the slide to the area where you want the viewer to move the mouse. In this example, we'll drag the outline that surrounds the words "rollover image" to the area of the map that corresponds to the close-up image (the area around Jerusalem).

Tip: You can't see the rollover images when you use the Play this slide function (by pressing F3). To see what the images will look like when the movie is played, use either Preview from this slide (F8) or Preview Next 5 slides (F10) from the Preview menu.

Figure 9-15. Preview the slide to see the designated rollover area.

When the viewer moves the mouse over the designated area (in Figure 9-15, it's the boxed area), the specified image displays.

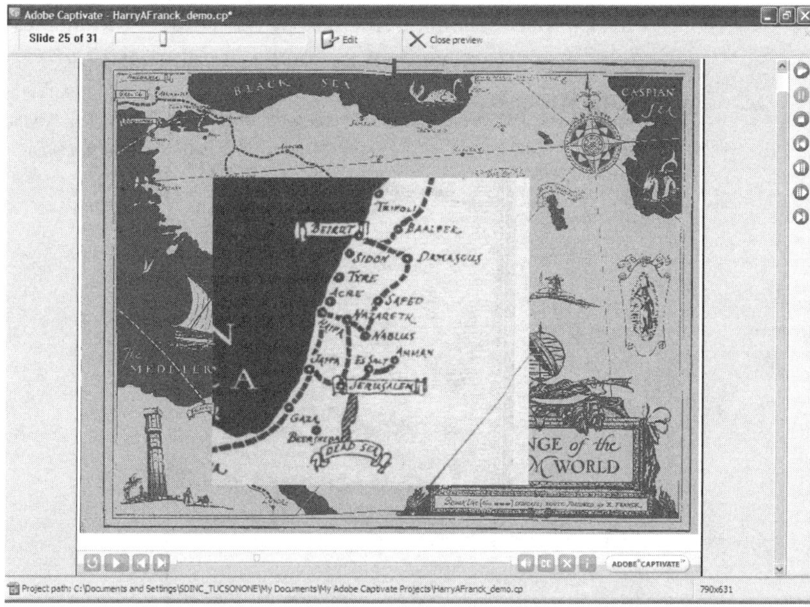

Figure 9-16. Move the mouse to display the rollover image.

Adding a Rollover Slidelet

A slidelet is a miniature slide that displays when the viewer rolls the mouse over a specified area. This gives you lots of options, since a slidelet can contain most of the elements that a full slide can contain.

Tip: Slidelets can be tricky to implement well. Remember that the slidelet displays on top of the current slide, which can make for a very busy screen. Also, it is easy to put too much into a slidelet, making each element very small (sometimes too small to read).

You'll need to define both the rollover area and the slidelet contents.

To add a rollover slidelet, follow these steps:

1. In Edit view, select the slide you want to edit.

2. From the Insert menu, select **Rollover Slidelet** to display the Slidelet properties window, as shown in Figure 9-17.

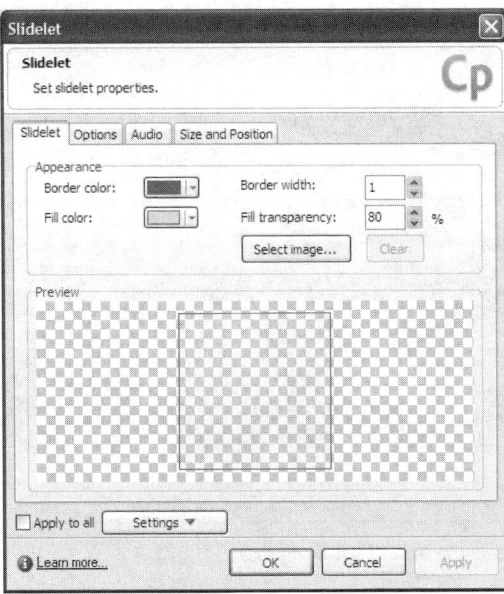

Figure 9-17. Set the slidelet properties.

3. If necessary, change the look of the slidelet by editing the following properties. As you make changes, the preview in the center of the window changes to reflect each new selection.

Table 9-5. Slidelet properties

To change this:	Do this:
Border color	Click on the down arrow in the color box next to Border color to display the Color window, and then choose a color for the border around the outside edge of the rollover slidelet area box. This is usually a darker shade than the inside of the box.
Border width	Specify the width, in pixels, for the border or frame of the box.
Fill color	Click on the down arrow in the color box next to Fill color to display the Color window, and then choose a color for the interior of the box. This is usually a lighter shade than the frame of the box.
Fill transparency	Enter the percentage of transparency for the inside of the box. 0% would be completely solid; 100% would be completely transparent. Most of the time, you want something between these two values so that the rollover slidelet area box is noticeable and yet the text behind the box still shows through.
Slidelet background	Click Select image and browse to the image you want as the slidelet background.

4. The changes you make to the properties will be applied to all subsequent rollover slidelet area images. If you want to apply these changes to all rollover slidelet area images that are already in the movie, click **Apply to all** to apply the current settings as defined in the properties window. To view or change the properties settings, click the **Settings** button.
5. You can click the Options tab to set transitions, as described in Chapter 7, or click the Audio tab to set audio properties, which are described in Chapter 8.
6. Click **OK** to display the new rollover slidelet in your slide. By default, the rollover area (labeled "Rollover Slidelet") and the content box (unlabeled) are in the center of the slide.
7. Click and drag the rollover area box—it's difficult to see, particularly if the slide is very busy—from the center of the slide to the area where you want the mouse movement to trigger the rollover slidelet display.
8. To set the rollover properties, double-click on the rollover area box, or right-click the box and click **Properties** to display the Rollover Slidelet properties window. This defaults to the appearance properties you set when creating the slidelet, but also gives you a few extra options.

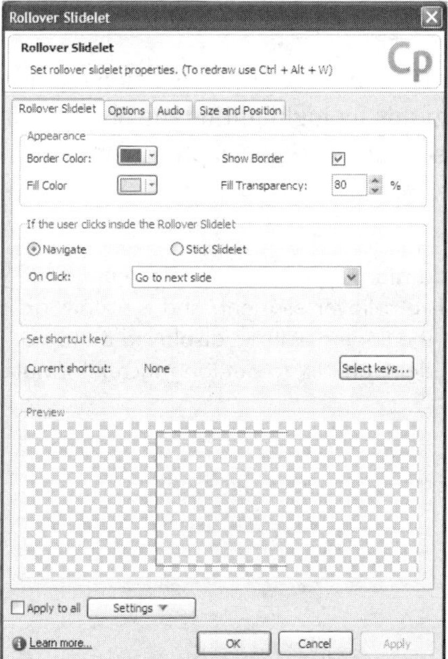

Figure 9-18. Set rollover area properties.

9. Define the actions you want to occur if the user clicks inside the slidelet rollover area. Remember, most rollover areas don't have a clickable functionality, so many users will not expect to click in the area. Click **OK** when finished.

Table 9-6. Rollover slidelet properties

Set this:	For this action:
Navigate	If the viewer clicks in the rollover area, take the action specified in the On Click drop-down box (such as Go To Next Slide or Continue).
Stick Slidelet	Leave the slidelet on the screen, even after the viewer moves the cursor out of the rollover area.
Shortcut Key	Specify a key (or combination of keys) that trigger the display of the rollover content.

10. Most of the tabs are similar to functions you've seen on other property windows (such as audio settings, size and position, and most of the options. The Options tab does include one extra option that you won't see for other elements. Click the **Options** tab and select the **Show Runtime Shadow** check box to display a shadow behind the slidelet when it displays. This can help to differentiate the slidelet content from the slide behind it.

11. Click and drag the content box to the location where you want it to appear when the viewer rolls the mouse over the designated rollover area.

12. Define the content for the rollover by inserting elements into the content box; you do this by highlighting the box and choosing elements from the Insert menu. See Chapter 7 for details on the available elements.

TIP: Though you can add many types of elements to the content box, remember that this is a rollover element, and is usually displayed temporarily. Also, the content will be displayed on top of whatever else is on the slide. Don't try to put too much information in a rollover slidelet.

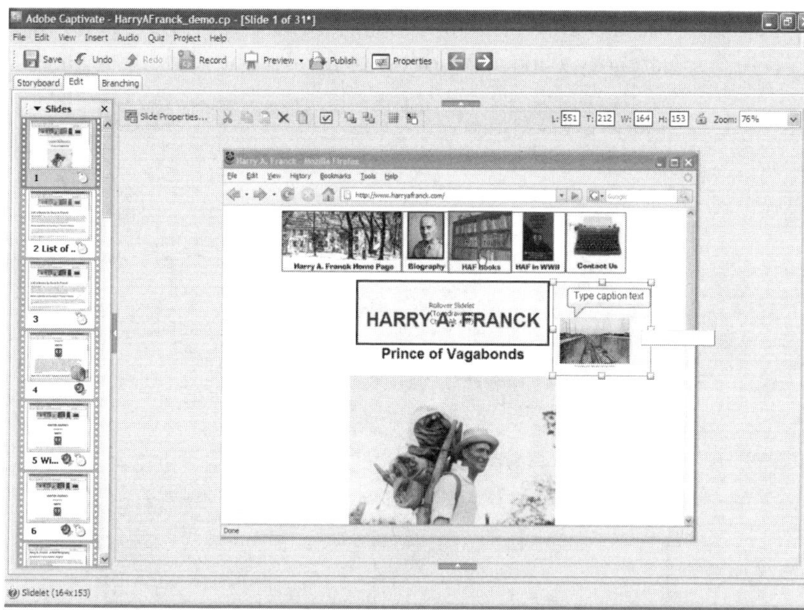

Figure 9-19. A slidelet consists of a rollover area and a content box.

Adding Interactive Elements While Recording

When you record tasks for a movie, Captivate can automatically add various visual elements for certain actions. For example, if you're recording an assessment simulation type of movie, failure and hint captions will automatically be added whenever you click on a menu item or link. To specify whether or not Captivate should add interactive elements automatically for you, you have to edit the recording options. To do this, follow these steps:

Note: You do not have to have an open movie to change the recording options.

1. From the Edit menu, choose **Preferences**, then in the **Recording** category, choose **Mode(s)** to display the current settings.

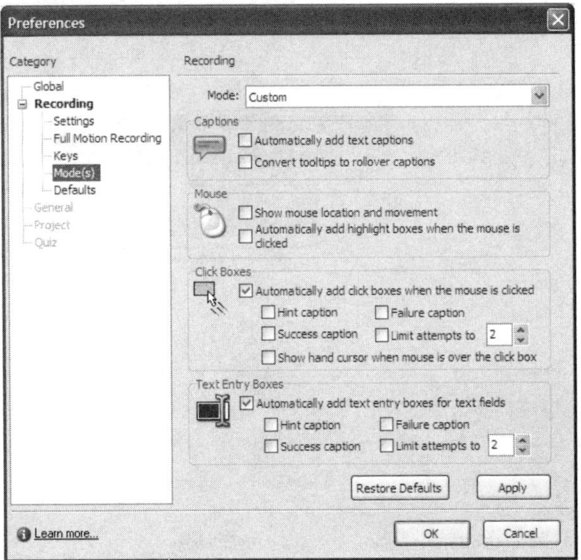

Figure 9-20. Specify recording settings in the Preferences window.

2. Choose the recording mode from the drop-down list. There are four options:
   - Demonstration—This mode automatically adds captions and highlight boxes, and records mouse movement.
   - Assessment Simulation—This mode adds click boxes and failure boxes but does not insert captions or mouse movement.
   - Training Simulation—This mode adds click boxes and hints but no mouse movements.
   - Custom—This mode allows you to set the recording options manually but defaults to including text captions.
3. For each mode, specify the options that you want Captivate to automatically add by choosing the appropriate check boxes.
4. Click **OK** to close the Preferences window. The options you've set will be used for all subsequent recordings (both for new projects and recording additional slides in an existing project).

Summary

This chapter covered the basics of adding interactive elements to your slides, such as for demonstrations and simulations. The following chapter takes this interactivity a step further into e-learning, where you can create quizzes in a variety of question formats, and store or export your viewer's quiz results.

Chapter 10

Creating e-Learning Content

In the previous chapter, you learned how to add interactive elements to a slide and how to display different captions or continue on to different slides based on whether or not the viewer performed certain tasks correctly. Taking this one step further, Captivate can store the results of all those interactive tasks, making the entire movie into a quiz that you can automatically grade and score and even integrate into other learning management systems.

Captivate also offers a powerful, easy-to-use feature called a question slide that automatically creates interactive slides in a variety of question formats, such as multiple choice, true or false, or short answer. Like the other interactive elements, you can specify what displays when the viewer gets a question right or wrong. And like the other interactive elements, questions can be included in quizzes.

Captivate quizzing functions let you define quiz properties that apply to all interactive elements as well as to dedicated question slides. You can even set up a question pool so that the questions that display in the finished movie will vary from viewer to viewer. You can define the defaults for elements such as "Try again" messages or the appearance of "Next" and "Submit" buttons. You can also export the results of any quiz to a learning management system.

Before you begin to create questions and quizzes, you'll need to make some basic decisions:

- Decide what you want the viewer to do and what format you want to use to request the viewer input. There are two ways to get and store input from the viewer:

    - Report on interactive elements, such as whether or not the viewer clicked in the right place or entered the correct text in a text entry box. This type of interaction takes place on normal slides during the course of the movie. You'll need to create the interactive element (such as a click box or button) as well as the instructions for it (usually with a text caption and optional highlight box).
    - Have the viewer read and answer question slides. A question slide is a unique type of slide that sits between the other slides in your movie and displays a question in any of a variety of formats (such as multiple choice or short answer questions). The interactivity is already built in, and all you have to do is input the questions and answers. You can also include some questions that will be graded (pass or fail) and others that are not graded (survey questions).
- Decide what you want to have happen if the viewer enters the correct answer or clicks in the right spot, and what you want to have happen if the viewer doesn't do the right thing. For example, you can pause the movie until the viewer clicks the right location or answers the question correctly, or display a different slide depending on whether the input is right or wrong. The display of different slides lets you give the viewer choices in the way the movie displays. This is described more in Chapter 11, "Working with the Branching View."
- Decide whether or not to use the quizzing functions to store and display a summary that shows how the viewer did overall. This is in addition to the success or failure captions that display for each interactive element or question. You can even decide to track some interactive elements and not others within the movie.
    - If you use a quiz, decide what a passing score should be, what should happen when the viewer gets a passing score, and what should happen when the viewer doesn't pass. For example, will there be an option to try again? Will you let the viewer keep watching the movie or go to another area? You could also run some JavaScript based on the viewer's score (pass or fail).
    - If you use a quiz, decide what you will do with the data once it's collected. You can have the results e-mailed to you, or create output files that you can then integrate with other programs.

- Decide if you want to use the Question Pool functionality to let Captivate generate random questions at specified places throughout the movie.

As you can see, Captivate offers a lot of options and thus gives you a lot of control over the movies you create.

Working with Question Slides

Captivate lets you insert eight types of question slides into your movie. For each slide, you'll need to define one question and enter answers. You'll also need to set the question slide options, such as which slide to display when the viewer answers correctly and whether or not to display buttons that allow the viewer to skip a question.

You'll also need to specify whether or not you want to track the answers for each question with the reporting function.

Entering Questions and Answers

Each of the eight types of question slides has its own requirements for entering the question and answer (or in some cases, multiple answers).

Table 10-1. Types of question slides

For this type of question:	Do this:
Multiple choice	Enter a list of possible answers, and indicate whether the viewer can choose one or more than one and which one or ones are correct.
True/False	Indicate which is correct.
Fill-in-the-blank	Supply the correct answer or a list of answers from which the viewer must choose. If you give a list of answers, indicate which are correct.
Short answer	Enter the correct answer.
Matching	Supply two lists of items that the viewer must pair up (one from column a, one from column b) and the correct matches.
Hot Spot	Similar to a multiple choice question, the hot spot question displays a number of areas on the slide (the hot spots) that the viewer must click. You can specify as many as 10 hot spots, and specify one or more that are correct.

For this type of question:	Do this:
Sequence	Similar to a Matching question, this type of question asks the viewer to put the possible answers in order or sequence This can be done by typing the letters of each answer (like a matching question) or by dragging the answers around on the slide to put them in the order you've specified as correct.
Rating Scale (Likert)	Give a list of statements that the viewer must rate on a scale that you define. This type of question is not graded—there is no "right" or "wrong."

Defining Multiple Choice Questions and Answers

Multiple choice question slides allow the viewer to choose from a list of answers that you provide. You can specify one correct answer, or several. If there are several correct answers in your list, the viewer would have to select all of them in order for the answer to be considered correct (no partial scores here!).

To add a multiple choice question slide, follow these steps:

1. In either Storyboard or Edit view, choose where you want the slide to be placed by selecting the slide just before the question. Captivate will insert the new slide immediately after the selected slide.

2. From the Insert menu, choose **Slide** and then **Question Slide** to display the list of question types.

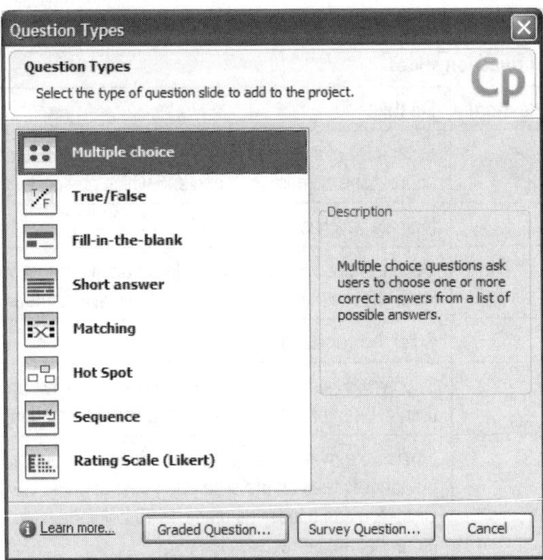

Figure 10-1. Select from the list of question types.

3. Click on **Multiple choice** from the list.
4. Specify whether this question will be graded (that is, part of a quiz) or not by clicking either **Graded Question** or **Survey Question**. Survey question results will be tabulated, but they will not be used to determine a score for the viewer. Once you've clicked either of these buttons, the Question Types window closes and displays the appropriate Multiple Choice Question window.

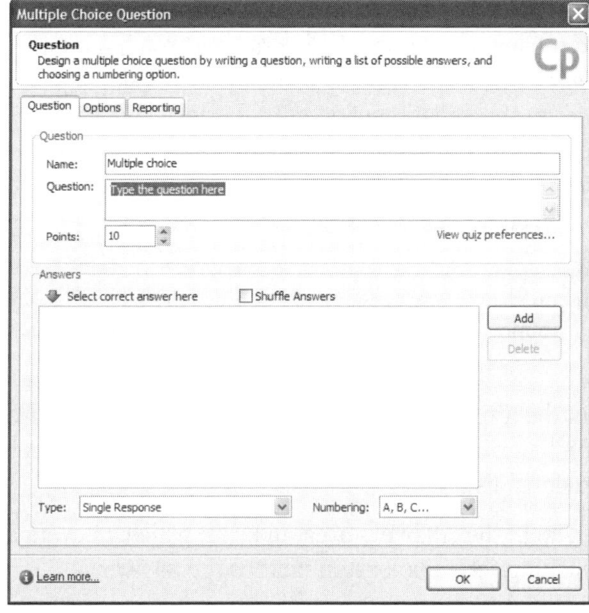

Figure 10-2. Enter a question and multiple answers.

5. Enter a name in the Name box. This text will be displayed across the top of the slide when the movie is played. It won't be stored or tracked anywhere else.

Tip: You can type unique names for each question, or you can use the name to categorize your questions for the viewer. For example, you might have the first few questions (regardless of question type) named Navigation Tasks, the next few named Message Board, and the final ones named Feedback (or whatever categories fit your movie).

6. Type the question, exactly as you want it to display, in the Question box. You can include text, numbers, and special characters including punctuation, and you may include instructions if necessary.
7. If you specified a graded question, you can enter a number in the Points box to indicate the value or weight of the question within the context of the quiz. If you specified a survey question, this box is not available.
8. Type the answers in the Answers area. You must enter at least two answers, but you can enter as many as you need. The answers will appear in the question slide in the order in which they display here. You can delete answers by highlighting the answer and either clicking the Delete button or pressing the Delete key on your keyboard.

Tip: You can click in each row or you can use the up and down arrow keys to move from one answer to the next within the Answers area.

9. From the Type box, choose whether you want to indicate just one correct answer or several by choosing an option from the drop-down list.
10. Back up in the Answers area, indicate which answers are correct by clicking the radio button next to the answer.
11. Select the **Shuffle Answers** check box to display the available answers in a different order each time the slide is displayed. Captivate will keep track of the correct answer, regardless of the order in which the answers are displayed. If this box isn't checked, the slide will always display the answers in the same order (so, in Figure 10-3, answer "B" will always be correct).
12. From the Numbering box, choose an option from the drop-down list to indicate whether you want the answers to be listed as uppercase letters, lowercase letters, or numbers. The choice you make will be reflected in the answers that are currently displayed in the Answers area.

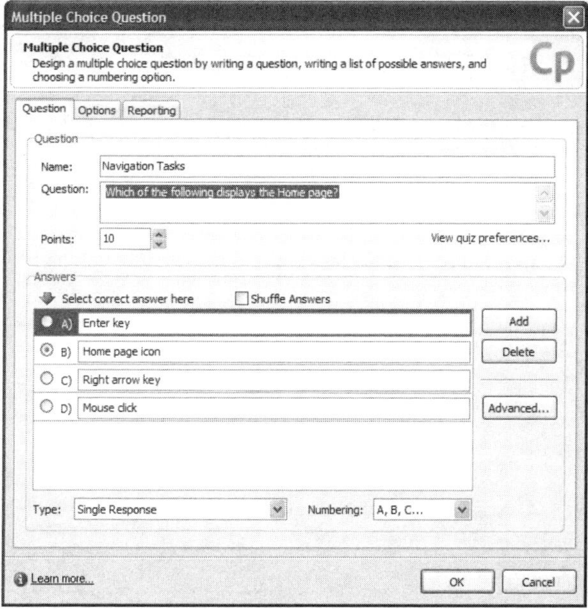

Figure 10-3. Specify the correct answer.

13. You may set options for this question as described in a later section in this chapter, or you can leave the default settings so that all your questions will act the same way.
14. You may set reporting options for this question as described later in this chapter.
15. Click **OK** when you are done to display the new question slide. Note that the slide displays the correct answer or answers as selected.

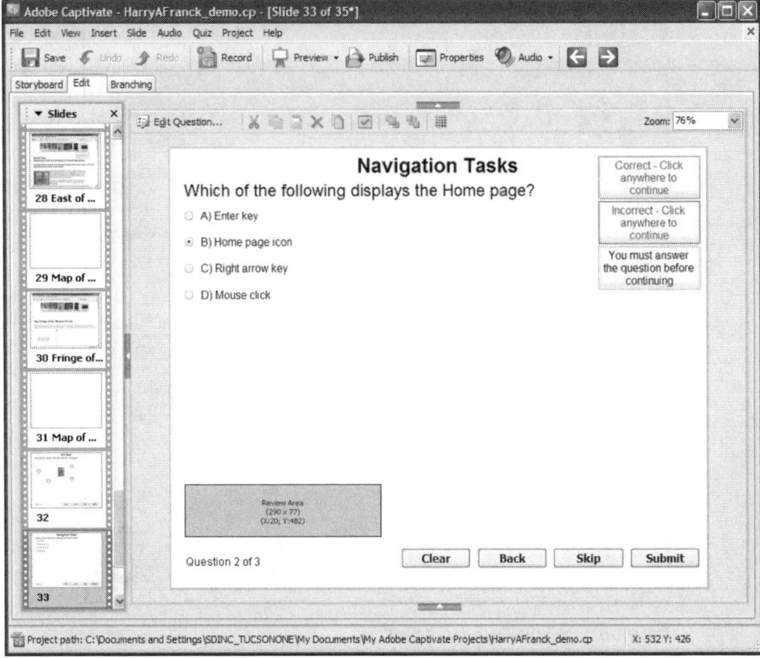

Figure 10-4. A multiple choice question slide.

Defining True/False Questions and Answers

A true/false question slide only gives the viewer two possible answers. You can choose whether the two answers will be True and False or Yes and No.

To add a true/false question slide, follow these steps:

1. In either Storyboard or Edit view, choose where you want the slide to be placed by selecting the slide just before the question. Captivate will insert the new slide immediately after the selected slide.

2. From the Insert menu, choose **Slide** and then **Question Slide** to display the list of question types.

Figure 10-5. Select from the list of question types.

3. Click **True/False** from the list.
4. Specify whether this question will be graded (that is, part of a quiz) or not by choosing either **Graded Question** or **Survey Question**. Survey question results will be tabulated, but they will not be used to determine a score for the viewer. Once you've clicked either of these buttons, the Question Types window closes and displays the appropriate True/False Question window.

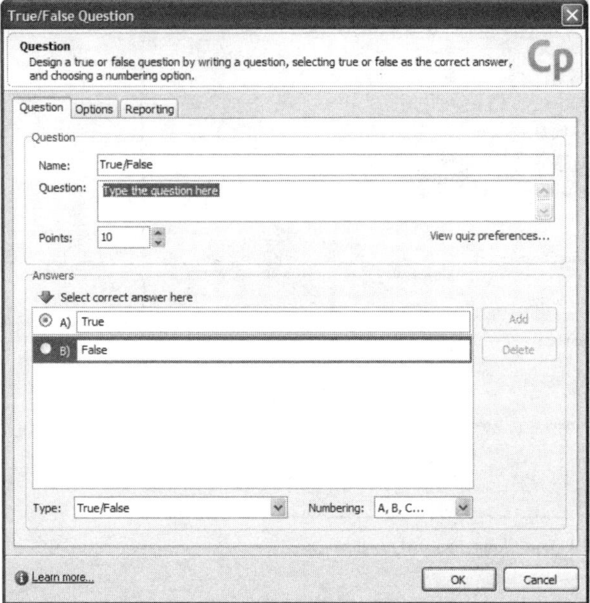

Figure 10-6. Enter a question and specify the correct answer.

5. Enter a name in the Name box. This text will be displayed across the top of the slide when the movie is played. It won't be stored or tracked anywhere else.

Tip: You can type unique names for each question, or you can use the name to categorize your questions for the viewer. For example, you might have the first few questions (regardless of question type) named Navigation Tasks, the next few named Message Board, and the final ones named Feedback (or whatever categories fit your movie).

6. Type the question, exactly as you want it to display, in the Question box. You can include text, numbers, and special characters including punctuation, and you may include instructions if necessary.
7. If you specified a graded question, you can enter a number in the Points box to indicate the value or weight of the question within the context of the quiz. If you specified a survey question, this box is not available.

8. From the Type box, choose either **True/False** or **Yes/No** from the drop-down list. If you want the answers to be anything else, you must edit them in the Answers section.
9. Back up in the Answers area, indicate which answer is correct by clicking the radio button next to the answer.
10. From the Numbering box, choose an option from the drop-down list to indicate whether you want the answers to be listed as uppercase letters, lowercase letters, or numbers. The choice you make will be reflected in the answers that are currently displayed in the Answers area.
11. You may set options for this question as described in a later section in this chapter, or you can leave the default settings so that all your questions will act the same way.
12. You may set reporting options for this question as described later in this chapter.
13. Click **OK** when you are done to display the new question slide.

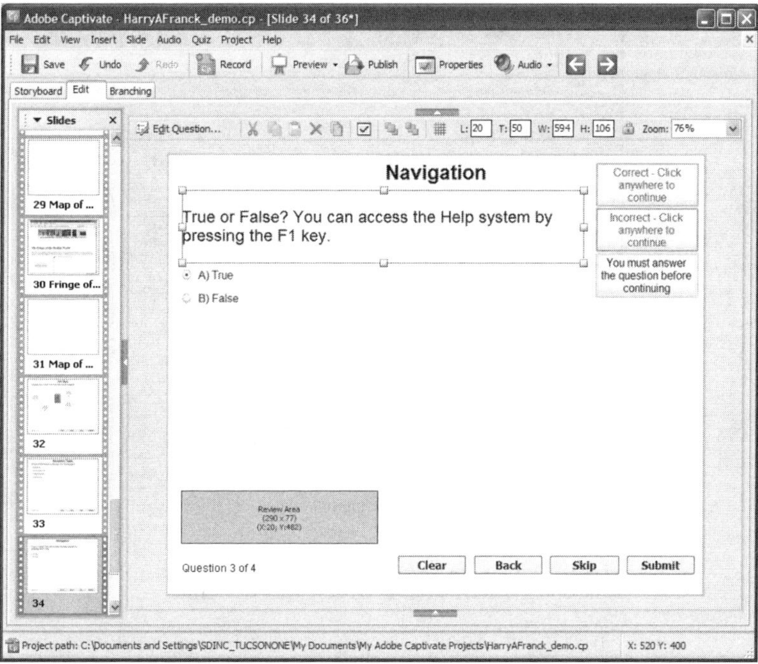

Figure 10-7. A true/false question slide.

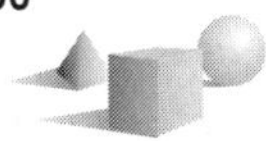

Tip: If the question you entered doesn't appear in full on the slide, you can make the text box bigger (or move elements around as needed) as described in Chapter 7, "Editing a Single Slide."

Defining Fill-in-the-Blank Questions and Answers

A fill-in-the-blank question slide starts with a question that is really a sentence with one or more blank spaces where words should be. You can either let the viewer type in the correct answer or you can provide a list of possible answers from which the viewer should choose.

To add a fill-in-the-blank question slide, follow these steps:

1. In either Storyboard or Edit view, choose where you want the slide to be placed by selecting the slide just before the question. Captivate will insert the new slide immediately after the selected slide.
2. From the Insert menu, choose **Slide** and then **Question Slide** to display the list of question slide types.

Figure 10-8. Select from the list of question types.

3. Choose **Fill-in-the-blank** from the list.
4. Specify whether this question will be graded (that is, part of a quiz) or not by choosing either **Graded Question** or **Survey Question.** Survey question results will be tabulated, but they will

not be used to determine a score for the viewer. Once you've clicked either of these buttons, the Question Types window closes and displays the appropriate New fill-in-the-blank question window.

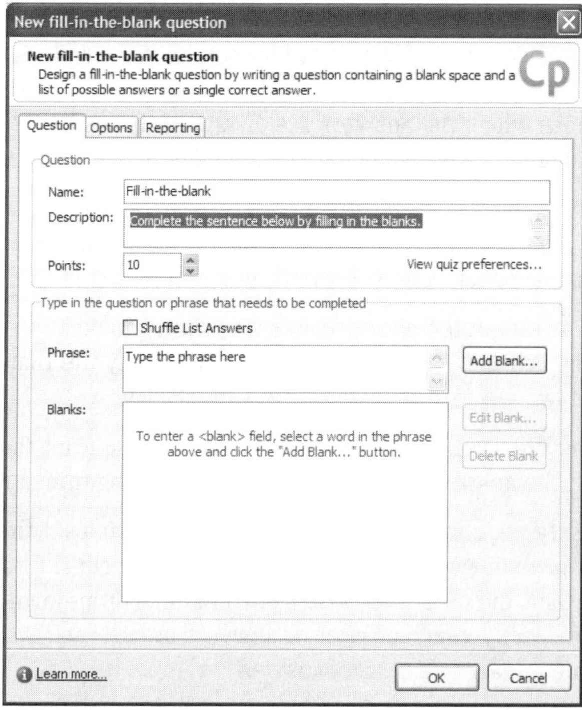

Figure 10-9. Enter a question and multiple answers.

5. Enter a name in the Name box. This text will be displayed across the top of the slide when the movie is played. It won't be stored or tracked anywhere else.

Tip: You can type unique names for each question, or you can use the name to categorize your questions for the viewer. For example, you might have the first few questions (regardless of question type) named Navigation Tasks, the next few named Message Board, and the final ones named Feedback (or whatever categories fit your movie).

6. Type a description in the Description box. This will appear on the slide beneath the title in slightly smaller text.

7. If you specified a graded question, you can enter a number in the Points box to indicate the value or weight of the question within the context of the quiz. If you specified a survey question, this box is not available.
8. Select the **Shuffle List Answers** check box to display the available answers in a different order each time the slide is displayed. Captivate will keep track of the correct answer, regardless of the order in which the answers are displayed. If this box isn't selected, the slide will always display the answers in the same order.
9. Type the phrase, exactly as you want it to display, in the Phrase box. Do not include the missing word! You can include text, numbers, and special characters including punctuation.
10. When you get to where the missing word should be in your phrase, click the **Add Blank** button to display the Blank Answer window.
11. In the Blank Answer window, choose how you want the viewer to input the answer (either by typing or selecting from a list).
12. Specify the correct answer or answers. If you want the user to type in an answer, any item in the list will be considered correct. If you want the user to choose from a list in a drop-down box, you must specify which answer or answers are correct. You must select at least one correct answer

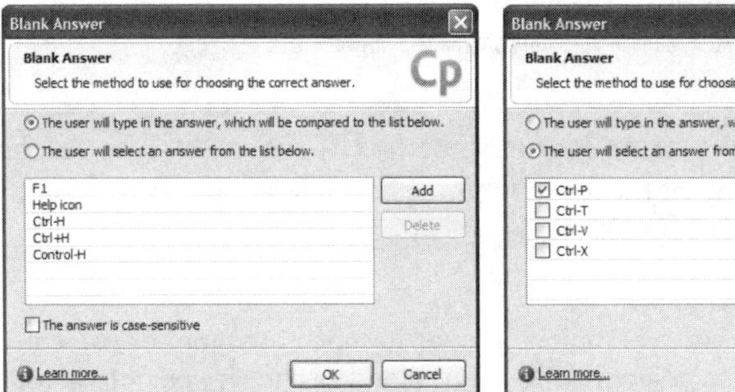

Figure 10-10. Specify the correct answer or answers for fill-in-the-blank question slides.

13. To edit the correct answers, you can use the Add or Delete button, or simply use your arrow keys to move from one answer row to the next.

14. Select **The answer is case-sensitive** if you want the viewer to enter the answer with the exact capitalization that you've specified. In other words, if you select this check box and have "Home" as a possible answer, the answer "home" would be considered incorrect. Ensure this box is not checked to allow both "Home" and "home" as correct answers.

15. Click **OK** to close the Blank Answer window and return to the New fill-in-the-blank question window. You can open the Blank Answer window again later if you need to by highlighting the answer and clicking on the **Edit Blank** button. Note that the question window displays only the correct answers.

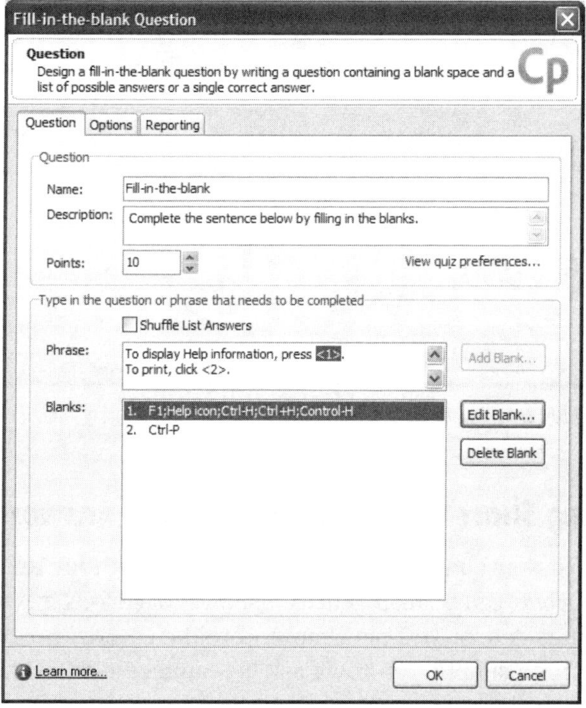

Figure 10-11. Correct answers display in the Blanks box.

16. Repeat steps 10 through 15 for each blank you want included in this question.

17. You may set options for this question as described in a later section in this chapter, or you can leave the default settings so that all your questions will act the same way.

18. You may set reporting options for this question as described later in this chapter.
19. Click **OK** when you are done to display the new question slide.

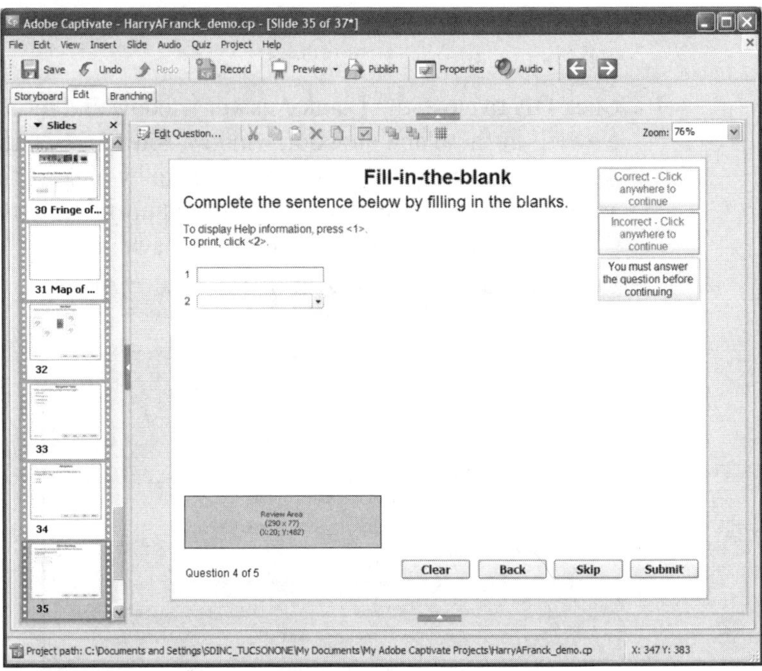

Figure 10-12. A fill-in-the-blank question slide.

Defining Short Answer Questions and Answers

A short answer question requires that the viewer type text into a text box. This text can be matched against a list of correct answers that you've provided, or you can simply store the entered text with the quiz results. For example, you could ask for comments or let the viewer submit suggestions with a short answer.

To add a short answer question slide, follow these steps:

1. In either Storyboard or Edit view, choose where you want the slide to be placed by selecting the slide just before the question. Captivate will insert the new slide immediately after the selected slide.

2. From the Insert menu, choose **Slide** and then **Question Slide** to display the list of question slide types.

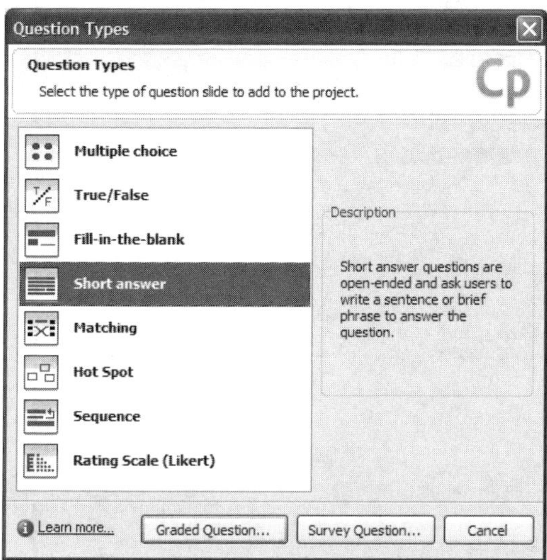

Figure 10-13. Select from the list of question types.

3. Click **Short answer** from the list.
4. Specify whether this question will be graded (that is, part of a quiz) or not by choosing either **Graded Question** or **Survey Question.** Survey question results will be tabulated, but they will not be used to determine a score for the viewer. Once you've clicked either of these buttons, the Question Types window closes and displays the appropriate New short answer question window.

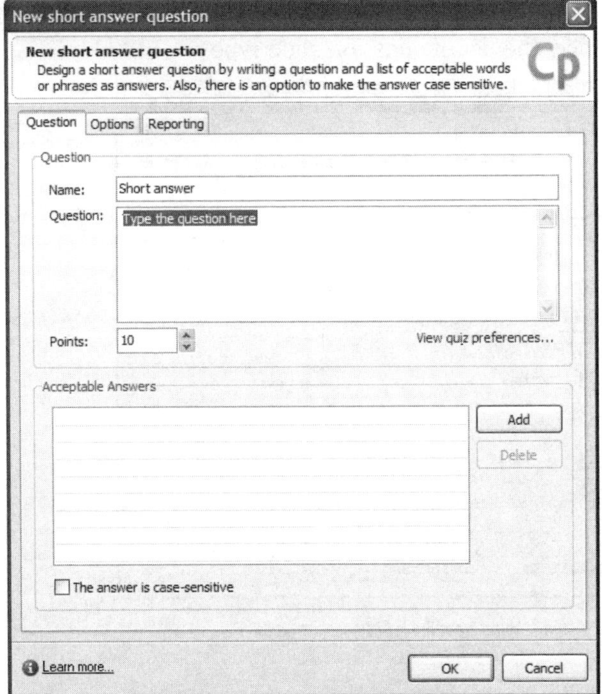

Figure 10-14. Enter a question and (optional) multiple answers.

5. Enter a name in the Name box. This text will be displayed across the top of the slide when the movie is played. It won't be stored or tracked anywhere else.

Tip: You can type unique names for each question, or you can use the name to categorize your questions for the viewer. For example, you might have the first few questions (regardless of question type) named Navigation Tasks, the next few named Message Board, and the final ones named Feedback (or whatever categories fit your movie).

6. Type the question, exactly as you want it to display, in the Question box. You can include text, numbers, and special characters including punctuation, and you may include instructions if necessary.

7. If you specified a graded question, you can enter a number in the Points box to indicate the value or weight of the question within the context of the quiz. If you specified a survey question, this box is not available.

8. If you chose a graded question, click **Add** and enter the correct answers in the box. If you initially chose a survey question, the viewer's text will not be marked correct or incorrect, but it will be stored as an answer and output in the same way as other questions in the quiz. You must have reporting functions (described later in this chapter) turned on in order to store any answer.

9. If you want to specify a correct answer, you can type an answer into each of the rows in the answer list area. The viewer will have to type the exact string in order for the answer to be considered correct. Each row represents a separate and equally "correct" answer. Note that you can type more than the displayed length—the characters will scroll within each row.

Tip: You can click in each row or you can use the up and down arrow keys on your keyboard to move from one answer to the next within the answer list area.

10. Choose whether you want to require the viewer to enter the exact short answer, including all upper- and lowercase letters, by selecting or deselecting the check box labeled **The answer is case-sensitive.**

11. You may set options for this question as described in a later section in this chapter, or you can leave the default settings so that all your questions will act the same way.

12. You may set reporting options for this question as described later in this chapter.

13. Click **OK** when you are done to display the new question slide.

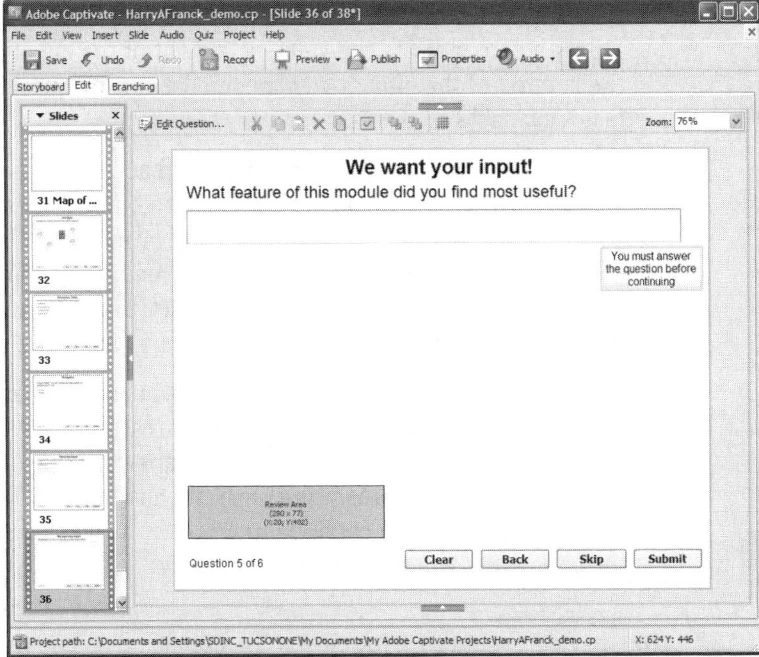

Figure 10-15. A short answer question slide.

Defining Matching Questions and Answers

A matching question slide has two lists on it. The viewers must match the items in the first list to the items in a second list. They do this by typing the letter or number of each entry from the second list into a box next to each entry in the first list. To set this up, you must enter the two lists and indicate which items match each other.

To add a matching question slide, follow these steps:

1. In either Storyboard or Edit view, choose where you want the slide to be placed by selecting the slide just before the question. Captivate will insert the new slide immediately after the selected slide.

2. From the Insert menu, choose **Slide** and then **Question Slide** to display the list of question slide types.

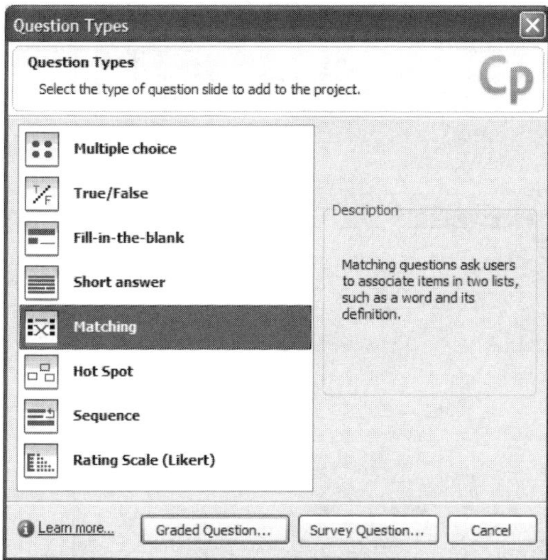

Figure 10-16. Select from the list of question types.

3. Click on **Matching** from the list.
4. Specify whether this question will be graded (that is, part of a quiz) or not by choosing either **Graded Question** or **Survey Question**. Survey question results will be tabulated, but they will not be used to determine a score for the viewer. Once you've clicked either of these buttons, the Question Types window closes and displays the appropriate New matching question window.

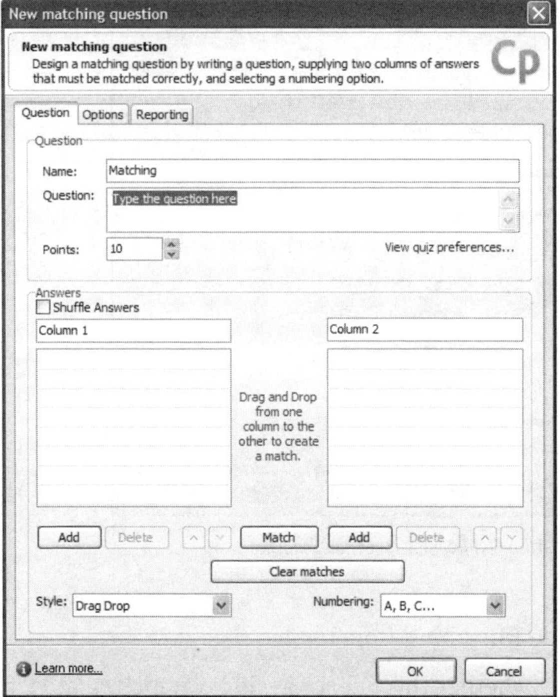

Figure 10-17. Enter two lists.

5. Enter a name in the Name box. This text will be displayed across the top of the slide when the movie is played. It won't be stored or tracked anywhere else.

Tip: You can type unique names for each question, or you can use the name to categorize your questions for the viewer. For example, you might have the first few questions (regardless of question type) named Navigation Tasks, the next few named Message Board, and the final ones named Feedback (or whatever categories fit your movie).

6. Type the question, exactly as you want it to display, in the Question box. You can include text, numbers, and special characters including punctuation, and you may include instructions if necessary.

7. If you specified a graded question, you can enter a number in the Points box to indicate the value or weight of the question within

the context of the quiz. If you specified a survey question, this box is not available.

8. Select the **Shuffle Answers** check box to display the available answers in a different order each time the slide is displayed. Captivate will keep track of the correct answer, regardless of the order in which they are displayed. If this box isn't checked, the slide will always display the answers in the same order.

9. In the Answers area, the default names for the two lists are Column 1 and Column 2. If you want to, you can click in either list title box to change these to more specific names for your two lists.

10. In each of the two columns, enter a list of answers. You can click Add to add a new entry with default text, or simply click in the row to enter text. You can use up and down arrow buttons at the bottom of each list to move the entries within each list, or click the Delete button or key as necessary to remove entries.

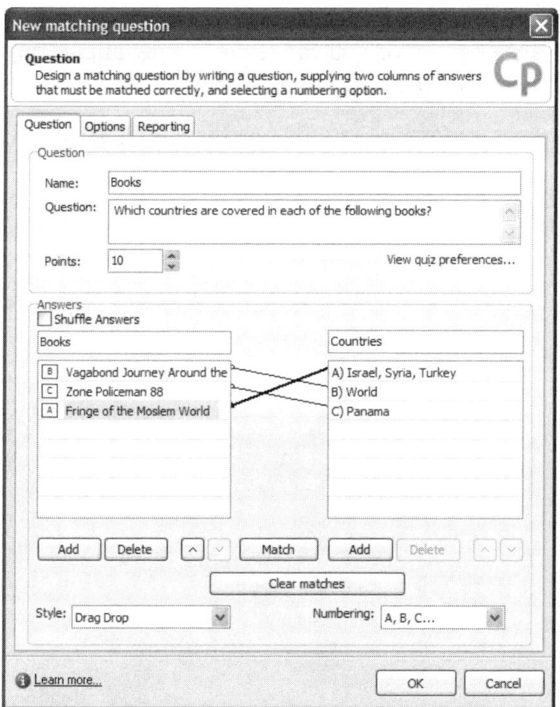

Figure 10-18. Indicate which items are "matches."

11. Specify the correct correlations between the two columns by clicking once on an answer in the first column, clicking once on the corresponding answer in the second column, and then clicking the **Match** button. You'll see a line connect the two "matched" entries. Repeat for each of the matches. Note that you can match any answer from the first column to any in the second column, even one that's already been matched.

Tip: You can also match entries by clicking on an entry in column 2 and dragging it to the matching answer in column 1.

12. Specify the way you want the viewer to make matches, either by dragging and dropping or by choosing a different option from the Style drop-down list.
13. Specify the Numbering for the questions. You can use capital letters (A, B, C), lowercase letters (a, b, c), or numbers (1, 2, 3).
14. You may set options for this question as described in a later section in this chapter, or you can leave the default settings so that all your questions will act the same way.
15. You may set reporting options for this question as described later in this chapter.
16. Click **OK** when you are done to display the new question slide.

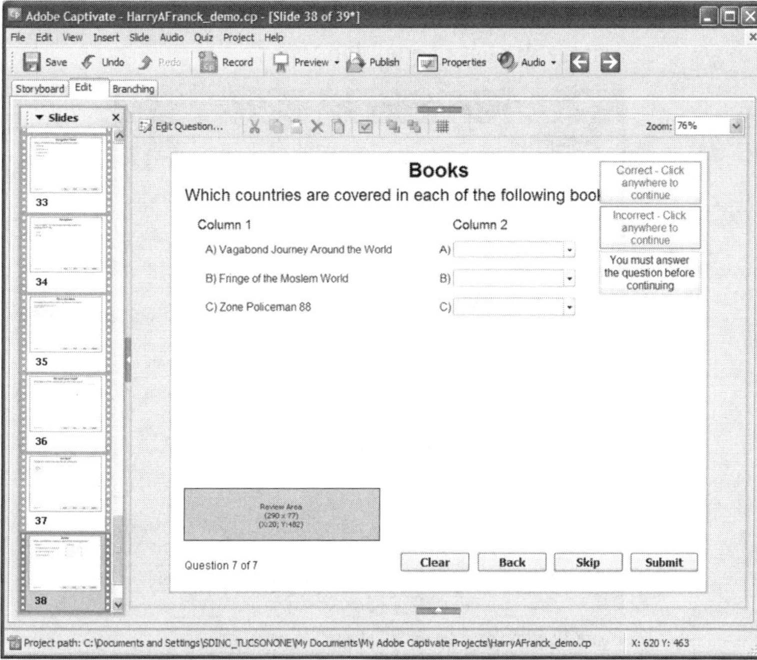

Figure 10-19. A matching question slide.

Defining Hot Spot Questions and Answers

A hot spot question lets you define areas on the slide (the hot spots) that the viewer must click. You can specify as many as 10 hot spots, and specify one or more that are correct. For example, you might want the viewer to click on a set of icons or other images. Or you might make the hot spots over portions of the slide to simulate clicking navigation areas. Like multiple choice questions, the viewer must select all of the correct hot spots (and none of the incorrect ones) in order to get this question correct. To add a hot spot question slide, follow these steps:

1. In either Storyboard or Edit view, choose where you want the slide to be placed by selecting the slide just before the question. Captivate will insert the new slide immediately after the selected slide.

2. From the Insert menu, choose **Slide** and then **Question Slide** to display the list of question types.

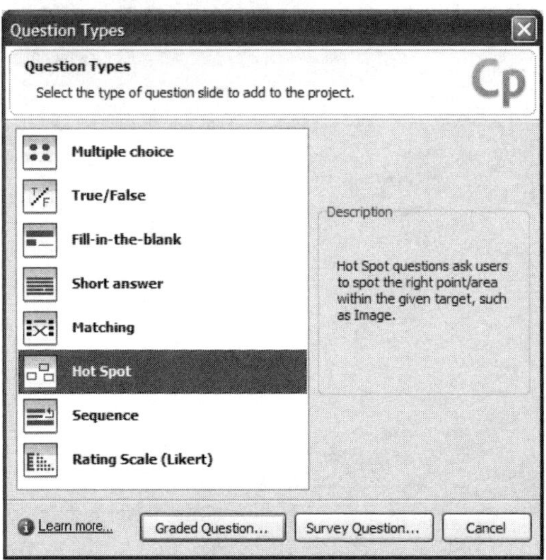

Figure 10-20. Select from the list of question types.

3. Click on **Hot Spot** from the list of types.

4. Specify whether this question will be graded (that is, part of a quiz) or not by choosing either **Graded Question** or **Survey Question.** Survey question results will be tabulated, but they will not be used to determine a score for the viewer. Once you've clicked either of these buttons, the Question Types window closes and displays the appropriate Hot Spot Question window.

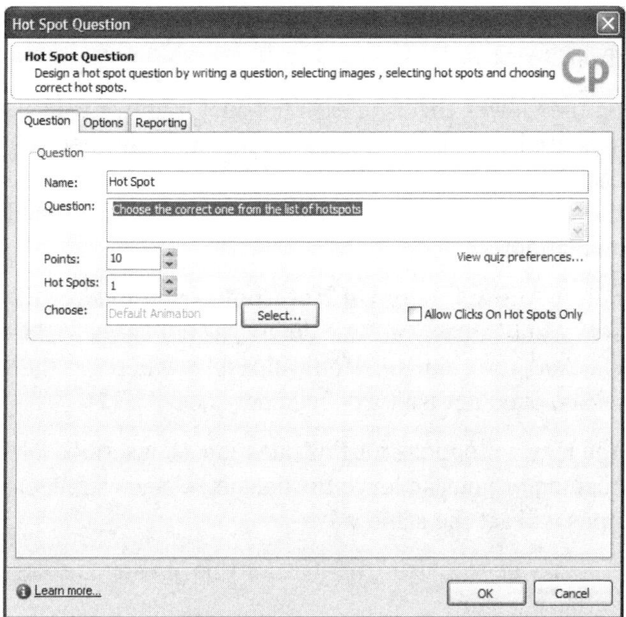

Figure 10-21. Enter a question and specify the number of hot spots.

5. Enter a name in the Name box. This text will be displayed across the top of the slide when the movie is played. It won't be stored or tracked anywhere else.

Tip: You can type unique names for each question, or you can use the name to categorize your questions for the viewer. For example, you might have the first few questions (regardless of question type) named Navigation Tasks, the next few named Message Board, and the final ones named Feedback (or whatever categories fit your movie).

6. Type the question, exactly as you want it to display, in the Question box. You can include text, numbers, and special characters including punctuation, and you may include instructions if necessary.

7. If you specified a graded question, you can enter a number in the Points box to indicate the value or weight of the question within the context of the quiz. If you specified a survey question, this box is not available.

8. Specify the number of hot spots you want to use for this question (from 1 to 10).
9. As the viewer clicks on each hot spot, Captivate displays a small animated icon that indicates the hot spot has been selected. You can change this animation by clicking the **Select** button next to the Choose box, then choosing from the list of available animations.
10. Select **Allow Clicks On Hot Spots Only** to force the viewer to select only areas you have defined as hot spots. If this box is not checked, the animated icon will display wherever the viewer clicks, even if it isn't a defined hot spot.
11. You may set options for this question as described later in this chapter, or you can leave the default settings so that all your questions will act the same way.
12. You may set reporting options for this question as described later in this chapter.
13. Click **OK** to display the hot spots on your slide. In Figure 10-22, we've got four hot spots.

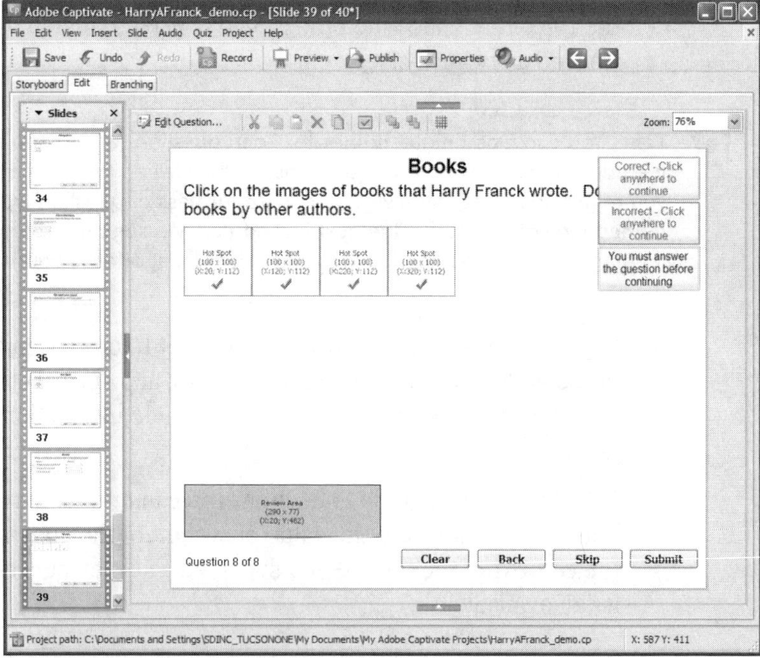

Figure 10-22. The hot spots display on the question slide.

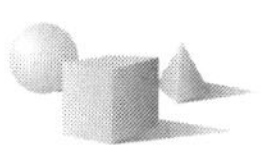

14. Next, you'll want to add the images (or background) that will display on the finished slide by selecting the **Insert** menu, then **Image**, then selecting the image. You can edit, move, or resize the images or do any of the other tasks described in Chapter 7, "Editing a Single Slide."
15. Edit, move, or resize each hot spot box so that it displays over the appropriate images or slide area that you want the viewer to click. This is the same technique you might use to place a highlight box or click box.
16. Specify which hot spots are "correct" by editing the properties for each hot spot element. Access the properties by selecting the hot spot, then clicking the **Properties** icon, or by right-clicking on the hot spot and choosing Properties, or by double-clicking the hot spot element. The properties window looks much like properties windows for other elements, and allows you to specify color and shading, as well as size and position.

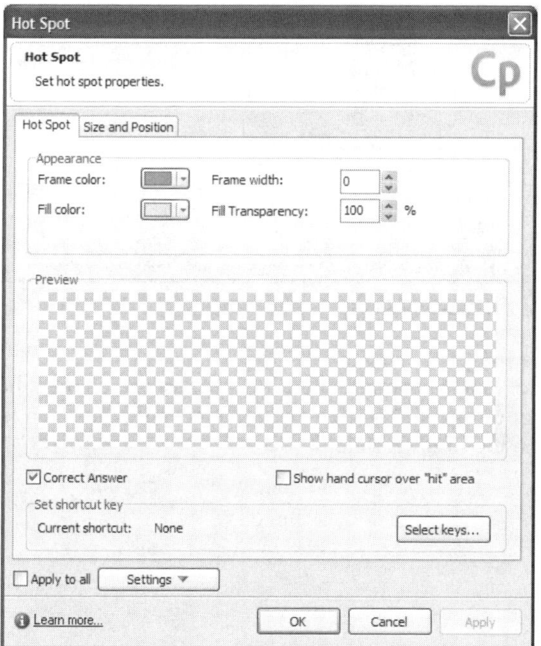

Figure 10-23. Specify the correct hot spots.

17. Select the **Correct Answer** check box for each correct hot spot, and ensure that this box is not checked for each incorrect hot spot. Click **OK** when finished, then repeat for each hot spot on the slide. When viewing the slide within Captivate, the correct hot spots will display with a green check mark; the check mark does not display on incorrect hot spots.

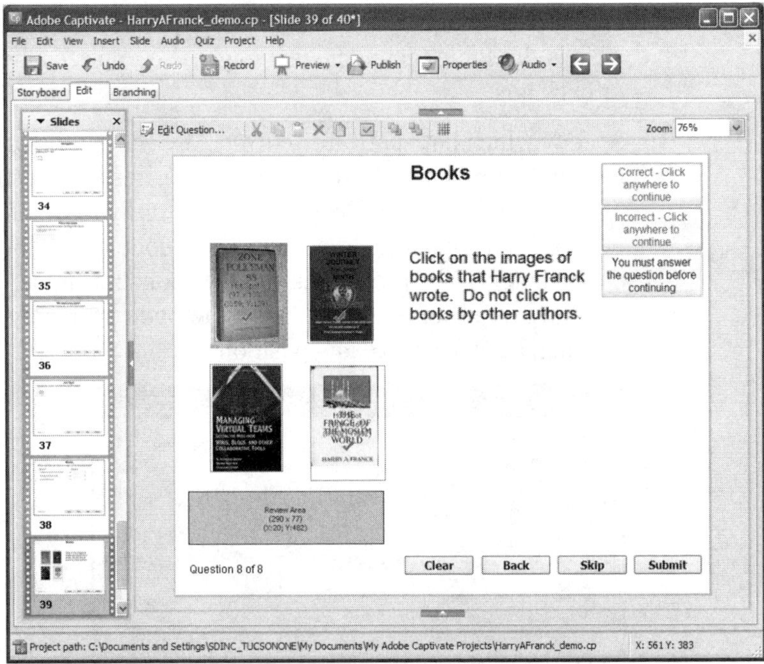

Figure 10-24. A hot spot question slide.

Tip: Note that in this example, the slide's "question" element has been moved and resized. You don't have to leave the question text centered at the top of each slide!

Defining Sequence Questions and Answers

A sequence question asks the viewer to put the possible answers in order or sequence. This can be done by typing the letters of each answer (like a matching question) or by dragging the answers around on the slide to put them in the order you've specified as correct.

To add a sequence question slide, follow these steps:

1. In either Storyboard or Edit view, choose where you want the slide to be placed by selecting the slide just before the question. Captivate will insert the new slide immediately after the selected slide.
2. From the Insert menu, choose **Slide** and then **Question Slide** to display the list of question types.

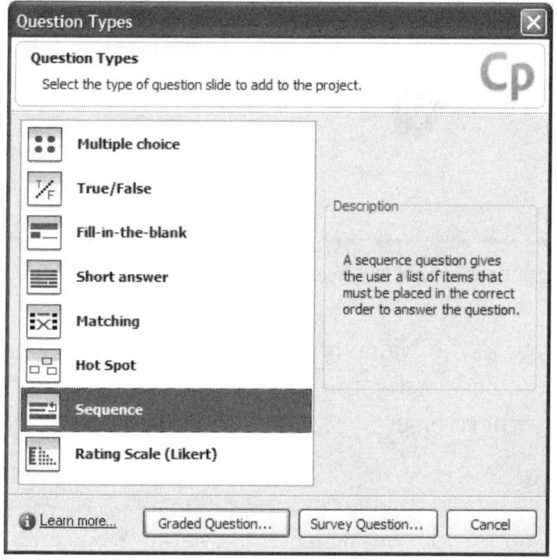

Figure 10-25. Select from the list of question types.

3. Click on **Sequence** from the list of types.
4. Specify whether this question will be graded (that is, part of a quiz) or not by choosing either **Graded Question** or **Survey Question**. Survey question results will be tabulated, but they will not be used to determine a score for the viewer. Once you've clicked either of these buttons, the Question Types window closes and displays the appropriate Sequence Question window.

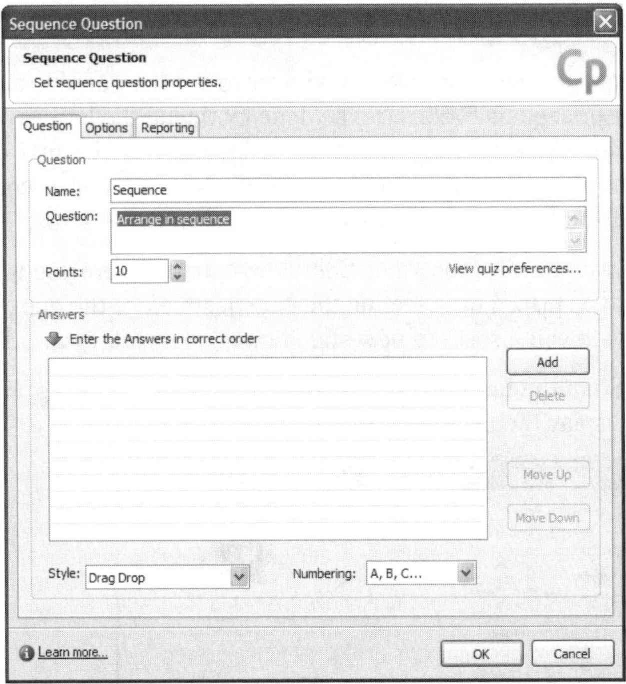

Figure 10-26. Enter a question and multiple answers.

5. Enter a name in the Name box. This text will be displayed across the top of the slide when the movie is played. It won't be stored or tracked anywhere else.

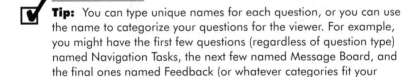

Tip: You can type unique names for each question, or you can use the name to categorize your questions for the viewer. For example, you might have the first few questions (regardless of question type) named Navigation Tasks, the next few named Message Board, and the final ones named Feedback (or whatever categories fit your movie).

6. Type the question, exactly as you want it to display, in the Question box. You can include text, numbers, and special characters including punctuation, and you may include instructions if necessary.

7. If you specified a graded question, you can enter a number in the Points box to indicate the value or weight of the question within the context of the quiz. If you specified a survey question, this box is not available.
8. Type each answer into a row in the Answers area. You must enter at least two answers, but you can enter as many as you need. You must enter them in the correct order—Captivate will scramble them at run time. Highlight an answer and click the Move Up or Move Down button to rearrange the answers as needed. You can also delete answers by highlighting the answer and clicking the Delete button or pressing the Delete key on your keyboard.

Tip: You can click in each row or you can use the up and down arrow keys to move from one answer to the next within the Answers area.

9. From the Style box, specify how you want the viewer to choose the correct sequence, either by dragging and dropping the answers or by choosing a different option from the drop-down list.
10. From the Numbering box, choose whether you want the answers to be listed as uppercase letters, lowercase letters, or numbers. The choice you make will be reflected in the answers that are currently displayed in the Answers area.
11. You may set options for this question as described in a later section in this chapter, or you can leave the default settings so that all your questions will act the same way.
12. You may set reporting options for this question as described later in this chapter.
13. Click **OK** when you are done to display the new question slide. Note that within the Captivate project, the slide displays the answers in the correct order. However, when you preview or run the movie, the appearance will vary depending on whether you chose Drag Drop or a different option from the Style list in step 9.

Adobe Captivate - HarryAFranck_demo.cp*

Slide 40 of 41 Edit Close preview

Sequence

Arrange the following book titles in correct order, oldest first.

A)

B)

C)

D)

Question 1 of 9 Clear Back Skip Submit

Project path: C:\Documents and Settings\SDINC_TUCSONONE\My Documents\My Adobe Captivate Projects\HarryAFranck_demo.cp 790x631

Figure 10-27. A sequence question using drop-down answer boxes.

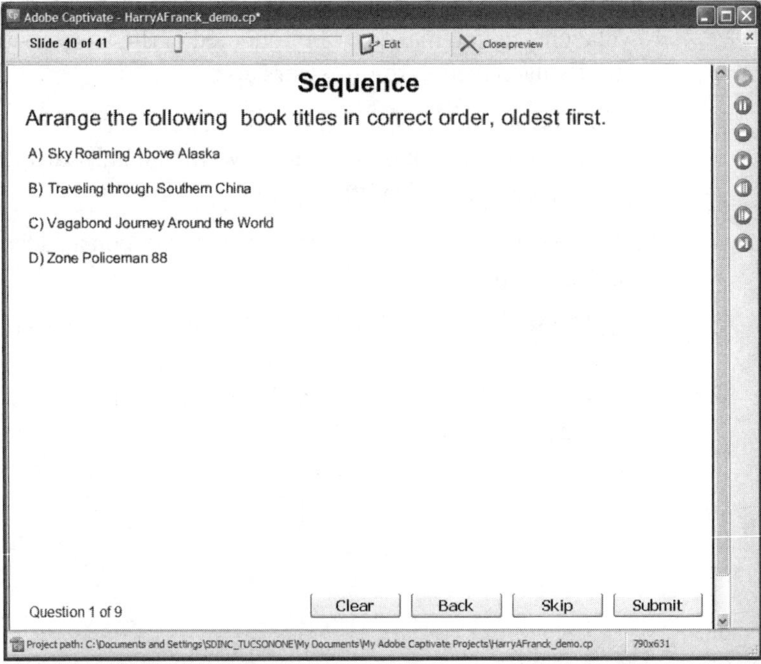

Figure 10-28. A sequence question using drag-and-drop answers.

Defining Rating Scale (Likert) Questions and Answers

A rating scale (Likert) question asks respondents to rate a statement in terms of how strongly they agree or disagree with the statement. The Likert scale is usually five to seven possible responses, such as "strongly agree," "somewhat agree," "neutral," "disagree," etc. This is by default a subjective type of question, asking for the viewer's opinion, so there are no right or wrong answers.

Captivate gives you a lot of control over how your Likert question slide looks. You can control the number of possible responses on your scale. For example, for some questions you might want to include five options, to allow the viewer to select the middle one as a neutral response. For others you might want to list an even number of responses, to make sure that the viewer chooses one side or the other. You can label all of the elements on the scale or just some of them, and you can use whatever text you want for the labels.

For example, some possible scales might be:

Disagree				Agree
1	2	3	4	5

Strongly Disagree	Somewhat Disagree	Somewhat Agree	Strongly Agree
1	2	3	4

Love it	It's OK	Hate it
1	2	3

Strongly Disagree		Neutral		Strongly Agree
1	2	3	4	5

Figure 10-29. Sample Likert scales.

To add a Likert question slide, follow these steps:

1. In either Storyboard or Edit view, choose where you want the slide to be placed by selecting the slide just before the question. Captivate will insert the new slide immediately after the selected slide.
2. From the Insert menu, choose **Select** and then **Question Slide** to display the list of question slide types.

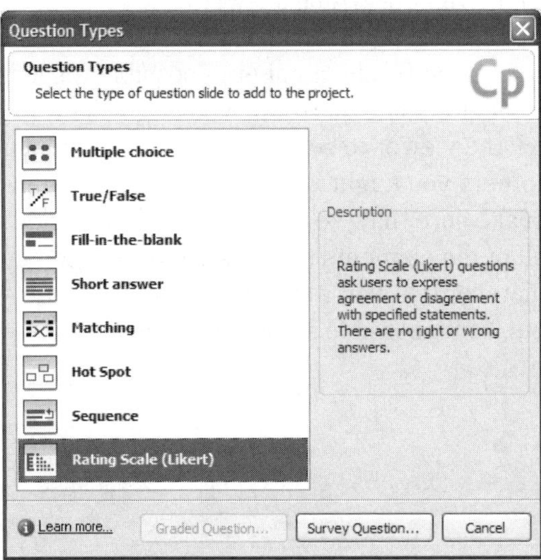

Figure 10-30. Select from the list of question types.

3. Click on **Rating Scale (Likert)** from the list of question types.
4. Click the **Survey Question** button to display the New Rating Scale (Likert) question window.

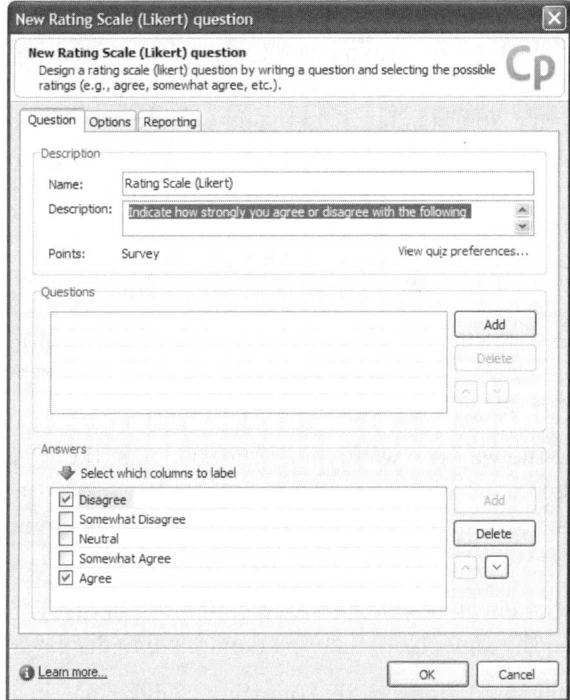

Figure 10-31. Enter the questions and scale you want to use.

5. Enter a name in the Name box. This text will be displayed across the top of the slide when the movie is played. It won't be stored or tracked anywhere else.

Tip: You can type unique names for each question, or you can use the name to categorize your questions for the viewer. For example, you might have the first few questions (regardless of question type) named Navigation Tasks, the next few named Message Board, and the final ones named Feedback (or whatever categories fit your movie).

6. Enter a description that defines what you want the viewer to do on this slide. You may also want to include information about what you plan to do with the information, since it won't be part of the graded portion of a quiz.

7. Type the questions, exactly as you want them to display, in the Questions box. You can include text, numbers, and special characters including punctuation, and you may include instructions if necessary. You can click **Add** to add a new entry with default text, or simply click in the row to enter text. You can use up and down arrow buttons to the right of each list to move the entries within each list, or click the **Delete** button as necessary to remove entries.

Tip: You can click in each row or you can use the up and down arrow keys on your keyboard to move from one answer to the next within the Answers area.

8. Define the way you want your scale to look in the Answers area. You can modify the existing text by double-clicking on it and typing new text, or you can delete text with the Delete button. To add more answer types, click **Add** and type new text.
9. Click the check box next to each column label that you want to display on the slide. Note that you don't have to display all the labels.
10. You may set options for this question as described in a later section in this chapter, or you can leave the default settings so that all your questions will act the same way.
11. You may set reporting options for this question as described later in this chapter.
12. Click **OK** when you are done to display the new question slide.

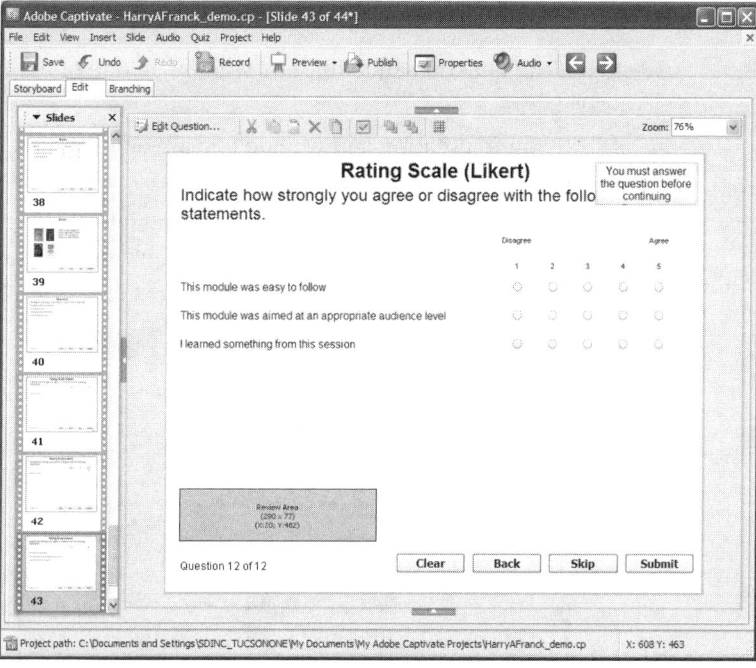

Figure 10-32. A Likert question slide.

Defining Question Slide Options

Like other interactive elements, question slides give you the option of defining what happens in the movie based on whether the viewer gets the question right or wrong. You can also specify whether the question should be graded (and specify which answers are right) or whether it is simply a survey question (no right or wrong, but the answers are stored). Finally, you can choose which buttons display on the bottom of the question slide (such as Next or Back).

Tip: Although you can define buttons that display for individual slides, you may find it easier to define buttons through the Quiz Preferences window. This way, you'll ensure that the buttons are positioned consistently throughout the movie.

To define question slide options, follow these steps:

1. Open the question slide options window in one of the following ways:
   - If you're creating a new slide and already have the question window open, click the **Options** tab.
   - If you're editing an existing question slide, open the slide in Edit view, click the **Edit Question** button that is in the upper-left corner of the slide, and then click the **Options** tab.

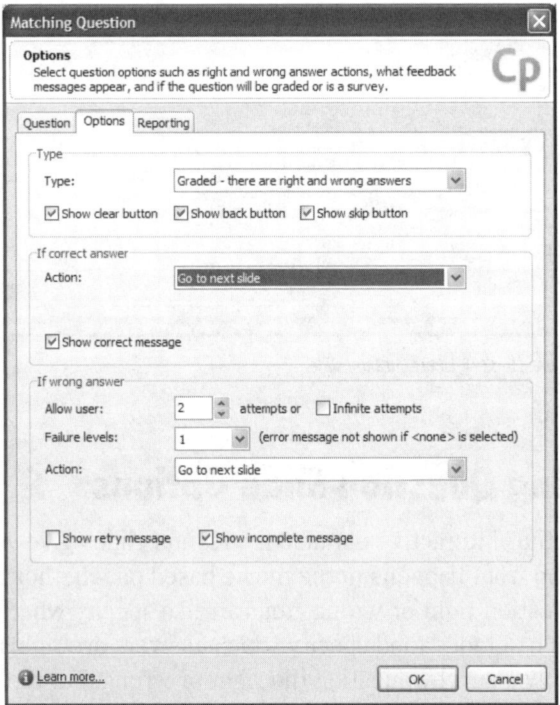

Figure 10-33. Enter question slide options.

2. Choose the type of question this slide will contain, either a graded question with one or more correct answers, or a survey question. The available options on the rest of the window will vary, depending on which question type you choose.

Note: The Type field is unavailable for Likert questions since they ask for opinions and cannot be graded.

3. Click the check boxes to specify which buttons you want to display across the bottom of the question slide. Available options include:
   - Clear—The viewer can click this button to remove any answers from the screen and start over.
   - Back—The viewer can click this button to go to the previous slide.
   - Skip—The viewer can click this button to go to the next slide without submitting any answers to the current question.

Note: All question slides will also have a Submit button that the viewers must click in order for their responses to be recorded. The default text for these buttons is stored in the Preferences window's Quiz category options, or you can edit the buttons directly on each slide.

4. If you chose a graded question type, choose a destination from the Action drop-down list to specify what you want the movie to display when the viewer enters and submits a correct answer. Valid options include:

Table 10-2. Destination options based on viewer success (or failure) to perform certain actions

Choose this option:	For this effect:	Also enter this information:
Continue	Continue playing the rest of the current slide and the rest of the movie.	None necessary
Go to previous slide	Display the previous slide, and then continue the movie from that point, even if all the actions for the current slide have not yet been performed.	None necessary
Go to next slide	Continue on to the next slide in the movie, even if all the actions for the current slide have not yet been performed.	None necessary
Jump to slide	Display the specified slide and continue the movie from there.	Choose from the drop-down list of slides. Note that slide labels, if any, appear in the list instead of slide numbers. This makes it easy to find the slide you're looking for!

Choose this option:	For this effect:	Also enter this information:
Open URL or file Open other movie	Display the specified URL or file in the viewer's default browser, or play another Flash movie. The viewer must have an active Internet connection to view URLs, and the specified file or movie must exist on the viewer's system. Note that the URL will not be visible on the finished movie.	Enter the URL or file name, or browse to the location of the file by clicking the button with three dots (...). For movies, you can also choose from a drop-down list. Click the black triangle button to choose the type of window in which the URL or file will display. Valid options are Current, New, Top, or Parent.
Send e-mail to	Create an e-mail message to send to a specified address in the viewer's default e-mail program. The viewer will still have to fill in the message and subject and hit Send.	Enter the e-mail address to which you want the e-mail sent. Click the check box to indicate whether or not the current movie should continue playing.
Execute JavaScript	Run JavaScript commands.	Enter the JavaScript code you want to run.

5. Select **Show correct message** if you want the slide to display a message when the viewer answers the question correctly. This option does not display if you chose a survey question type.
6. *If you chose a graded question type,* determine the number of incorrect answers the viewer can enter. By default, Captivate allows the viewer an unlimited (infinite) number of tries to get the correct answer. If you want to limit the number of attempts, click the **Infinite attempts** check box to deselect it, then specify the number of attempts you want to give to the viewer. If you leave Infinite attempts selected, the movie will pause until the viewer gets it right. If you specify a number of attempts, choose an option from the **Action** drop-down list to specify what you want the movie to display after the last unsuccessful attempt. Valid options are the same as for successful actions and are listed in Table 10-2.
7. *If you chose a graded question type*, specify the messages that you want to display (if any) when the viewer submits an incorrect answer. Click the check box to turn on or off the display of the following possible messages:
   - Show retry message—Displays when the viewer enters an incorrect answer and has not yet reached the limit set in step 6, above.

- Show incomplete message—Displays a message when the viewer does not enter any answer by the time limit set in the reporting options.

8. *If you chose a survey question type*, you'll only have one Action drop-down list. Choose from this list to specify what you want the movie to display after the viewer enters and submits an answer. Valid options are the same as those for graded questions and are listed in Table 10-2.
9. You may set reporting options for this question as described later in this chapter.
10. Click **OK** when you are done to display the question slide with the options you've set.

Tracking Results with Reporting Options

To set an e-learning system to track the results of the viewer's actions, you'll need to first set the reporting options within Captivate. These options are the same for individual interactive elements on a standard slide and for question slides.

To report results, follow these steps:

1. Open the element or question reporting window in one of the following ways:
   - If you're creating a new slide and have the element or question window open, click the **Reporting** tab.
   - If you're editing an existing element, open the slide in Edit view, double-click the element on the slide, and then click the **Reporting** tab.
   - If you're editing an existing element or question slide, open the slide in Edit view, click the **Edit Question** button in the upper-left corner of the slide, then click the **Reporting** tab.

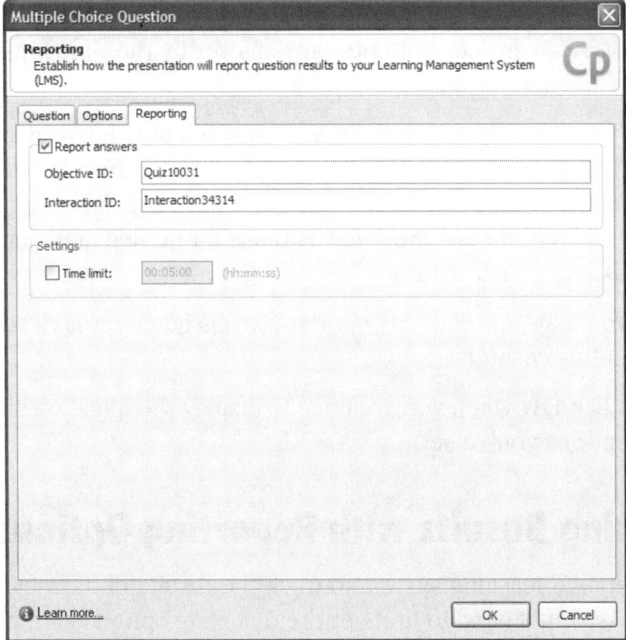

Figure 10-34. Set the reporting options on interactive elements and question slides.

2. *For interactive elements only,* choose whether or not you want the results of the viewer's actions included in the quiz by selecting (or deselecting) the **Include in Quiz** check box. This check box must be selected in order to store the viewer's answers and access the other options on the Reporting tab.

3. Click the **Report answers** check box to store the viewer's answers and add to the overall score for all questions and interactive elements that have this option checked. The answers will be handled as specified in the Preferences window's Quiz category options. If you don't check this box, the viewer can still work through the questions or perform interactive tasks, but you will not get a record of them.

Note: If you want to track the answers for a quiz without adding to the overall score, you can always set the points for a correct response to zero.

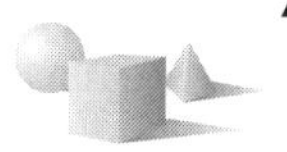

You can change either or both of the following additional items:

- Objective ID—Enter the ID for the objective, if you have one. If you're exporting to a learning management system, use the ID set in that system. If you're just going to be reviewing answers without a coded system, you may want to change this item to a text ID. For example, for our sample movie, we may have objectives of Navigation, Message Board, and Books. You can use the same objective ID for more than one question or interactive element.
- Interaction ID—This is the unique code that identifies this particular question or interactive element. If you're using a learning management system, enter the ID assigned by that system. If you're not using a learning management system, you can set whatever ID you want for each question. For example, you could use straight numeric coding (questions 1, 2, 3, etc.) or you could enter coding for category of question, type of question, or however you want to track items. You can use text or numbers in your Interaction ID. Note that the system will assign a sub-code to questions that have multiple sections. For example, in a Likert question with an Interaction ID of 22934, each statement would be given an Interaction ID such as 22934_1, 22934_2, etc.

4. *For question slides only*, you can set a time limit in which the viewer must specify the answer. The time limit is in hours, minutes, and seconds, and defaults to 5 minutes (00:05:00). Remember that you need to allow enough time for the viewer to read and understand the question, then enter the answer or answers.

Tip: The timer ends when the viewer clicks the Submit button, and the movie goes on to the next thing specified by either the correct or incorrect answer. If you're using time limits, make them longer than you think the average viewer will need.

5. Click **OK** when you are done to close the window.

Working with Question Pools

If you want to randomize the questions in your movie—that is, specify that a random question should appear at specified points throughout the project—you can use the Question Pools function. This function allows you to create sets or pools of questions, and then instead of entering a question slide in the movie, you can enter a placeholder slide that will be replaced with one of the question slides from the specified pool. You can also have multiple pools. For example, if your project has different sections, such as one on navigation and another on history, you would create two separate pools (one for navigation and one for history). This way, you could ensure that the questions that display in each section apply to that section. Similarly, you could have beginner, intermediate, and advanced level pools, then display questions from each at appropriate points in the movie.

There are three ways to add a question pool to your project:

- Create the pool and the questions in it from the Question Pools Manager.
- Create your question slides, then import them into a question pool.
- Import a question pool from a different Captivate project.

Creating a Pool of Questions

The first step in creating a pool of questions is to create the pool file. Do this through the Question Pools Manager.

1. From the Quiz menu, choose **Question Pools Manager**. The Manager window displays a lot of information about the questions in each pool and the pools in the project.

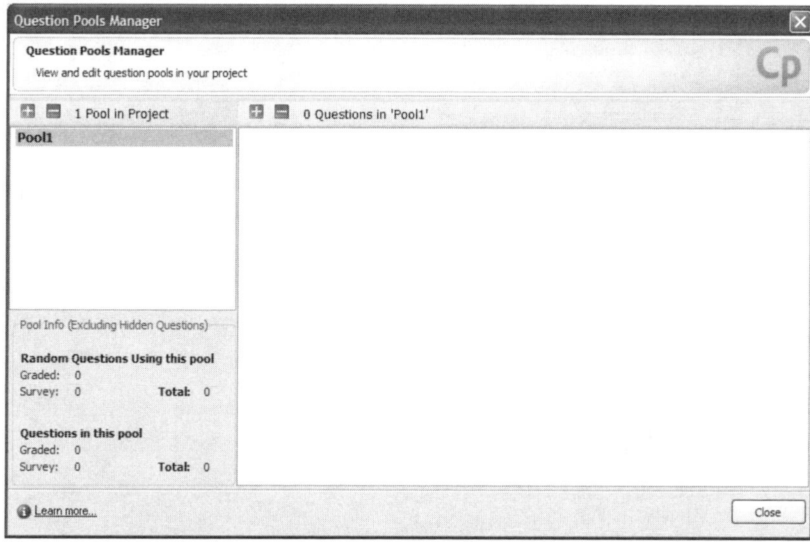

Figure 10-35. Display the Question Pools Manager.

2. To work with a pool, click on the line that contains the pool name. Note that Captivate starts you off with one empty pool file called "Pool1."
3. To rename a pool, double-click on the pool name, then type a new name. You can use up to 100 letters or numbers, but no special characters or spaces.

Tip: Use a name that identifies the type of questions you intend to store in the pool. Names like "AdvancedNavigation" or "HistoryQuestions" are more descriptive than "Pool1."

4. Click the plus symbol above the large white questions area to display the list of available question types (such as true/false, multiple choice, and hot spot questions), then choose from the list of question types to create each question as described in the earlier sections of this chapter. As you add questions, they are displayed in the questions area, along with a symbol that indicates the type of question.

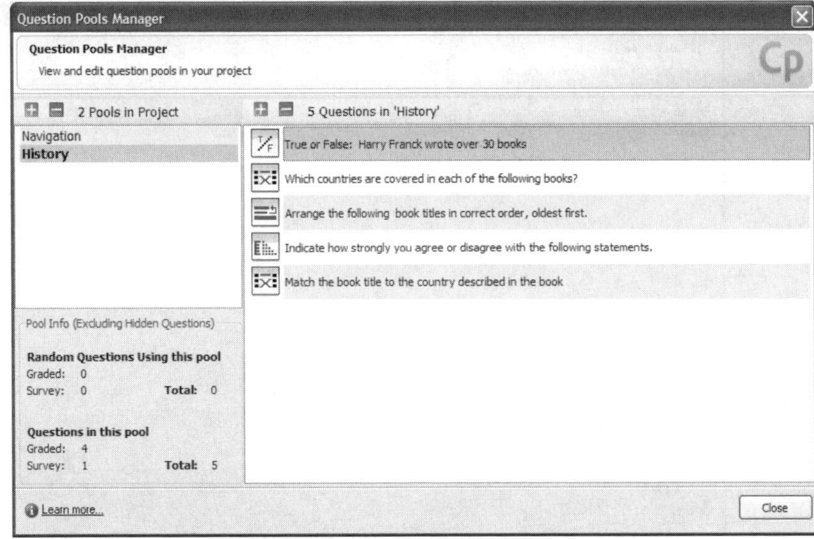

Figure 10-36. The Question Pools Manager displays the questions in the pool.

5. To remove a question from a pool, select the question and click the minus symbol above the question list.
6. Click the **Close** button to return to the main Captivate window.

Importing Questions into a Pool

Once you've created a pool, you can import questions to the pool in one of the following ways:

- Move existing question slides from the project into the pool (see the following section).
- Copy questions from another pool in the project.

Move a Question Slide into a Pool

If your movie project already contains question slides, you can move those slides into a pool. Note that this will remove the questions from the original location in the movie. Follow these steps:

1. Display the question slide you want to import into a pool in the Edit view.

2. Right-click on the slide in either the filmstrip area or the main area of the Edit view, then choose **Move Question to** to display a list of existing pool names.

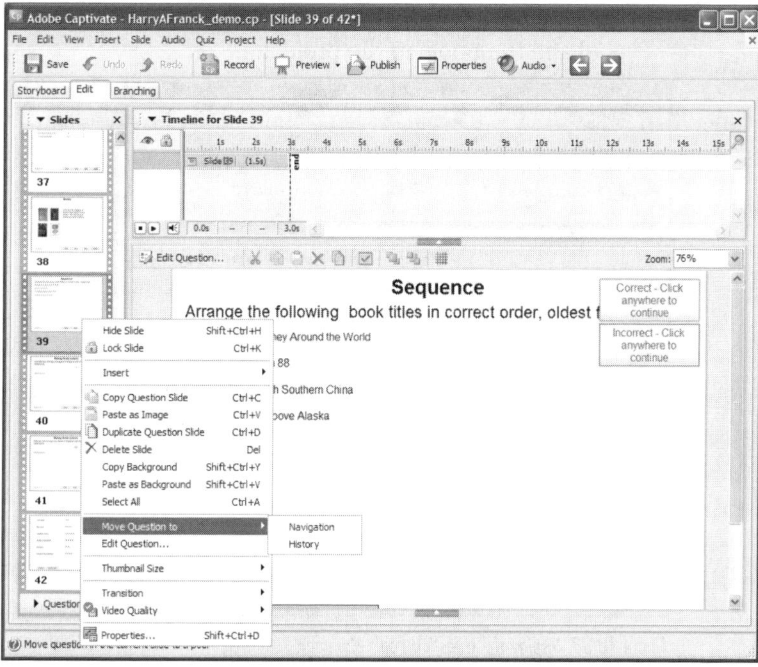

Figure 10-37. Move a slide into a pool with the right-click menu.

3. Choose the name of the pool into which you want to move the question. The question is removed from the Edit view and stored in the specified pool. In the example above, the two available pools are called Navigation and History. You can access the slide for further editing through the Question Pools Manager.

Copy Questions from Another Pool

If you have several pools in your project already, you can copy or move questions from one pool to another. For example, you may want to include all the "easy" questions in the more difficult pools. You can also copy a question slide (including all the graphics, fonts, links, elements, placements, etc.) and then just change the text to create new questions. Rather than recreate every question slide from scratch, you

can create them once and then just copy them as needed. To do this, follow these steps:

1. From the Quiz menu, choose **Question Pools Manager**. The Manager window displays information about the questions in each pool and the pools in the project.

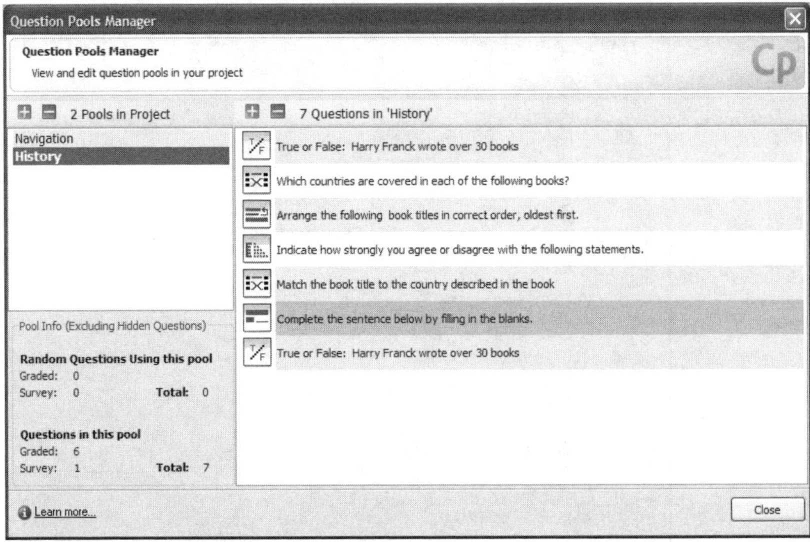

Figure 10-38. Display the Question Pools Manager.

2. Click on the name of the pool that contains the questions you want to copy or move to display the available questions in that pool.
3. To copy a slide, right-click on the question, then choose **Copy Question Slide** (or press **Ctrl+C**), then open the destination pool, right-click, and choose **Paste Question Slide** (or press **Ctrl+V**).
4. To move a slide from one pool another, simply drag the question from the list on the right side of the screen to the destination pool name on the left side of the screen. This will remove the question from the original pool (and from the displayed list of questions).
5. Click **Close** when you're done.

Import an Entire Question Pool

If you have an existing question pool in one movie, you can copy the entire pool or specified questions from that pool into another movie. This can be useful if you want consistency across your movies, or if you have a core set of questions about your navigation or company that you want to include in all your output.

Tip: Be careful when importing question pools from one movie to another. If large questions are imported into a movie with a smaller size, the question slides may lose navigation buttons or other important elements.

To import a pool, follow these steps:

1. Open the project to which you want to copy the questions (the destination project).
2. From the Quiz menu, choose **Import Question Pools** to display a list of other Captivate projects.
3. Choose the project that contains the existing question pools and click **Open** to display the question selection screen.

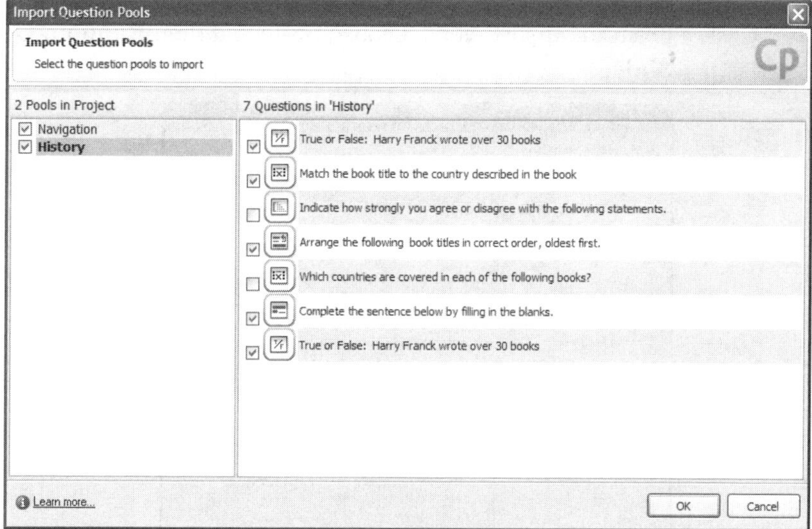

Figure 10-39. Import questions from one movie to another.

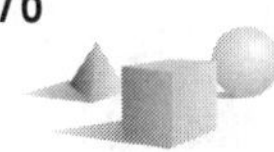

4. When you begin the import process, Captivate has all pools and all questions in each pool selected by default. Click on the pool name to display the questions in each pool. Click on the check box next to any question to deselect it if you don't want to import that question. Click on the check box next to the pool name to deselect an entire pool of questions.
5. Click **OK** when you've finished identifying the questions that you want to import. Captivate copies all of the selected pools and questions to the current project file.

Incorporating the Questions from Pools into Your Movie

Once you have defined the question pools, you still have to specify where the questions will display in your movie. Do this by inserting one or more random question slides. Captivate will insert one random question from the specified pool for each random question slide in the movie. The number of questions that actually appear in the movie is determined by the number of random question slides you include, not by the number of questions in the pool.

1. From the Insert menu, choose **Slide** and then **Random Question Slide**.

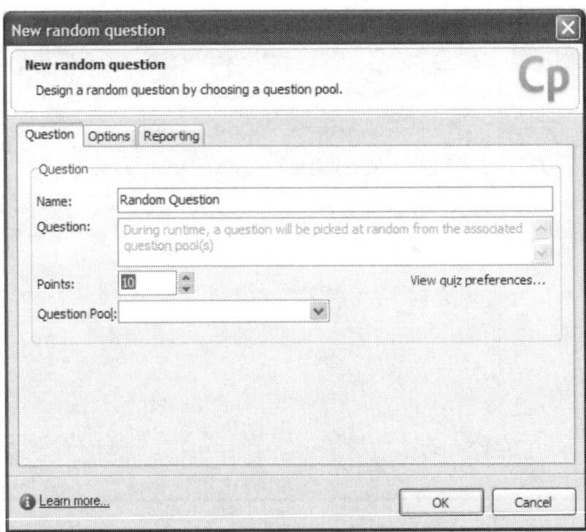

Figure 10-40. Create a random question slide.

2. Enter a name in the Name box. This text will be displayed across the top of the slide when the movie is played. It won't be stored or tracked anywhere else.
3. You can enter a number in the Points box to indicate the value or weight of the question within the context of the quiz. Note that this may not apply if the randomly selected question is a survey type question.
4. Choose a pool from the Question Pool drop-down list.
5. Click **OK** to display the random question slide. Note that most of the elements for a random question slide are defined by the question slides in the specified pool. Therefore, this random question slide will not have timeline information or any elements other than placeholder information such as the name of the pool.

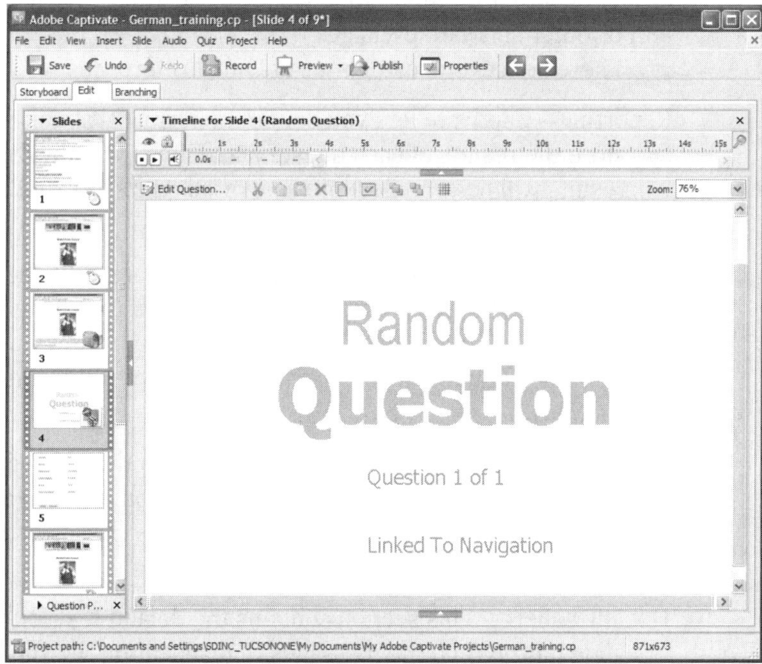

Figure 10-41. The random question slide is a placeholder.

6. If necessary, repeat steps 1 through 5 to add more questions. The number of questions that actually appear in the movie is determined by the number of random question slides you include, not

by the number of questions in the pool. If, for example, you want to include a five-question quiz in your movie, you'll need to add five random question slides.

Setting Quiz Preferences

As you create interactive elements and question slides, you specify which ones will be part of the quiz for the current movie. The Quiz Preferences apply to all questions in the quiz. For example, use the Preferences window to control the overall scoring of a quiz, specify what the viewer will see based on the overall score, and define the default text for question slides and quiz results. You can also define the format of output for integration with your learning management system or other software package.

There are several categories of Quiz Preferences:

Reporting—Captivate lets you define the format that will be used to store the results of each question and how the individual question results will be compiled into an overall quiz score and/or passed to an external learning management system.

Settings—This section lets you specify whether or not the viewer will be allowed to review the quiz answers, how to display progress, and whether or not to display a total score for the viewer. This section also contains the default text for question slide messages and captions.

Pass or Fail—Just as you can define different actions based on whether the viewer passes or fails a specific question, you can also define what happens based on whether the viewer passes or fails the entire quiz.

Default Labels—This section contains the default text for question slide buttons and the messages that appear on the slide after the viewer submits an answer. Note that you can change these for each slide; this section defines the default values only.

PENS (Package Exchange Notification Services)—If your movie contains e-learning components that you want to integrate with an external learning management system, you must set the PENS preferences to define the way the two systems will communicate

with each other. Note that these preferences define how you send the data; you define the format of the data in the Quiz Reporting area.

Setting Reporting Preferences

To define the way that the movie will store, display, and/or output overall quiz results, follow these steps:

1. From the Edit menu, select **Preferences**, then choose **Reporting** from the Quiz category, or from the Quiz menu, select **Quiz Preferences** to display the Preferences window's Reporting options.

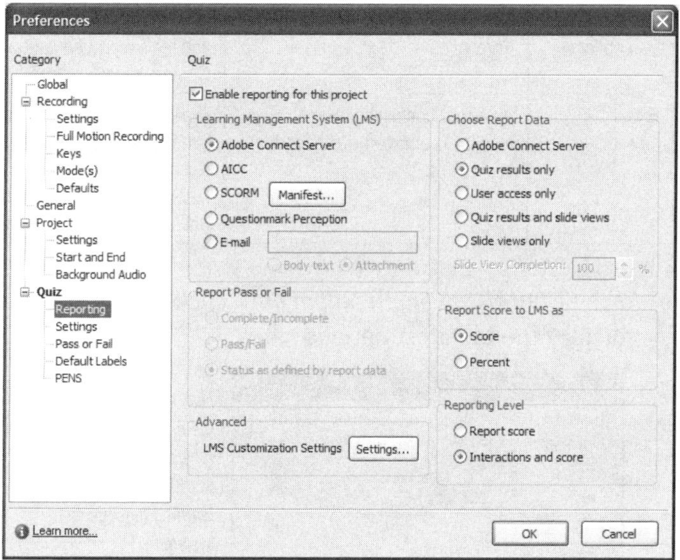

Figure 10-42. Set the reporting preferences for the whole quiz.

2. If you want to store the quiz results for each learner, click the **Enable reporting for this project** box. You must check this box in order to set the other output options.

3. Choose what you want the system to do with the results of your quizzes by choosing from the Learning Management System (LMS) options.

Table 10-3. Quiz results output options

Click this:	To store results in this format:	You'll also need to:
Adobe Connect Server	Published directly to a server running Adobe Connect Professional	Import the project from the Adobe Connect library to an available Adobe Connect meeting.
AICC	Aviation Industry CBT Committee approved format, commonly used by learning management systems	Import the published Captivate files into your AICC-compliant learning management system.
SCORM	Sharable Content Object Reference Model format	Define the options for a manifest file (see step 4) and import the generated imsmanifest.xml and the associated .swf file to your SCORM-compliant learning management system.
Questionmark Perception	Compatible with Questionmark Perception	Import the published Captivate .swf file and the associated .qml file into your Questionmark Perception software.
E-mail	An e-mail containing the quiz results in comma-delimited format	Type a complete e-mail address into the text box. When you get the results by e-mail, you can copy and paste them into other programs, such as spreadsheet or database software packages.

4. *For SCORM-compliant output only,* click the **Manifest** button to display the Manifest options window.

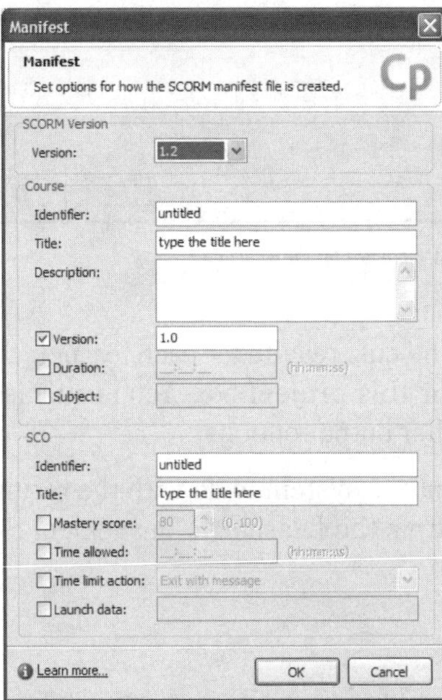

Figure 10-43. Enter the manifest options for use with a SCORM-compliant learning management system.

Complete the manifest file information as described in Table 10-4, and then click **OK** to close the Manifest options window.

Table 10-4. Manifest file options for SCORM-compliant output

In this field:	Do this:
Version	Choose the version number from the drop-down list.
Course Identifier	Type a unique identifier for the Captivate movie.
Course Title	Enter a title that the viewers will see when they're within the learning management system.
Description	Enter a description that the viewers will see for this movie from within the learning management system.
Version	Enter a number that indicates the version of this movie. By default, the version number is 1.0.
Duration	You can specify the approximate time it takes to complete the Captivate movie. Type in the estimated time in hours, minutes, and seconds (hh:mm:ss).
Subject	You can enter keywords that identify the movie by typing them into the Subject field.
SCO Identifier	Type the identifier that the learning management system will use to distinguish this movie from other Sharable Content Objects (SCO).
SCO Title	Enter a description that the viewers will see for this movie from within the learning management system.
Mastery score	If you want, you can enter the minimum passing score by typing a number from 0 to 100, where 100 means the viewer must get every question correct in order to pass. Be sure this score matches the score you set in the Pass or Fail options. The Pass or Fail score is used to indicate a score to the learner, but this SCO Mastery score is used to communicate a score to the LMS. Select this option to specify a passing score for the Captivate movie.
Time allowed	If you want, you can enter a time limit for the viewer to complete the entire quiz. If you enter a time limit, you must also enter a time limit action (see below).
Time limit action	If you entered a Time allowed value, choose from the list of possible actions to take if the viewer exceeds the time limit. Valid options are: • Exit with message (stop the movie and display a time limit exceeded message) • Exit without message (stop the movie) • Continue with message (continue the movie and display a time limit exceeded message) • Continue without message (continue the movie)
Launch data	If the learning management system requires initialization data, enter it here.

5. From the Choose Report Data area of the Preferences window, specify the information you want to store.

Table 10-5. Data output by quizzes

Select:	To perform this data transfer:
Adobe Connect Server	Passes the quiz reporting data to the Connect Enterprise Server.
Quiz results only	Reports quiz results.
User access only	Reports each time a viewer opens at least one slide, but doesn't track the quiz answers.
Quiz results and slide views	Displays both the quiz results and the number of slides the viewer displayed.
Slide views only	Reports how many individual slides users viewed as a percentage. For example, if a viewer displays 8 out of 10 slides, a slide view of 80% is reported.

Tip: If you're working with a learning management system, check to make sure the system can import individual interactions before attempting to report data output.

6. In the Report Pass or Fail area, choose **Complete/Incomplete** to tell the movie viewer when the quiz is complete but not whether the score was pass or fail, choose **Pass/Fail** to let the viewer know the status, or choose **Status as defined by report data** to let this parameter be defined by the report data.
7. For Report Score to LMS as, choose **Score** to send the number of questions right (as in 6 out of 10), or choose **Percent** to send the results as a percentage (for example, 75% correct).
8. Choose a Reporting Level of either **Report score** (to get just the results) or **Interactions and score** (to get more detailed information about each viewer's actions).
9. Click the **Settings** button to define advanced LMS options for Resume Data and Escape Version and Session ID. See your LMS documentation for appropriate escape characters for your system. Click **OK** when you are done with the LMS Customization Settings window.

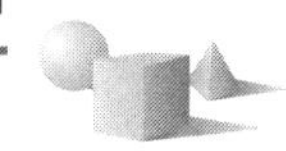

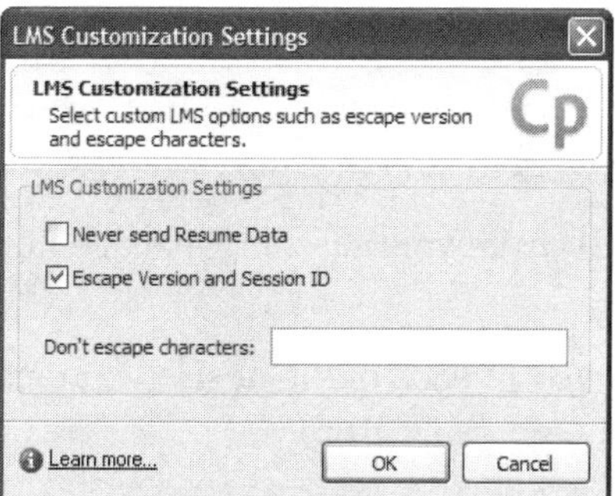

Figure 10-44. Set LMS customization settings.

10. Click **OK** when you are done to close the Preferences window.

Defining Overall Quiz Settings

If you chose to display the score after the viewer completes the quiz, Captivate will create a special slide that displays the results. To specify quiz settings, follow these steps:

1. From the Edit menu, select **Preferences**, or from the Quiz menu, select **Quiz Preferences** to display the Preferences window.
2. Select **Settings** to display the quiz settings options.

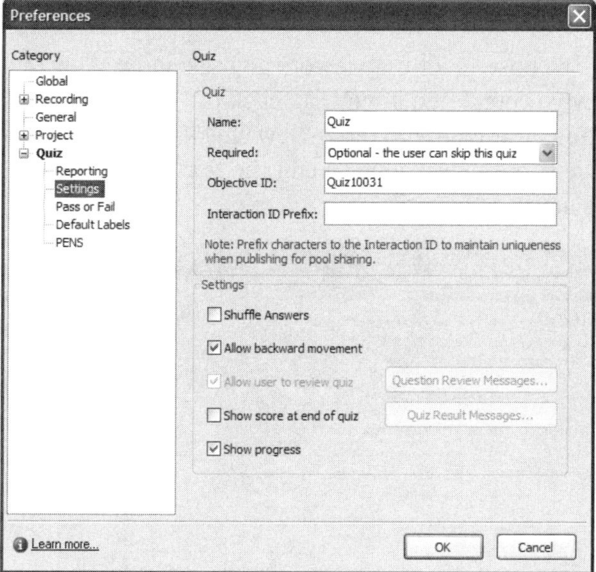

Figure 10-45. Define quiz settings.

3. Type a unique name for the quiz.
4. From the Required drop-down list, choose whether or not you want to allow the viewers to skip the quiz.
5. Enter the Objective ID from your learning management system if you have one.
6. Click the check box next to each of the desired options in the Settings area to select it (see Table 10-6).

Table 10-6. Quiz navigation and display settings

When you choose this:	This happens:
Shuffle Answers	Displays answers in random order.
Allow backward movement	Displays the Back button and lets viewers see slides that contain questions they've already answered.
Allow user to review quiz	Allows viewers to go back to see how they did on each question after they've completed the quiz. Their answer and the correct answer for each question displays in the review area for each slide while the viewer is reviewing the quiz.
Show score at end of quiz	Select this option to display a summary slide at the end of the quiz. See the following section in this chapter for more detail on defining this summary slide.
Show progress	Select this option to display the number of the current slide.

7. If you chose to let the viewers go back and review the quiz after they've completed it, you can click the **Question Review Messages** button next to the review check box to display the default review messages. You can edit the text or type new text in any of the message boxes.

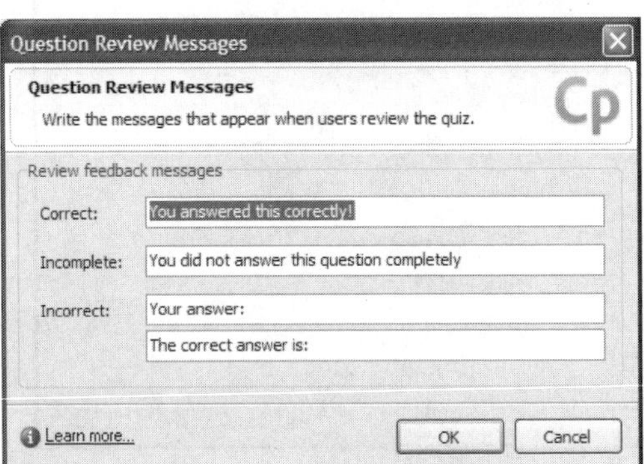

Figure 10-46. Change the default review feedback messages.

8. Click **OK** when you are done to close the Question Review Messages window.
9. Click the **Quiz Result Messages** button to display or edit the default messages.

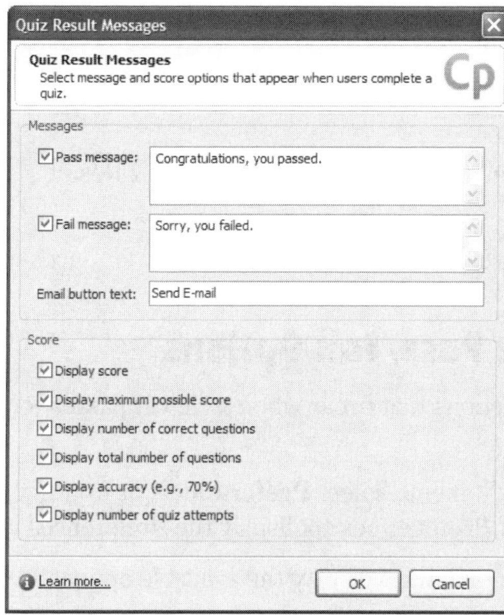

Figure 10-47. Change the result slide messages.

10. Click the check box next to each feedback message that you want to display. Note that the summary/review slide is generated by the Flash movie and does not appear in your Captivate Storyboard view.

    Available feedback messages are listed in Table 10-7.

Table 10-7. Feedback message options

This message:	Displays when:
Pass message	The viewer answers the question correctly. This is also called a "success message."
Fail message	The viewer answers the question incorrectly. This is also called a "failure message."
Display score	Check this box to display the number of points on the summary slide.
Display maximum possible score	Displays the score for 100% correct answers.

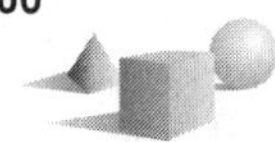

This message:	Displays when:
Display number of correct questions	Displays the number of questions the viewer answered correctly.
Display total number of questions	Displays the total number of questions displayed. Note that if the quiz includes branching, this number may vary for each movie.
Display accuracy	Displays the percentage of correct answers.
Display number of quiz attempts	Indicates how many times the viewer has taken the quiz.

11. When you finish, click **OK** to close the Quiz Result Messages window.
12. Click **OK** to close the Preferences window for quiz settings.

Defining the Pass/Fail Options

To specify the actions that occur when a viewer passes (or fails) a quiz, follow these steps:

1. From the Edit menu, select **Preferences**, or from the Quiz menu, select **Quiz Preferences** to display the Preferences window.
2. Select **Pass or Fail** to display the available options.

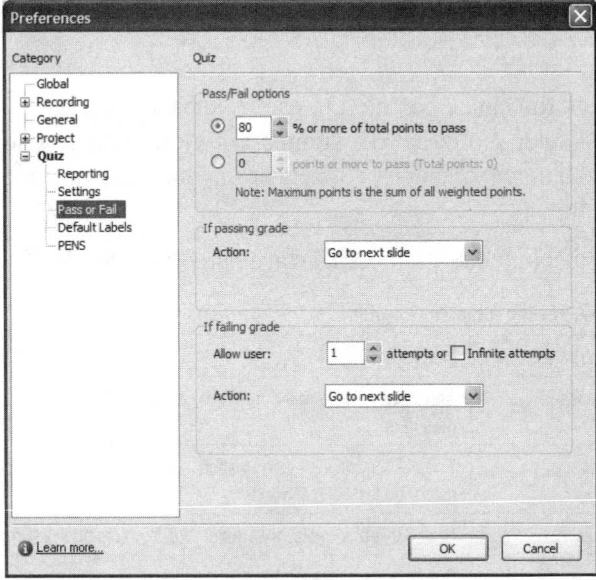

Figure 10-48. Change the default review pass or fail messages.

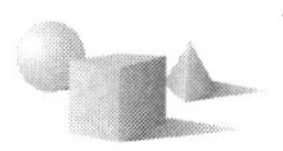

3. Specify the lowest percentage that will be considered a passing score OR specify the total number of points that constitute a passing score.

4. Specify what you want the movie to display when the viewer passes the quiz by choosing from the If passing grade **Action** drop-down list. Valid options are given in Table 10-8.

Table 10-8. Action options for passed (or failed) quizzes

Choose this option:	For this effect:	Also enter this information:
Continue	Continue playing the rest of the current slide and the rest of the movie.	None necessary
Go to previous slide	Display the previous slide, and then continue the movie from that point, even if all the actions for the current slide have not yet been performed.	None necessary
Go to next slide	Continue on to the next slide in the movie, even if all the actions for the current slide have not yet been performed.	None necessary
Jump to slide	Display the specified slide and continue the movie from there.	Choose from the drop-down list of slides. Note that slide labels, if any, appear in the list instead of slide numbers. This makes it easy to find the slide you're looking for!
Open URL or file Open other project	Display the specified URL or file in the viewer's default browser, or play another Flash movie. The viewer must have an active Internet connection to view URLs, and the specified file or movie must exist on the viewer's system. Note that the URL will not be visible on the finished movie.	Enter the URL or file name, or browse to the location of the file by clicking the button with three dots (...). For movies, you can also choose from a drop-down list. Click the black triangle button to choose the type of window in which the URL or file will display. Valid options are Current, New, Top, or Parent.
Send e-mail to	Create an e-mail message to send to a specified address in the viewer's default e-mail program. The viewer will still have to hit Send.	Enter the e-mail address to which you want the e-mail sent. Click the check box to indicate whether or not the current movie should continue playing.
Execute JavaScript	Run JavaScript commands.	Enter the JavaScript code you want to run.
No Action	Take no action, not even continue the movie.	None necessary

5. Enter the number of times the viewer can attempt to take a quiz. By default, Captivate allows the viewer an unlimited (infinite)

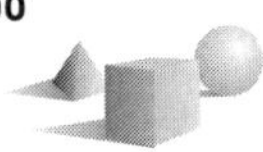

number of tries. If you want to limit the number of attempts, deselect the **Infinite attempts** check box, and then specify the number. If you leave Infinite attempts selected, the movie will pause until the viewer gets it right. If you specified a number of attempts, choose an option from the If failing grade **Action** drop-down list to specify what you want the movie to display after the last unsuccessful attempt. Valid options are the same as for successful actions and are listed in Table 10-8.

6. When you finish, click **OK** to close the Preferences window.

Defining the Default Buttons and Messages

To specify the default messages and the button text that display on question slides, follow these steps:

1. From the Edit menu, select **Preferences**, or from the Quiz menu, select **Quiz Preferences** to display the Preferences window.
2. Select **Default Labels** to display the default button text and message options.

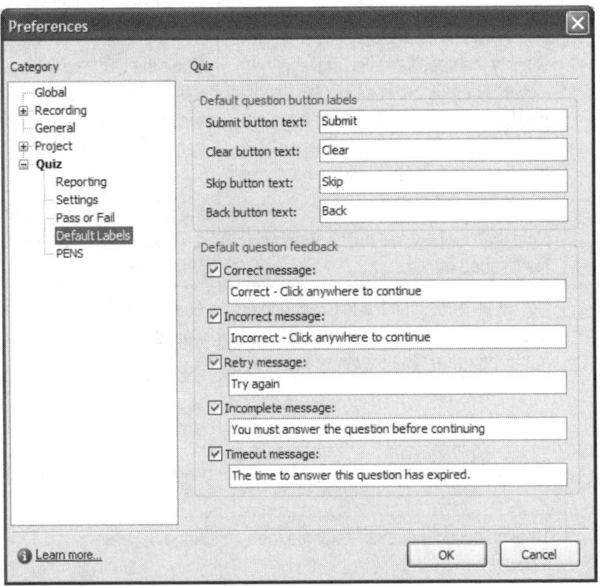

Figure 10-49. Set the default button text and feedback messages.

3. If you have the movie review buttons displayed, Captivate automatically uses the text in these default button fields. You can type new text for the buttons if you like.

Tip: It's best not to get too creative with button names. You want to ensure that the viewers understand the intent of the buttons right away.

4. Click the check box next to each feedback message that you want to display. You can edit the text in individual slides, or you can edit the text for each message here; all subsequent messages of that type will use your new text. Available feedback messages are listed in Table 10-9.

Table 10-9. Feedback message options

This message:	Displays when:
Correct message	The viewer answers the question correctly. This is also called a "success message."
Incorrect message	The viewer answers the question incorrectly. This is also called a "failure message."
Retry message	The viewer answers the question incorrectly, but there are remaining attempts available.
Incomplete message	The viewer does not answer the question at all or does not answer all portions of the question.
Timeout message	The viewer does not answer the question in the allotted amount of time.

5. When you finish, click **OK** to close the Preferences window.

Editing Question Slides

Captivate question slides are like other types of slides in that they have a background and a variety of elements placed on top of the background. You can add elements such as text captions or images and move any of these elements around as needed. You can also change the font, re-enter text, or align the elements with other objects on the slide as described in Chapter 7.

The true power of question slides, though, is that you don't have to create all the elements individually. When you create a question slide, Captivate automatically creates text elements, boxes, captions, and a variety of other elements required for each question slide format. For example, a matching slide automatically includes text captions that are designated as a slide title, a question, and titles for each column. This type of slide can include success and failure captions like other interactive elements, plus additional types of captions (incomplete and timeout). There are predefined buttons that allow the viewer to work through a question slide, and there is a special category of captions that only display after the viewer has completed a quiz.

Although you can edit each element individually, it's easier and more efficient to use the Edit Question button that displays in the upper-left corner of each question slide. This button displays the same windows that you used to create the question slide (described in the earlier sections of this chapter) and allows you to access most of the element properties. However, if you want to change the placement of a question slide element or the font or size of the text that displays in captions or messages, do this from the Captivate Edit view.

Setting Font Properties on Question Slides

1. In Edit view, select the slide you want to edit.
2. Double-click on the message that you want to change. Figure 10-50 shows the Failure Caption window that contains the default text and default settings for caption type and font and other properties.

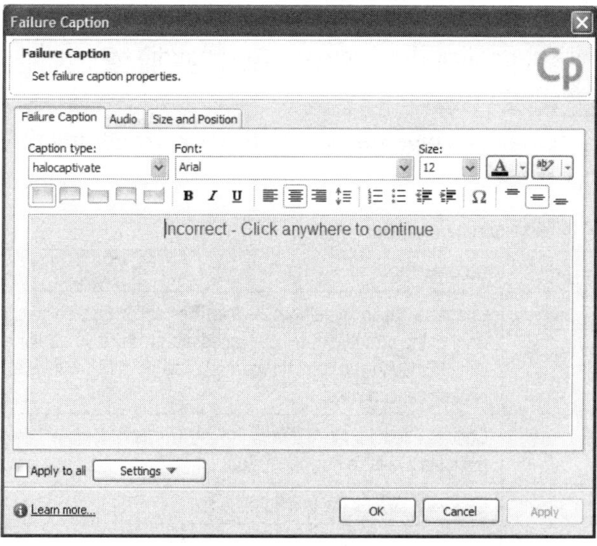

Figure 10-50. Edit font or size or style in the caption window.

3. Type the text you want to display in the text caption area.
4. The changes you make to the properties will be applied to all subsequent messages of that type. If you want to apply these changes to all messages that are already in the movie, click **Apply to all** to apply the current settings as defined in the properties window. To view or change the properties settings, click the **Settings** button.

Figure 10-51. Apply settings to previously created captions.

5. You can click the Size and Position tab to set the default size and position, or click the Audio tab to set audio properties as described in Chapter 8.

6. If necessary, change the look of the text by editing the following properties:

Table 10-10. Text caption properties

To change this:	Do this:
Caption type	Choose a caption type from the list. The caption type defines the shape and color of the outline that will be placed around the text, as well as the default text color (although you can change this). The icons below this field display the look of each caption type.
Font	Choose a font for the text from the list. The list of fonts will be determined by the fonts available on your system.
Size	Choose a size for the text from the list.
Color	Click the down arrow next to the letter A to choose a new color for the text. The text color does not change the color of the caption type outline.
Highlight	Click the down arrow next to the highlight icon (a pen with ab next to it) to choose a color that will appear behind the text. Note that this is a color for the text background, and does not necessarily fill the caption outline.
Caption outline style	Many of the caption types include outlines that point in different directions. In the example above, the "halocaptivate" type has options that point in four different directions as well as an option with no direction. Click any one of the type icons to select it for the current text caption.
Text style	If you want, set standard text options such as font appearance, bullets, numbering, and alignment.

Note: Selecting the Apply to all check box applies the caption style, font type, font size, font color, and transition properties to all messages in the movie. It does not change the wording of the text for messages of this type.

7. Click **OK** to close the window.

Defining the Review Area

Another type of element generated by question slides is the review area. This is a type of highlight box that indicates where on the slide the results of each question will be displayed when the viewer reviews the answers after completing all of the questions in the movie.

The review area displays on the slide as a shaded box so that you can adjust its placement if necessary, but does not appear on the slide. Only the review statements display in the final movie, and they will only appear when the viewer goes back to review the results of a completed quiz.

To move the review area, simply click and drag the shaded box to a new location.

To edit the content of the text that introduces the answers for the current slide, double-click in the review area to display the Review Area window. Note that changes you make here apply only to the current slide.

Figure 10-52. The Review Area window.

Summary

This chapter reviewed the components that make up the Captivate e-learning functions. You learned about questions and quizzes and the reporting capabilities of Captivate. The following chapter describes how to work with the Branching view in Captivate.

Chapter 11

Working with the Branching View

Branching (sometimes called "contingency branching") allows you to display different slides based on the way each viewer responds to interactive or question slides. For example, you could set up a question slide that indicates whether the viewer is a beginner, intermediate, or expert at the movie topic, then display the appropriate lessons for each level. Or you might set different slide sets (branches) for different job descriptions, different regions, or whatever category makes sense for your movie.

Displaying Branches

When you added interactivity (see Chapter 9) or created question slides (see Chapter 10), you had the option to specify an action based on how the viewer interacted with the slide elements or answered the questions. If you chose "Jump to" and specified any slide other than the next one, you created a branch within your movie.

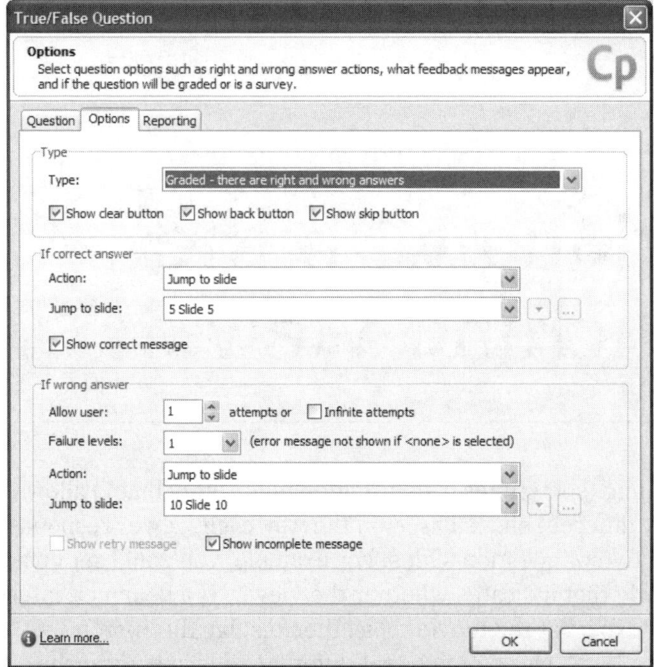

Figure 11-1. Branching based on a True/False question slide.

Captivate can display the branches and links between slides in the Branching view. To display the Branching view, click the Branching tab. For example, the simple branch shown in Figure 11-1 would display as shown in Figure 11-2.

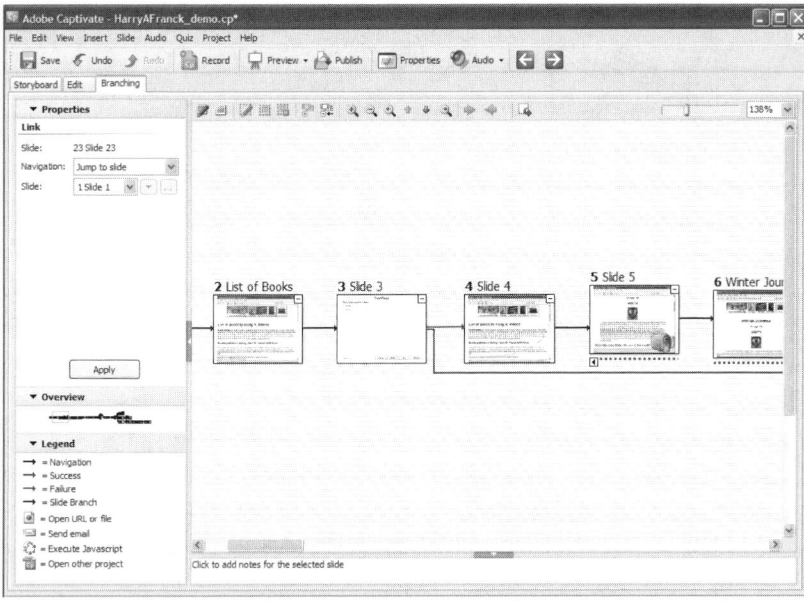

Figure 11-2. A True/False question slide creates two branches.

Note that there are now two lines coming from slide 3 (the True/False question slide). The green line points to the slide that displays when the question is correctly answered. The longer red line points to the slide that displays if the question is answered incorrectly (even though it is off the edge of the display).

A slide that doesn't use correct and incorrect designations (such as a slide with a series of buttons on it) would display branch lines in black (for "Jump to slide" settings) or blue (for "Next slide" settings).

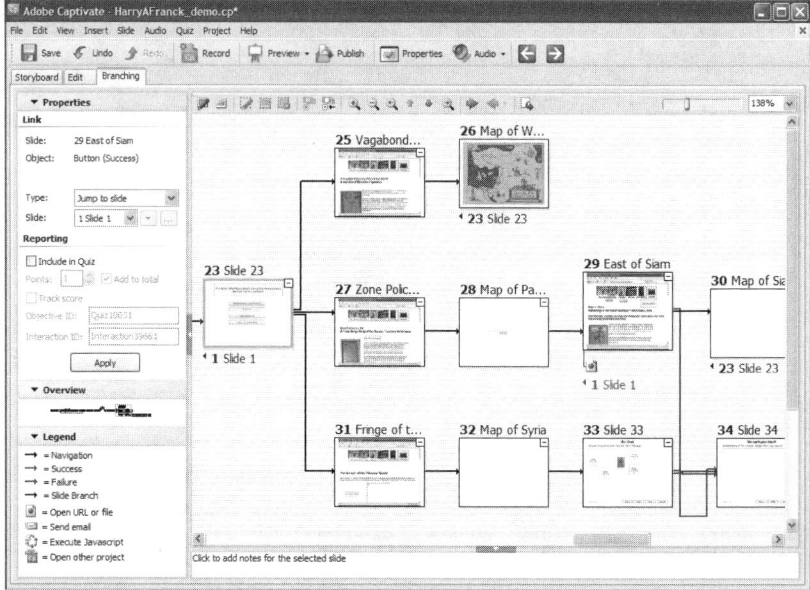

Figure 11-3. Multiple branches show slide navigation options.

In Figure 11-3, Slide 23 has three buttons that each begin a new path (starting with slides 25, 27, and 31). Slide 29 shows several possible navigation paths. There is a button that links to an outside URL (the square icon under slide 29). There is also an interactive element, that, if performed correctly, returns the viewer to slide 1, or, if done incorrectly, displays slide 34. If neither of these buttons are selected, the movie continues on to slide number 30.

The left panel of the branching display shows three additional sets of information:

- The Properties area displays the navigation panels for the selected slide or link. At the page level, this is the same as the properties that display while editing a slide or element. At the link level, the Properties area shows the object (button, click box, etc.) properties.
- Overview shows a miniaturized representation of the entire movie, with a square around the slides that are currently displayed.
- The Legend area displays a reminder of the meanings of the colors and icons on the Branching view.

Changing Branching Display

If you have a lot of slides in your movie, you probably won't be able to see them all at once on the branching display. There are several options for displaying slides in Branching view:

- Use the Overview panel to display different areas of the movie.
- Zoom in or out to display the slides larger or smaller, to the left or to the right, or up or down, depending on the size and complexity of your movie.
- Group the slides and then view the groups at the same size as one individual slide.
- "Browse In" to hide all slides before the specified slide.

Overview

The Overview shows a miniaturized representation of the entire movie, with a square around the slides that are currently displayed. A quick way to change the display is to click on the square in the Overview panel and slide it to a new position in the movie.

Zooming

You can view other parts of your movie using the scroll bars across the bottom and side of your window, or you can use the zoom buttons on the menu above the branching display. There are four zoom buttons, identified by small magnifying glass icons:

- Zoom In (+)—Click (or click and hold) this icon to make the displayed slides appear larger. The larger your slides, the fewer that will fit on the current display area.
- Zoom Out (–)—Click (or click and hold) this icon to make the displayed slides appear smaller. The smaller your slides, the more that will fit on the current display area.
- Zoom Left (←)—Click (or click and hold) this icon to display the earlier slides in the movie. Note that this particular Zoom icon does not change the size of the displayed slides.

- Zoom Right (→)—Click (or click and hold) this icon to display the later slides in the movie. Note that this particular Zoom icon does not change the size of the displayed slides.

Captivate also offers a zoom slider that allows you to change the Branching view from 25% (very small) to 400% (huge) of the original size. You can either slide the rectangular control in the center of the slider, or type (or select) a percentage in the Zoom percentage box in the upper-right corner of the window.

Grouping

If your movie has a lot of slides, you can create slide groups to make them easier to manage. A slide group can display as either collapsed (taking up the space of a single slide) or expanded (each slide in the group taking up a full slide space).

Tip: Grouping slides is a tool for managing slides within Captivate. Group functions do not carry over to the finished movie.

You can perform functions on a slide group just as you do on a single slide (such as moving, deleting, or hiding). In addition, you can assign a border color to all slides in a group for easy identification.

Creating a Slide Group

To create a slide group, follow these steps:

1. Select the slides that you want to group, either by using the mouse to draw a box around the selected slides, or by clicking one slide and then holding down the Shift key to select additional slides.

Note: Slides must be concurrent in order to group them. For example, you can group slides 8, 9, 10, and 11, but you cannot make a group of just slides 8, 10, and 12.

2. Once the slides are selected, you can create a group in any of the following ways:
    - Click the **Create Group** icon (a square with a dotted line around it) at the top of the Branching view window.
    - Right-click and choose **Slide Group**, and then choose **Create**.

- From the Slide menu, choose **Group** and then **Create.**
- Hold down Ctrl and Alt, then type the letter G (**Ctrl+Alt+G**).

3. The selected slides are grouped into a single group slide with their numbers and descriptions displayed on it.

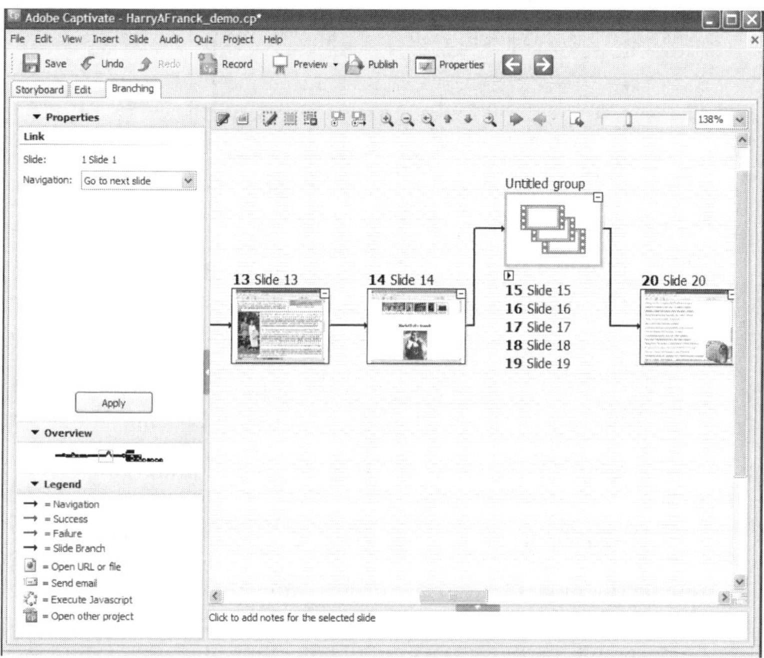

Figure 11-4. Grouped slides collapse into a smaller space than individual slides.

4. To rename the group to something meaningful, open the Slide group properties window in one of the following ways:
   - Click the **Edit Group** icon (a square with a pen symbol on it) at the top of the Branching view window.
   - Double-click on the icon of the new group.
   - Right-click and choose **Slide Group**, and then choose **Edit.**
   - From the Slide menu, choose **Group** and then **Edit.**
   - Hold down Ctrl and Alt, then type the letter E (**Ctrl+Alt+E**).

Figure 11-5. Slide group properties window

5. From the Color pop-up menu, select a color. This color will display on the border of all the slides in the group when the group is expanded. It will NOT appear in the finished movie.
6. In the Title box, type a name for the group. The name will display on the Branching view at the top of the grouped slides, and at the bottom of the collapsed group in the Edit and Storyboard views.
7. Click **OK** to close the properties window.

Expanding or Collapsing a Slide Group

Once you've created the groups, an icon for the group will display instead of the individual slides in all three views (Storyboard, Edit, and Branching). To see the individual slides instead of the icon for a group, do any one of the following:

- Select the group you want to expand, then click the **Expand** icon at the top of the Branching view window.
- Click the **Expand All** icon at the top of the Branching view window to expand all groups.
- Hover the mouse over the icon for a group to display small images of each slide in the group.
- Click the small triangular button beneath the icon for a group (and above the list of slide names).
- Right-click on the icon for a group and choose **Slide Group**, then choose **Expand** or **Expand All**.
- From the Slide menu, choose **Group**, and then **Expand** or **Expand All**.

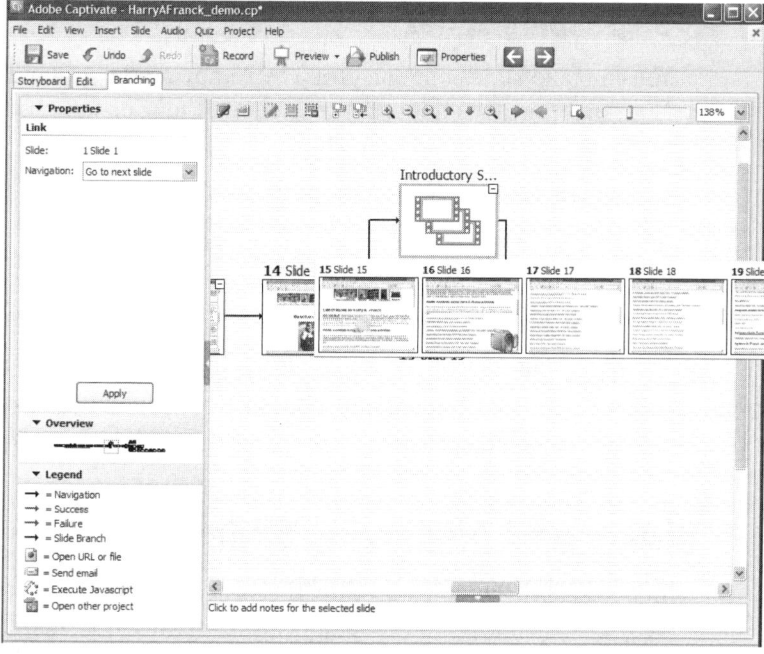

Figure 11-6. Display slides in a group with the mouse.

As you can see, there are many ways to expand a group. You can collapse an expanded group into the single group icon in similar ways:

- Select any slide in the group you want to collapse, then click the **Collapse** icon at the top of the Branching view window.
- Click the **Collapse All** icon at the top of the Branching view window to collapse all groups.
- Click the small triangular button beneath the first slide in the group.
- Right-click on any slide in the group and choose **Slide Group**, and then **Collapse** or **Collapse All**.
- From the Slide menu, choose **Group**, and then **Collapse** or **Collapse All**.

Ungrouping Slides

You can take slides out of a group by removing the group element. Note that this does not remove or delete the slides themselves! To ungroup slides, follow these steps:

1. Select a slide group.
2. Do one of the following:
   - Click the **Remove Slide Group** icon at the top of the Branching view window.
   - Right-click and choose **Slide Group**, and then **Remove**.
   - From the Slide menu, choose **Group**, and then **Remove**.
   - Hold down Ctrl and Alt, then type the letter P (**Ctrl+Alt+P**).

Hiding and Displaying Slides

In particularly complex layouts, the Branching view window can get very busy and it can become difficult to identify the slides you want to see. You can temporarily clear space on the display by hiding slides either before or after a specified slide.

Hiding or Displaying Slides before a Specified Slide

The Browse Into option collapses all slides before the slide into which you're browsing. The slides aren't removed from the movie, just temporarily hidden when you work on other slides. To hide or redisplay slides, follow these steps:

1. From the Branching view, select a slide.
2. Click the **Browse Into** icon (right arrow) in the Branching view toolbar or right-click and then choose **Branch Into**. All slides that precede the selected slide will be hidden.
3. To redisplay the hidden slides, click the **Browse Back** icon (left arrow) or right-click on the first displayed slide and choose **Browse Back**.

Hiding or Displaying Slides after a Specified Slide

Each slide icon has either a plus sign or a minus sign in the upper-right corner. When the minus sign is displayed, all slides subsequent to that slide are also displayed. If you see a plus sign, that indicates that the subsequent slides are temporarily hidden. To hide or redisplay slides, follow these steps:

1. From the Branching view, select a slide. In Figure 11-7, slide 27 is selected.

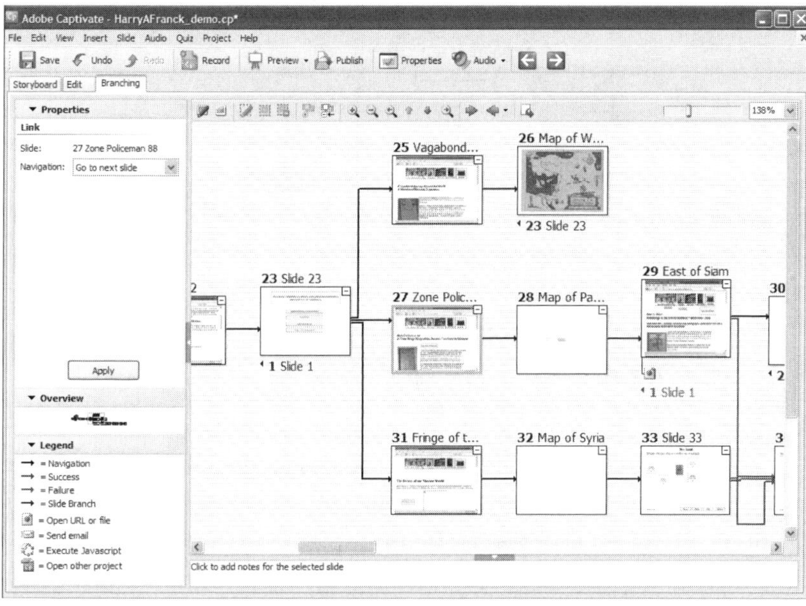

Figure 11-7. The selected slide has an orange outline.

2. Click the minus sign on the selected slide, or right-click the selected slide, then choose **Collapse Slide Path.**

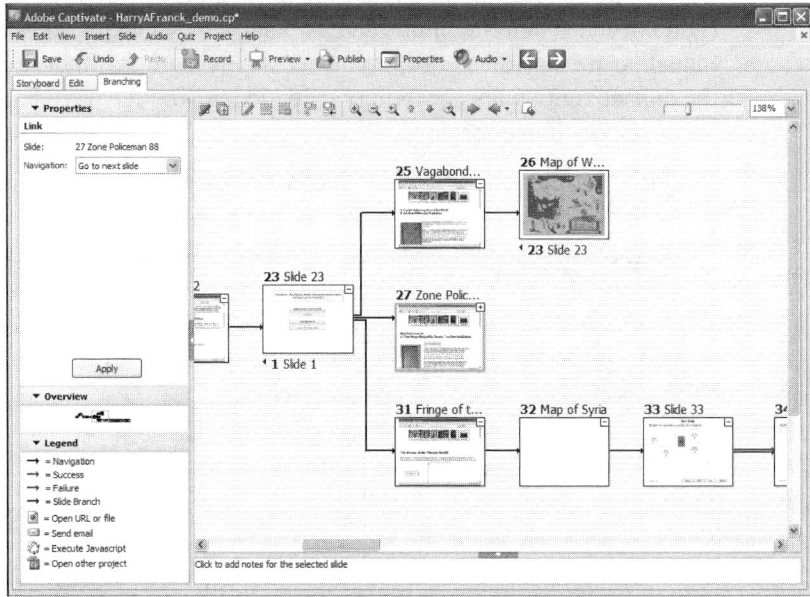

Figure 11-8. The small "plus" sign on slide 27 indicates there are hidden slides.

3. To redisplay the hidden slides, click the plus sign on the selected slide or right-click the slide and choose **Expand Slide Path.**

Editing Navigation in the Branching View

In addition to changing the way the Branching view displays your slides, you can also make changes to the navigation right in the Branching view, either to an entire slide's navigation or to the properties for specific links within the slide.

To change properties for a slide, simply click the slide to display the current properties. For example, slide number 22 in Figure 11-9 simply goes to the next slide.

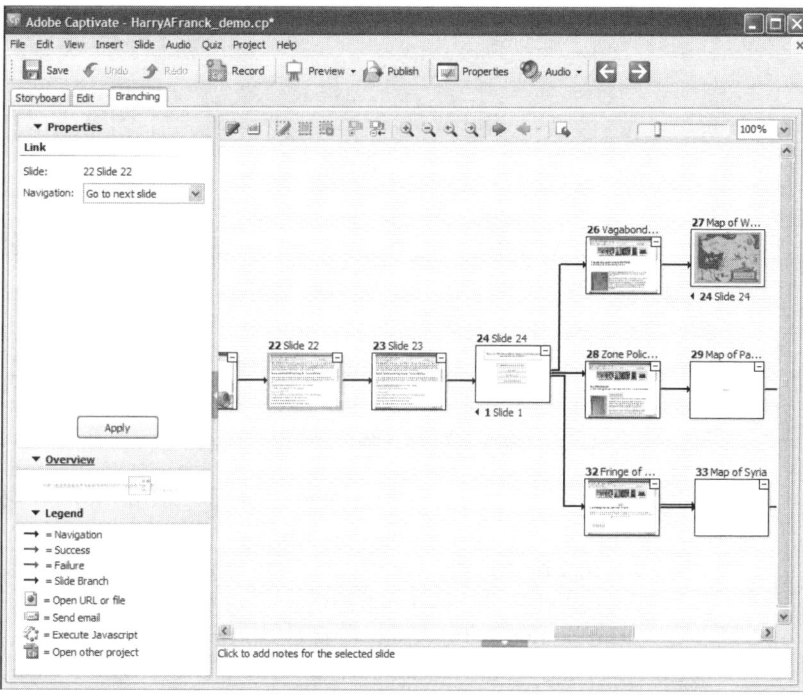

Figure 11-9. Slide 22 navigates to the next slide.

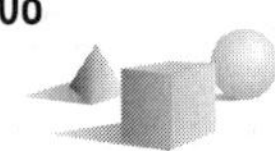

If you look at slide number 24 in Figure 11-9, you'll see that there are three possible navigation paths (to slide 26, 28, or 32). To view the navigation properties for any one of these paths, click on the path itself (not on the slide).

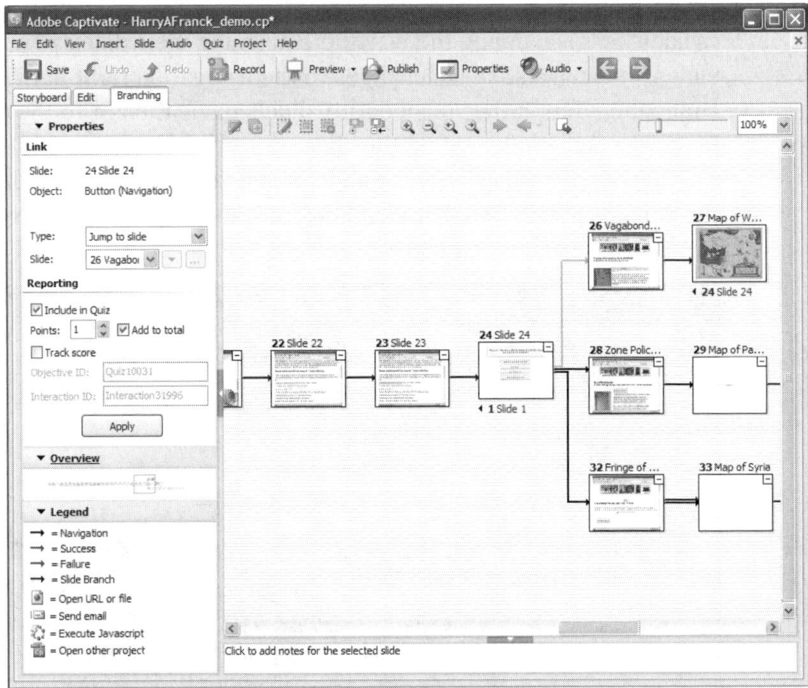

Figure 11-10. Display the navigation for a button in slide 24.

In Figure 11-10, the line that represents a specific button on slide 24 has been selected (on your screen it would appear orange). The properties for that button display in the Properties panel of the Branching view. You can change the navigation if you need to (see Chapter 9) or change the reporting functions (see Chapter 10). For example, if the button is strictly a navigation device, you may not want it included in a quiz.

Exporting Branching View

The Branching view is a handy graphic representation of your entire movie. You can export the Branching view to a BMP or JPEG file. The exported image will include only those slides currently displayed in your Branching view. This can be helpful, for example, if you want to ensure that reviewers or testers check all possible paths. If you have collapsed groups or other types of hidden slides, they will not be on the resulting image file. To export the displayed Branching view, follow these steps:

1. Ensure that the Branching view displays the slides you want in the exported image.
2. Choose one of the Export functions:
   - Click the **Export Branching View** icon.
   - Right-click anywhere on the Branching view, then select **Export Branching View**.
   - From the File menu, select **Export** and then **Branching View**.

   The Save As window displays.
3. Type a name for the file in the File Name box.
4. Select either JPEG or Bitmaps from the File Type drop-down list. If you don't specify a type, the system will default to JPG.
5. Click **Save**.

Summary

This chapter described how to work with the Branching view, including grouping slides and changing the Branching view display. The next chapter will discuss how to use some of the software tools that come with Captivate.

Chapter 12

Using Captivate Tools

Captivate comes with a variety of useful tools that help you do better work and create better, more useful movies.

Spell checker—The spell checker in Captivate works just like spell checkers in other software packages. You can choose from a list of languages or change the dictionary that the spell checker uses.

Slide Notes—Add notes for your own use to any slide. You'll be able to see the notes from a variety of places within Captivate, but they won't be visible to the viewer once the movie is published. You can use these notes as references when editing or reviewing your movies, or as a guide when you're narrating. You can even print the notes.

Templates—Once you've got a movie with all the settings you like, you can save it as a template. Then, when you start a new movie, use the template to ensure consistency across projects. You'll also save time since you won't have to reset all the movie parameters.

Sizing tools—Anytime you're delivering electronic information, you need to be aware of your file size and the size of the images on the screen. Captivate has a couple of functions that help you manage your movie size.

MenuBuilder—This tool creates a special slide that points to multiple Captivate movies and works like—that's right!—a menu.

User Assistance—Of course, Captivate comes with online documentation that you can access either as PDF files or online Help, including context-sensitive Help. In addition, there are a number of other resources that can answer your questions and help to solve problems you may encounter.

Using the Captivate Spell Checker

Captivate can check the spelling of most of the text in your movie. It does this by comparing the text you entered to valid words in the Captivate dictionary. To use the spell checker, follow these steps:

1. Do any one of the following to start the spell checker:
   - From the Edit view or Storyboard view Movie menu, choose **Check spelling**.
   - From the MenuBuilder Tools menu, choose **Spelling and Grammar**.
   - From anywhere within Captivate, press the **F7** key.
2. If no spelling mistakes are found, a message displays and you are done! If Captivate finds a word that isn't in the dictionary, the Check spelling window displays the suspect word and several words around it.

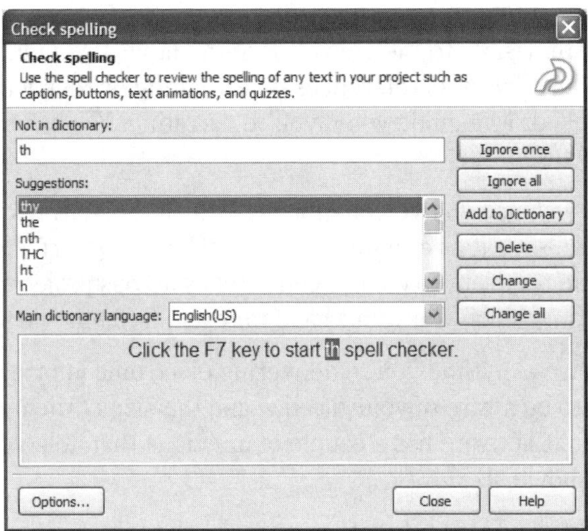

Figure 12-1. Captivate finds misspellings.

3. The misspelled word appears in the Not in dictionary box, and the sentence in which the word was found displays toward the bottom of the window. If the spell check identified a correctly spelled word as not in the dictionary (common for proper names and technical words), do one of the following:

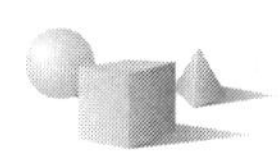

Table 12-1. Leave correctly spelled words alone

Click this button:	To do this:
Ignore once	Leave the word as it is, this time only.
Ignore all	Leave the word as it is for this sentence and for every other instance of the word in this movie.
Add to Dictionary	Leave the word as it is, and add the word to the dictionary so that it will be recognized when you spell check other movies.

4. If the word is incorrect, click on the correct form of the word in the Suggestions box (or type the correct word in the Not in dictionary box) and then do one of the following:

Table 12-2. Fix misspellings

Click this button:	To do this:
Delete	Delete the word from the movie.
Change	Insert the correction into this sentence in the movie.
Change all	Insert the correction into all places that use the misspelled word throughout the movie.

5. As you click to correct or ignore each word, Captivate automatically continues the check. If you want to stop the spell check at any time, click the **Close** button.
6. When the check is complete, a message displays. Click **OK** to close the message window.

Setting Spell Check Options

Captivate makes a few assumptions about the way you want to check your spelling. For example, words are checked against an English language (as spoken in the United States) dictionary, and words in all capital letters are ignored. To change any of these settings, follow these steps:

1. Do either of the following to display the Options window:
   - If you have the Check spelling window open, click **Options**.
   - From anywhere within Captivate, from the Options menu, choose **Preferences**, and then click the **Change** button under Spelling Preferences.

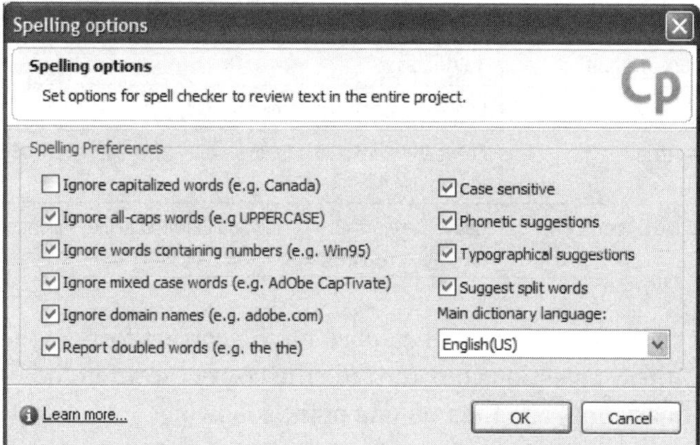

Figure 12-2. Set spell checker options.

2. Select the options you want to use the next time you run the spell checker.

Table 12-3. Spell check options

Select this:	To cause the spell checker to do this:
Ignore capitalized words	Skip over all words that start with an uppercase letter such as "Captivate."
Ignore all-caps words	Skip over all words that are all uppercase letters, such as acronyms.
Ignore words containing numbers	Skip over all words that contain numeric digits, such as phone numbers or zip codes.
Ignore mixed case words	Skip over all words that have a combination of uppercase and lowercase letters in positions other than the first letter. For example, select this to cause the spell checker to ignore words such as "JavaScript" or "RoboHelp."
Ignore domain names	Skip over all words that may be Internet domain names (or URLs) such as "www.harryafranck.com."
Report doubled words	Display instances where the same word appears twice in a row such as "the the."
Case sensitive	Consider the capitalization when determining if a word matches an entry in the dictionary. If the word in the dictionary is capitalized (as in proper nouns), then the word in your movie must be capitalized or it will be considered a misspelling.
Phonetic suggestions	List words in the Suggestions box that sound like the misspelled word.
Typographical suggestions	List words in the Suggestions box that use letters similar to the misspelled word.

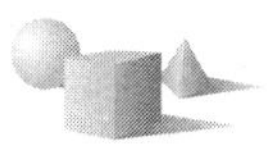

Select this:	To cause the spell checker to do this:
Suggest split words	List word pairs in the Suggestions box for misspelled words that appear to be missing a space between two words, such as "twowords."

3. If you want to specify a dictionary other than the United States English one, choose from the list of dictionaries on your system in the Main dictionary language list. All of the dictionaries available on your system display in the list.
4. When you finish selecting spelling options, click **OK**.

Adding Notes to Slides

A note in Captivate is an organizational tool that you can see while you're working with the Captivate project, but doesn't display in the finished movie. When you add notes to a slide, you can view the notes while editing the slide or while recording audio for the slide. For example, you could type the voice-over script into the notes area and then read it while recording the audio for that slide. Notes can also store information about the origins of imported objects or comments about what you plan to add to a slide. You can also print the notes as part of handouts if you want to.

To add notes to a slide or to view existing notes, follow these steps:

1. Do one of the following to display the Slide Properties window:
   - From Edit view, double-click on the slide background.
   - From Storyboard view or the filmstrip in Edit view, right-click on a slide and choose **Properties**.
   - In either view, from the Slide menu, choose **Properties**.

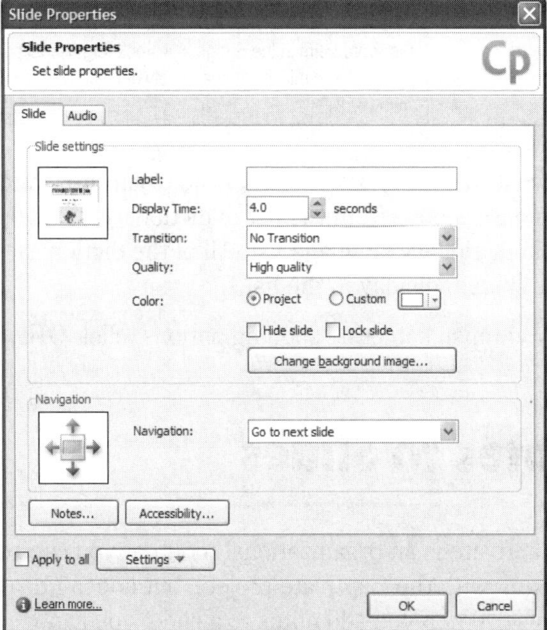

Figure 12-3. Enter notes from the Slide Properties window.

2. On the Slide Properties window, click the **Notes** button to display the Slide notes window.

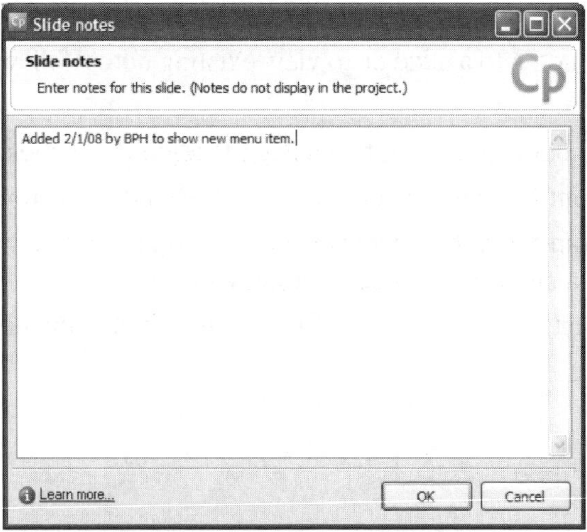

Figure 12-4. Type notes into the Slide notes window.

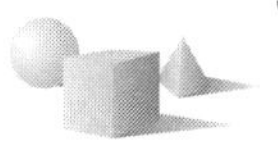

3. Type the notes you want to add to the slide. This is a free-form text box; you can type anything you want into it, and make the notes as detailed as you need them to be.
4. Click **OK** to store the notes and close the Slide notes window.

Tip: You'll know when there are notes associated with a slide because the Notes button on the Slide Properties window will display as bold.

5. Click **OK** to close the Slide Properties window.

Working with Templates

As you've seen throughout this book, Captivate gives you a lot of options for the way the individual slides look (and sound) and the way the movie runs. It can be very time-consuming to set all of these options, so Captivate allows you to save the settings from a finished movie as a template that you can use to create other movies. This not only saves time, but it also ensures that your movie settings are consistent from one project to the next. If you use a template to create a movie, you can always change any of the settings as needed.

Tip: Captivate templates are basic movie projects with all settings and often with slides. These are not the same as the MenuBuilder templates, which contain only information about the background for one menu slide, similar to a PowerPoint template. See the section on MenuBuilder later in this chapter for information about MenuBuilder templates.

When you're working with templates, you'll need to:

1. Create a movie with the settings you want, and then save it as a template.
2. Use the template to create new movies.
3. (*optional*) As time goes by, you may need to change your template. You can edit templates directly, or simply make changes within a movie and then save the new movie to the existing template name.

Creating a Template

To use templates, you'll have to first create a movie that has the settings you want. This can be as simple as a blank movie with publishing and playback controls, or as complex as a multi-slide movie with sample text and audio, imported images, interactive elements, and a complete quiz already set up.

To create a template, follow these steps:

1. Create the movie that will serve as the basis of the template.
2. From the File menu, choose **Save as Template** to display the Save As window with the Templates folder already selected.

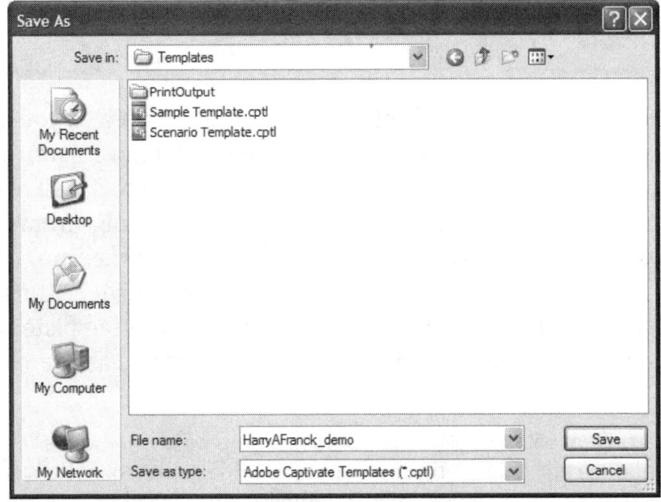

Figure 12-5. Save a movie as a template.

3. Type a name for the template in the File name box. Captivate defaults to using the same name as the movie you've created, and automatically adds the .cptl extension.

Tip: Choose a name that is not too specific, since you'll be using this template in a variety of other projects. For example, although the movie in Figure 12-5 was called HarryAFranck_demo, we saved the template as simply Demo.cptl.

4. Click **Save** to save the template to the Templates folder and display the template in your Captivate view.
5. From the File menu, choose **Close** to close the template.

Using a Template to Record a New Movie

Once you've created a template, you can use it to serve as the basis for subsequent movies. For the most part, recording a movie with a template is very similar to recording a new movie (as described in Chapter 4). There are a few minor differences:

- The size of the recording area is defined in the template. You can move the area around on your screen or resize a window to fit into the recording area, but you cannot change the size or shape of the recording area.
- There is at least one slide in the template, and often many slides. Once you've set the recording area, you'll see a window that asks where you want to add the new slides you'll be recording.

To record a new movie using a template, follow these steps:

1. Do one of the following to display the list of available templates:
    - From the Captivate main menu, choose **Record or create a new project.**
    - From anywhere within Captivate, open the **File** menu and choose **Record/Create**, and then **New project.**

Note: If you have a movie open, this will close the current movie. If you haven't saved your movie, Captivate will prompt you to do so.

2. Browse to point to the template you want to use and click **Open** to display the selected template.
3. Click **OK** to display the Record additional slides window, as shown in Figure 12-6.
4. The Record additional slides window displays small images of each of the slides in the template. You can see the slide labels, if any. If there are no slide labels, the slides will be numbered. If the slide icon and label are grayed-out and appear lighter than other slides in the template, that indicates that the slide is hidden. You can

scroll through the slides in the template to see what is there, and click on a slide to highlight it.

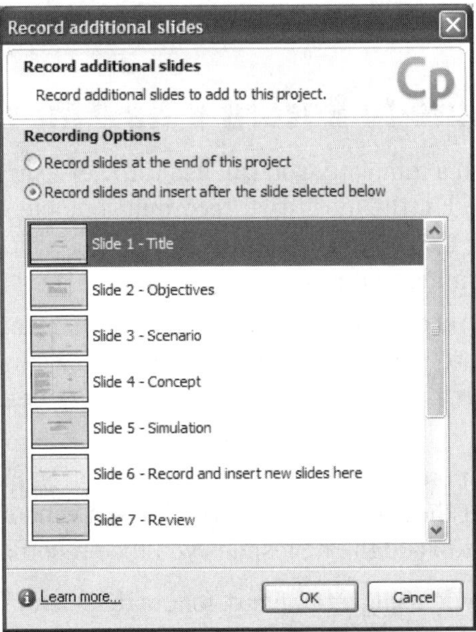

Figure 12-6. Specify where the new slides should go.

5. Click the option to specify whether you want to add new slides to the end of the slides in the project or into the middle of the movie immediately after the highlighted slide.
6. Click **OK** to close the Record additional slides window and display your own screen with the recording window and recording area outline.
7. Adjust the recording area to the part of the screen you want to record. You can move the area, or choose from the drop-down list of open windows to automatically move a window into the recording area. You cannot change the size of the recording area.
8. The movie will be recorded with the options set as specified in the template (including automatic captions, recording narration, and other settings). You can change these if you want to.
9. Click the **Record** button and perform the actions for your new movie.

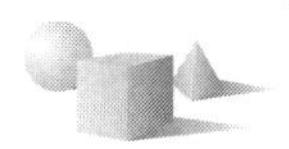

10. When finished, press the **End** key to generate the Captivate files and display your new movie in Storyboard view.

Editing a Template

There may come a time when you need to make changes to an existing template. To do this, you'll simply open the template, make the changes exactly as you would to a regular movie file, and then save the template. Captivate has a shortcut that displays the templates in the template directory so that you can get to them quickly and easily.

To open a template for editing, follow these steps:

1. From the File menu, choose **Edit template** to display the folder of Captivate templates.
2. Click the name of the template you want to edit.
3. Make changes as necessary.
4. From the File menu, choose **Save**. Note that the **Save as template** option isn't available—or necessary, since the open file is already a template.
5. From the File menu, choose **Close** to close the template.

Viewing and Changing Movie Size

When we talk about the size of a movie, there are really two considerations:

- The size of the movie "screen"—that is, the dimensions of the recording area that determine the width and height of the displayed movie on a monitor. This is originally set when you record the movie but can be changed if needed.
- The size of the file, in bytes. This is determined by a combination of the resolution, number of slides, types of elements, and dimensions of the displayed movie. Depending on your delivery mechanism (such as on CD or DVD, as a download from a web page, or stored on a server), you may need to be concerned with file size.

Viewing or Changing the Dimensions of a Movie

The specific height and width of your movie were set when you recorded or created it (see Chapter 4). For example, you may have specified a full-screen movie to be recorded at 640 pixels wide by 480 pixels tall. Or you may have dragged the recording area to a custom size. In general, the larger your movie dimensions, the larger the file size will be. Smaller dimensions, although easier to download, may be more difficult for viewers to see.

You can view the current dimensions of the movie in the Information area on the bottom of the left panel of the Storyboard view. For example, the movie in Figure 12-7 is a custom size of 790 x 631.

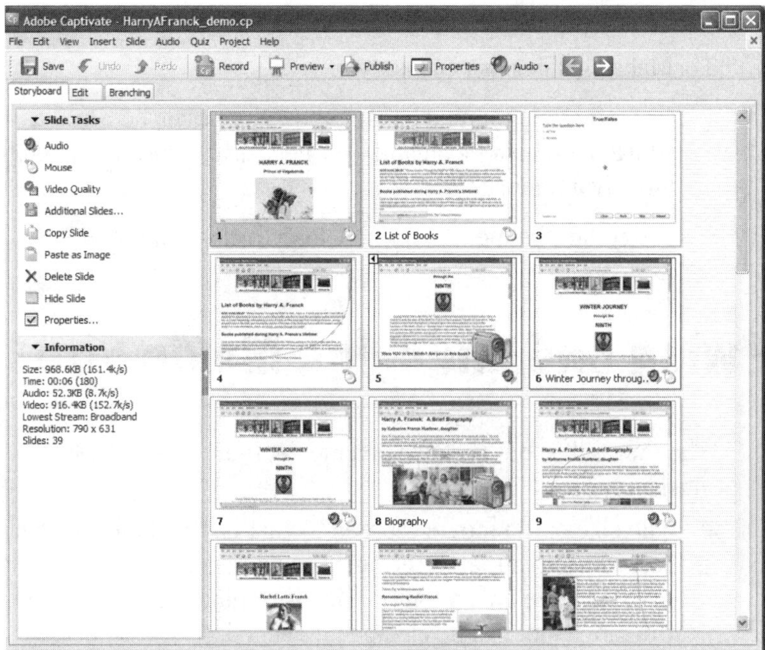

Figure 12-7. View the movie dimensions in Storyboard view.

Tip: Changing dimensions cannot be undone, so you should always make a backup of the movie before using this function.

Tip: When you reduce the dimensions of a movie, the image density is adjusted to be appropriate for the new movie size. If you are trying to enlarge a movie that had been reduced in the past, you may run into image quality problems. If you've saved the images (by themselves or in a backup of the original movie), you can import original quality images into the movie after enlarging it.

You can change the dimensions of a movie by following these steps:

1. From the Project menu, select **Resize Project** to display the Project resize window and view the current movie dimensions.
2. To change the dimensions of the movie, choose either **User defined (custom)** or **Preset size**.

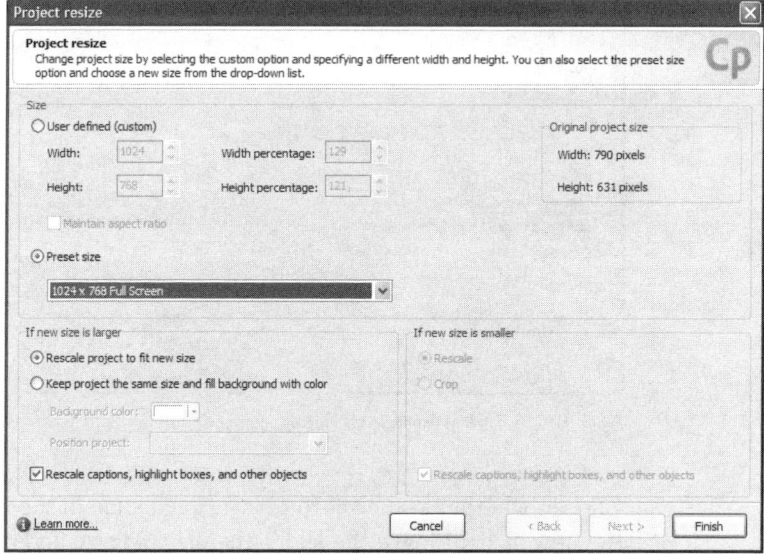

Figure 12-8. Display the Project resize window to change movie size.

3. *If you chose User defined*, specify whether or not you want to maintain the aspect ratio. If you select this check box, the relative height and width of the slides will remain the same after resizing. If you don't select this check box, you may get some unexpected distortion.
4. *If you chose User defined*, type either the number of pixels for each dimension or a percentage change. If you have selected Maintain aspect ratio, typing a new value in either the height or width

Chapter 12

dimension will automatically change the other dimension to maintain their relative sizes.

5. *If you chose Preset size*, choose from the drop-down list of available sizes. For example, you might choose 220 x 230 for a very small display or 1024 x 768 for a larger, full-screen display.

6. If the new size you've entcred is larger than the original size, the If new size is larger area becomes active.

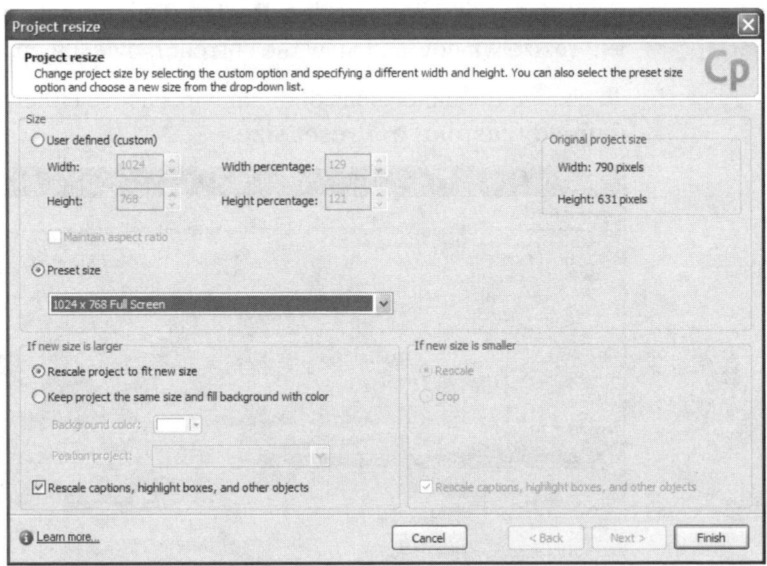

Figure 12-9. Define how Captivate will enlarge your movie.

Choose whether you want to rescale each slide in the movie to fit the new size, or leave the slides the original size and insert a solid color to fill in around the slides.

If you choose to keep the movie the same size, specify the color for the background by clicking on the **Background color** box, and specify where on the new slide the original slide will be placed (such as top center or bottom right).

Select the **Rescale captions** check box to enlarge the text captions and other elements so that they stay in the same proportion to the slide display.

Skip to step 11 when you are done.

7. If the new size you've entered is smaller than the original movie size, the If new size is smaller area becomes active.

   Choose whether you want to rescale each slide in the movie to fit the new size, or leave the slides the original size and just use whatever portion of the slide fits in the new movie space.

   Select the **Rescale captions** check box to reduce the text captions and other elements so that they stay in the same proportion to the slide display.

   Skip to step 11 when you are done.

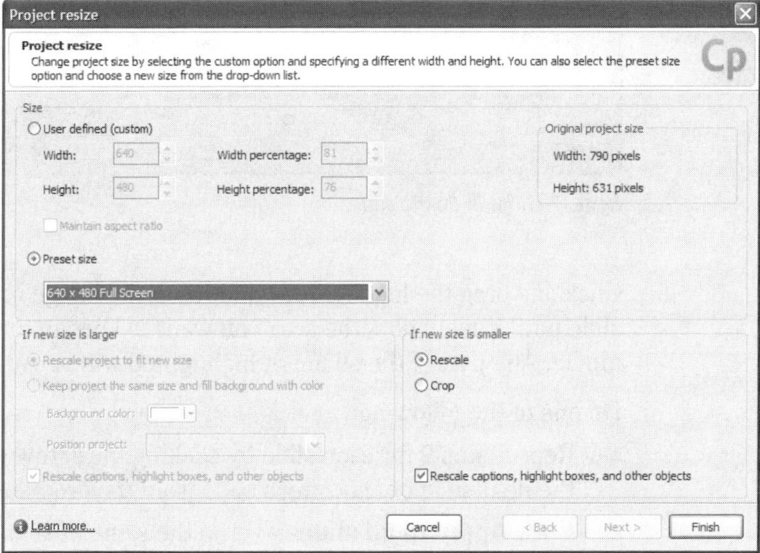

Figure 12-10. Define how Captivate will reduce the movie dimensions.

8. If you chose to crop the movie to a smaller size, the Next button becomes active. Click **Next** to display the Project resize window with an area you can use to indicate which portion of each slide you want to include in the resized movie.

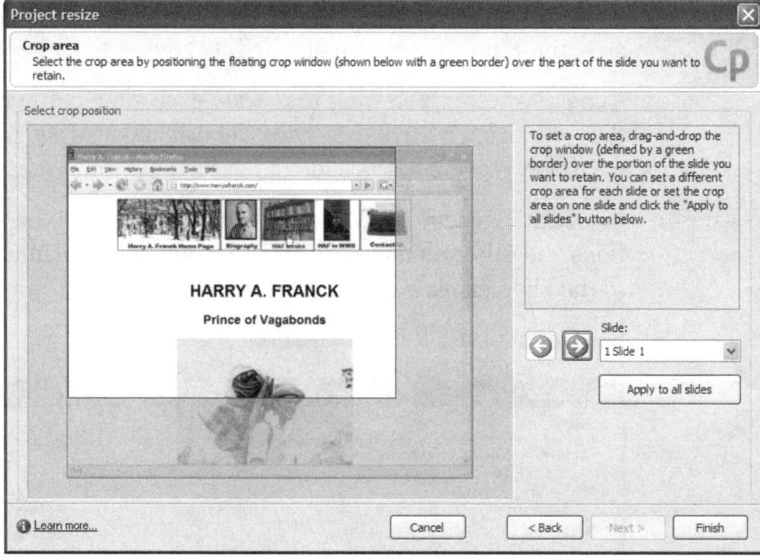

Figure 12-11. Specify the crop area.

9. Click and drag the highlighted window on the image in the original slide until it highlights the area you want to keep in the resized movie. Any part of the slide not highlighted will be cut away.
10. Do one of the following:
    - Repeat step 9 for each slide by clicking the arrow to display the next slide or choosing a slide from the drop-down list.
    - Click **Apply to all slides** to crop the same area on every slide.
11. Click **Finish** (from either the Project resize window or from the crop position window) to resize the movie.
12. A message displays, warning you that resizing cannot be undone. Click **OK** to complete the resizing process.

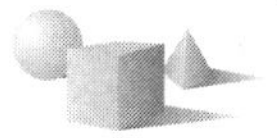

Viewing Movie File Size

Captivate can display file size in bytes for the entire movie, and break it down to display the size of each individual slide and all the elements on it. You can also see a graphic that represents how long the movie will take to download at various connection speeds.

To display the movie file size, follow these steps:

1. From the Project menu, choose **Bandwidth Analysis** to display the Bandwidth Monitor window. The first tab, Slide Summary, displays information about the size of each slide and the length of time it takes to play. The size of audio files, if any, is also identified.

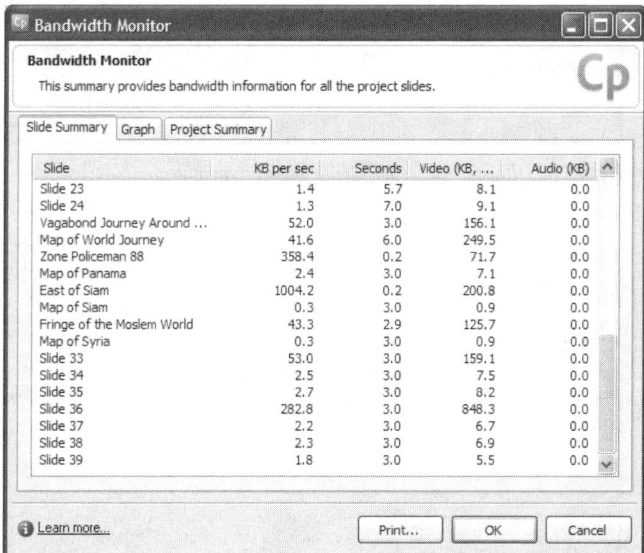

Figure 12-12. Display the size of each slide.

2. Click the **Graph** tab to display a visual representation of how long it will take to display the movie over different types of connections. The vertical axis on the left of the graph represents the amount of bandwidth the movie requires. The bottom, horizontal axis represents the display time of the movie. In Figure 12-13, the jagged black line represents the actual size of each slide. The horizontal lines represent the amount of time for each bandwidth, identified by color.

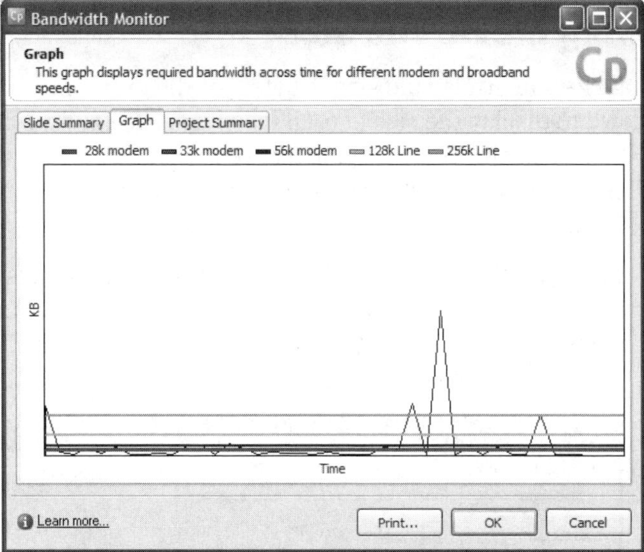

Figure 12-13. Display relative times for different bandwidths.

3. Click the **Project Summary** tab to display a summary of the movie information. This is the same information that displays in the Information panel at the left of the Storyboard view.

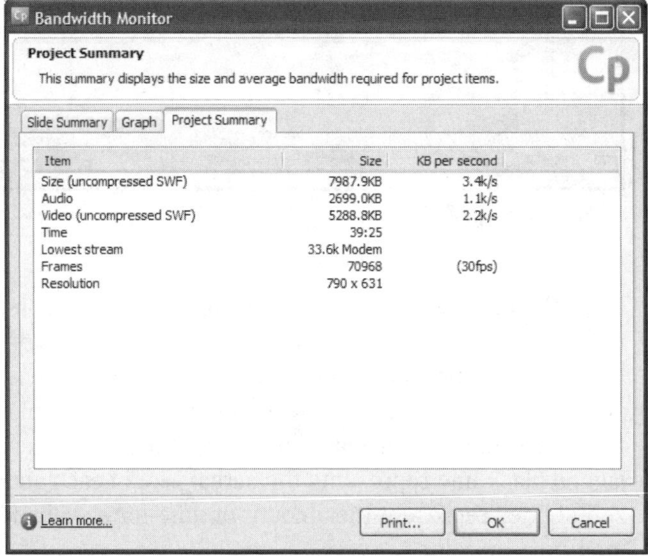

Item	Size	KB per second
Size (uncompressed SWF)	7987.9KB	3.4k/s
Audio	2699.0KB	1.1k/s
Video (uncompressed SWF)	5288.8KB	2.2k/s
Time	39:25	
Lowest stream	33.6k Modem	
Frames	70968	(30fps)
Resolution	790 x 631	

Figure 12-14. Display the summary.

4. For any of the Bandwidth Monitor window tabs, you can click **Print** to print a complete bandwidth analysis, including the slide summary, graph, and project summary information.

5. Click **OK** to close the Bandwidth Monitor window.

Combining Movies with MenuBuilder

The MenuBuilder tool makes it easy to create a special slide that displays a list of several Captivate movies from which the viewer can choose. You can then export the MenuBuilder project to create a Flash movie that combines the menu slide and the associated movies into a single file. You have a lot of control over the MenuBuilder output. For example, you can include menu items that point to other types of output, such as web pages or other files. You can specify whether or not MenuBuilder should include the associated movies in the output file or just point to them. And you have a variety of output formats and options for each. For example, if you're delivering your movies on a CD or DVD, you can create an executable file (.exe) and specify that the menu display automatically when the viewers put the disc into their computers.

Valid output formats for MenuBuilder are:

- Adobe Flash (.swf)
- Executable file (.exe)
- HTML file (.htm)
- Word document (.doc)
- Macintosh file (.hqx)

There are four main steps to working with MenuBuilder:

1. Create your project by defining the slide and the items that you want included in the menu. The easiest way to create a MenuBuilder project is with the MenuBuilder wizard, which guides you through the process. If you prefer, you can create a MenuBuilder project from scratch.

2. Make edits to the slide as needed, just as you would edit any other Captivate slide. You can add elements, like text and click boxes,

move them around on the slide, edit text fonts or sizes, change backgrounds, etc.

3. You can preview the slide to see what it will look like when exported, and check the links to make sure they work as you expect.
4. Export the project to create the file or files you need.

Tip: MenuBuilder is a fast and efficient way to bundle several movies into a single output file. However, it is somewhat more limited in functionality than other parts of Captivate. Depending on your output needs, you may be better able to create the type of menu you want in Captivate without the MenuBuilder tool.

Creating a New Project with the MenuBuilder Wizard

The MenuBuilder wizard is a series of windows that steps you through the various parameters you need to enter in order to create a new MenuBuilder project. To use the MenuBuilder wizard, follow these steps:

1. From anywhere within Captivate, open the **File** menu and choose **Record/Create** and then **MenuBuilder project**.

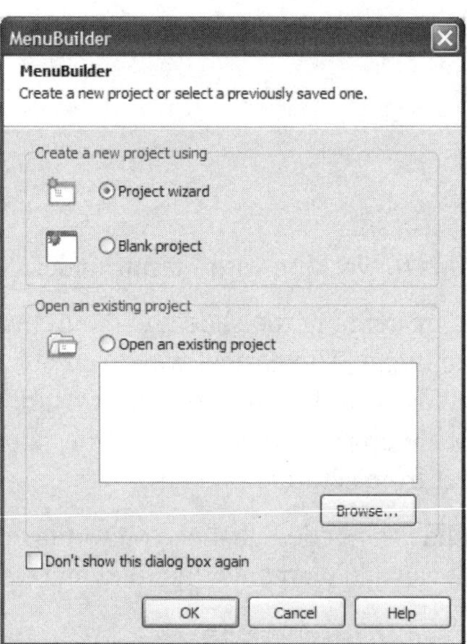

Figure 12-15. Start a new MenuBuilder project.

Note: If you have a movie open, this will close the current movie. If you haven't saved your movie, Captivate will prompt you to do so.

2. Select **Project wizard** to have Captivate step through the creation of the new project.
3. Click **OK** to display the next wizard window.

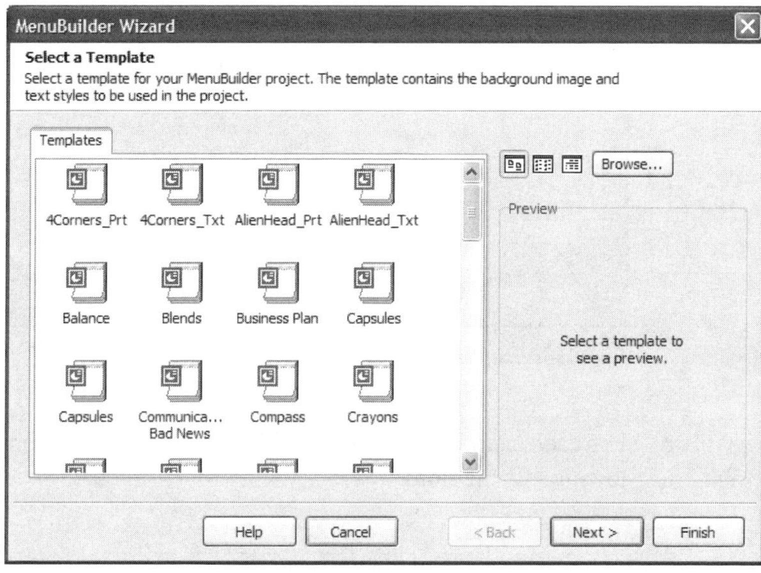

Figure 12-16. Choose a template for the menu slide.

4. MenuBuilder uses the same types of templates as PowerPoint. If you have PowerPoint installed on your system, the predefined PowerPoint templates will appear in this window along with any MenuBuilder templates you've created. You can click on any of the displayed templates to see a preview of the template style in the Preview area. Select the template you want to use, if any, and then click **Next** to display the next wizard window.

Tip: You can stop the wizard at any point after this by clicking Finish. Captivate will create the MenuBuilder project with as many settings as you've entered to that point.

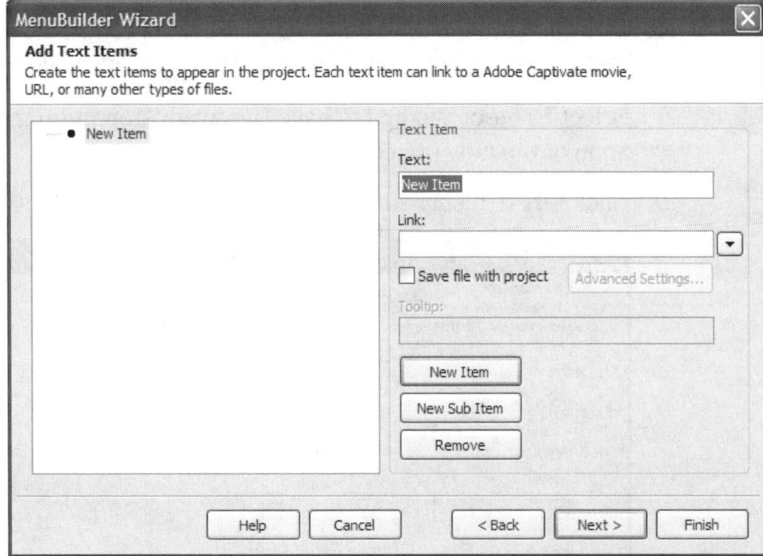

Figure 12-17. Enter the menu items.

5. For each item that you want to display in the menu, enter the following information:

Table 12-4. Defining links

In this area:	Do this:
Text	Type the text that you want to display on the menu.
Link	Type the destination, or what you want to display when this menu item is clicked. You can choose from the drop-down list to specify a type of file or to access the Browse button, which lets you link to any type of file.
Save file with project	*For Flash movie links only*, select this box if you want to include the entire movie with the menu when you export it. If this box is not selected, you'll have to ensure that the viewer has the same access to the files and that they are in the same location as the information you enter here.
Tooltip	Type text that will display when the viewer rolls the mouse over the link.

Note: Published Captivate movies have two components—an SWF file and an associated HTM file. Both files will be needed to link to the movie from MenuBuilder, but you'll only have to select the HTM file. MenuBuilder will automatically link to the SWF file and include both files with the project if you select the Save file with project check box.

6. *For URL or HTML links only,* you may click the **Advanced Settings** button to set display options for the browser window that contains the link.

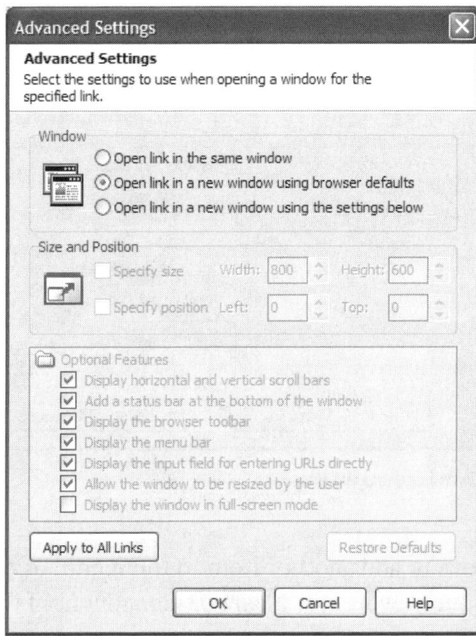

Figure 12-18. Define the window for links to URL and HTML links.

7. *For URL or HTML links only*, in the Advanced Settings window, choose whether you want to open the specified link in the same window that the menu is in, in a new window using the viewer's system defaults, or in a window that you've defined. If you choose to define the window, check the features you want to display or allow. When you're done defining the window, click **OK** to close the Advanced Settings window and return to the text items window.

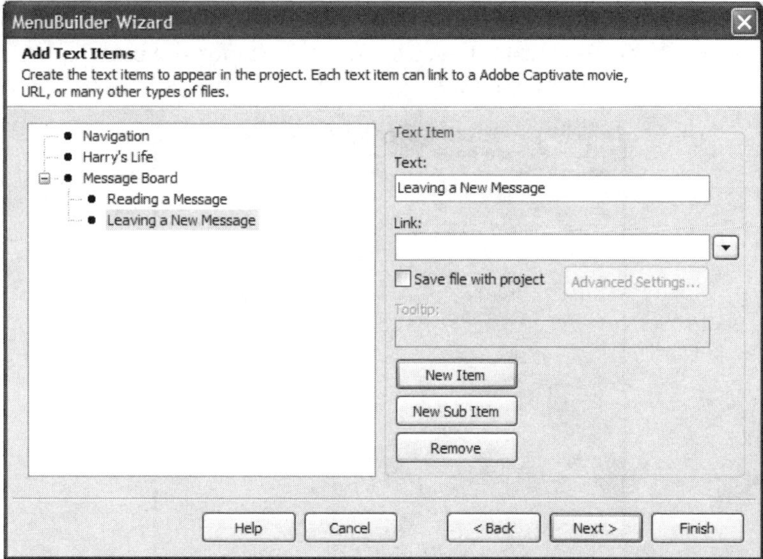

Figure 12-19. Enter menu items and sub-items.

8. Click **New Item** to add another item to the menu, or click **New Sub Item** if your new item is a part or component of the first item. (For example, in Figure 12-19, there are two sub-items under the main item Message Board.) Then repeat steps 5 through 7.
9. If necessary, you can highlight an item you've entered and click **Remove** to delete that item from the menu. Remove does not delete the original files, just the menu item that points to the files.
10. When done, click **Next** to display the next wizard window.

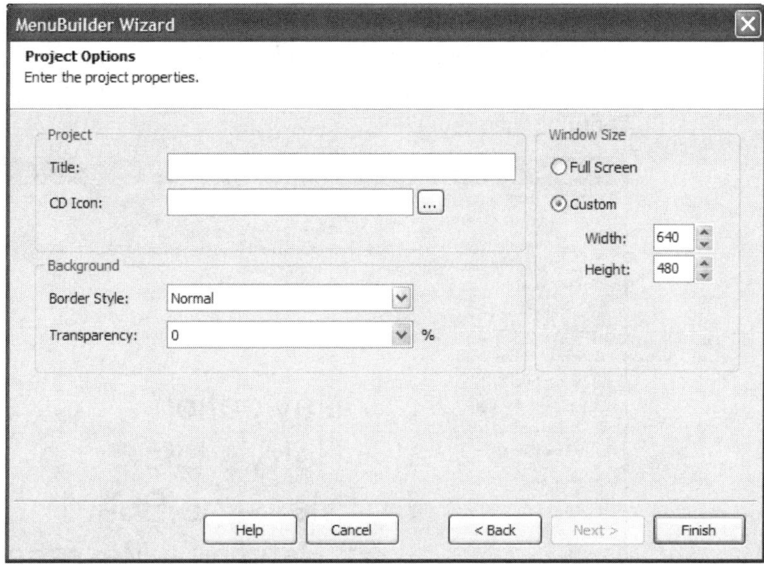

Figure 12-20. Name the project and define window size.

11. Type a title for the project. This is the name that will display at the top of the finished menu slide.
12. For EXE output only, select an icon that will represent the file. If you don't specify an icon, MenuBuilder will default to the Captivate icon. You can use any existing icon file (extension .ico).
13. Define the background you want for the menu slide. You can choose any of the border styles from the drop-down list. These will change the way the line around the edge of the slide looks. You can also set the background to be more or less transparent. The higher the transparency number of the background, the less visible it will be.
14. Choose the window size, either **Full Screen** or **Custom**. If you choose Custom, you'll have to enter the dimensions you want for the menu slide.

15. Click **Finish** when you are done to display the menu slide you've made in the MenuBuilder window. You'll see the slide, as well as a variety of icons that represent the tools you can use to further refine your menu slide.

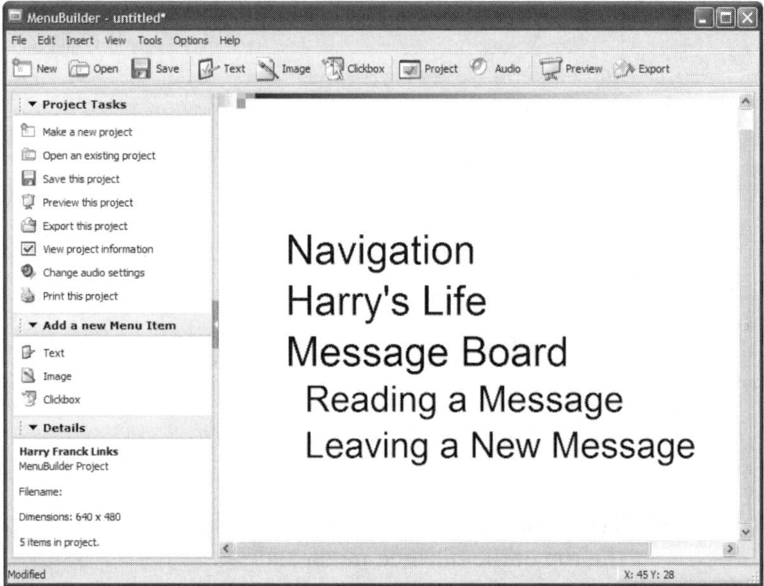

Figure 12-21. The MenuBuilder window displays the menu slide and editing tools.

16. Edit the project as needed as described in later sections of this chapter.
17. Save the project in one of the following ways:
    - Click **Save this project** from the Project Tasks list on the left of the screen.
    - Click the **Save** icon from the top of the screen.
    - From the File menu, choose **Save**.
    - Press **Ctrl+S** on your keyboard.

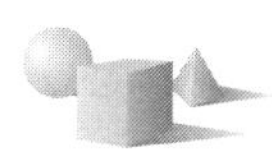

Creating a New Project without the MenuBuilder Wizard

If you don't want to use the MenuBuilder wizard, you can simply create a blank menu slide and then edit it to add elements individually. To create a new project with a blank slide, follow these steps:

1. From anywhere within Captivate, open the **File** menu and choose **Record/Create** and then **MenuBuilder project**.

Note: If you have a movie open, this will close the current movie. If you haven't saved your movie, Captivate will prompt you to do so.

2. Click **Blank project**, and then click **OK**. The new blank menu slide displays in the MenuBuilder window.

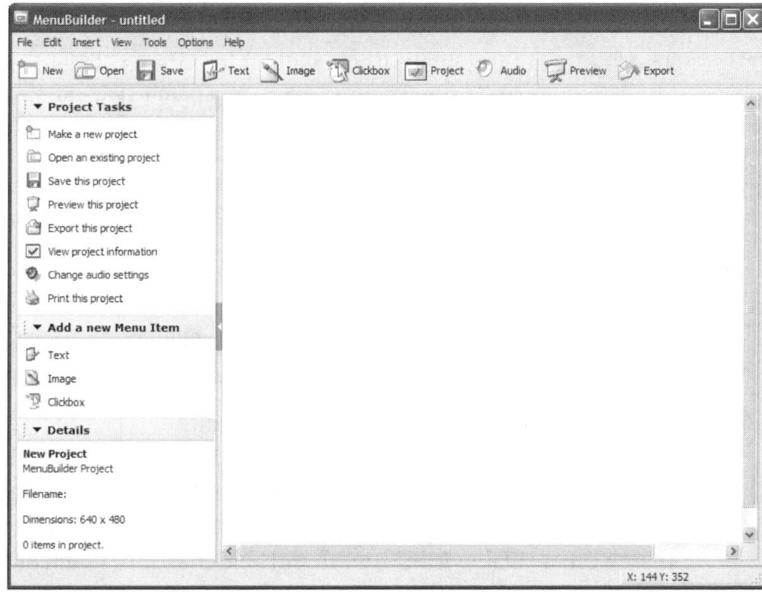

Figure 12-22. Open a blank project.

3. Edit the project as described in the following sections of this chapter.

4. Save the project in one of the following ways:
   - Click **Save this project** from the Project Tasks list on the left of the screen.
   - Click the **Save** icon from the top of the screen.
   - From the File menu, choose **Save**.
   - Press **Ctrl+S** on your keyboard.

Adding and Editing Menu Items

The MenuBuilder window displays the current menu slide on the right side of the screen and a variety of tools that let you edit the slide on the left side of the screen. There are three main types of elements you can add to MenuBuilder slides; although they use the same names as slides that are not menu slides, the functions are slightly different within MenuBuilder.

Text—Most of the menu items will be text items. These look much like regular Captivate text captions, except that they also have an associated click box that is the same size as the text.

Image—You can insert an image into a menu slide. Like other types of images, you can crop or resize as needed. The MenuBuilder images, like MenuBuilder text items, can be clicked to display other movies or sites.

Clickbox—An area where the viewer can click on the screen, very much like click boxes elsewhere within Captivate.

You can easily add any of the three menu item types to your menu slide, whether or not the slide was created with the wizard. You can also edit the properties of any menu item to change the way it looks or acts when clicked. Editing the text menu items gives you more options than were available from the MenuBuilder wizard (such as font style or size).

Adding or Editing a Text Menu Item

To add or edit a text item on a MenuBuilder slide, follow these steps:

1. Create the menu slide using one of the two methods described earlier in this chapter. The menu slide displays in the MenuBuilder window.
2. Do either of the following to display the New text window:
   - To add a new text menu item, on the left side of the MenuBuilder window, under Add a new Menu Item, choose **Text**.
   - To edit an existing text menu item, double-click on the text you want to edit.

Figure 12-23. Define the text properties.

3. Do one of the following to define the way the text looks:
   - Choose a predefined heading style from the Style drop-down list. If you used a template to create the menu slide, these headings are imported from that template. You can select **Custom** to create a new style for this slide.
   - Choose a font and text size from the two drop-down lists next to Font, and choose either bold or italic if desired.

The text in the Preview area will change to reflect your style and font selections.

4. In the Text box, type or edit the text. This is the text that will appear on the menu. The text in the Preview area will change to reflect edits.
5. In the Link box, type the destination or what you want to display when this menu item is clicked. You can choose from the drop-down list to specify a type of file or to access the Browse button, which lets you link to any type of file.

Note: Published Captivate movies have two components—an SWF file and an associated HTM file. Both files will be needed to link to the movie from MenuBuilder, but you'll only have to select the HTM file. MenuBuilder will automatically link to the SWF file and include both files with the project if you select the Save file with project check box.

6. *For Flash movie links only*, select the **Save file with project** check box if you want to include the entire movie with the menu when you export it. If this check box is not selected, you'll have to ensure that the viewer has the same access to the files and that they are in the same location as the information you enter here.
7. In the Tooltip box, type text that will display when the viewer rolls the mouse over the link.
8. *For URL or HTML links only*, you may click the **Advanced Settings** button to set display options for the browser window that contains the link.

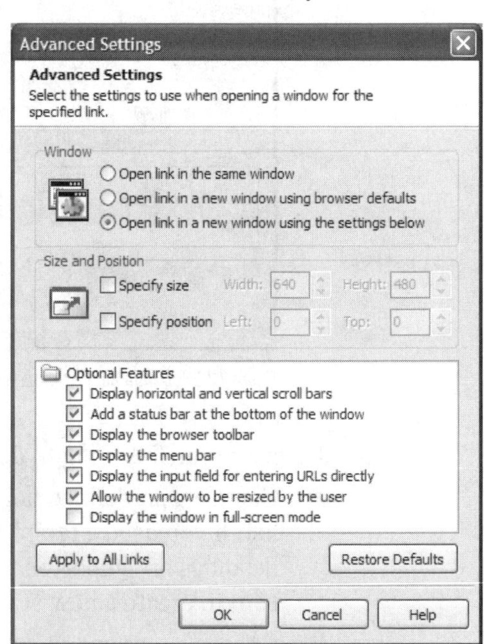

Figure 12-24. Define the window for links to URL and HTML links with the Advanced Settings window.

9. *For URL or HTML links only*, in the Advanced Settings window, choose whether you want to open the specified link in the same window that the menu is in, in a new window using the viewer's system defaults, or in a window that you've defined. If you choose to define the window, check the features you want to display or allow. When you're done defining the window, click **OK** to close the Advanced Settings window and return to the New text window.
10. You can change the color of the text by clicking in the color box next to Normal Color and then choosing from the color palette. You can also specify a Hover Color to have the text change color when the viewer moves the cursor over the text link.
11. Once you've set the text menu item properties, you can click **Apply changes to all items** to use these settings for all other text items in the menu.
12. Click **OK** to close the New text window and display the text in the menu slide.

Note: If you added a new text item, it displays in the center of the menu slide. You can click and drag it to a new location.

Adding or Editing an Image Menu Item

To add or edit an image item on a MenuBuilder slide, follow these steps:

1. Create the menu slide using one of the two methods described earlier in this chapter. The menu slide displays in the MenuBuilder window.
2. Do either of the following to display the New image window:
   - To add a new image menu item, on the left side of the MenuBuilder window, under Add a new Menu Item, choose **Image**, then browse to the image file you want to use and click **Open**.
   - To edit an existing image menu item, double-click on the image you want to edit.

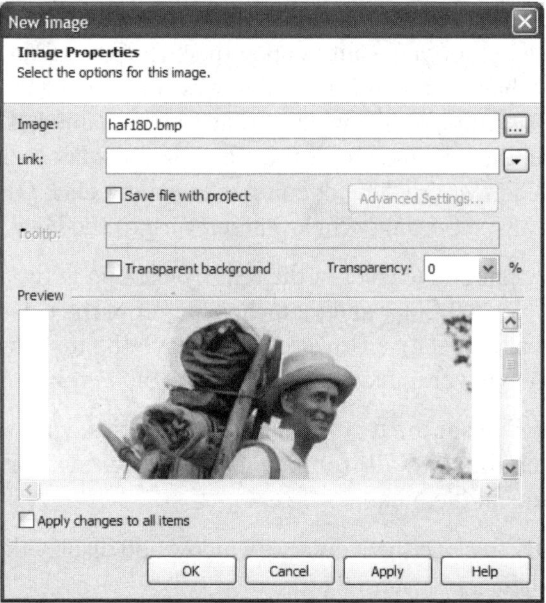

Figure 12-25. Define the menu item image properties.

Note: If the image is too large for the specified menu slide size, a window displays asking whether you want to crop the image (displaying as much of the upper-right corner of the image as will fit on the slide) or resize (reducing the image until it fits on the menu slide).

3. You can type the name of a different file in the Image box to change the image or click the button to the right to browse to a new file.
4. In the Link box, type the destination, or what you want to display when this menu item is clicked. You can choose from the drop-down list to specify a type of file or to access the Browse button, which lets you link to any type of file.

Note: Published Captivate movies have two components—an SWF file and an associated HTM file. Both files will be needed to link to the movie from MenuBuilder, but you'll only have to select the HTM file. MenuBuilder will automatically link to the SWF file and include both files with the project if you select the Save file with project check box.

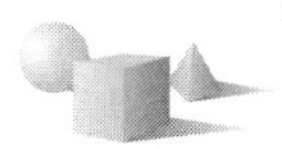

5. *For Flash movie links only,* select the **Save file with project** check box if you want to include the entire movie with the menu when you export it. If this check box is not selected, you'll have to ensure that the viewer has the same access to the files and that they are in the same location as the information you enter here.
6. In the Tooltip box, type the text that will display when the viewer rolls the mouse over the link.
7. *For URL or HTML links only,* you may click the **Advanced Settings** button to set display options for the browser window that contains the link.
8. *For URL or HTML links only,* in the Advanced Settings window, choose whether you want to open the specified link in the same window that the menu is in, in a new window using the viewer's system defaults, or in a window that you've defined. If you choose to define the window, check the features you want to display or allow. When you're done defining the window, click **OK** to close the Advanced Settings window and return to the New image window.
9. You can set the background of the image to be transparent by selecting the **Transparent background** check box.

Tip: All portions of the image that have the same color levels as the pixel in the lower-left corner of the image will be set to transparent. They will not show up on the menu slide, and anything behind the pixels of that color will show through.

Note: Be careful to check your images after you import them, particularly if you use a transparent background. Captivate will make all areas the color of the background transparent. For example, if you have an image of a black circle with white lettering and a white background, and you make the white background transparent, then Captivate will make all white portions of the image transparent (including the letters). If this isn't the look you wanted, use a graphics program to make the background or the letters slightly different shades of white.

10. You can set a transparency level for the entire image by entering a number in the Transparency % box. The higher the transparency setting, the fainter the image will appear.

11. Once you've set the image item properties, you can click **Apply changes to all items** to use these settings for all other image items in the menu.
12. Click **OK** to close the New image window and display the image in the menu slide.

Note: If you added a new image item, it displays in the center of the menu slide. You can click and drag it to a new location, or use the handles on the sides and corners to resize it.

Adding or Editing a Click Box Menu Item

To add or edit a click box item on a MenuBuilder slide, follow these steps:

1. Create the menu slide using one of the two methods described earlier in this chapter. The menu slide displays in the MenuBuilder window.
2. Do either of the following to display the New clickbox window:
   - To add a new click box menu item, on the left side of the MenuBuilder window, under Add a new Menu Item, choose **Clickbox**.
   - To edit an existing click box menu item, double-click on the click box you want to edit.

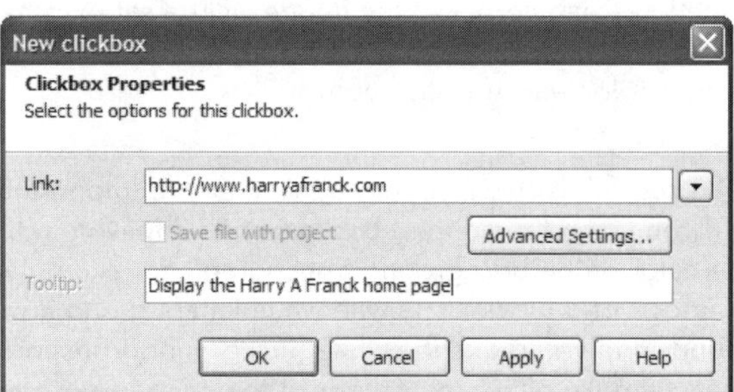

Figure 12-26. Define the click box properties.

3. In the Link box, type the destination, or what you want to display when this menu item is clicked. You can choose from the drop-down list to specify a type of file or to access the Browse button, which lets you link to any type of file.

Note: Published Captivate movies have two components—an SWF file and an associated HTM file. Both files will be needed to link to the movie from MenuBuilder, but you'll only have to select the HTM file. MenuBuilder will automatically link to the SWF file and include both files with the project if you select the Save file with project check box.

4. *For Flash movie links only*, select the **Save file with project** check box if you want to include the entire movie with the menu when you export it. If this box is not selected, you'll have to ensure that the viewer has the same access to the files, and that they are in the same location, as what you're entering the information here.
5. In the Tooltip box, type text that will display when the viewer rolls the mouse over the link.
6. *For URL or HTML links only*, you may click the **Advanced Settings** button to set display options for the browser window that contains the link.
7. *For URL or HTML links only*, in the Advanced Settings window, choose whether you want to open the specified link in the same window that the menu is in, in a new window using the viewer's system defaults, or in a window that you've defined. If you choose to define the window, check the features you want to display or allow. When you're done defining the window, click **OK** to close the Advanced Settings window and return to the New clickbox window.
8. Once you've set the clickbox properties, you can click **Apply changes to all items** on the New image window to use these settings for all other click box items in the menu.
9. Click **OK** to close the New clickbox window and display the click box in the menu slide.

Note: If you added a new click box item, it displays in the center of the menu slide. You can click and drag it to a new location, or use the handles on the sides and corners to resize it.

Moving Menu Items on MenuBuilder Slides

After you've created a text, image, or click box menu item within MenuBuilder, you can move it to a desired location or line it up with other elements.

Follow these steps:

1. Select the item or items you want to move. To select multiple items, hold down the **Shift** key as you click on each one. You'll know an item has been selected when the outline of the item displays.

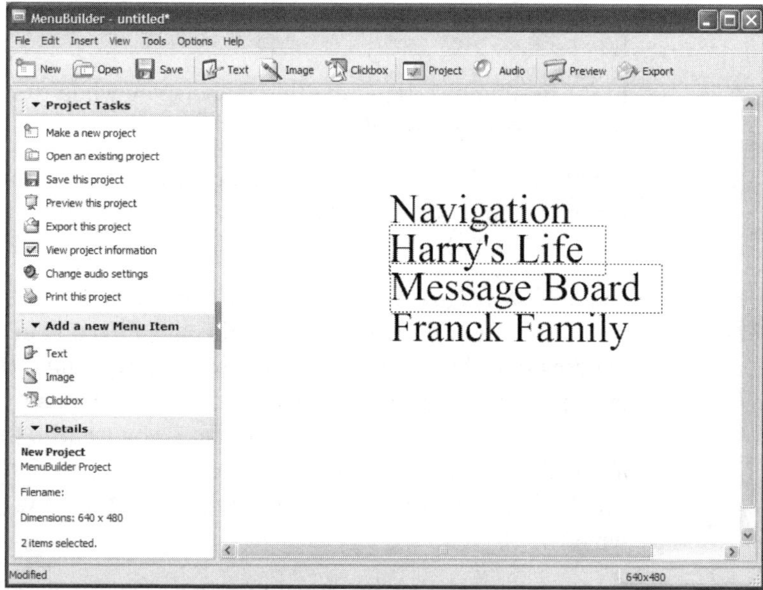

Figure 12-27. A menu slide with two text items selected.

2. To move the selected items, drag them to a new location.

Tip: For finer control over movement, hold down the Shift key and press an arrow key to move the selected items one pixel in the direction of the arrow.

3. To line up the selected items relative to each other, from the Edit menu, choose **Align**. The Alignment window displays.

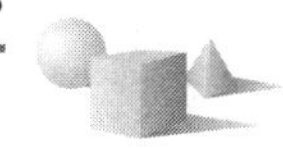

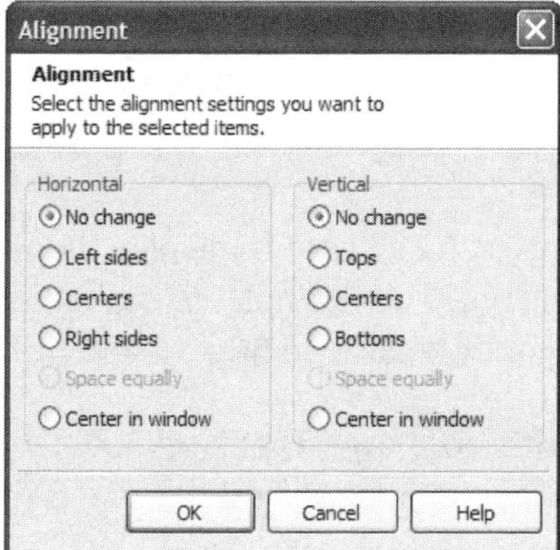

Figure 12-28. Choose from available alignment options.

4. Choose how you want to line up the items by clicking on the appropriate options, and then click **OK** to close the Alignment window.

Resizing Images and Click Boxes in MenuBuilder

There are three resizing methods in MenuBuilder. You can click and drag to change any dimension of the item, you can resize items to a specific height and width in pixels or change the size of a group of items to match the smallest (or largest) item in the group, and you can resize the item or items relative to their original size (scaling). The aspect ratio (the proportion of height to width) for scaled items remains the same as in the original. To resize items, follow these steps:

1. Select the item or items you want to resize.
2. Do one of the following:
   - Select the item and drag the handles (the square boxes on the sides and corners) to resize.

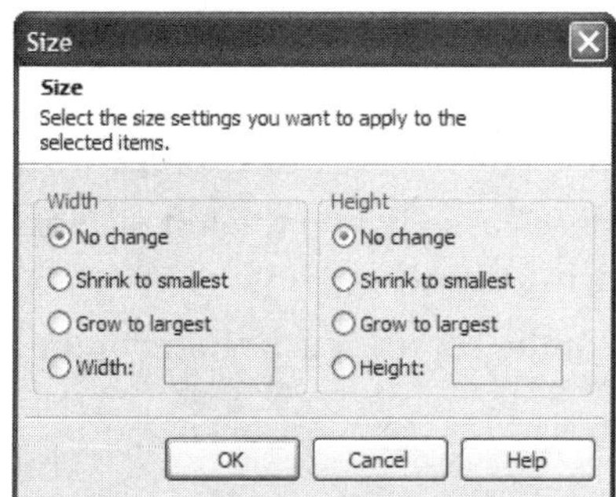

Figure 12-29. Resize selected items.

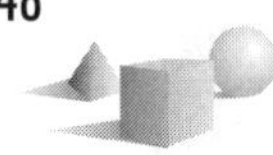

- From the Edit menu, select **Size** to display the Size window, then choose the appropriate actions. If you choose Width or Height, you'll need to enter the dimension you want for the finished item in pixels.
- From the Edit menu, select **Scale** to display the Scale window, then enter a percentage. For example, to scale the image to be half the size it originally was, type **50**.

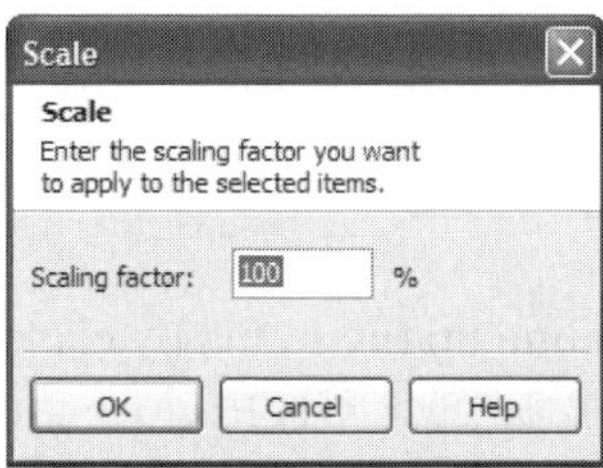

Figure 12-30. Rescale selected items.

Tip: The scaling factor is applied to each dimension, not to the area of the image or click box. For example, you have an image that is 100 x 100 pixels (for a total area of 10,000 pixels) and want to reduce it to half the original size. When you enter a scaling factor of 50%, the resulting image would be 50 x 50 pixels (for a total area of 2,500 pixels). Each dimension has been reduced 50%, and the total area is now one-fourth the size of the original item.

3. Click **OK** to close the displayed window, if any, and view the resized items.

Setting Project Options

Up to this point, you've been working with the individual menu items. You can also adjust other components on the slide by using the MenuBuilder Project Options window. Follow these steps:

1. Do one of the following to open the MenuBuilder Project Options window:
   - From the Options menu, choose **Project Options**.
   - From the Project Tasks list on the left side of the screen, click **View project information.**
   - From the top of the screen, click the **Project** icon.

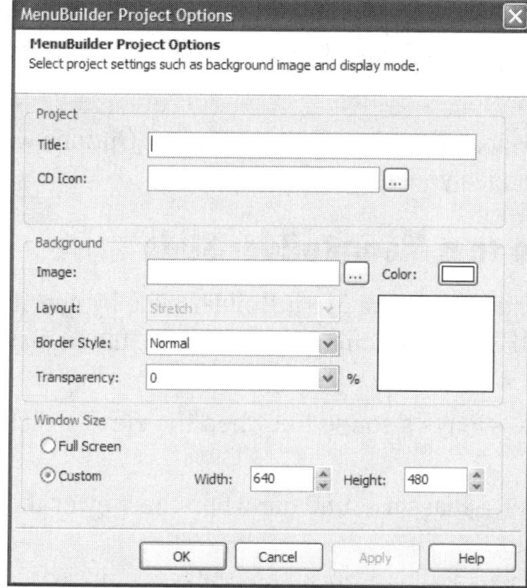

Figure 12-31. Name the project and define the window size.

2. Type a title for the project. This is the name that will display at the top of the finished menu slide.
3. *For EXE output only*, select an icon that will represent the file. If you don't specify an icon, MenuBuilder will default to the Captivate icon. You can use any existing icon file (extension .ico).
4. Define the background you want for the menu slide in one of the following ways:
   - Enter the name of an image file that will be the slide background. When you enter an image name, you'll have the option of specifying how the image should be resized to fill the slide background (centered on the slide, stretched to fit, or repeated (tiled) as needed).
   - Choose a solid color background by clicking the color box next to Color.
5. You can choose any of the border styles from the drop-down list. These will change the way the line around the edge of the slide looks.
6. You can set the background to be more or less transparent. The higher the transparency percentage of the background, the less visible it will be.

7. Choose the window size, either **Full Screen** or **Custom**. If you choose Custom, you'll have to enter the dimensions you want for the menu slide.
8. Click **OK** to close the MenuBuilder Project Options window and view the changes you've made.

Adding Audio to a MenuBuilder Slide

You can add sound effects to a MenuBuilder slide by specifying an existing WAV, MP3, or WMA file and setting the file to play at one of four times:

- Mouse Click—Plays a sound file when the viewer clicks the mouse.
- Mouse Hover—Plays a sound file when the viewer moves the cursor over a link.
- On Start—Plays a sound file when the menu slide first displays.
- Background—Plays a sound file for the duration of the menu slide display.

The files must exist already (you can't record in MenuBuilder), and you can't associate them with specific menu items. For example, when you specify a mouse hover sound, the same sound plays for each of the links in the menu.

To add audio files to your MenuBuilder slide, follow these steps:

1. Do one of the following to open the MenuBuilder Audio Options window, as shown in Figure 12-32:
   - From the Options menu, choose **Audio Options**.
   - Press the **F5** key on your keyboard.
   - From the Project Tasks list on the left side of the screen, click **Change audio settings**.
   - From the top of the screen, click the **Audio** icon.
2. Type the location of the audio file, or use the Browse button next to each of the action text boxes to point to the file you want to play for each action.
3. Click the **Audio** icon next to any of the listed actions to hear the sound currently associated with that action.

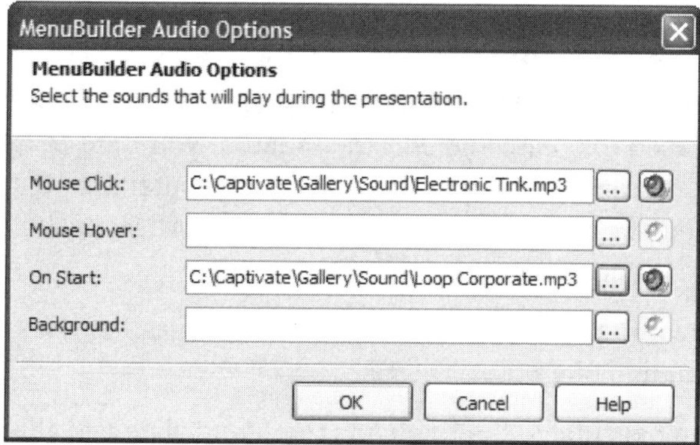

Figure 12-32. Choose audio files for certain actions.

4. When you're done, click **OK** to close the MenuBuilder Audio Options window.

Previewing Projects in MenuBuilder

Before you export your MenuBuilder project to create the files that incorporate all the movies in your menu, it's a good idea to preview the menu slide. You can see exactly how the menu will look to the viewers, and you can check the links for each menu item to make sure they work the way you expect.

To preview a menu slide, do one of the following:

- From the File menu, choose **Preview**.
- Press the **F4** key on your keyboard.
- From the Project Tasks list on the left side of the screen, click **Preview this project**.
- From the top of the screen, click the **Preview** icon.

The preview will open in its own window. You can roll the cursor over any of the links to see the color change, if any, or click any menu item to start movies, go to web pages, or send e-mail (or whatever you've defined for each link).

Exporting MenuBuilder Projects

When you save your MenuBuilder projects, you're saving all the files that you used to create and edit the menu. If you want to create a new file that you can give to other people to view outside of Captivate, you'll need to export the project. You can export MenuBuilder projects in several different formats including:

Flash Movie—You can choose to include the Flash movies to which the menu points.

EXE—An executable file that runs the menu slide and all the files it points to.

HTML—A basic web page. The background of your slide will be exported to a JPG file.

Word—An image of the menu slide, plus a list of the elements on the menu slide.

Mac—A movie that can be played on a Macintosh system.

To export a project and make files you can distribute, follow these steps:

1. Do one of the following to display the first MenuBuilder Export Options window:
   - From the File menu, choose **Export**.
   - From the Project Tasks list on the left side of the screen, click **Export this project**.
   - From the top of the screen, click the **Export** icon.

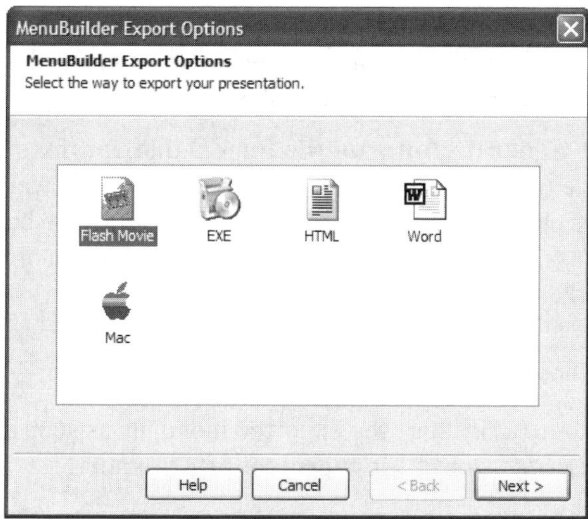

Figure 12-33. Select the type of output.

2. Choose a project type and then click **Next** to display the second Export Options window.

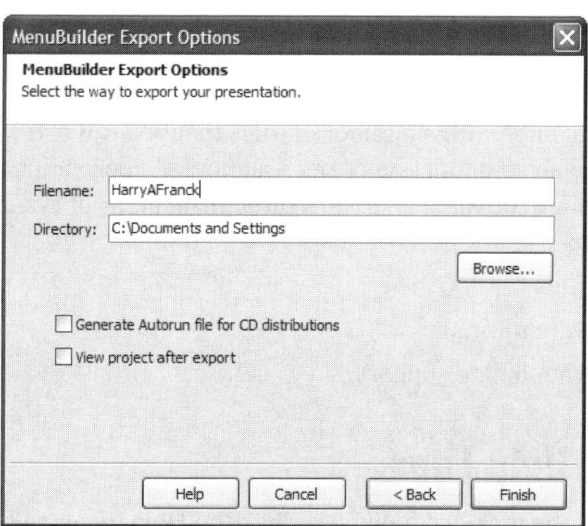

Figure 12-34. Enter output name and directory.

3. In the Filename box, type a name or edit the default name if needed.

4. In the Directory box, type a directory or edit the default directory if needed. You can also click **Browse** to display the default folder, and then browse to a different folder.
5. Select **Generate Autorun file for CD distributions** to create a text file that will start the movie at the menu slide when the viewer places the CD in his drive. You must include both the output files and the autorun file (named autorun.inf) in order for this to work.

Note: This option is not available for Word output.

6. To automatically start the exported menu file as soon as it has been created, select **View project after export.**

Note: This option is not available for Word or Mac output.

7. Click **Finish** to create and save the specified files.

Using User Assistance

Captivate comes with a number of tools that you can use when you aren't sure about a function or need additional information about something within Captivate. There are three main areas of available user assistance:

- Help files
- Captivate tutorials
- Captivate online support

Viewing Help Files

To display the included help files, click the Help menu and choose **Adobe Captivate Help** (or press **F1** from anywhere within Captivate).

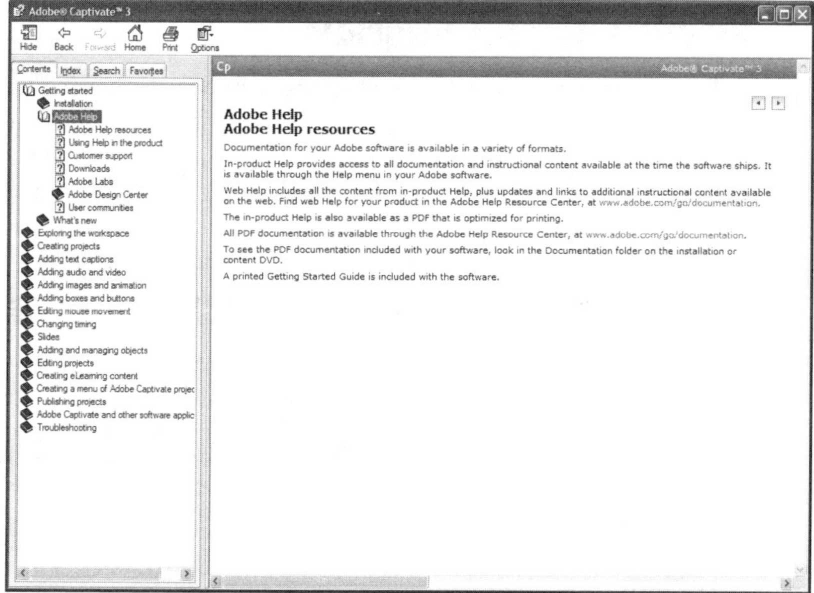

Figure 12-35. Captivate Help resources.

You can find information in several ways:

- Choose the **Search** tab and enter a word or phrase in the search box of the Help window.
- Click on the main topics on the left side of the screen to display additional information.
- Click the **Index** tab to see an alphabetical list of topics.
- Click the **Favorites** tab to see definitions for Captivate terminology.
- From within each displayed topic, click any underlined word to display more information on that word or phrase.

When you're finished, close the online Help window by clicking the Close icon in the upper-right corner of the Help window.

Viewing Helpful Tutorials

In addition to traditional Help systems, Captivate comes with a variety of tutorials that you can view. These movies step through some of the Captivate processes and are most useful for those who are just getting started. When you first start Captivate, the list of available tutorial topics is displayed on the right side of the screen, or you can open the list from the Help menu by choosing **Getting Started Tutorials.**

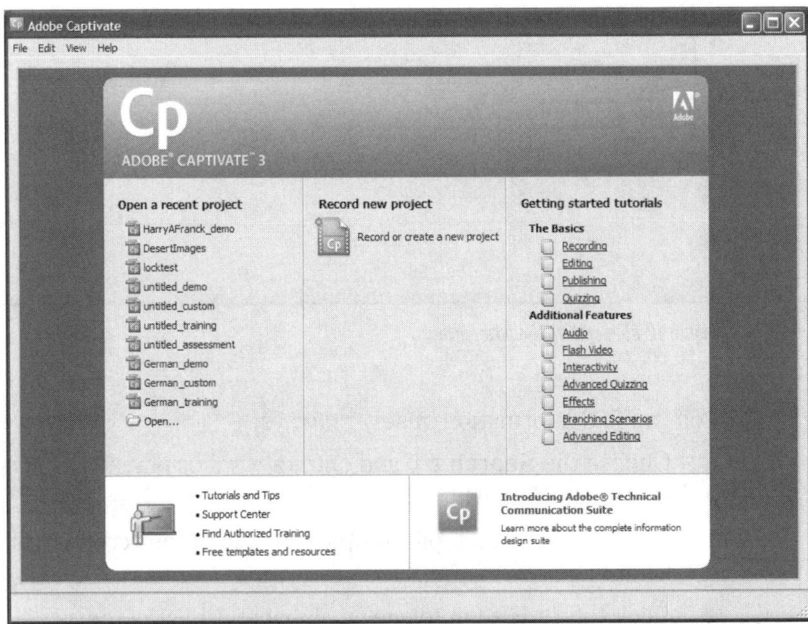

Figure 12-36. Captivate offers Getting started tutorial movies.

Use the playback controls along the bottom of the movie screen to start, stop, pause, or otherwise navigate through the movie. When you're finished, close the movie window by clicking the Close icon in the upper-right corner.

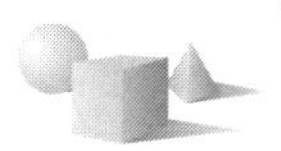

Captivate Online Support

Adobe hosts a variety of online support areas from which you can find answers to your Captivate questions. You can use any browser to view the support pages at http://www.adobe.com/support/captivate/ or you can go to the Help menu and choose either **Support Center** (for most users) or **Developer Center** (for more advanced users).

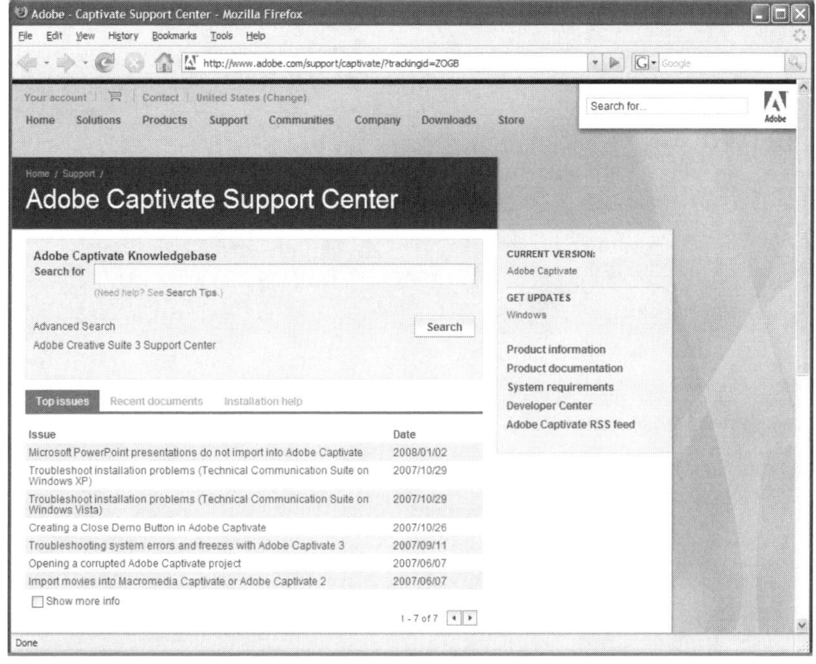

Figure 12-37. Access Captivate online support.

From this site, you can ask questions, view articles, download files, look at documentation, even participate in the Adobe online forums where other Captivate users share problems—and resolutions—with each other.

Another useful resource is the Adobe Captivate Exchange (http://www.adobe.com/cfusion/exchange/index.cfm?event=productHome&exc=22&loc=en_us.) This site offers custom buttons, captions, icons, sounds, and more.

Summary

This chapter reviewed the tools that help you work with Captivate and help you to make better, more efficient movies. The following chapter discusses how to set global properties that determine how your movie looks when it is finished.

Chapter 13

Refining the Movie

Up to this point, we've been working with individual slides and the elements on those slides. You also need to take a look at your movie as a whole. This chapter describes some of the features that help you refine your movie, including moving slides around within the movie and managing the movie files.

Working with Multiple Slides

The Storyboard view allows you to do some of the tasks that you can do in Edit view. The main difference is that in Storyboard view, you can apply your changes to multiple slides at once.

As you've already seen, the Storyboard view displays all of the slides in your movie. When you first open a movie in Captivate, the movie is automatically displayed in Storyboard view.

The left side of the Storyboard view displays a list of tasks you can perform on the slides and some information about the movie as a whole, such as the running time, movie size, and resolution. This information only displays after you've published the movie at least once.

The right side of the Storyboard view displays miniature versions of each slide called thumbnails. If you've entered slide labels, they display beneath each slide next to the slide number; otherwise, just the slide number displays. There are also icons that indicate the type of components that are associated with each slide.

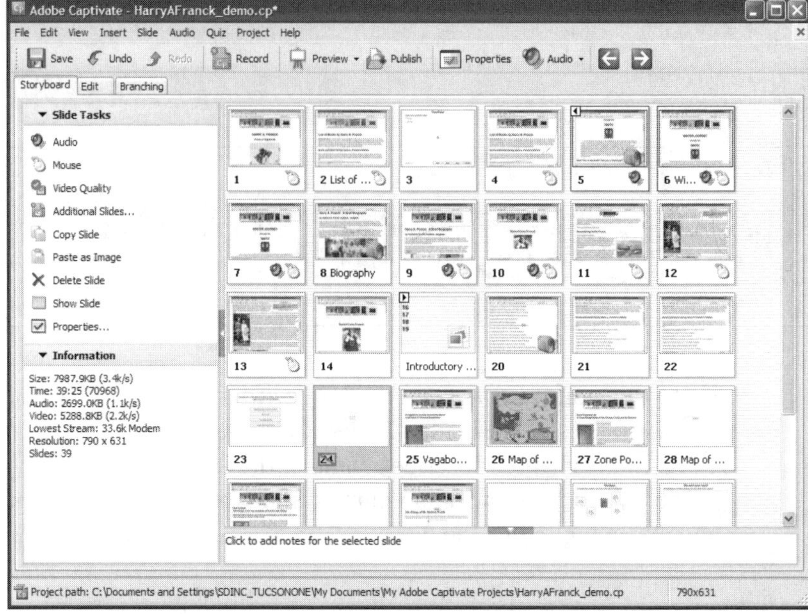

Figure 13-1. Display a movie in Storyboard view.

Table 13-1. Storyboard view icons

This icon:	Indicates this:
	The slide contains a full-motion recording, usually a small, high-resolution movie of scroll bar movement or a drag-and-drop action.
	The slide contains an audio element. Note that this icon only displays for slide-level audio, not for audio associated with individual elements such as click boxes or captions.
	The slide is locked so that the elements on it cannot be changed.
24	The slide is hidden, so that although it displays in Captivate, it will not display in the published movie. The hidden icon displays over the slide number (in this example, slide 24).
	The slide contains information for cursor movement (the beginning and end points of the track along which the cursor moves).
	The slide represents a group of slides. The numbers of the slides in the group appear in the upper-left corner of the slide icon.

These icons also display on the filmstrip in the Edit view (see Chapters 6 and 7 for details about working in Edit view) and Branching view

(see Chapter 11). Most of the tasks that you can do in the Edit view filmstrip can also be accomplished in the Storyboard view.

Changing the Storyboard View Display

In Storyboard view, you can specify which elements of the Storyboard view display and the size of the slide thumbnails.

Modifying the Thumbnail Display

By default, the thumbnail images of each slide start out as medium-sized images, but you can change the size of each slide icon (called thumbnails) at any time. You can either make the icons smaller (so you can see more slides at once) or make them larger to display more detail on each one. Follow these steps:

1. From the Storyboard view screen, click **View** to display the viewing options.
2. Click **Thumbnail Size** to display the available options (small, medium, or large).
3. Click the size you want for your thumbnails.

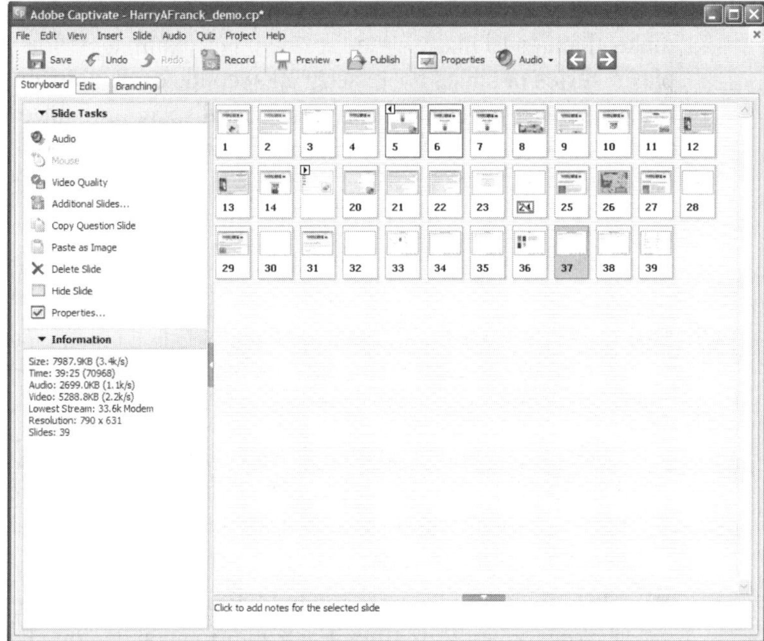

Figure 13-2. Display the storyboard with small icons.

Displaying or Hiding the Left Panel Information

The left panel of the Storyboard view contains two elements. The top of the panel contains a list of common tasks that you can perform on the selected slides. The bottom shows information about the movie. You can hide or redisplay either at any time by clicking on the title of each section (Slide Tasks or Information). For example, if the movie information is displayed, click on the word Information to hide it. If the information is already hidden, click on the word Information to redisplay it.

You can also hide or redisplay the entire panel by clicking the arrow icon between the the left and right panels. This is a narrow arrow, in the center of the dividing border between the two elements. The direction of this arrow will vary depending on whether or not the panel is currently displayed.

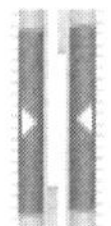

Figure 13-3. Display or hide the left panel with the arrows.

Selecting Slides

One of the most useful features of the Storyboard view is the option to make changes to many slides at once. For example, if you want to display a series of slides for exactly 10 seconds each, you could go into the properties for each slide and set the display time for each one. Or you can select them all in Storyboard view and change the setting just once.

To select slides, do any of the following:

- Click on a slide once to select it.

Tip: Don't double-click; that will open the slide in Edit view. If you double-click by accident, simply click the Storyboard tab to return to Storyboard view.

- Click on one slide and hold down the **Shift** key before clicking another slide. Both slides you clicked and all of the slides in between them will be selected. Use this method to select a consecutive series of slides.
- Click on one slide, and then hold down the **Control** key before clicking on another slide. Each additional slide you click while

holding down the Control key will be selected. Use this if you want to select every fifth slide, or only those slides with questions on them, or some other set of slides that aren't next to each other.

- Hold down the **Control** key and press the **A** key (**Ctrl+A**) to select all slides. You can also choose **Select All Slides** from the Edit menu.

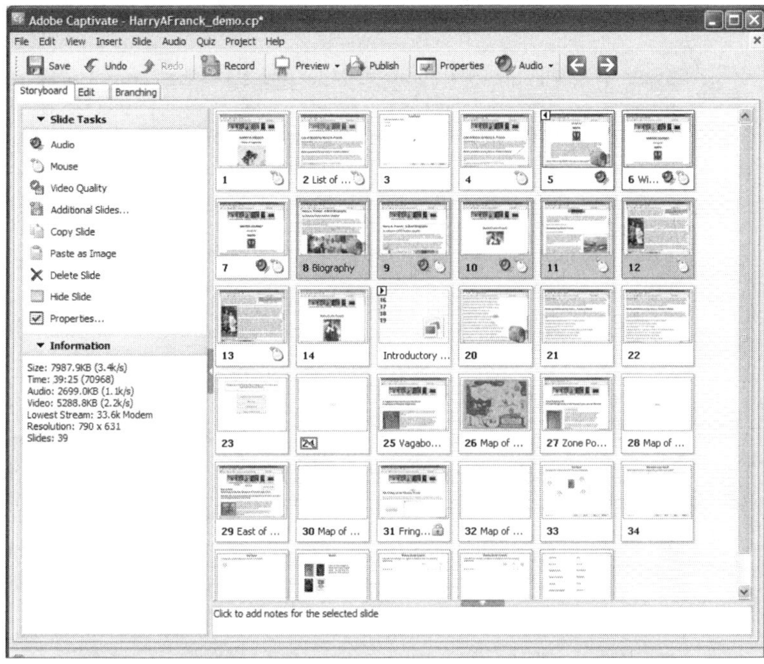

Figure 13-4. Select multiple slides.

Selected slides display in the Storyboard view with a shaded background. Any task you choose from the Slide Tasks list on the left of the Storyboard view will be applied to all of the selected slides. For example, in Figure 13-4, you can see that slides numbered 8 through 12 have been selected. The other slides above and below them are not selected. You could delete them all by choosing Delete Slide from the Slide Tasks list, or copy them all, or modify the slide properties such as transitions or timing.

Note: When you have multiple slides selected, some functions will not be available (such as adding a label). These functions will display in pale gray and you won't be able to click on them.

Rearranging Slides

After you've recorded a movie, you may decide that a particular set of slides belongs in a different part of the movie. Or you may want to set all the animation, transitions, and interactive elements for one section, then copy and paste those slides for modification in another section. These sorts of tasks are easy to do in Storyboard view.

Tip: When you move slides, all the slides will be renumbered so that the numbering remains sequential—that is, if you cut slide #3, the old slide #4 becomes the new slide #3 and all subsequent slides are renumbered. You may want to assign a label to slides you're moving so that you can keep track of them more easily.

There are several methods you can use to move slides around within your movie:

- Select the slides or slides you want to move, click and hold down the left mouse button, and drag the slides to a new location in the Storyboard.
- Select the slide or slides and copy them to the clipboard with the Copy Slide command in the Slide Tasks list, the Copy function in the Edit menu, or the Ctrl+C key combination.
- Cut slides from your movie and copy them to the clipboard with the Delete Slide command in the Slide Tasks list, the Cut function in the Edit menu, or the Ctrl+X key combination.
- Paste slides from the clipboard to wherever the cursor is by choosing the Paste as Image command in the Slide Tasks list, the Paste function in the Edit menu, or the Ctrl+V key combination.

Changing Movie-wide Settings

Some of the Captivate functions apply to the entire movie, not just individual slides. For example, you can set a background color that displays if the content of a slide doesn't fill the whole screen, or change the movie speed or color quality.

Choosing a Background Color

The background of a movie is the portion of the screen not covered by the content of a slide. For example, if you import an image that does not fill the entire screen, the background of the slide will show through around the border of the image. Note that the background color won't show through on all slides—if your slide content, such as a screen capture, covers the entire screen, the background won't show.

To set the background for a movie, follow these steps:

1. From any view, open the **Edit** menu, and then select **Preferences** to display the Preferences window.
2. Click **Project** in the Category list to display the project preferences options.

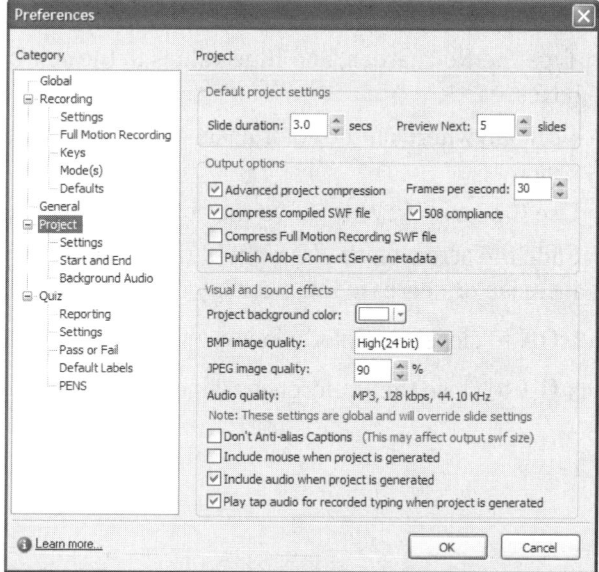

Figure 13-5. Set the background color in the Preferences window.

3. The current background color is displayed in the Project background color box. The default is white. Click on the color box to display a set of predefined colors. You can also click on the down arrow to display the Color window.

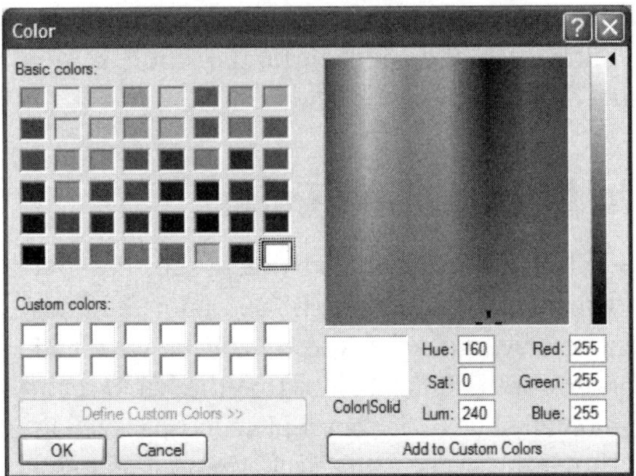

Figure 13-6. Choose a background color.

4. Select the color you want for the background in any of the following ways:
   - Click on a color in the Basic colors grid.
   - Type the Hue, Saturation, and Luminosity values in the appropriate boxes.
   - Type the Red, Green, and Blue values in the appropriate boxes.
   - Click anywhere on the color chart on the right side of the window.
   - Use the arrow keys to move the color selection indicator.
   - Slide the arrow on the far right of the window up or down to increase or decrease the intensity of the current color.
5. Click **OK** to close the Color window.
6. Click **OK** to close the Preferences window.

Changing Display and Audio Quality

When you first recorded your Captivate movie, you specified the quality you wanted for both the video and audio quality. You can override those settings in the Preferences window.

1. From any view, open the **Edit** menu, and then select **Preferences** to display the Preferences window.
2. Click **Project** in the Category list to display the preferences options.
3. Set the image quality as a percentage of the original input quality. Thus, if you start with very high-quality JPEG graphics, you can probably reduce the quality and still get decent images. However, if your graphics start out at low quality, you want to leave this setting high. You can set different quality levels for JPEG and for BMP images.

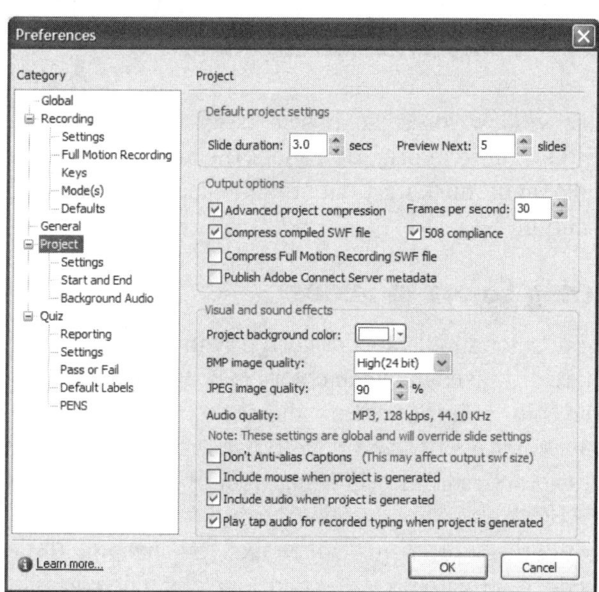

Figure 13-7. Set image quality in the Preferences window.

4. Set the audio quality by clicking on the displayed audio quality description to display the Audio settings window. For example, in Figure 13-7, the audio quality is MP3, 128 kbps, 44.10 KHz.

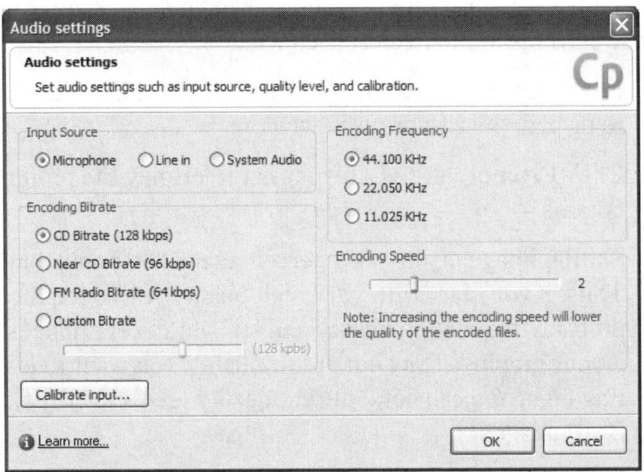

Figure 13-8. Set audio quality in the Audio settings window.

From this window you can choose a variety of audio settings. See Chapter 8 for more information about the audio options. Remember, your audio input must start out at high quality in order to get high-quality output.

Correcting Colors in Slides

In general, color should appear correctly in Captivate movies. However, there are cases in which colors may appear inaccurately, such as when the color scheme varies radically between slides. So if Slide A uses color palette ABC, and Slide B uses color palette XYZ, and the two palettes are radically different, Slide B might resort to using palette ABC.

Most of these problems can be fixed by changing the video quality of the slide. Captivate provides four levels of video quality, even though the Standard option is suggested for most uses.

To change video quality in a slide:

1. Open a Captivate project.
2. Double-click on the slide containing the colors you want to correct.

3. From the Slide menu, select **Properties** to display the Slide Properties window.

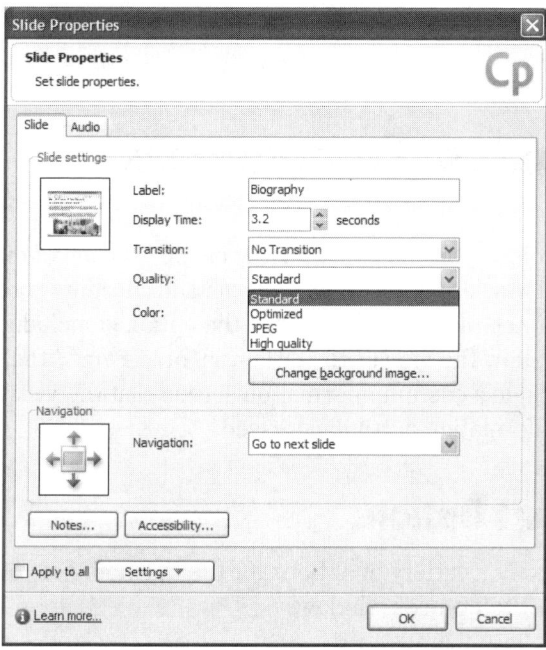

Figure 13-9. Set color quality in the Slide Properties window.

4. Select one of the video options from the Quality drop-down list:
   - Standard—The default format for slides. Standard is the most efficient choice for the majority of screen shots because it uses 256 optimized colors. Standard slides also compress well, which results in smaller file sizes.
   - Optimized—Better resolution than the standard quality.
   - JPEG—This option is best used when the slide contains a photograph. You can change the quality and compression ratio for JPEG images in the Preferences window.
   - High quality—Compared to the standard format of 256 colors, this format uses 16 million colors for the slides. This option should only be used if the Standard and JPEG options do not offer the correct color depth. The file size increases dramatically using this option.

Note: Selecting the JPEG or High quality format may increase the file size and the time it takes to download your movie. You should only use a format other than Standard when necessary and appropriate.

Adding Custom Components

For each project, you can add a variety of special components to polish the finished movie. For example, you can add a loading screen at the beginning of the movie, and you have the option of including playback controls to allow the viewer to start, stop, or "rewind" the movie. You can also include a custom information screen that the viewer sees when the Information button is pressed.

Movie Start Options

You can specify a variety of options for the beginning of your movie through the Preferences window.

Loading screen—This displays an image (such as a clock or an icon that says "Loading…") while your movie is being prepared for the viewer. For short movies displayed from a hard drive, the loading process may be so short that you don't even see the loading screen. For longer movies, particularly those distributed over the Internet, you may want to include a loading screen to indicate that the movie will start soon.

Password protection—You can limit the viewers of a movie by requiring that a password be entered before the movie plays. You can set one password for each movie.

Expiration date—Depending on the content of your movie, you may want to limit the number of days that viewers can access your movie. Do this by setting an expiration date for the movie.

Fade in—Rather than have the first screen on your movie appear suddenly, you can specify a fade-in effect.

Tip: Always test your movie from the final location—with all files and folders in place. Sometimes, if you're running in a development environment or on a local hard drive, the movie start options (particularly the loading screen) may not display as they will on the finished project.

To define the way your movie begins, follow these steps:

1. From any view, open the **Edit** menu, and then select **Preferences** to display the Preferences window.
2. Click the **Start and End** option under the Project category on the left side of the screen.

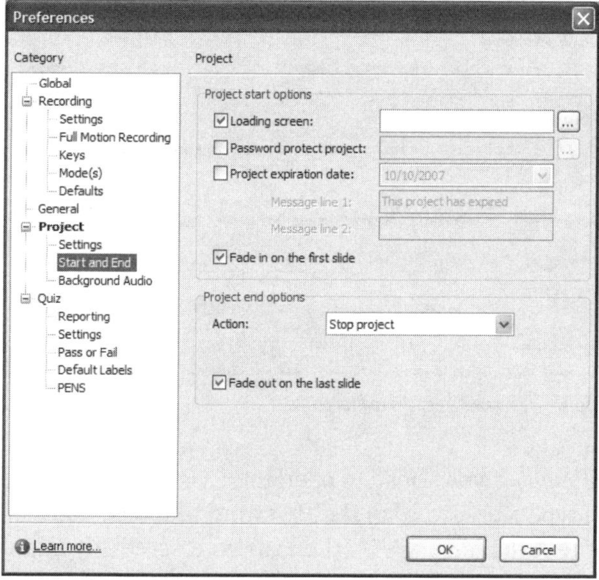

Figure 13-10. Set project start preferences.

3. To specify a loading screen, click the **Loading screen** check box, and then type the location and file name of the image you want to use into the Loading screen text box. You can also click the **Browse** button to browse to the file location. Loading screens, icons, and/or animations must be in one of the supported formats (JPG, JPEG, GIF, PNG, BMP, ICO, EMF, WMF, or SWF).

Tip: Captivate comes with a variety of animations that you can use as loading screens. By default, they're stored in the Captivate\Gallery\Preloaders folder.

4. If you want the viewer to enter a password before viewing the movie, click the **Password protect project** check box. If you select this option, you must also enter a password, either by typing it into the text box or clicking the button to the right of the box to display the Password options window. Passwords may contain any combination of letters and numbers and may also include the underscore character (_), but no other punctuation or spaces.

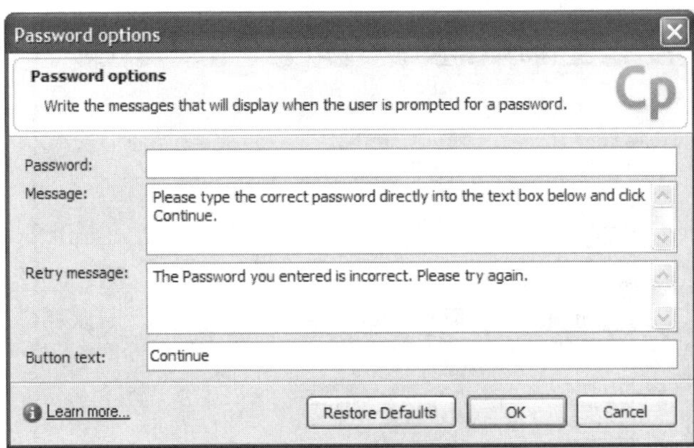

Figure 13-11. Password options control access.

5. (*optional*) If you chose to open the Password options window, you can type a password in the Password text box. You can also change the text that displays on the Password screen by entering text in the appropriate fields. Click **OK** when you are done to return to the Preferences window. You may leave the default text (shown in Figure 13-11) or edit any or all of the following:
   - Message—This text appears on the screen along with a text entry box.
   - Retry message—This text appears only if the viewer enters an incorrect password.
   - Button text—This text appears on the button that the user must click after typing in the password.

6. If you want to set an expiration date, click the **Project expiration date** check box and then enter a date. Viewers will be able to view the movie up through the end of the day you've specified.

Note: Captivate compares the expiration date of the movie to the date as set on the viewer's system. If the viewer's system has an incorrect date, the viewer may not be able to see the movie (or may be able to see a movie after you've set it to expire).

7. (*optional*) If you've set an expiration date, you can also modify the text that appears on the screen when the viewer attempts to open an expired movie. You have up to two lines of text.
8. Click the **Fade in on the first slide** check box to have the beginning of your movie appear on the screen gradually.
9. Click **OK** when you are finished to close the Preferences window.

Movie End Options

You can also specify what happens at the end of the movie. There are a variety of options, including simply stopping or closing the movie, replaying the movie again from the beginning, and starting some other movie. To set the movie end action, follow these steps:

1. From any view, open the **Edit** menu, and then select **Preferences** to display the Preferences window.
2. Click the **Start and End** option under the Project category on the left side of the screen.

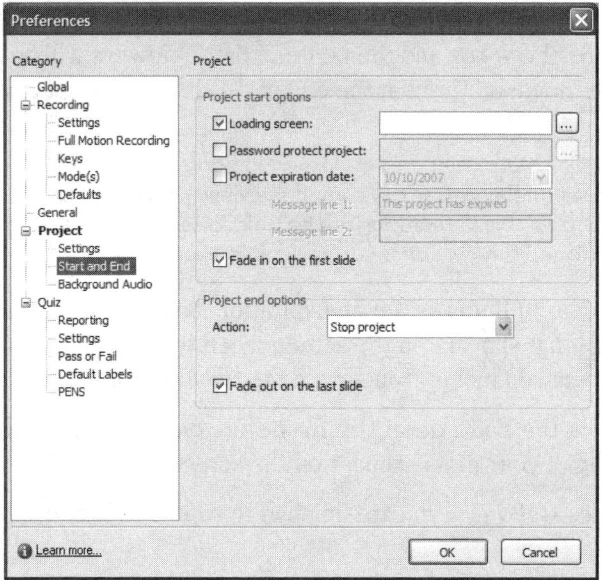

Figure 13-12. Set end preferences.

3. Choose an action from the Project end options Action drop-down list. Available options include:

Table 13-2. Options for the end of a movie

Choose this action:	For this result:
Stop project	The movie simply stops at the last slide.
Loop project	The movie restarts from the beginning. This is often useful for kiosk-type delivery.
Close project	The movie stops at the last slide and closes the movie viewer.
Open URL or file	After the last slide plays, either a new file or a web page will display. You must enter the name of the file or URL of the page by typing it in the box or by browsing to the file location or URL. You can also click the pop-up menu to select the window in which the URL or file should appear (Current window, New window, Parent window, or Top window).
Execute JavaScript	Run specified JavaScript when the movie ends. Click the Browse button to enter the JavaScript code you want to run.
Open other project	Play another movie as soon as this one ends. You must enter the name by typing it in the box or by browsing to the file location. You can also click the pop-up menu to select the window in which the movie should appear (Current window, New window, Parent window, or Top window).
Send e-mail to	Send an e-mail as soon as the movie has finished. You must type the full e-mail address (for example, bphuettner@p-ndesigns.com).

Note: As you make selections for the project end actions, additional fields or buttons will display that are appropriate for the selected action.

4. Click **Fade out on the last slide** to display the last slide and then gradually have it fade from view. This fading will happen immediately before other actions you may have specified in step 3.

5. Click **OK** to close the Preferences window.

Movie Skins

You can control the final look and feel of your movie using Captivate "skins." A skin defines the playback controls, the background that displays behind your slides, and the information that displays when the viewer presses the Info (i) button on the playback controls. You can also use skins to define a menu that will display in addition to the playback controls.

Captivate comes with a variety of predefined skins. You can edit any of these skins, or create your own skin so that you can reuse it in other movies.

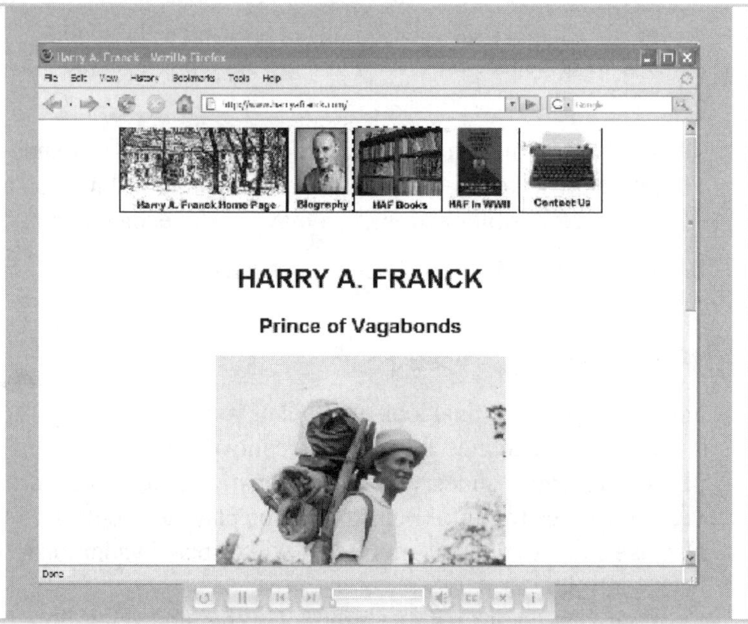
Harry A. Franck - Mozilla Firefox
Harry A. Franck Home Page
Biography
HAF Books
HAF in WWII
Contact Us
HARRY A. FRANCK
Prince of Vagabonds
Done

Harry A. Franck - Mozilla Firefox
Harry A. Franck Home Page
Biography
HAF Books
HAF in WWII
Contact Us
HARRY A. FRANCK
Prince of Vagabonds

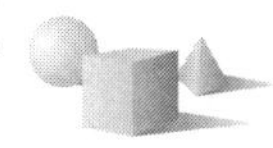

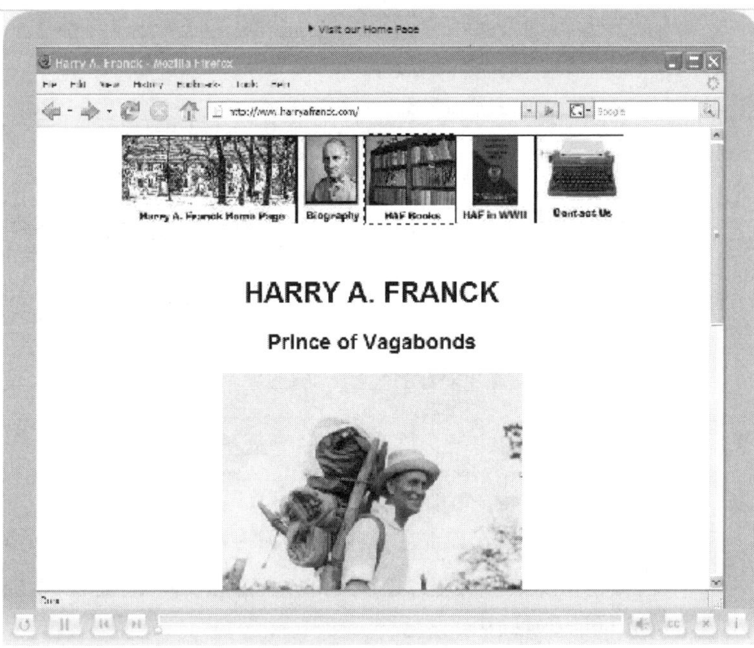

Figure 13-13. Different skins change the look of your movie.

Changing the Skin

To change the look and feel of your movie, you can use any one of the predefined skins that are shipped with Captivate.

1. From any view, open the **Project** menu, and then select **Skin** to display the Skin Editor.
2. Click the **Playback Control** tab to display the Playback control options.

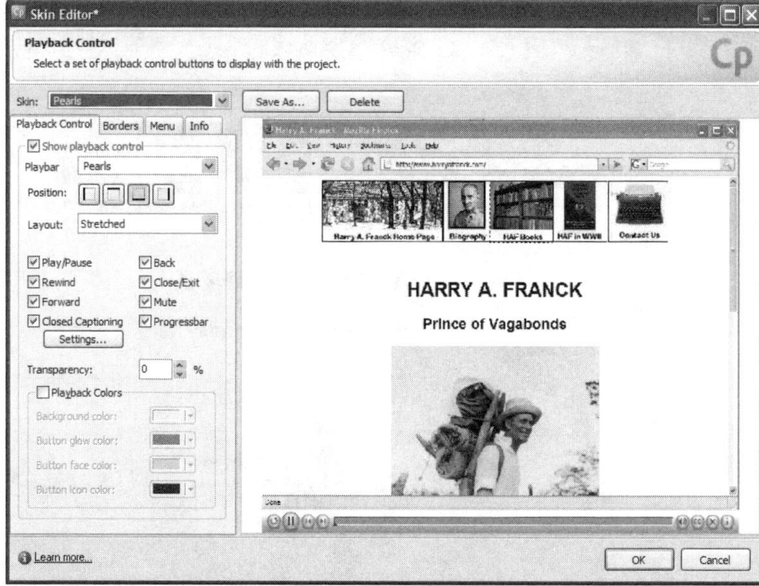

Figure 13-14. Choose a skin.

3. Choose a skin from the drop-down list at the top of the Skin Editor. The preview of the movie with the new skin displays on the right side of the screen.
4. You can make changes to any skin as described in the following sections; then click the **Save As** button to store your changes. Or you can just use the predefined options.
5. Click **OK** when you're finished changing the skin.

Changing Playback Controls

For each movie, you have the option to include playback controls that determine which buttons display while the viewer is playing the movie. You can choose from a variety of playback control styles that come with Captivate. Some have many buttons, such as forward one slide, forward to the end of the movie, go back one slide, go back to the beginning, pause, stop, etc. You can also specify where the playback controls will display.

Figure 13-15. A variety of playback controls.

Note: These are not the same as the controls available when you're previewing a movie. Playback controls usually (though not always) have an information button (designated by the letter i).

To select the playback controls for the current movie, follow these steps:

1. From any view, open the **Project** menu, and then select **Skin** to display the Skin Editor.
2. Click the **Playback Control** tab to display the Playback control options.

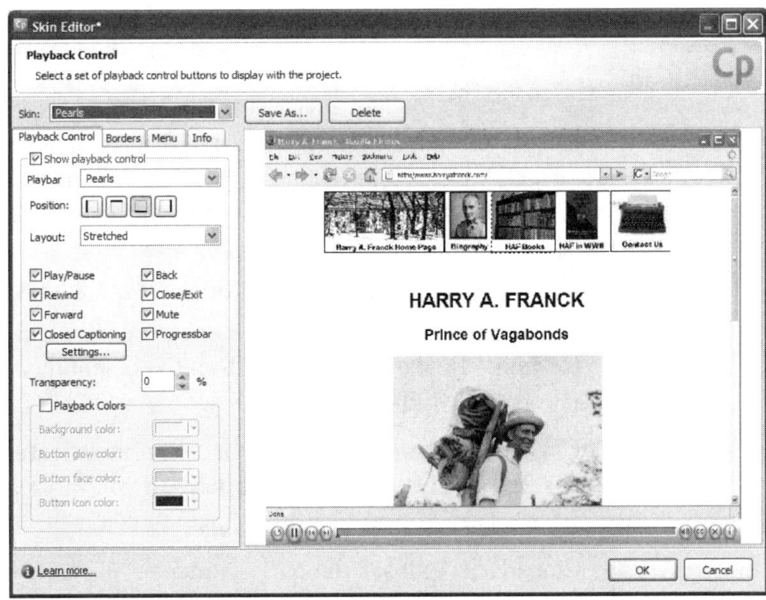

Figure 13-16. Set playback control options in the Skin Editor.

3. Click the **Show playback control** check box to display the controls and activate the playback options. If this check box is not selected, no playback controls will display on the finished movie.

4. Choose the location for the playback controls by clicking on one of the Position icons. You can place the controls on the left, top, bottom, or right side of the movie viewer screen.

Tip: Make sure you preview your movie with the playback controls to ensure that your controls don't cover important captions or other buttons. Some playback controls are much larger than others, and switching controls without testing can give unexpected results. You'll also want to think carefully about choosing controls that omit, for example, an exit button, particularly for a full-screen movie that may have no other way of ending early if the viewer needs it to.

5. Choose the layout of the playback controls within the location you specified by choosing an option from the Layout drop-down list. These options will vary depending on the location you chose. For example, if you chose a vertical orientation (left side or right side), you'll be able to specify whether the controls should be on the top or bottom of that side. You also have the Stretched option, which displays the controls from one edge of the screen to the other. As you specify these options, the preview panel reflects the changes as you make them.

6. Choose the playback controls you want displayed by selecting the style check boxes. Note that some Playbar options have more buttons than others, and a few are oriented vertically. The check boxes may include some or all of the following:
   - Play/Pause—Plays the movie (or restarts the movie after the viewer pauses it).
   - Rewind—Restarts the movie from the beginning.
   - Forward—Displays the next slide.
   - Closed Captioning—Displays an icon that activates text descriptions of the movie as it plays (if you've created them).
   - Back—Displays the previous slide.
   - Close/Exit—Closes the movie window.
   - Mute—Displays an audio control icon.
   - Progressbar—This is the visual representation of where the viewer is within the movie. For example, if the viewer is looking at slide 10 of 100, the progress bar will display across one-tenth of the available bar length. If the viewer is looking at

slide 80 of 100, the progress bar will show that the movie is 8/10ths of the way complete.

7. If you chose to display closed captioning, click the **Settings** button to display the Closed Captioning settings window. You can define the number of lines on which the captions display, as well as the font, size, background, and transparency of the displayed text. Remember, you must create the captions for each audio file as described in Chapter 8. Click **OK** to close the Closed Captioning settings window.

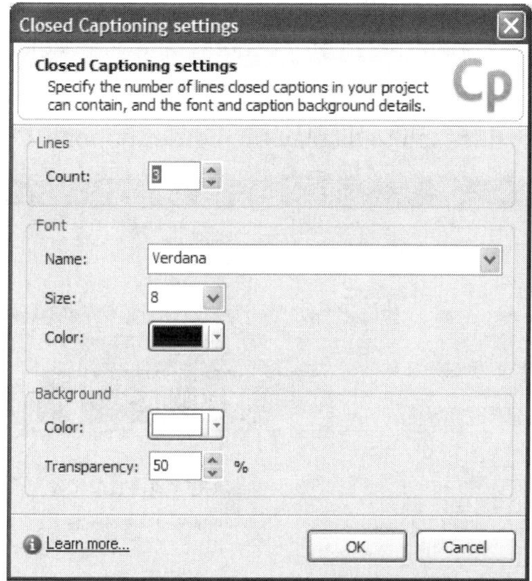

Figure 13-17. Define how the closed captions will display.

8. You can set the transparency of the playback control background by either using the up and down arrows to increment the transparency by steps of 10%, or by typing a specific transparency percentage. Note that a transparency of 0 is solid (nothing shows through) and a transparency of 100 removes the control background entirely (the playback buttons appear to "float" on the movie).

9. (*optional*) Predefined playback controls have predefined control colors. You can change these colors by selecting the Playback Colors check box to activate the color controls. As you choose new colors for each of the options, the colors display on the preview.

10. Click **Save As** if you want to store your changes to the skin (to the current name or to a new custom name). If you don't save the changes you've made, they'll be applied to the current movie only. Click **OK** when you're done to close the Skin Editor.

Defining Borders

The borders on the final movie are the areas around the captured area. By enlarging the border behind the location you've chosen for the playback controls, you can ensure that those controls don't cover important areas of your movie.

1. From any view, open the **Project** menu, and then select **Skin** to display the Skin Editor.
2. Click the **Borders** tab to display the border options.

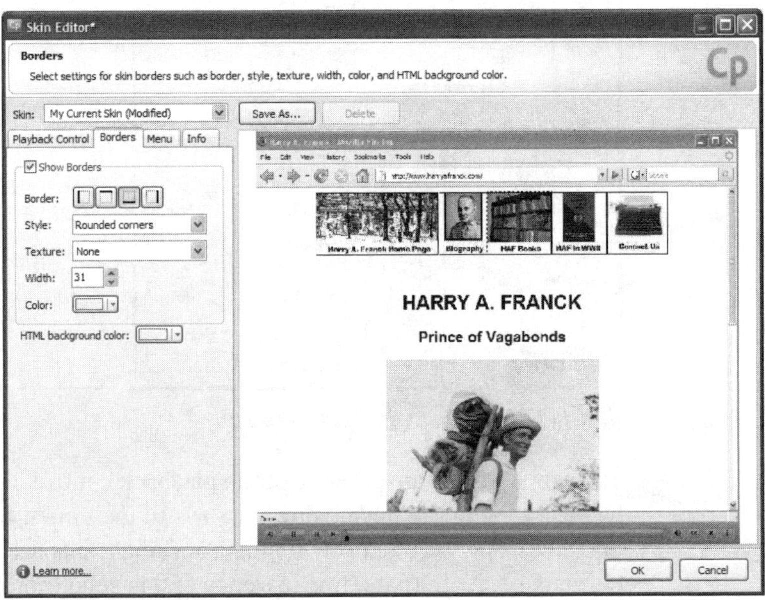

Figure 13-18. Enlarge or shade around the edges of your movie.

3. Click the **Show Borders** check box to display the defined borders and activate the border options. If this check box is not selected, no borders will display on the finished movie.
4. Select which borders to display by clicking the Border icons. Note that unlike the Position setting, which allows you to select any one icon, the Border setting lets you choose as many borders as you

need. As you click on each icon, the selected border displays on the preview portion of the window.

5. Select a Style of either **Rounded corners** or **Square edge**. Note that this style applies to the outer edges of the borders around the movie, not the captured movie itself.

6. Choose either a Texture (by selecting a graphic from the drop-down list) or a Color (by clicking on the color box and choosing a color) for the borders. If you choose a texture, the selected graphic will be used as the selected border edges. For example, Figure 13-19 shows the texture "thatch" on all four sides of the movie (and a rounded corner style).

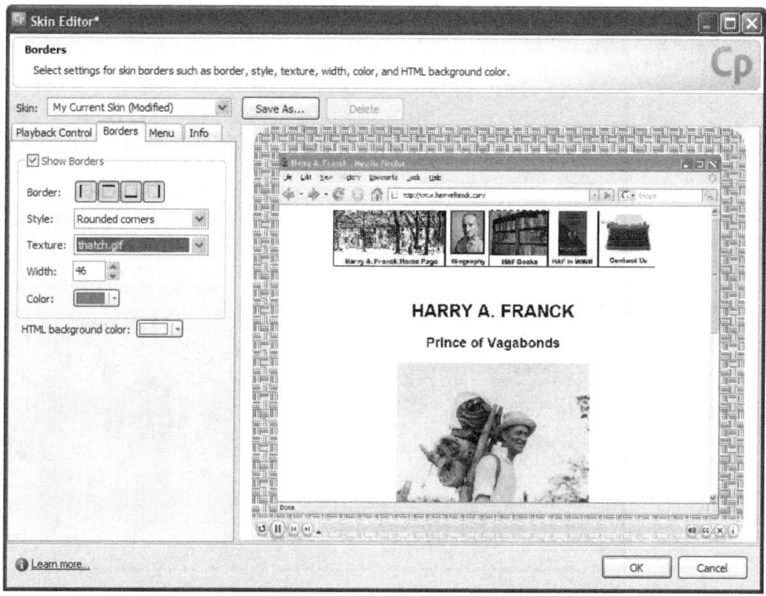

Figure 13-19. A movie with textured borders.

7. Specify the Width (in pixels) for the border. The border should be at least as large as your playback controls on the edge where the playback controls are displayed (the bottom edge in Figure 13-19).

8. Choose a color that will display behind the movie (for example, show through the rounded corners).

9. Click **Save As** if you want to store your changes to the skin (to the current name or to a new custom name). If you don't save the

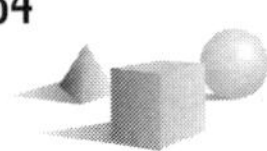

changes you've made, they'll be applied to the current movie only. Click **OK** when you're done to close the Skin Editor.

Creating a Menu

Captivate allows you to create a unique menu that displays at run time. You can define the appearance of the menu and the actions that occur when the menu sub-items are selected.

1. From any view, open the **Project** menu, and then select **Skin** to display the Skin Editor.

2. Click the **Menu** tab to display the menu options.

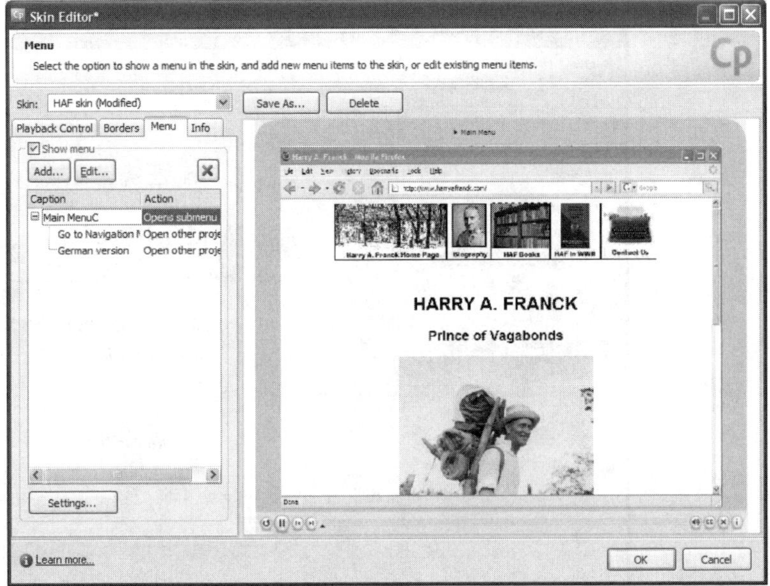

Figure 13-20. Define a menu that displays at run time.

3. If this movie already has a menu, it will display in the Menu panel on the left side of the window. To edit the Main Menu item, highlight it and click **Edit.** If you don't yet have a menu, this area will be blank. To add a menu, click the **Add** button. Either way, the Add/Edit menu item window displays.

Note: If you already have a menu in this file, the Add button will add menu sub-items. If you don't have a menu yet, the Add button creates the Main Menu.

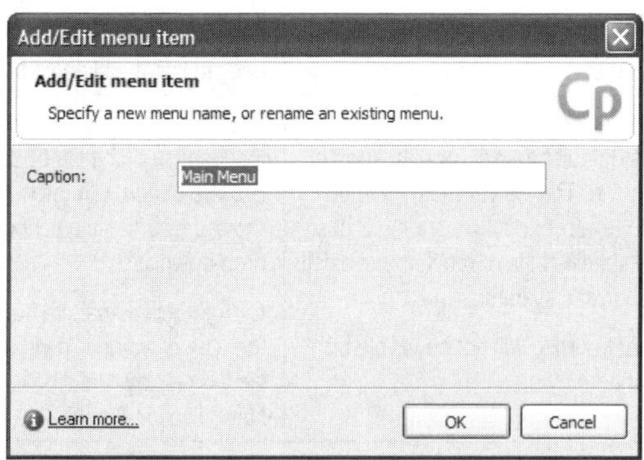

Figure 13-21. Define text for the Main Menu item.

4. Type the name of the menu in the Caption text box, then click **OK** to close this window.
5. Click the **Add** button to add new items to the Main Menu (or highlight an existing item and click **Edit**). The Add/Edit menu item window is again displayed, this time with additional options.

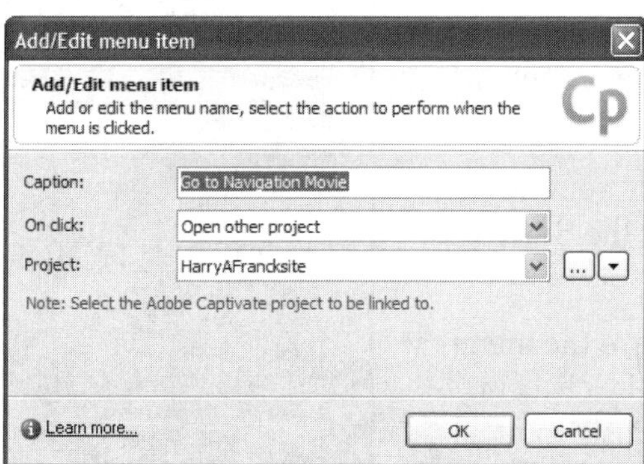

Figure 13-22. Define how the menu items work.

6. Type the name of the menu item in the Caption text box.
7. Choose an action from the **On click** drop-down list to specify a destination display when the viewer clicks the menu item:

Table 13-3. Destination options for menu items

Choose this option:	For this effect:	Also enter this information:
Jump to slide	Display the specified slide and continue the movie from there.	Choose from the drop-down list of slides. Note that slide labels, if any, appear in the list instead of slide numbers. This makes it easy to find the slide you're looking for!
Open URL or file Open other project	Display the specified URL or file in the viewer's default browser, or play another Flash movie. The viewer must have an active Internet connection to view URLs, and the specified file or movie must exist on the viewer's system. Note that the URL will not be visible on the finished movie.	Enter the URL or file name, or browse to the location of the file by clicking the Browse button with three dots (...). For movies, you can also choose from a drop-down list. Click the black triangle button to choose the type of window in which the URL or file will display. Valid options are Current, New, Top, or Parent.
Send e-mail to	Create an e-mail message to send to a specified address in the viewer's default e-mail program. The viewer will still have to fill in the message and subject and hit Send.	Enter the e-mail address to which you want the e-mail sent. Click the check box to indicate whether or not the current movie should continue playing.
Execute JavaScript	Run a specified JavaScript.	Enter the JavaScript code here.

8. Click **OK** to close the window. The item appears in the list of menu captions.

9. To change the color and placement of your new menu, click the **Settings** button.

10. Specify where the menu will display by choosing one of the Position radio buttons, then choose the colors and font for the menu items. Click **OK** when you're done to close the window.

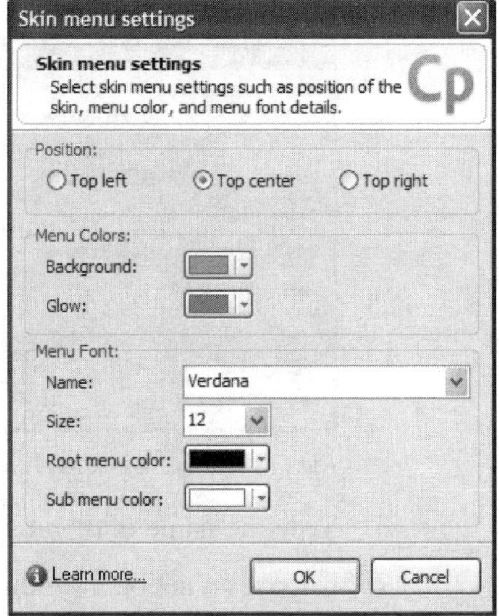

Figure 13-23. Define how the menu items display.

11. Click **Save As** if you want to store your changes to the skin (to the current name or to a new custom name). If you

don't save the changes you've made, they'll be applied to the current movie only. Click **OK** when you're done to close the Skin Editor.

Displaying Movie Information

If you display movie controls on the finished movie, the controls will always include an information button. The button itself will vary according to the style of controls you choose, but it will always be designated with the letter **i**. To specify the information that displays when the viewer clicks the information button, follow these steps:

1. From any view, open the **Project** menu, and then select **Skin** to display the Skin Editor.
2. Click the **Info** tab to display the information display options.

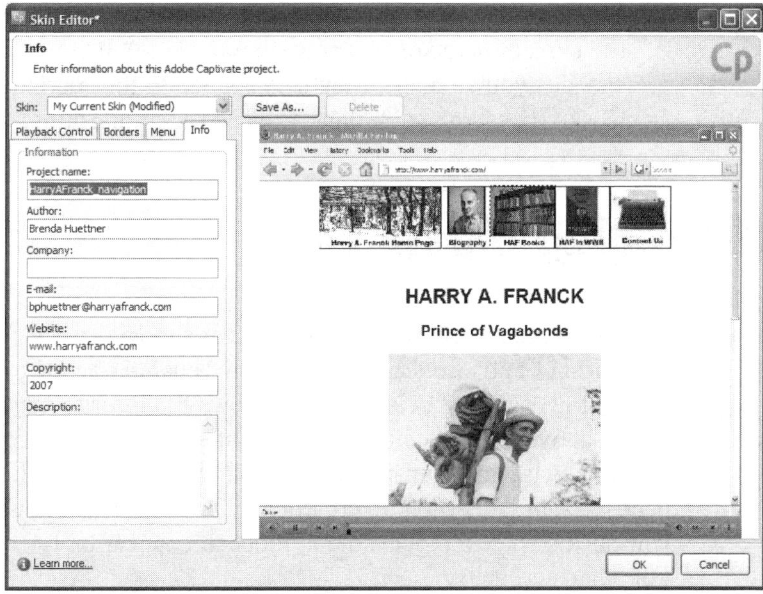

Figure 13-24. Enter information about the movie.

3. Type information in any or all of the text boxes.

Note: Although you can leave the information boxes empty, you must enter at least the name and description for full compliance with the U.S. government Section 508 accessibility rules.

Table 13-4. Information fields

This field:	Should contain this information:
Project name	A unique name for the movie. If you're generating accessible movies, this name will be read by screen reader software at the beginning of the movie. Note that this does not display in the information window.
Author	The name of the author of the movie (or department, if more applicable).
Company	The company name.
E-mail	An e-mail address to which people can write with problems, if they encounter any.
Website	The web address (URL) for your company or organization.
Copyright	The copyright information for your movie.
Description	A short description of the movie. If you're generating accessible movies, this description will be read by screen reader software at the beginning of the movie. Note that this does not display in the information window.

4. Click **Save As** if you want to store your changes to the skin (to the current name or to a new custom name). If you don't save the changes you've made, they'll be applied to the current movie only. Click **OK** when you're done to close the Skin Editor.

Managing Movie Files

You can set Captivate to automatically save movies with a global setting within Captivate. But if you want to rename or copy or delete a movie, the easiest way is to use Windows Explorer to manipulate your files. Captivate stores information about each movie in Captivate project files (with an extension of .cp). You can delete these files, if necessary, or copy them to create new files. Back within Captivate, you can also hide a movie so that it doesn't appear on the opening Captivate screen.

Saving Movies

As you've seen throughout this book, it is easy to save a movie periodically while you're working on it. There are three ways to save a movie:

- Click the **Save** icon on the toolbar.

- From the File menu, choose **Save.**
- Press **Ctrl+S** on the keyboard.

Working with Movie Files in Windows Explorer

You can view all of your movie projects, or delete or copy them, or perform any of the other tasks that are normally handled by the Windows operating system. To do this, follow these steps:

1. Open Windows Explorer, then navigate to the location of the Captivate movie.

Tip: As you create movie projects, Captivate stores the files by default in the folder \My Documents\My Captivate Projects. If you've saved movies to a location other than this (using the Save As command), you'll need to browse to wherever your movies are stored.

2. Captivate creates a number of files of various types while you're working within the project. Click the file icon (or name) to select it.

Table 13-5: Captivate file types

This extension:	Indicates this file type:
.cp	The Captivate project files. All other files are created from this one.
.htm	An HTML file that is created specifically to play a Flash movie file.
.swf	The Flash movie file itself.
.mpg	MenuBuilder files that point to a variety of other files.

3. Choose any of the displayed tasks (Rename, Move, Copy, Delete). You can also right-click on the file icon (or name) to display a pop-up menu of tasks.

Tip: It is easy to recreate deleted .htm or .swf files from your Captivate project file (.cp). However, if you delete the Captivate project file, you'll have to start all over again to create that particular movie. Make sure you are completely finished with a project file before you delete it—better yet, archive the project for future reference. You may be able to borrow tricks or slides from one movie for use in another later.

Hiding Movies

When you start Captivate, it displays a list of the most recently created movies. You can remove a movie project from this list if desired. For example, if you've got several versions of a movie and only want the most recent one to display, you can "hide" the older versions. To do this, follow these steps:

1. From the main Captivate opening window, right-click on the movie that you want to hide to display a pop-up menu.
2. Choose **Hide movie** to display a confirmation dialog.
3. Click **Yes** to remove the movie from the list of recently viewed movies. The project remains in the folder and can still be accessed using the Open button.

Summary

This chapter reviewed some of the tasks you might perform on movies and projects, including setting start and end options and managing movie files. The following chapter discusses the various output options for Captivate projects.

Chapter 14

Generating Captivate Output

After you've created your slides, added objects and interactivity, and defined the movie-level components, the final step is to generate the movie output. Captivate gives you a variety of output options, such as stand-alone executable files or HTML files for web-based delivery.

Another type of Captivate output lets you specify just parts of the movie, such as pulling out the text captions (for translation or review purposes) or creating a variety of paper-based handouts.

There are also options that you can set to ensure your movie is compatible with the U.S. Section 508 accessibility guidelines.

Publishing a Movie

There are a variety of output options available when you generate (or "publish") a movie project.

Flash (SWF)—This option creates a standard Flash file (.swf) that can be played by a Flash viewer. You can have Captivate automatically generate an HTML file that will use the default browser viewer, or create a zipped file for easier transportation between systems.

Adobe Connect—Adobe Connect is a web-based meeting and presentation server software package. You can export Captivate movies directly to an Adobe Connect server.

Standalone—This option can produce a Windows executable file (.exe), a Linux Projector file (.exe), or a Macintosh Projector file (.hqx).

Viewers of the movie would not need to have any viewing software on their systems to run a stand-alone movie.

In addition, you can e-mail or FTP Flash files, executable files, or even the original project files directly from Captivate, and print captions as Word files.

Publishing Projects as Flash Files

When you publish Captivate projects as Flash SWF movie files, you can automatically create zip files (for easier distribution) or HTML files for use with web pages. You can also specify whether the movie should play as a full-screen movie or at the size you specify when recording.

To publish a project as a Flash movie file, follow these steps:

1. Click the Publish icon or select **Publish** from the File menu to display the Publish window.
2. Click the **Flash (SWF)** icon to display the Flash options.

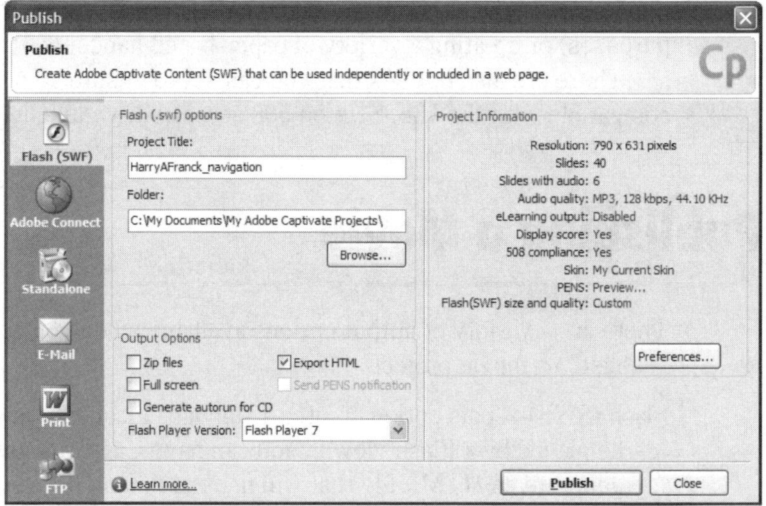

Figure 14-1. Set the publishing options.

3. The Project Title text box defaults to the name you entered for the project file. You can leave this as-is or type a new name. It isn't necessary to include the file extension—Captivate will add .swf to the finished file name.

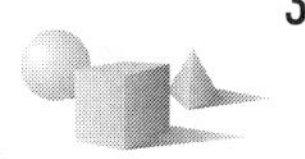

4. The Folder text box defaults to the folder that stores the project files. You can leave this as-is, type a new folder location, or click the Browse button to browse to the output location.
5. Select any of the following from the Output Options area:

Table 14-1. Flash movie output options

Select this option:	To create this:
Zip files	A zip file containing your Flash file. The zip file will have the same name entered in the Project Title field with the extension .zip.
Full screen	A Flash file and two HTML files that you'll use to play the Flash file in full-screen mode. The HTML files both have the same name as the Project Title (and the extension .htm), but one also has "_fs" appended to the file name. When you open *filename*_fs.htm, the movie will play full screen. Note that this option is not available if you have selected AICC or SCORM options (see Chapter 10).
Generate autorun for CD	A Flash file and an autorun file (called autorun.inf). If you copy both of these files to a CD or DVD, the movie file will play automatically when the user starts the disc (depending on the user's system).
Export HTML	A Flash file and an HTML file that can be used to display the Flash file in a browser. The HTML file will have the same name entered in the Project Title field with the extension .htm.
Send PENS notification	Notification to the specified learning management system (if you've defined it in the Quiz Preferences area).
Flash Player Version	Output that can be read by the specified version of the Flash Player.

6. The Project Information area on the right of the screen displays the current preference settings for the movie, such as the resolution (in pixels) and audio information. To change the options listed in this area, click **Preferences** to display the Preferences window. The output options on this window are described later in this chapter in Table 14-4; other preferences are described in Chapter 13.
7. When you are done, click **Publish** to generate the output file or files.

Publishing to Adobe Connect

If you use the Adobe Connect collaboration and meeting application, you can publish your movie directly to the Adobe Connect server.

To send a Captivate project directly to a Connect server, follow these steps:

1. Click the Publish icon or select **Publish** from the File menu to display the Publish window.
2. Click the **Adobe Connect** icon to display the server options.

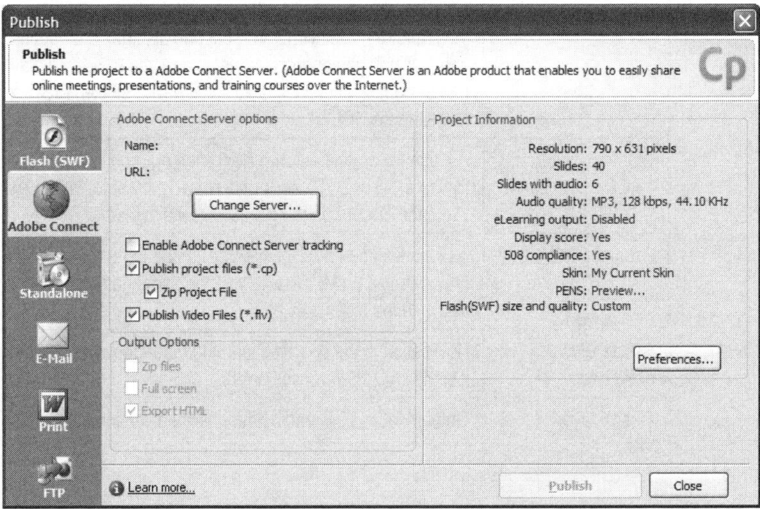

Figure 14-2. Set the Connect publishing options.

3. Click the **Change Server** button to display the list of Connect options available on your system.

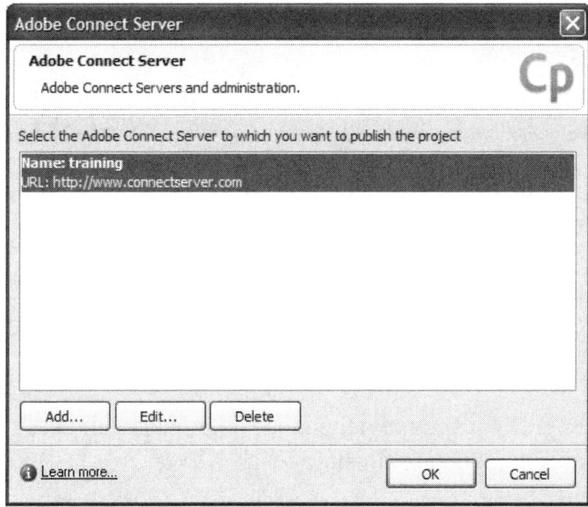

Figure 14-3. Choose a Connect server.

4. Select the server you want to use by clicking on the server name or URL. If the server isn't listed, you can click the **Add** button to enter information about a new server. You must enter both the name and URL of the server. Click **OK** when you are done to close the Adobe Connect Server window.

5. Select the check boxes for the output options you want.

Table 14-2. Adobe Connect output options

Select this option:	To do this:
Enable Adobe Connect Server tracking	Allow the Adobe Connect server to track viewer interactions within the Captivate movie.
Publish project files (*.cp)	Copies the source Captivate file (along with the output SWF file) to the Connect server.
Zip Project file	Zips the Captivate source file before storing it on the Connect server.
Publish Video Files (*.flv)	Copies FLV files (if any) from the Captivate project to the Connect server.

6. The Project Information area on the right of the screen displays the current preference settings for the movie, such as the resolution (in pixels) and audio information. To change the options listed in this area, click **Preferences** to display the Preferences window. The output options on this window are described later in this chapter in Table 14-4; other preferences are described in Chapter 13.

7. Set the preferences you want; then click **OK** to close the Preferences window.

Note: This window is discussed in more detail in Chapter 13.

8. When you are done, click **Publish** to display the Adobe Connect login screen.
9. Sign in to Adobe Connect using your login name and password.
10. Select a location on the server to store the Captivate movie.
11. Click **Publish to This Folder** to display the available options.
12. Type a title for the movie, choose a language, and enter a speaker name. When you are finished, click **Next**.
13. When the movie has been published to the server, a confirmation dialog displays. Click **OK** to close the confirmation dialog.

Publishing Projects as Stand-alone (EXE) Files

A stand-alone file is an executable file that does not require a browser for viewing. The Flash movie file is embedded in the executable file.

To generate a stand-alone movie file, follow these steps:

1. Click the Publish icon or select **Publish** from the File menu to display the Publish window.
2. Click the **Standalone** icon to display the executable options.

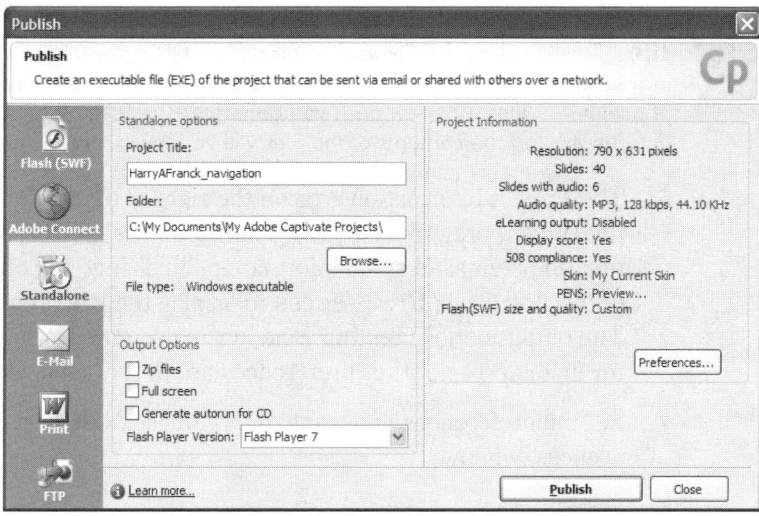

Figure 14-4. Set the publishing options.

3. The Project Title text box defaults to the name you entered for the project file. You can leave this as-is or type a new name. It isn't necessary to include the file extension—Captivate will add .exe to the finished file name.
4. The Folder text box defaults to the folder that stores the project files. You can leave this as-is, type a new folder location, or click the Browse button to browse to the output location.
5. Select any or all of the following from the Output Options area:

Table 14-3. Executable output options

Select this option:	To create this:
Zip files	A zip file containing your executable file. The zip file will have the same name entered in the Project Title field with the extension .zip.
Full screen	An executable file plays the movie in full-screen mode.
Generate autorun for CD	An executable file and an autorun file (called autorun.inf). If you copy both of these files to a CD or DVD, the movie file will play automatically when the user starts the disc by placing it in the disc drive or by clicking on the drive icon.
Flash Player Version	Output that can be read by the specified version of the Flash Player.

Tip: If you're using the Generate autorun for CD option, keep your movies in separate folders. This prevents Captivate from overwriting prior autorun files with new ones you generate. They are all named autorun.inf; just the contents of the files will vary by movie title.

6. The Project Information area on the right of the screen displays the current preference settings for the movie, such as the resolution (in pixels) and audio information. To change the options listed in this area, click **Preferences** to display the Preferences window. The output options on this window are described later in this chapter in Table 14-4; other preferences are described in Chapter 13.
7. Set the preferences you want, and then click **OK** to close the Preferences window.

Note: This window is discussed in more detail in Chapter 13.

8. When you are done, click **Publish** to generate the output file or files.

Setting Movie Preferences

During the publishing process, you can view the movie settings on the right side of the screen. If you need to change these settings, click the Preferences button to display the Preferences window, as shown in Figure 14-5.

Refer to Table 14-4 to choose the output, visual, and sound options on the Preferences window. You can also refer to Chapter 13 for more details about the Preferences window.

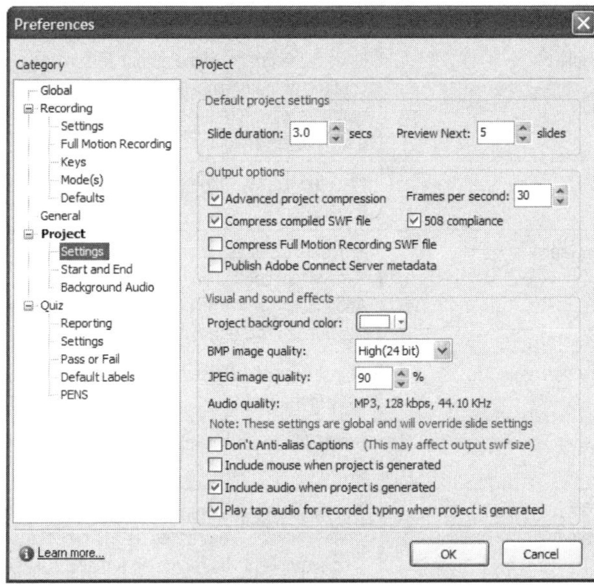

Figure 14-5. Set the movie output, visual, and sound options.

Table 14-4. Movie output, visual, and sound options

Select this:	To cause this:
Advanced project compression	Compress the movie by removing information that is shared among slides. This will reduce the movie size but may also impact movie quality. As always, be sure to test your movie after it is finished!
Compress compiled SWF file	Compress the SWF file. Note that compressed SWF files can only be used with Flash 7 or later.
Compress Full Motion Recording SWF file	Compress the full motion recordings within the movie.
Publish Adobe Connect Server metadata	Add information to the project file (SWF) that makes it easier to integrate the project into Adobe Connect Enterprise.
Frames per second	Determines the speed at which the movie will be played.
508 compliance	Select this option if you need to deliver Section 508-compliant Flash files. See the section called "About Accessibility" later in this chapter.
Project background color	Specify a color for the background of the movie slides.
BMP image quality	Specify the quality of the output BMP images.

Select this:	To cause this:
JPEG image qualiity	Specify the quality of the output JPG images as a percentage of the original file resolution. Note that lower numbers will decrease both the size of the file and the quality of the images.
Audio quality	Click the display of the current settings to display additional audio options.
Don't Anti-alias Captions	Prevents Captivate from using the anti-alias feature on transparent caption text in the published file. Anti-aliasing smooths out the text edges in the published file, but can make the resulting file size larger.
Include mouse when project is generated	Select this option to include any recorded mouse movement in the movie.
Include audio when movie is generated	Select this option to include any added audio files in the movie.
Play tap audio for recorded typing when movie is generated	This option plays tapping sounds in the final movie whenever keys are pressed as you record the movie. (For example, if you record an e-mail message being sent, you most likely type an e-mail address. Using this option, a tapping sound is played for each of the keystrokes.)

Sending Movie Files

Once you've published a movie to any of the available formats, you can send the files to other people by e-mail, on CD, over a web site, or by any other method that works for you. In addition to sending files after they've been published, Captivate allows you to send a movie either by e-mail or by FTP at the same time as you publish it.

Sending Movies through E-mail

To publish a project as a movie and send it through e-mail all at once, follow these steps:

1. Click the Publish icon or select **Publish** from the File menu to display the Publish window.
2. Click the **E-Mail** icon to display the e-mail options.

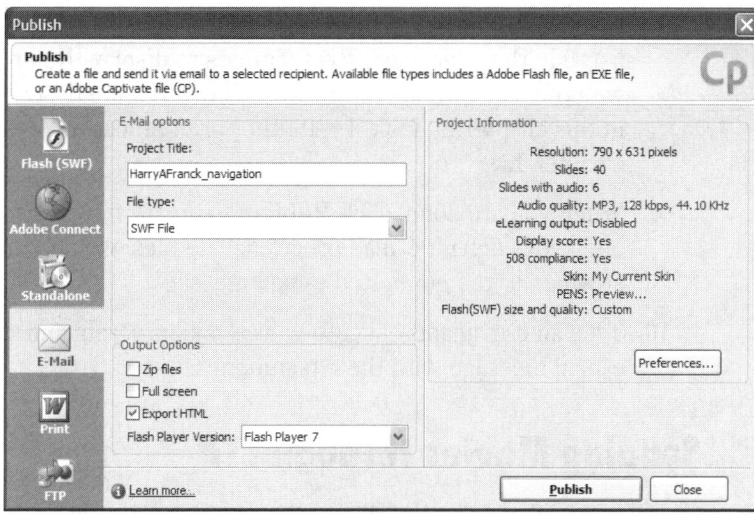

Figure 14-6. Enter e-mail options.

3. The Project Title text box defaults to the name you entered for the project file. You can leave this as-is or type a new name. It isn't necessary to include the file extension—Captivate will add .swf to the finished file name.
4. Specify which of the file types you want to generate by choosing from the drop-down list under File type:
   - SWF File—Creates and sends a Flash format file.
   - Windows Executable—Sends a stand-alone executable file with the extension .exe that runs on any Microsoft Windows-based system.
   - Project Files (.cp)—Sends the source Captivate files.
   - XML—Sends an XML version of the project.
5. (*optional*) Select the **Zip files** option to compress all output files into a single file with the extension .zip.
6. (*optional*) Select the **Full screen** option to create and e-mail a full-screen version of the movie.
7. (*optional*) Select the **Export HMTL** option to create an HTML file that will run the exported SWF file.
8. The Project Information area on the right of the screen displays the current preference settings for the movie, such as the

resolution (in pixels) and audio information. To change the options listed in this area, click **Preferences** to display the Preferences window. The output options on this window are described earlier in this chapter in Table 14-4; other preferences are described in Chapter 13.

9. When you are done, click **Publish** to create the specified files and open your default e-mail program. The files will automatically be attached to the generated e-mail message.
10. Type an e-mail address into your e-mail program and send the e-mail message with the attachment.

Sending Movies through FTP

You can publish your Captivate projects as movies directly to a web site using the standard file transfer protocol (FTP). You must have permission to access the destination site, which often means you'll need a user name and password.

To publish a movie and send it through FTP, follow these steps:

1. From the File menu, select **Publish** to display the Publish window.
2. Click the **FTP** icon to display the FTP options.

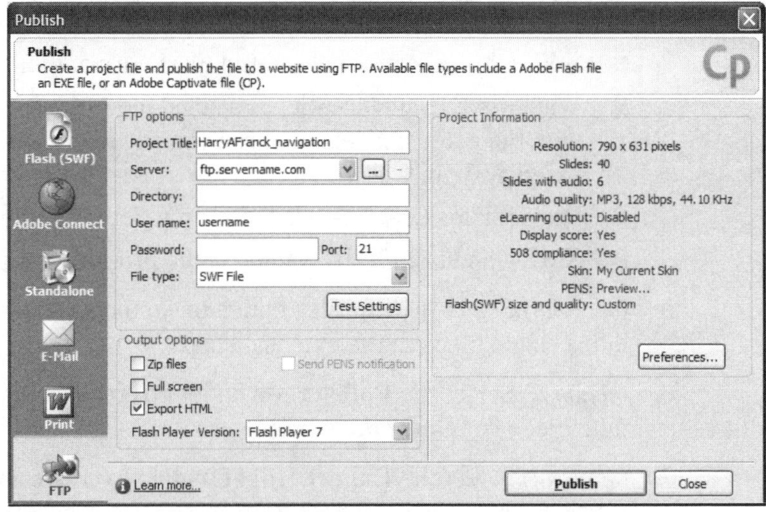

Figure 14-7. Enter FTP options.

3. The Project Title text box defaults to the name you entered for the project file. You can leave this as-is or type a new name. It isn't necessary to include the file extension—Captivate will add .swf to the finished file name.
4. In the Server text box, enter the server that hosts the destination for the movie files. You must type the "ftp" and the extension. For example, you might send it to ftp.harryafranck.com.
5. Enter the directory on the server for the files you're sending. Remember, you must have access to this directory.
6. Enter your user name and password, if required. Once you've entered this information, you may click the **Test Settings** button to make sure that you do have access and all systems are working before generating and sending the movie files.
7. Enter the port for this system. Captivate defaults to Port 21 because it is the most commonly used.
8. Specify which of the file types you want to generate by choosing from the drop-down list for File type:
   - SWF File—Creates and sends a Flash format file.
   - Windows Executable—Sends a stand-alone executable file with the extension .exe that runs on any Microsoft Windows-based system.
   - Project Files (.cp)—Sends the source Captivate files.
9. Select any of the following in the Output Options area:

Table 14-5. FTP output options

Select this option:	To send this:
Zip files	A zip file containing your Flash file. The zip file will have the same name entered in the Project Title field with the extension .zip.
Full screen	A Flash file that plays in full-screen mode. Note that this option is not available if you have selected AICC or SCORM options (see Chapter 10).
Export HTML	A Flash file and an HTML file that can be used to display the Flash file in a browser. The HTML file will have the same name entered in the Project Title field with the extension .htm.
Send PENS notification	Notification to the specified learning management system (if you've defined it in the Quiz Preferences area).
Flash Player Version	Output that can be read by the specified version of the Flash Player.

10. The Project Information area on the right of the screen displays the current preference settings for the movie, such as the resolution (in pixels) and audio information. To change the options listed in this area, click **Preferences** to display the Preferences window. The output options on this window are described earlier in this chapter in Table 14-4; other preferences are described in Chapter 13.
11. Click **Publish** to create the movie and send it by FTP to the designated server.

Exporting and Importing Text Captions

You can export text captions from an existing Captivate movie into a Word document (DOC) or into an XML localization translation file format (XLIFF). The formatting from Captivate (font, color, size, etc.) will be preserved in the output document. You can then make changes using any of the Word features (such as global change and replace) or send your captions out for translation if necessary. Once you've made the changes, you can import the captions back into the original movie.

Exporting Captions to a Word File

Note: You must have Microsoft Word installed on your computer in order to export text captions to a Word document.

To export, edit, and import text captions using a Word document, follow these steps:

1. From the File menu, select **Export**, and then choose **Project captions and closed captions** to display a standard Save As window.
2. Captivate defaults to using the same name and same directory as the project for your exported caption text. You can leave this name as-is or type a new file name for the DOC file. You can also specify a different directory or folder.
3. Click **Save** to store the captions in a Word file (.doc format) and display a confirmation dialog.

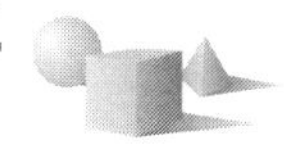

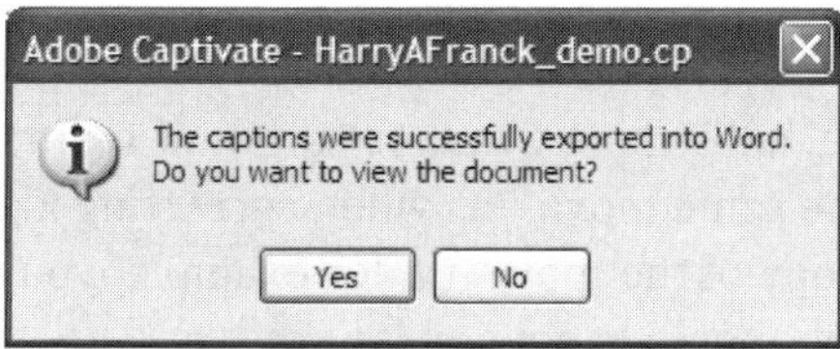

Figure 14-8. View the captions after exporting them.

4. Click **Yes** to view the Word document containing the captions. The Word document contains information about all the captions in the movie (text captions, success captions, failure captions, etc.) in a table. The actual text is contained in two identical columns.

5. Make any necessary changes to your captions by editing the text in the Updated Text Caption Data column, as shown in Figure 14-9.

Note: Do not change anything in the first two columns (Slide ID and Item ID). Captivate uses this information when you import the captions back into the project. You can change the text in the Original Text Caption Data column if you like, though you may prefer to keep this text as-is to track the changes as you make them. You can also use Microsoft Word's track changes feature for this purpose.

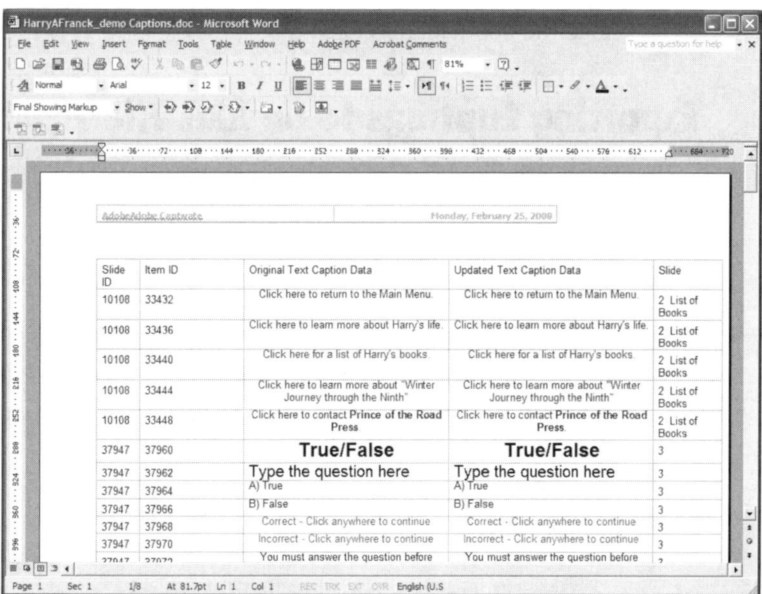

Slide ID	Item ID	Original Text Caption Data	Updated Text Caption Data	Slide
10108	33432	Click here to return to the Main Menu.	Click here to return to the Main Menu.	2 List of Books
10108	33436	Click here to learn more about Harry's life.	Click here to learn more about Harry's life.	2 List of Books
10108	33440	Click here for a list of Harry's books.	Click here for a list of Harry's books.	2 List of Books
10108	33444	Click here to learn more about "Winter Journey through the Ninth"	Click here to learn more about "Winter Journey through the Ninth"	2 List of Books
10108	33448	Click here to contact **Prince of the Road** Press.	Click here to contact **Prince of the Road** Press.	2 List of Books
37947	37960	**True/False**	**True/False**	3
37947	37962	Type the question here	Type the question here	3
37947	37964	A) True	A) True	3
37947	37966	B) False	B) False	3
37947	37968	Correct - Click anywhere to continue	Correct - Click anywhere to continue	3
37947	37970	Incorrect - Click anywhere to continue	Incorrect - Click anywhere to continue	3

Figure 14-9. The captions in a Word file.

6. Save the Word document.
7. Back in Captivate, determine whether you want to import the captions back into the same movie (as when correcting a product name) or into a copy of the movie (if, for example, you want to make copies of the movie in several languages).

Tip: When you import the captions, the original captions will be overwritten. You may want to store a copy of the movie as a backup before importing.

8. Open the copy of the movie where you want the new captions.
9. From the File menu, select **Import**, and then **Project captions and closed captions** to display a window containing the files in the default folder.

Note: This option is only active for projects that have exported the captions already (or copies of projects that exported captions).

10. Select the file containing the new captions, and then click **Open** to import the edited captions into the current movie.
11. A message is displayed when the import is complete. Click **OK** to close the confirmation dialog.

Exporting Captions to an XML File

To export, edit, and import text captions using an XML localization interchange file format (XLIFF), follow these steps:

1. From the File menu, select **Export**, and then choose **XML** to display a standard Save As window.
2. Captivate defaults to using the same name and same directory as the project for your exported project text. You can leave this name as-is or type a new file name for the XML file. You can also specify a different directory or folder.
3. Click **Save** to store the captions in an XML file and display a confirmation dialog.

Relevant objects in the project are converted into XML format. A dialog box appears, confirming that the XML export was successful. Choose whether you want to view the XML file. If you click Yes, the XML file is opened in your computer's default XML viewer.

Printing Movie Components

Though you can't print animations, Captivate does allow you to print a variety of movie components:

- Handouts—Converts the project into a "handout" showing all the slides.
- Lessons—Converts the project into a lesson with questions and answer key.
- Step by Step—Converts the project into a short reference guide.
- Storyboard—Creates a Word document containing a project summary and view of each slide.

Printing Slide Handouts

The Handouts output type creates a Microsoft Word file. You have the option of including a variety of components in your handouts and determining the size of the slide images (much like PowerPoint handouts).

To publish a Captivate project as a handout, follow these steps:

1. From the File menu, select **Publish** to display the Publish window.
2. Click the **Print** icon to display the print options.
3. From the **Type** drop-down list, choose **Handouts** to display the Handouts options, as shown in Figure 14-10.

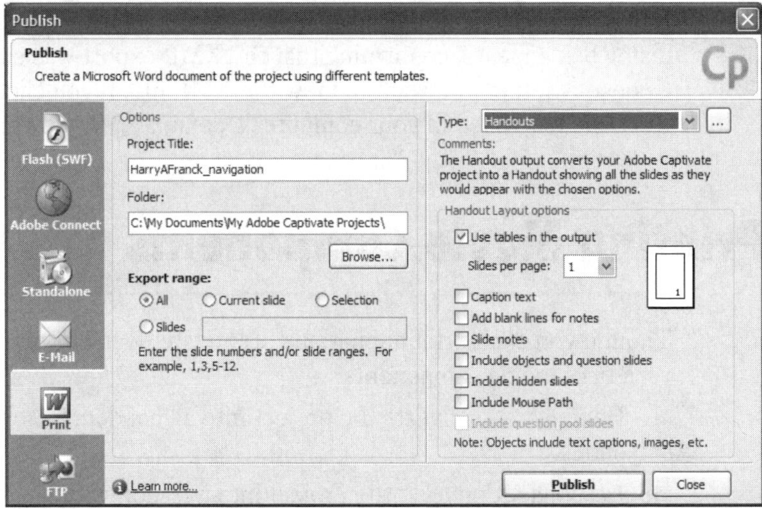

Figure 14-10. Publish slides as handouts.

4. The Project Title text box defaults to the name you entered for the project file. You can leave this as-is or type a new name. It isn't necessary to include the file extension—Captivate will add .doc to the finished file name.
5. The Folder text box defaults to the folder that stores the project files. You can leave this as-is, type a new folder location, or click the Browse button to browse to the output location.
6. Specify which of the slides you want to export by entering an export range. Choose one of the following:
   - All—Export all slides
   - Current slide—Export only the one slide currently displayed in Edit view
   - Selection—Export all selected slides
   - Slides—Enter the numbers of the slides you want to export
7. Specify the layout options you want for the exported data.

Table 14-6. Options for printed handouts

Select this option:	For this result:
Use tables in the output	Allows you to specify the number of slides that you want to print on each page. If you don't select this option, Captivate prints one slide per page, with other selected options (such as printing lines for notes or caption text) displayed beneath each slide.
Slides per page	This option is only available if you've selected Use tables in the output. Choose the number of slides you want to print on each page by choosing from the drop-down list. You can choose one, two, four, six, or nine slides per page. A graphic shows how the finished page will look based on the number of slides you specify.
Caption text	Exports the text of all captions and prints them below the slide on which they appear.
Add blank lines for notes	Several lines appear to the right of each slide image on which readers can take their own notes if desired. This is similar to handout options in other software packages, such as PowerPoint handouts.
Slide notes	Exports the notes for each slide from the Slide Properties window. Tip: Before you actually hand out pages with your slide notes on them, proof-read your handouts! You may not want a message that was intended for internal use to be distributed to other people.
Include objects and question slides	Exports a graphic representation of all objects on your slides (including captions and highlight boxes). Note that if you have your captions stacked (that is, if the success, failure, and retry captions all display in the same location), then only the topmost one will appear on the slide. This option automatically includes the mouse movement for slides that have mouse movement turned on.
Include hidden slides	Exports the hidden slides. If you don't want the hidden slides on your handouts, make sure this option is not selected.
Include Mouse Path	Draws the mouse path on slides where a mouse movement is turned on.
Include question pool slides	Includes the question pool slides in the handouts. Note that this option is only available if you checked the Include objects and question slides option.

Tip: As you add options that display outside of the slides, such as slide notes, blank lines, or caption text, the slide image itself gets smaller. If you have a larger number of slides per page (six or nine) the images may be too small to read. Options that display on top of the slide, such as mouse path and include objects, can make the slides very busy and difficult to read. Always print and proof your handouts before distributing them!

8. Click **Publish** to create a Word file that contains your slides along with any selected options.
9. A confirmation dialog displays. Click **View Output** to open Microsoft Word and display the handout file.
10. You can edit any of the components in the Word document, including text captions and header and footer text, and even delete slides if necessary.

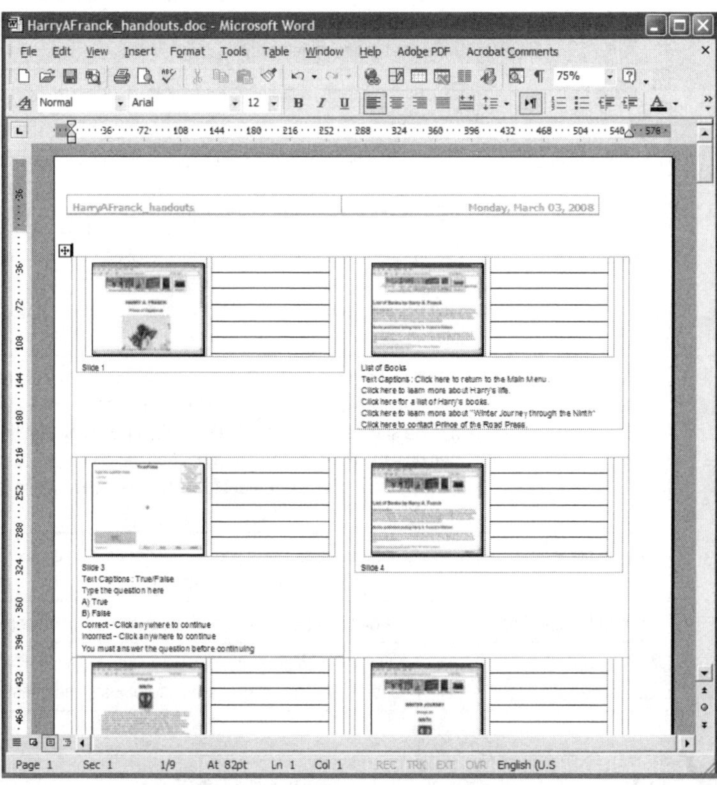

Figure 14-11. Handouts with six slides per page and blank lines for notes.

Tip: By default, Captivate creates the handouts using the Captivate.dot template that is stored in the \Program Files\Adobe\Captivate folder. The name Captivate and the current date are in the header, and the page number is in the footer. You can make edits to this template to change the headers, footers, page size, and other elements.

Printing Slide Lessons

Lessons are created as a Microsoft Word file. There will be one page for each slide. If you've used (and included) question pools, these will be included at the end of the other types of movie slides. Finally, the lesson file will include a list of the answers for each quiz question. You have the option of including a variety of components in your lesson.

To publish a Captivate project as a lesson, follow these steps:

1. From the File menu, select **Publish** to display the Publish window.
2. Click the **Print** icon to display the print options.
3. From the **Type** drop-down list, choose **Lesson** to display the lesson options, as shown in Figure 14-12.

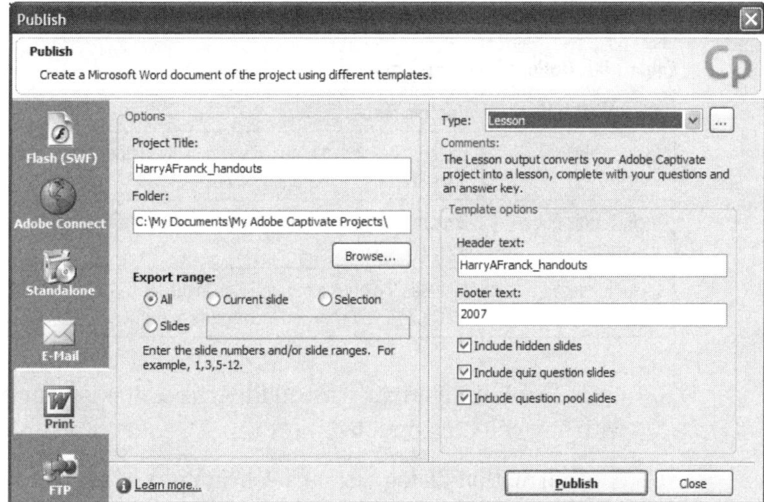

Figure 14-12. Publish slides as a lesson.

4. The Project Title text box defaults to the name you entered for the project file. You can leave this as-is or type a new name. It isn't necessary to include the file extension—Captivate will add .doc to the finished file name.

5. The Folder text box defaults to the folder that stores the project files. You can leave this as-is, type a new folder location, or click the Browse button to browse to the output location.
6. Specify which of the slides you want to export by entering an export range. Choose one of the following:
   - All—Export all slides
   - Current slide—Export only the slide currently displayed in Edit view
   - Selection—Export all selected slides
   - Slides—Enter the numbers of the slides you want to export
7. Enter the header and footer text that you want printed on the top and bottom of each lesson page and select the options you want included in the output:

Table 14-7. Options for printed lessons

Select this option:	For this result:
Include hidden slides	Exports the hidden slides. If you don't want the hidden slides on your lessons, make sure this option is not selected.
Include quiz question slides	Exports the question slides (and includes the answers at the end of the lesson file).
Include question pool slides	Includes the question pool slides in the lesson. Note that this option is only available if you checked the Include quiz question slides option.

8. Click **Publish** to create a Word file that contains your slides along with any selected options.
9. A confirmation dialog displays. Click **View Output** to open Microsoft Word and display the lesson file.
10. You can edit any of the components in the Word document, including text captions and header and footer text, and even delete slides if necessary.

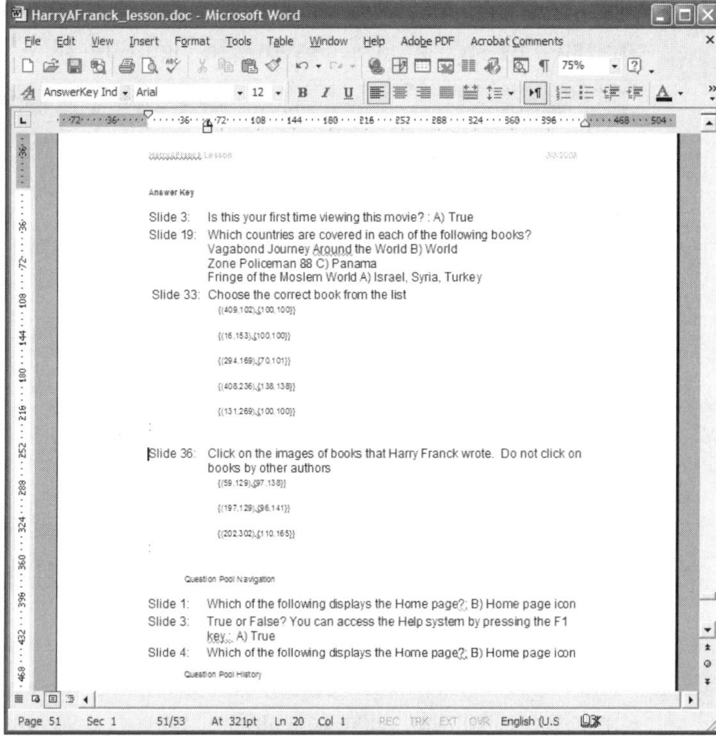

Figure 14-13. A lesson file may include question pool slides after the other movie slides.

Printing Slides Step by Step

This function creates a Microsoft Word file that contains one line for each interactive item in the movie (such as buttons or click boxes).

To publish a Captivate project as a step-by-step reference, follow these steps:

1. From the File menu, select **Publish** to display the Publish window.
2. Click the **Print** icon to display the print options.

3. From the **Type** drop-down list, choose **Step by Step** to display the step-by-step options, as shown in Figure 14-14.

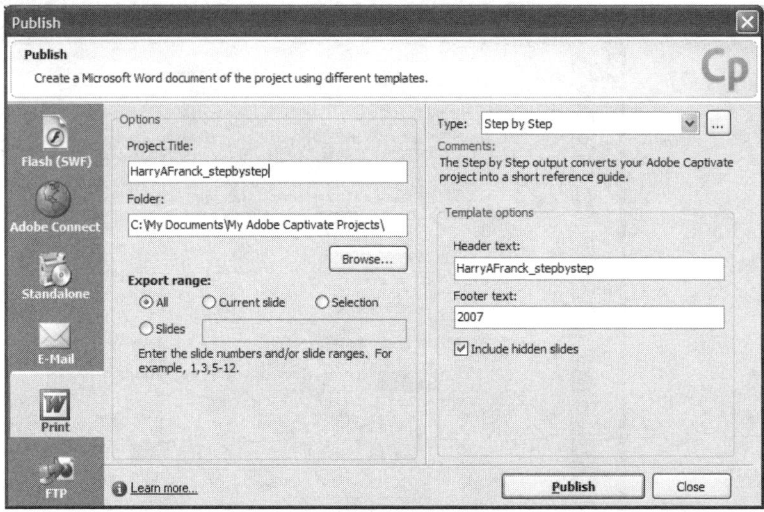

Figure 14-14. Publish slides as a step-by-step reference.

4. The Project Title text box defaults to the name you entered for the project file. You can leave this as-is or type a new name. It isn't necessary to include the file extension—Captivate will add .doc to the finished file name.
5. The Folder text box defaults to the folder that stores the project files. You can leave this as-is, type a new folder location, or click the Browse button to browse to the output location.
6. Specify which of the slides you want to export by entering an export range. Choose one of the following:
   - All—Export all slides
   - Current slide—Export only the slide currently displayed in Edit view
   - Selection—Export all selected slides
   - Slides—Enter the numbers of the slides you want to export
7. Enter the header and footer text that you want printed on the top and bottom of each page.

8. Select the **Include hidden slides** option to include the hidden slides in the output (or deselect this option to omit the hidden slides).
9. Click **Publish** to create a Word file.
10. A confirmation dialog displays. Click **View Output** to open Microsoft Word and display the step-by-step file.
11. You can edit any of the components in the Word document, including text captions and header and footer text, as well as delete slides if necessary.

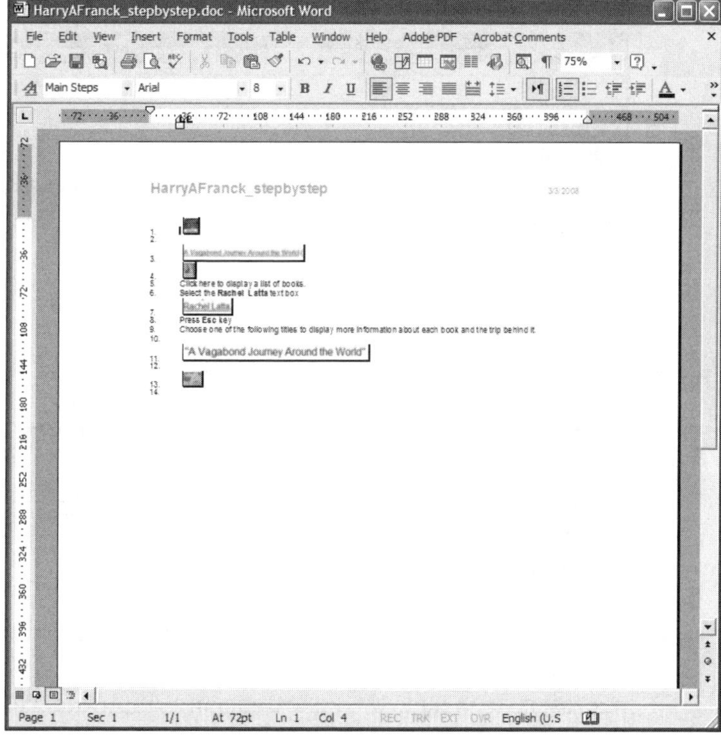

Figure 14-15. The step-by-step file has one line per interactive slide.

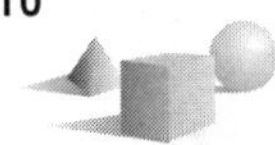

Printing Slides as a Storyboard

This function creates a Microsoft Word file that contains a project summary item and a detailed view of each slide.

To publish a Captivate project as a storyboard reference, follow these steps:

1. From the File menu, select **Publish** to display the Publish window.
2. Click the **Print** icon to display the print options.
3. From the **Type** drop-down list, choose **Storyboard** to display the storyboard options, as shown in Figure 14-16.

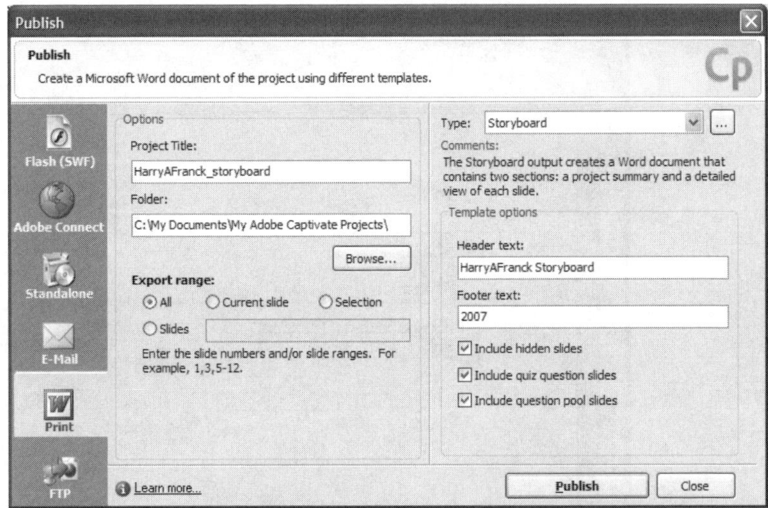

Figure 14-16. Publish slides as a storyboard.

4. The Project Title text box defaults to the name you entered for the project file. You can leave this as-is or type a new name. It isn't necessary to include the file extension—Captivate will add .doc to the finished file name.

5. The Folder text box defaults to the folder that stores the project files. You can leave this as-is, type a new folder location, or click the Browse button to browse to the output location.
6. Specify which of the slides you want to export by entering an export range. Choose one of the following:
   - All—Export all slides
   - Current slide—Export only the slide currently displayed in Edit view
   - Selection—Export all selected slides
   - Slides—Enter the numbers of the slides you want to export
7. Enter the header and footer text that you want printed at the top and bottom of each storyboard page and select the options you want included in the output.

Table 14-8. Options for printed storyboard

Select this option:	For this result:
Include hidden slides	Exports the hidden slides. If you don't want the hidden slides on your storyboard, make sure this option is not selected.
Include quiz question slides	Exports the question slides (and includes the answers at the end of the storyboard file).
Include question pool slides	Includes the question pool slides in the storyboard. Note that this option is only available if you checked the Include question slides option.

8. Click **Publish** to create a Word file that contains your slides along with any selected options.

9. A confirmation dialog displays. Click **View Output** to open Microsoft Word and display the storyboard file. The first section includes a summary of the movie, and the second section includes one page for each slide.

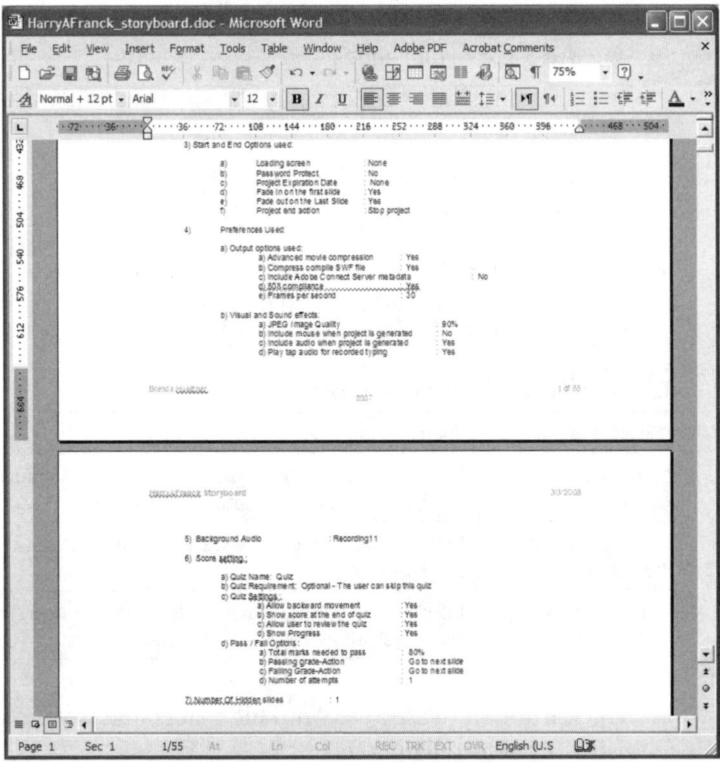

Figure 14-17. The storyboard summary includes information about the entire movie.

10. You can edit any of the components in the Word document, including text captions and header and footer text, as well as delete slides if necessary.

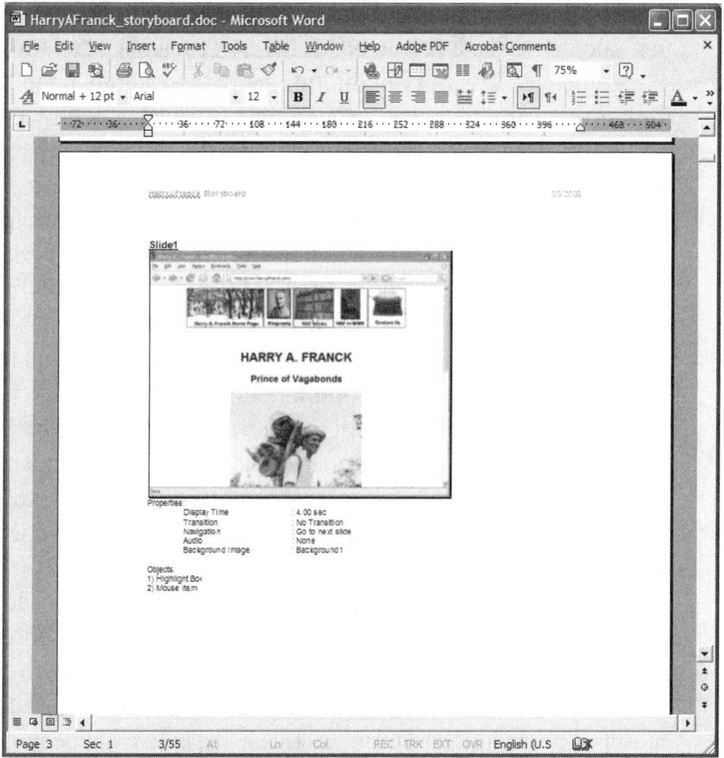

Figure 14-18. The storyboard file also includes a page for each slide.

About Accessibility

Accessibility is the term that many people use to indicate that a product, such as a Flash movie or HTML page, can be read (or accessed) by people with a variety of limitations. For example, people with limited or no vision may use screen reader software that reads printed text aloud. Or people with limited manual dexterity may prefer to use assistive devices with a keyboard instead of a mouse.

Many countries have adopted accessibility standards based on the Web Content Accessibility Guidelines from the World Wide Web Consortium (W3C). For information about the Web Accessibility Initiative, see the W3C web site at www.w3.org/WAI.

The United States government has mandated that all federal agencies' electronic and information technology be accessible to people with disabilities. This regulation, often referred to as Section 508, includes a detailed set of standards that many companies find useful even if they aren't selling to the U.S. government. For more information about the United States government regulation Section 508, see www.section508.gov.

Although Captivate does include an output option check box that creates 508-compliant output from information you've entered, it is primarily concerned with making your output available to screen reader software. You must still ensure that you've entered the required information. There are three areas to consider:

- Audio elements. If people with various degrees of deafness watch your movie, they may not be able to hear your audio elements. It is important that you check each audio file to ensure that any important information contained in the audio file is also available in a visual element. For example, if your audio simply contains background music, you don't need to do anything. If your audio includes instructions to the viewer, those instructions should also be printed on the slide (in any of the different text captions or even as part of the background). If you use audio to indicate success (such as applause) or failure (such as a buzzer), then there must also be a visual distinction between these two indicators.

Tip: To test your movie to see if it is compliant, you can turn the audio off (in the Properties window) and then publish and view your movie. Or you could simply view your movie with your computer sound system turned all the way down.

- Screen reader software cannot read pictures, so you must enter a text description for slides that contain images. Captivate can help you do this through the Slide Accessibility button. You must also set the 508 compliance check box to allow the screen reader to access these elements.
- In order for screen readers to read elements such as buttons, controls, and question slides, you must ensure that the information required by the screen readers is included in your Properties window. You must also set the 508 compliance check box to allow the screen reader to access these elements.

For more information about Captivate and accessibility, see www.adobe.com/accessibility/.

Entering Text Descriptions of Visual Elements

For each slide, you can enter descriptive text that will be read by screen reader software. You can enter brief text as a slide label, or you can enter more descriptive text in the accessibility text area (or you can enter both).

To enter text descriptions, follow these steps:

1. Do one of the following to display the Slide Properties window:
   - From Edit view, double-click on the slide background.
   - From Storyboard view or the filmstrip in Edit view, right-click on a slide and choose **Properties**.
   - In any view, from the Slide menu, choose **Properties**.

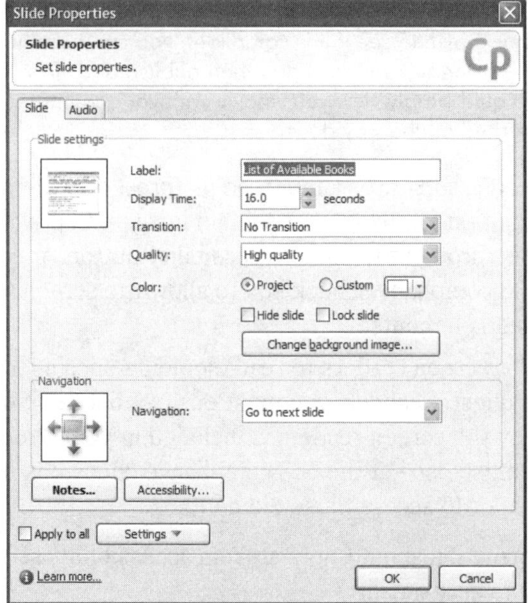

Figure 14-19. Accessibility options are accessed from the Slide Properties window.

2. Enter a label for the slide in the Label field.
3. Click the **Accessibility** button to display the Slide Accessibility Text entry window.

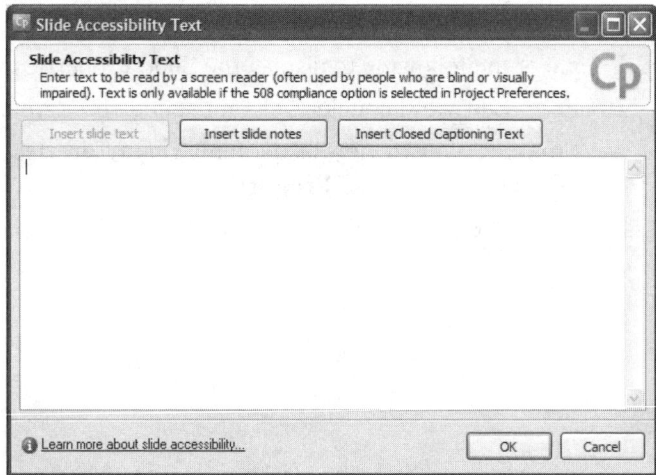

Figure 14-20. Enter slide accessibility text.

4. Enter the text in any combination of the following approaches:
   - Click the **Insert slide text** button to automatically insert the text from all captions on the current slide. This is most useful if you have only one caption, and it is fairly descriptive. Note that this button is only active if the current slide contains at least one text caption.
   - Click the **Insert slide notes** button to automatically insert the text from the slide notes. Note that this button is only active if the current slide contains slide notes.
   - Click the **Insert Closed Captioning Text** to automatically insert the text from all audio elements on the current slide. Note that this button is only active if the current slide contains at least one audio closed caption.
   - Begin typing new text.
5. When the text is displayed the way you want it, click **OK** to close the Slide Accessibility Text window.
6. From any view, open the **Edit** menu, and then select **Preferences** to display the Preferences window.
7. Click **Project** in the Category list to display the project preferences options.

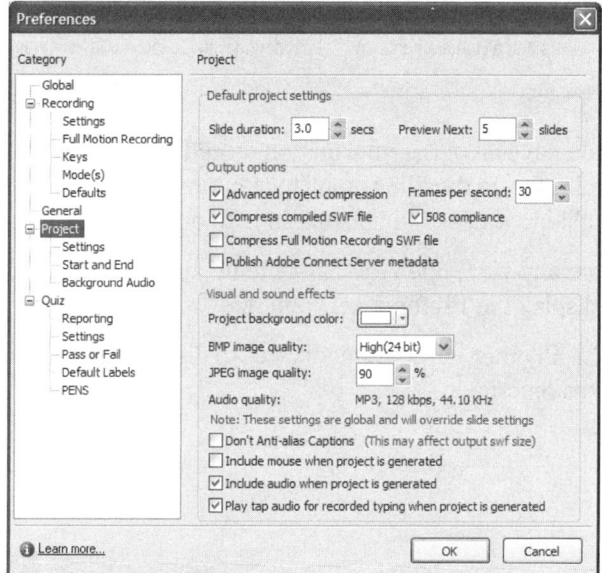

Figure 14-21. Set the 508 compliance option.

8. Ensure that the **508 compliance** option is selected. Even if you have all of the text entered and other properties set for compliance, the output will not allow screen readers to access this information unless this option is selected.
9. Click **OK** to close the Preferences window.
10. Publish the movie as described in earlier sections of this chapter.

Entering Additional Information for Screen Readers

In addition to the text for each slide, setting the 508 compliance option allows a screen reader to read a variety of elements as long as you've got them entered and turned on within the movie.

Table 14-9. Accessible information

For this element:	See this section and chapter:
Project name	"Displaying Movie Information," Chapter 13
Project description	"Displaying Movie Information," Chapter 13
Buttons	"Adding and Editing Interactive Elements," Chapter 9
Playback controls	"Changing Playback Controls," Chapter 13
Password protection prompt, if any	"Movie Start Options," Chapter 13
Question slides and all the elements on them	"Working with Question Slides," Chapter 10

After you have all of the information stored with your project, you must still turn on the 508 compliance option before a screen reader will be able to access the information. To do this, follow these steps:

1. From any view, open the **Edit** menu, and then select **Preferences** to display the Preferences window.
2. Click **Project** in the Category list to display the project preferences options.

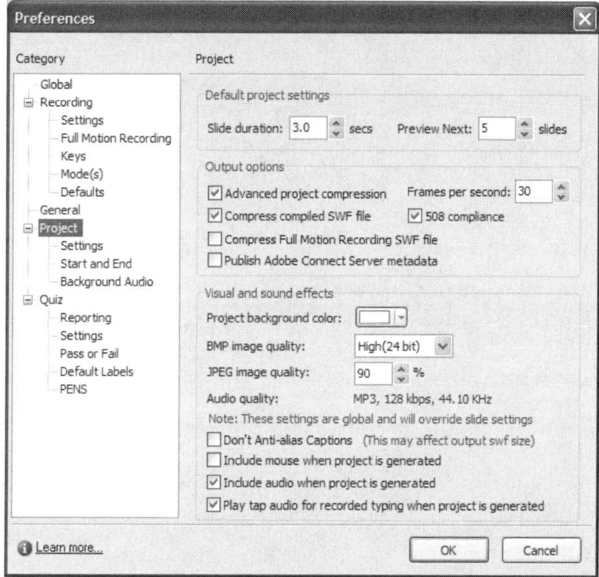

Figure 14-22. Set the 508 compliance option.

3. Select the **508 compliance** option. Even if you have all of the text entered and other properties set for compliance, the output will not allow screen readers to access this information unless this option is selected.
4. Click **OK** to close the Preferences window.
5. Publish the movie as described in earlier sections of this chapter.

Summary

This chapter discussed ways to publish your movie and the variety of output options available to you. In addition to creating Flash movies, you can also publish Word documents based on your movie project. This chapter also described some of the considerations to keep in mind when publishing accessible content.

Glossary

AICC: Aviation Industry CBT Committee (where CBT stands for computer-based training) is an international association of technology-based training professionals. The AICC has been developing guidelines for CBT and related training technologies since 1988. For more information about AICC and its guidelines, see www.aicc.org.

AVI: Audio Video Interleaved format files. Movie files with the .avi extension are generally compatible across multiple platforms and can be imported into Captivate files as either new movies or as animations within slides.

bandwidth: The amount of data that is transmitted from one computer to another, usually given in megabits (Mbit) per second. A larger file will require a larger bandwidth for transmission.

bit rate: The number of bits that are transferred per second, generally expressed as kilobits per second (kbps), megabits per second (Mbit), or gigabits per second (Gbit). A higher number here represents a faster transmission (or quicker download).

BMP: Microsoft Windows bitmap format for graphics.

branching: The mechanism by which you can display different slides depending on whether or not the viewer answers a question correctly. This is often used with e-learning applications to control the display based on student progress through a learning activity.

caption: A caption is simply a piece of text that highlights or points to a portion of the screen. Captivate contains a variety of caption types that display at different times depending on the viewer input. For example, a text caption might instruct the viewer to click on a certain icon. If the viewer performs the task as instructed, a success caption displays. If the viewer doesn't click the right area, you may choose to display either a retry caption or a failure caption.

CBT: Computer-based training; a catchall phrase that covers any type of instruction that is delivered via computer.

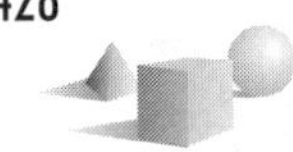

click box: A click box indicates an area on the screen that the viewer should click with the mouse. You can emulate the functionality of buttons or links within a Captivate movie by creating a click box over the button and specifying a destination file that will be displayed when the viewer clicks the click box.

compression: A method of reducing the size of a file using an algorithm to remove unneeded bits. Compression reduces file size, but can also reduce file quality.

.cp: The extension used for Captivate project files.

e-learning: Short for electronic learning, this is a growing field that encompasses distance learning, computer-based training, web-based training, and a variety of other education delivery mechanisms. Instructor input is minimal or nonexistent at the time the learner is actually taking the training, and thus must be integrated up front during design and development phases. e-learning also usually has an electronic or automated grading or evaluation component.

EMF: Enhanced Metafile format for Microsoft Windows graphics.

EXE: An executable file that runs a program or performs an action.

filmstrip: A representation of all of the slides in the movie that displays along one edge of the screen in Edit view.

Flash: A multimedia authoring program from Adobe that creates animations and movies. This term is also used to refer to the output of the Flash software or any other output that is compatible with the Flash Player (such as Captivate movies).

frames: In movie jargon, a frame is a single image that, when combined and played with other images, creates the illusion of movement on a screen. In Captivate, each slide is a frame that has additional functionality such as animations, click boxes, timing components, etc.

FTP: File transfer protocol that allows you to transfer information from one computer to another over a TCP/IP network.

GIF: Graphics interchange format for graphics, often used for web delivery because of its compression and small file size.

highlight box: A graphic on a slide that highlights a particular area, usually with colored borders and a partially transparent fill color.

HQX: Macintosh Projector file where the data is converted to ASCII format for better portability between systems.

HTML: Hypertext Markup Language uses tags and special encoding to create files that can be posted and displayed on the web and read by web browsers.

.ico: File extension used by files that display as icons on PC systems.

image: An image in Captivate can be any graphic or picture that you use in your movie. Valid image formats are JPG, JPEG, GIF, PNG, BMP, ICO, EMF, and WMF.

JPG or JPEG: Joint Photographic Experts Group format for images. This format is often used for web-based graphics.

LMS: Learning management system. A learning management system is software used to plan, implement, and assess learning processes. Different commercial LMS implementations will have different components (such as monitoring student progress, discussion lists, or even video conferencing).

Macintosh Projector file: Captivate creates this type of file with the .hqx extension so that it can be played on Macintosh systems, even though it was created on a Windows-based system.

MP3: MPEG format audio file using a compression scheme called audio layer 3.

pass rate: In e-learning applications, the total of correct answers required to "pass" a course. In Captivate, this can be expressed as a percentage or a raw number.

PENS: Package Exchange Notification Services, a type of update notification protocol standard created by the AICC (Aviation Industry CBT Committee) and used by many learning management systems.

PNG: Portable Network Graphic, a highly transportable image format.

POT: PowerPoint Template format.

PowerPoint: A widely used presentation software program from Microsoft.

Questionmark Perception: A web-based assessment delivery system widely used for computer-assisted evaluation of courses.

quiz: Within Captivate, a quiz is defined as all of the questions and click boxes in a single movie. You can exclude any of the questions or click boxes from the quiz as needed.

recording: In Captivate, recording is the process of capturing screens and storing audio and mouse movement elements for use in Captivate projects.

resolution (screen): Screen resolution is the number of pixels that can be displayed on a monitor, expressed as the number of horizontal pixels times the number of vertical pixels. For example, a standard screen size might be 1024 x 768.

scoring: The mechanism of determining how well a student does on a quiz. You can keep track of the number of questions the viewer gets right, or you can attach relative weights (or importance factors) to each question. You can also calculate a score and integrate it into an LMS.

SCORM: Sharable Content Object Reference Model is a specification created by the Advanced Distance Learning group and the United States Department of Defense to standardize the transfer of information between learning management systems. For more information on SCORM, see http://www.adlnet.org/.

storyboard: A storyboard is a planning device for movies that consists of a rough representation of both the visual and audio components, usually in paper format.

transition: In Captivate, a transition is the way a movie changes from one slide to the next.

transparency: The percentage of the background behind an image that shows through the image. A high transparency means that a lot of the background shows through the image, and 100% transparent means the image is invisible. A low transparency means that the image is quite dense, and very little of the background shows through.

weighting: A mechanism that attaches more importance to some quiz elements than others when calculating the final score. For example, introductory questions may be worth less than advanced questions. The advanced questions would have a higher weight.

WMF: Windows Metafile graphic format.

Additional Resources

As you work with Captivate, your movies are likely to get more sophisticated. There are a number of resources available on the Web that can help you get the most out of Captivate software as it evolves, as well as help you keep up with the latest in e-learning and Flash development. All URLs are accurate as of the time of this printing.

Captivate and Flash Resources

Flash Player download—You'll need this and the viewers of your movies will need this (http://www.adobe.com/shockwave/download/download.cgi?P1_Prod_Version=ShockwaveFlash).

Adobe Resource Center for Captivate—Lots of useful information, including tech notes and release notes as they come out (http://www.adobe.com/support/captivate/).

Adobe Resource Center for Flash—For more detailed information on the Flash output format (http://www.adobe.com/support/flash/).

Silke Fleischer's blog—Lots of great information as well as tips, tricks, and examples (http://blogs.adobe.com/silke.fleischer/).

Accessible Flash lessons—Discussion of how to ensure that your Flash files (however you create them) are accessible to all (http://www.webaim.org/techniques/flash/).

e-learning

e-learning guru site—Loads of terrific articles, tools, white papers, and links (http://www.e-learningguru.com/).

The E-Learning Guild—An organization for managers and creators of e-learning (http://www.elearningguild.com/).

American Society for Training Development—An organization for trainers of all types (http://www.astd.org/astd).

Society for Technical Communication (STC) Instructional Design and Learning (IDL) Special Interest Group (SIG)—Lots of good resources, including a directory of service providers (http://www.stcsig.org/idl/index.html).

Captivate Shortcut Keys

Captivate software often gives you many ways to perform the same task, such as choosing from a menu, clicking a link, or pressing a combination of keys on your keyboard. The following table lists the shortcut keys in order by the keys used.

To use shortcut key combinations, hold down the first key while pressing the second (and third, if any).

Shortcut Key	Action
F1	Open Adobe Captivate Help (To access dialog-level help, click the Help button on individual dialog boxes.)
F3	Test view current slide (Edit view only)
F4	Preview project
F5	Record audio
F6	Import audio
F7	Spelling and grammar check
F8	Preview project from current slide
F9	Show the Advanced interaction dialog box
F10	Preview current slide and following *n* slides
F11	View Adobe Captivate in full screen
F12	Preview project in web browser
Ctrl+A	Select all
Ctrl+C	Copy (slide in Storyboard view or filmstrip, and selected object in Edit view)
Ctrl+D	Duplicate (slide in Storyboard view or filmstrip, and selected object in Edit view)
Ctrl+E	Extend length of object display time to end of slide on Timeline (Edit view only)
Ctrl+F	Open the Find and Replace dialog box
Ctrl+G	Change slide to optimized quality
Ctrl+H	Change slide to high quality
Ctrl+I	Increase indent (selected object in Edit view)
Ctrl+J	Change slide to JPEG quality
Ctrl+K	Lock the slide

Shortcut Key	Action
Ctrl+L	Sync selected object to the playhead
Ctrl+M	Merge the selected object with background
Ctrl+N	Move to Slide Notes pane
Ctrl+O	Open project
Ctrl+P	Align selected object with playhead on Timeline (Edit view only)
Ctrl+Q	Insert Random Question Slide
Ctrl+R	Print the project (through the Publish dialog box)
Ctrl+S	Save
Ctrl+T	Change slide to standard quality
Ctrl+U	Edit with (in project Library)
Ctrl+V	Paste what is on the clipboard (e.g., slide, image, object, etc.)
Ctrl+X	Cut (selected object in Edit view)
Ctrl+Y	Redo
Ctrl+Z	Undo
Ctrl+=	Zoom in
Ctrl+-	Zoom out
Ctrl+Tab	To shift between Storyboard, Edit, and Branching view
Ctrl+Alt+B	Show Thumbnails (Edit view only)
Ctrl+Alt+D	Update Library
Ctrl+Alt+F	Find in Library
Ctrl+Alt+L	Show Library (Edit view only)
Ctrl+Alt+N	Show Slide Notes (Edit view only)
Ctrl+Alt+O	Record additional slides
Ctrl+Alt+R	Reset to original size
Ctrl+Alt+T	Show Timeline (Edit view only)
Ctrl+Alt+U	Library usage
Shift+Ctrl+A	Add animation object (Edit and Storyboard views only)
Shift+Ctrl+B	Add new button (Edit and Storyboard views only)
Shift+Ctrl+C	Add new caption (Edit and Storyboard views only)
Shift+Ctrl+D	View slide properties
Shift+Ctrl+E	Insert new zoom area (Edit and Storyboard views only)
Shift+Ctrl+F	Insert Flash Video (Edit and Storyboard views only)
Shift+Ctrl+G	Show the Go to Slide dialog box

Shortcut Key	Action
Shift+Ctrl+H	Hide/Show slide
Shift+Ctrl+I	Decrease indent (selected object in Edit view)
Shift+Ctrl+J	Insert blank slide (Edit and Storyboard views only)
Shift+Ctrl+K	Add new click box (Edit and Storyboard views only)
Shift+Ctrl+M	Add new image
Shift+Ctrl+N	Add new animation slide
Shift+Ctrl+O	Add new rollover image
Shift+Ctrl+P	Publish file
Shift+Ctrl+Q	Insert question slide
Shift+Ctrl+R	Insert rollover caption
Shift+Ctrl+S	Insert image slide
Shift+Ctrl+T	Insert text entry box
Shift+Ctrl+U	Insert mouse
Shift+Ctrl+V	Paste as background
Shift+Ctrl+W	Insert PowerPoint slide
Shift+Ctrl+X	Insert text animation
Shift+Ctrl+Y	Copy background
Shift+Ctrl+Z	Insert hover area

Index

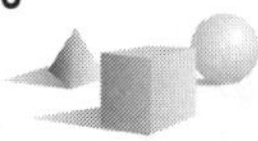

N

O

P

Q

Looking for More?

Check out Wordware's market-leading Game Development and Graphics Libraries featuring the following titles.

LightWave 3D 8 Cartoon Character Creation
Vol. 1: Modeling & Texturing
1-55622-253-X • $49.95
6 x 9 • 496 pp.

LightWave 3D 8 Cartoon Character Creation
Vol. 2: Rigging & Animation
1-55622-254-8 • $49.95
6 x 9 • 440 pp.

Modeling, UV Mapping, and Texturing 3D Game Weapons
1-55622-870-8 • $39.95
6 x 9 • 368 pp.

Polygonal Modeling: Basic and Advanced Techniques
1-59822-007-1 • $39.95
6 x 9 • 424 pp.

Advanced Lighting and Materials with Shaders
1-55622-292-0 • $44.95
9 x 7 • 360 pp.

Design First for 3D Artists
1-55622-085-5 • $49.95
9 x 7 • 336 pp.

The Mechanics of Anime and Manga
1-59822-019-5 • $29.95
7.25 x 10.25 • 328 pp.

Maya 8.0 Character Modeling
1-59822-020-9 • $44.95
6 x 9 • 504 pp.

The Art of Flash Animation: Creative Cartooning
1-59822-026-8 • $34.95
6 x 9 • 480 pp.

LightWave v9 Texturing
1-59822-029-2 • $44.95
6 x 9 • 648 pp.

LightWave v9 Lighting
1-59822-039-X • $44.95
6 x 9 • 616 pp.

3ds max Lighting
1-55622-401-X • $49.95
6 x 9 • 432 pp.

Y8, Newgrounds Kongregate

Visit us online at www.wordware.com for more information.
Use the following coupon code for online specials: capt0497